W9-BRN-861

RED-HANDED

ALSO BY PETER SCHWEIZER

Architects of Ruin: How Big Government Liberals
Wrecked the Global Economy—
and How They Will Do It Again If No One Stops Them

Clinton Cash: The Untold Story of How and Why Foreign Governments
and Businesses Helped Make Bill and Hillary Rich

Secret Empires: How the American Political Class Hides Corruption
and Enriches Family and Friends

Profiles in Corruption: Abuse of Power by America's Progressive Elite

RED-HANDED

How American Elites
Get Rich Helping
China Win

PETER SCHWEIZER

HARPER

An Imprint of HarperCollins*Publishers*

RED-HANDED. Copyright © 2022 by Peter Schweizer. All rights reserved. Printed in the United States of America. No part of this book may be used or reproduced in any manner whatsoever without written permission except in the case of brief quotations embodied in critical articles and reviews. For information, address HarperCollins Publishers, 195 Broadway, New York, NY 10007.

HarperCollins books may be purchased for educational, business, or sales promotional use. For information, please email the Special Markets Department at SPsales@harpercollins.com.

FIRST EDITION

Library of Congress Cataloging-in-Publication Data

Names: Schweizer, Peter, 1964– author.
Title: Red-handed : how American elites get rich helping China win / Peter Schweizer.
Description: First edition. | New York : Harper, 2022. | Includes index. |
Identifiers: LCCN 2021039597 (print) | LCCN 2021039598 (ebook) |
    ISBN 9780063061149 (hardcover) | ISBN 9780063061163 (ebook)
Subjects: LCSH: Elite (Social sciences)—Political activity—United States. |
    Political corruption—United States. | United States—Foreign relations—China. |
    China—Foreign relations—United States.
Classification: LCC HN90.E4 S35 2022 (print) | LCC HN90.E4 (ebook) |
DDC 305.5/20973—dc23
LC record available at https://lccn.loc.gov/2021039597
LC ebook record available at https://lccn.loc.gov/2021039598

22 23 24 25 26 LSC 10 9 8 7 6 5 4

To W—

". . . a brother is born for adversity."

—Proverbs 17:17

The welfare of the people . . . has always been the alibi of tyrants . . . giving the servants of tyranny a good conscience.

—*Albert Camus*

CONTENTS

1: The Rope   1

2: The Bidens   9

3: Capitol Hill   46

4: Silicon Valley   83

5: Wall Street   121

6: Diplomats   150

7: The Bush and Trudeau Dynasties   186

8: Higher Education   211

9: Fighting Back   237

Acknowledgments   247

Notes   249

Index   331

1

THE ROPE

The world is undergoing great changes unseen in a century, but time and momentum are on our side. This is where our force and vigor reside, and it is also where our determination and confidence reside.[1]
—*President Xi Jinping, January 2021*

"The capitalists will sell us the rope with which to hang them."
There is little evidence that Vladimir Lenin uttered those exact words. What he did say, however, was more precise, if less catchy: "They [capitalists] will furnish credits which will serve us for the support of the Communist Party in their countries and, by supplying us materials and technical equipment which we lack, will restore our military industry necessary for our future attacks against our suppliers. To put it in other words, *they will work on the preparation of their own suicide.*"[2]

On another occasion, a Soviet source reports him having written: "The whole world's capitalists and their governments, as they pant to win the Soviet market, will close their eyes to the above-mentioned reality and will thus transform themselves into men who are deaf, dumb and blind. They will give us credits . . . they will toil to *prepare their own suicide.*"[3]

While Lenin's Soviet Union receded into the pages of history, the Leninist mentality is still a current event. And today on Wall

Street, in Silicon Valley, and in Washington, too many play "deaf, dumb, and blind" while selling rope. And the buyer is Beijing.

Throughout this book, I will refer to the challenges we face from Beijing. By "Beijing," I mean the dictatorial regime of the Chinese Communist Party (CCP), which controls the People's Republic of China. The threat we face is from political Beijing, not the Chinese people. Indeed, it would be accurate to say that the Chinese people are the biggest victims of the CCP.

By "rope," I am talking very specifically about technology, money, intelligence, or even political support given to the communist regime. This rope enhances the military or strategic capabilities of Beijing, anything that advances their position in competition with the United States. I am not talking simply about general commerce with China.

For decades, the proverbial wisdom has been that China was going to liberalize. We were told by political figures and members of the business class that China would become more open. China was not a threat; it was a Western wannabe. Give them free trade, access to technology, and American capital, and they would become more like us. This attitude has proliferated into a new establishment consensus, one that conveniently enriches many American elites. Beijing is happy to encourage this false assumption to advance their own very different political agenda.

Of course, China has not liberalized. It has become more aggressive and repressive. Yet those elites who advised us on such a course of action got fabulously wealthy along the way.

Should we let lobbyists represent Chinese companies in the corridors of American power? Should we be investing our 401(k)s in Chinese companies? Should we keep thinking—against all evidence—that we can "engage" with China and make it a positive force on the planet?

Twenty-five years ago, it might have been reasonable for America's elite to believe they could make Beijing more America-friendly by cultivating relationships with certain Chinese officials, but the exact opposite has happened. Beijing forged ties and gave money and deals to certain American elites, who became more friendly to the Beijing regime.

The culpability of those elites in what we are experiencing today—an increasingly powerful and aggressive China—cannot be overestimated.

Members of this special class either seek or are approached with lucrative deals, market access, and accolades. In return, naïvely or not, strategic and economic benefits flow to the Beijing regime. This has been a vital approach pursued by the communist government, a strategy first proposed by Mao in 1956: *yang wei Zhong yong*, or "make the foreign serve China." More than sixty years later, the strategy has only become more aggressive. Beijing offers deals, inducements, praise, and access to seduce foreign elites into serving their interests.[4] As Professor Anne-Marie Brady, a premier specialist in Chinese influence operations, puts it, "Beijing forges close partnerships of mutual advantage with highly prominent foreign figures who can bring commercial or political advantages to China."[5]

In the world of espionage, practitioners use the term "elite capture" to describe successful efforts to essentially buy off members of a country's leadership. Opportunities to get wealthy are a key motivator. Beijing hopes that at a minimum this approach will neutralize members of the elite by making them less critical or resistant to their policies, or at a maximum turn them into actual advocates for Beijing's position. But for some, there are other motives beyond just money.

As we will see, too many of America's political, tech, and finance elites share an infatuation with dictatorship. They seem quite content with—indeed, even endorse—the notion that we should trust people to pick their breakfast cereal but not their government leaders. They believe the Beijing dictatorship is more efficient—even a better system overall—than representative democracy. Their endorsements are often quoted by Chinese government media. In short, American elites are granting legitimacy to the Chinese government and are rewarded with large financial deals.

Some prominent figures will point to a negative statement they have made about the Beijing regime as evidence that they are tough on China. But this is largely a diversion. To be clear, Beijing does not require American collaborators to toe the party line. Beijing pragmatically accepts some level of public criticism from the elites with whom it is working. The idea is known as "big help with a little badmouth." Tolerating some dissent and criticism from its foreign partners is wise because it maintains their partners' cloak of credibility in the eyes of the American public.[6] As long as these elites deliver on key policies and actions that benefit the regime, some criticism is acceptable.

So, who exactly are these American elites who, in deed if not in word, wittingly or unwittingly, promote the dictatorial Beijing regime? Some of the most prominent names in Big Tech, Wall Street, and American politics figure into this story.

This book will bring into focus what many of us have known, anecdotally, for decades: leading Americans have collaborated extensively with a brutal regime for personal gain.

We will continue to consider the case, with new evidence, of arguably the most powerful man in the world making excuses for Beijing while his family secured multiple deals with Beijing worth tens of millions of dollars. This, through the courtesy of individuals with direct ties to Chinese intelligence.

We will bring to light another presidential family that has benefited through two generations from deals with Beijing—a family whose members now appear on Chinese state television touting the regime's accomplishments.

We will turn to Capitol Hill and draw the curtain back on the U.S. Speaker of the House, whose family has enjoyed profitable, decades-long dealings with Beijing, allowing it to influence their positions on the most important issues of the day.

We will meet a powerful U.S. senator, chair of the Senate Intelligence Committee, who has excused Beijing's actions while her family secured a string of deals with China.

We will be introduced to former U.S. senators and members of Congress who are now on the payroll of Beijing and military-linked firms, lobbying on their behalf in the corridors of Washington.

We will be introduced to several former U.S. ambassadors to China who are now getting rich working for Chinese entities in the United States.

We will learn about a former U.S. senator and U.S. secretary of defense now helping Chinese state-owned enterprises compete against U.S. companies.

We will expose the former high-ranking U.S. intelligence and security officials now helping Beijing more easily acquire U.S. technologies.

From Silicon Valley, we will meet some of the richest tech entrepreneurs in the world and their troubling bonds with Beijing, as well as their defense of its virtues in government media outlets.

We will show how the head of the largest financial firm on Wall Street praises the regime and even helped the Communist Party solidify its hold over foreign corporations. We will also reveal how and why one of the most powerful men on Wall Street invested $100 million into a Chinese Communist Party propaganda project.

Too many of America's rich and powerful turn a blind eye to the nature of their business partners. This is not exactly a win–win scenario.

We do not have to go into a full history of the Chinese Communist Party regime to see Beijing's true colors—and ultimate motives.

They are currently on display in Nanjing province, where they are violently repressing millions. President Xi Jinping's regime has set up reeducation camps, or "free hospital treatment for the masses with sick thinking," as Beijing calls them.[7] The CCP justified the camps because of a series of violent attacks by extremists in the region. Xi ordered his security apparatus to carry out a "smashing, obliterating offensive," according to leaked documents. "Round up everyone who should be rounded up. . . . Even grandparents and family members who seemed too old to carry out violence could not be spared."[8] The result is "the largest mass incarceration of an ethnic-religious minority since the second world war."[9]

Beijing also sanctions the forceable harvesting of the body organs of detained political and religious prisoners. An international tribunal in London, headed by Sir Geoffrey Nice, who led the prosecution of war criminal Slobodan Milošević, has laid out volumes of evidence, including the testimony of doctors who have been forced to perform these procedures.[10]

Beijing's suppression of COVID-19 warnings has impacted human lives and economies worldwide. On December 30, 2019, a Chinese medical doctor named Li Wenliang commented to colleagues about a new and aggressive virus. When he did so on a chat app, he was detained by the Public Security Bureau, who charged that he had "severely disturbed the social order."[11]

By the end of January 2020, after becoming increasingly ill from the virus, he posted the letter he had been forced to sign on Weibo, a massive Chinese public messaging website. This is how his nation and the world learned about the true danger of the COVID virus.[12] Other brave Chinese doctors and journalists who tried to alert the world about the virus disappeared at the hands of the Beijing regime, which was more concerned about its political viability than the health of its people—or for that matter, the health of people around the world.

Beijing continues to take a position of non-cooperation in global efforts to find out the true origins of the virus.

You can add to this list the practice of crimes against Christians, the Falun Gong, citizens of Hong Kong, the people of Tibet, and others. By now, the Chinese military is openly talking about using new kinds of biological warfare, including "specific ethnic genetic attacks," which should come as no surprise.[13]

Constant surveillance and censorship, detention without trial, torture and forced confessions, other forms of physical and psychological abuse, and excessive use of the death penalty are all a standard part of life for the mainland Chinese people under the CCP.

As Maya Angelou once said, "When someone shows you who they are, believe them the first time."[14]

This is the regime with whom the American elites addressed in this book are in bed.

The brutal nature of the regime is only the beginning of the problem. Beijing aspires to replace the United States as the most powerful nation on the globe. Do not take my word for it: the Chinese leadership itself speaks openly about that ambition. China's state news agency, Xinhua, boosts the party line, "By 2050, two centuries after the Opium Wars, which plunged the 'Middle Kingdom' into a period of hurt and shame, China is set to regain its might and re-ascend to the top of the world." China's President Xi has a specific 2049 plan to accomplish that goal.[15]

Xinhua elsewhere declares the superiority of the communist dictatorship over the representative democracy of the United States.

"After several hundred years, the Western model is showing its age. It is high time for profound reflection on the ills of a doddering democracy which has precipitated so many of the world's ills and solved so few."[16]

President Xi commonly uses the expression that he is seeking for China a "strong nation dream." The phrase comes from a 2009 book published in China called *The China Dream*. The author, Colonel Liu Mingfu of the People's Liberation Army (PLA), is quite explicit about what that means. "China's grand goal in the 21st century is to become the world's No. 1 power," he says bluntly. "The competition between China and the United States will not be like a 'shooting duel' or a 'boxing match' but more like a 'track and field' competition. It will be a protracted 'Marathon.'"[17]

But this "China dream," as expressed by President Xi, is a nightmare for the rest of the world. The American elites featured in this book are in various ways feeding the beast that would make this nightmare a reality. And they get paid well doing it.

Throughout American history, there have been concerns about powerful American leaders aligning themselves with our foreign adversaries. Nothing comes close in magnitude to the problem of the buying off of these elites. It represents the most dire national security threat our country faces today. As Professor Walter Russell Mead wrote in the *Wall Street Journal*, "America's greatest risk isn't the vulnerability of its voting machines to foreign hackers or the susceptibility of party apparatchiks to phishing scams. It is the erosion of ethical standards in the American political and business establishments that most exposes the U.S. to the kind of foreign interference against which [George] Washington warned."[18]

2

THE BIDENS

You all heard that Trump said Biden's son has securities companies all over the world," the speaker said in a smooth, elegant Mandarin voice. "But who helped Biden's son build his global companies?"[1]

The question came from a slender Chinese academic named Di Dongsheng as he stood in front of a large audience in Shanghai. It was November 28, 2020, just weeks after the U.S. presidential election. Beyond the hundreds who had gathered in the auditorium, many more watched the streamed version online, courtesy of Guan Video, an influential Chinese nationalist website.[2] Di is more than a random academic: as an associate dean at Renmin University, an elite institute in Beijing that boasts prominent alumni high in the Communist Party and government, including politburo members and ambassadors, he sits near the center of power. Di has also worked with the Chinese government's official propaganda organs to spread pro-Beijing material in the United States, including Washington, D.C.[3]

The speech was part of a prestigious forum that featured talks by Chinese luminaries such as the former directors general of the Asian Development Bank and of the International Department of China's Central Bank.[4]

Di's remarks struck a nerve. The crowd, no doubt including high-ranking Communist Party officials, was actively engaged. They smiled, laughed, and applauded as he discussed the global stage and

China's influence in the United States. Di noted that Beijing had "old friends . . . inside America's core circle of power," mentioning Wall Street in particular as a strong ally. He reassured the audience that Beijing could settle issues with "people at the top" in the United States. When he asked that question—rhetorically—about Biden's son's deals, the audience laughed knowingly. "There are indeed buy-and-sell transactions involved in here," Di added. "So I think at this particular time, it is of strategic and tactical value for us to show good will."[5] Di's comments about Chinese influence among elites in the United States were unusually candid for a Chinese official in public—direct and on the nose. The fact that he referenced Chinese commercial dealings with the Biden family—which I was the first to expose in 2018—was particularly surprising. Apparently, they surprised Beijing too, which promptly removed the speech from the country's social media platforms after it started to go viral.[6]

The answer to Di's question is that financiers with close ties to the highest levels of Chinese intelligence helped Hunter Biden build or join several global companies. There are important reasons for Beijing to want their commercial ties with the Biden family to remain obscured.

The greater puzzle is, why would the Biden family want commercial ties to China? Could Hunter Biden not trade on his last name to open doors in less authoritarian countries?

Chinese officials have cultivated these commercial ties for more than a decade. Other Biden family members have happily pursued financial relationships, too, eager to cash in with lucrative deals. Since I first broke the story about these ties in 2018, I have gained access to an abundance of new documentary evidence.

In short, the new evidence makes clear that the Biden family received some $31 million from Chinese businessmen with very close ties to the highest levels of Chinese intelligence during and after Joe Biden's tenure as vice president. Indeed, as of this writing, some of those financial relationships remain intact. One is struck by the extraordinary concentration of intelligence ties by the businesspeople making these deals with the Bidens. These ties reach the highest levels of Chinese intelligence, including the former head of the Ministry of State Security, the head of foreign intelligence recruitment for Chinese intelligence, and a cluster of United Front organizations used for intelligence operations in the West. (We will later learn of the significance of these United Front organizations—something Xi and other communist officials consider a "magic weapon" in their struggle against the West.)[7]

The new sources of information also provide even more evidence that this is a story about not just Hunter Biden, but Joe Biden himself. To some degree, for the period our research covers, Hunter Biden and Joe Biden had intertwined finances. Hunter Biden privately complained to family members about paying his father's bills. "I love all of you," he wrote to his daughter Naomi on January 3, 2019. "But I don't receive any respect and thats fine I guess -works for you apparently. I Hope you all can do what I did and pay for everything for this entire family Fro 30 years. It's really hard. But don't worry unlike Pop I won't make you give me half your salary."[8]

Other correspondence confirms that the vice president of the United States, signified by the initials "JRB" for Joseph Robinette Biden, was mentioned in emails discussing payments or financial opportunities.[9]

The idea that his father might be participating in Hunter Biden's dealings was potentially realized when Hunter Biden or his business partner, Eric Schwerin, arranged for private phone lines for the vice president, at a cost ranging from $190 to several hundred dollars a month.[10] This would allow for a non-official channel of communication. It is neither legal for the vice president of the United States to accept gifts from a company, nor clear why the vice president of the United States needs an undisclosed means of communication.[11]

According to Hunter, he (or Rosemont Seneca Partners) had been paying for multiple phone lines for his father for eleven years—all while he was in office as a senator or vice president. Using the lowest number of payments for "JRB," we found that for the cost of Joe's phone line(s) ($190), that amounts to over $25,000. Interestingly, in February 2017, Hunter moved to put at least one phone number back under Joe Biden's name after he left office because, "he wants to *start* paying it."[12]

There are myriad other examples of communications between Hunter Biden and his partners at Rosemont about paying the bills of then vice president Joe Biden. These included paying for contractors making renovations on Joe Biden's Delaware home. Schwerin wrote to Hunter in June 2010, asking him which ones "should get paid out of 'my' account and which should be put on hold or paid out of the 'Wilmington Trust Social Security Check Account.'" In addition, Schwerin explains, "There is about $2,000 extra in 'my' account beyond what is used for monthly expenses." In a follow-up email on June 8, Schwerin told Hunter that "Mike Christopher," one of the contractors who worked on Joe Biden's Delaware home, "is hassling" him. He said that he was "paying a couple of the smaller things since I haven't heard from your Dad." In yet another instance, Hunter made reimbursements to Joe Biden for a Ford Raptor truck, in an email marked "payment to JRB from RHB - autopay owasco acct."[13]

The new sources of information presented here include:

- *The Hunter Biden Secret Service Travel Logs*
  The Secret Service keeps travel logs on the family members of the president and vice president when they travel with them. Hunter Biden's Secret Service travel logs, covering the years from 2009 to 2014, were obtained through the Freedom of Information Act and by the U.S. Senate Oversight Committee.

- *The Bevan Cooney emails*

   This collection of more than twenty-five thousand emails contains the correspondence of Hunter Biden business associate Bevan Cooney between 2010 and 2016. Cooney's emails show communication to and from Hunter Biden and include an abundance of attachments and documents. Cooney granted us access to his complete email collection.

- *The United States Senate Oversight Committee Report*

   Issued in September 2020, the U.S. Senate committee report on Hunter Biden's activities included dozens of U.S. Treasury Department Suspicious Activity Reports (SARS), which detailed some financial transactions of Hunter Biden and his firms. (Note: a supplement to the report was released in November 2020.)

- *The Tony Bobulinski emails and messages*

   Bobulinski, a successful financier and businessman, was brought into the Biden orbit in 2017 to help put together and run an investment fund that the Chinese would finance. Bobulinski shared those records with the U.S. Senate Oversight Committee.

- *Jason Galanis materials*

   We were given access to materials involving Hunter Biden business partner Jason Galanis.

- *The Hunter Biden emails from his laptop*

   These emails number close to twenty-five thousand and include emails and messages sent to colleagues, partners, and family members. Hunter Biden has never denied that the emails are genuine, even admitting that they could be his. Were the emails false, we could assume that he would vigorously challenge their authenticity. He has not.[14]

As we first reported in *Secret Empires*, in 2009, Hunter Biden joined forces with his close friends and fellow Yale students Devon Archer and Christopher Heinz to set up a series of businesses. They first established Rosemont Capital and, soon after, Rosemont Seneca Partners. They also set up Rosemont Realty and Rosemont Seneca Technology Partners. Rather than locate the shop in Manhattan, the world's financial capital, Rosemont Seneca leased space in Washington, D.C. "They occupied an all-brick building on Wisconsin Avenue . . . just two miles from both Joe Biden's office in the White House and his residence at the Naval Observatory."[15]

Hunter Biden and his partners constructed a remarkable constellation of limited liability companies, many of which served as passthroughs, to manage the flow of foreign money. These included Oldaker, Biden, and Belair, LLP; Seneca Global Advisors; Rosemont Seneca Advisors; RSP Investments; Eudora; RSTP I; RSTP II Alpha and Bravo, Owasco, and Skaneateles. Numerous emails—including corporate documents—between the two clearly indicate that the management of those LLCs and Hunter Biden's finances were handled by his colleague Eric Schwerin, a former Clinton administration official.[16]

Hunter Biden's defenders present a wholly benign narrative: he had a small role in medium-sized deals with profit-driven Chinese investors drawn in only by his business acumen. The facts add up to something else entirely.

As you have seen, there are indications that Hunter and Joe Biden's financial fortunes have been fused. Barely a year and a half into the Obama administration, Hunter Biden and his business partners in Rosemont Seneca began drawing up a memo called "JRB Future Memo" about commercial opportunities for Joe Biden after he left the Obama administration. "Mike has a pretty good draft of this done," Schwerin wrote to Hunter Biden. "Does it make sense to see if your Dad has some time in the next couple of weeks while you are in DC to talk about it? Your Dad just called me (about his mortgage) and mentioned he'd be out a lot soon and not really back until Labor Day so it dawned on me it might be a good time (also he could use some news about his future earnings potential!)."[17]

What "future earnings" the vice president would be discussing with Schwerin, the manager of Hunter Biden's LLCs, is unclear, as is why the vice president would be talking about his mortgage with the same manager.

The Bidens—father and son together—apparently followed a business model offering access to the highest levels of power in Washington in exchange for big-money international deals.

Locating Rosemont Seneca Partners in Washington, D.C., fits with this model, because access to the White House, particularly for foreign elites, represented a central selling point in securing private deals.

This setup is what Hunter clearly had in mind when dealing with foreign elites, and is best demonstrated by an email Hunter sent to a prospective partner in Mexico, Miguel Aleman. In a February 2016 email, Hunter, who was arriving in Mexico City aboard Air Force Two with his father, was furious because he had granted Aleman access to the highest reaches in Washington, but the deals he wanted in return had yet to materialize.

We are arriving late tonight on Air Force 2 to MX City. We will be there for Thursday - I'm attending meeting w/ President N [of Mexico] w/ Dad. Jeff is with me on [p]lane and [he] will be with us all day. Would love to see [you] but you never respond. I am really upset by it. You respond when it's something you need. You are the most generous person I know but WTF. We have so many great things to do together and I want you at the plane when the VP lands with your Mom and Dad and you completely ignore me. I've looked at what your family has done and want to follow in that tradition and you always say you will help but I haven't heard from you since I got you a mtg for Carlos and your Dad. We have been talking about business deals and partnerships for 7 years. And I really appreciate you letting me stay at your resort villa . . . *but I have brought every single person you have ever asked me to bring to the F'ing WHite House and the Vice President's house and the inauguration and then you go completely silent - I don't hear from you for months. I don't know what it is that I did but I'd like to know why I've delivered on every single thing you've ever asked - and you make me feel like I've done something to offend you.*[18] (Emphasis added)

In the case of the Aleman family, access to the White House did not land Hunter a profitable accord. China, however, was a completely different story.

Hunter's Rosemont Seneca quickly set its sights on "Zhongguo—the Middle Kingdom."[19] As we will see, a number of Chinese officials, several with intelligence connections, were all too happy to go into business with the son of the vice president. It is likely this is because they have different goals than just making money.

Doing business in China often entails having the right political contacts and relationships; having a powerful family name can be of enormous benefit.

In one case, to do business in China, as I first reported in *Secret Empires*, Hunter Biden and his partners at Rosemont joined forces with another politically connected consultancy called the Thornton Group. James Bulger, the nephew of the infamous mob hit man James "Whitey" Bulger, heads the Massachusetts-based firm. Whitey was the doyen of the Winter Hill Gang of the South Boston mafia. On the hook for nineteen murders, he took off. He was later found, arrested, tried, and convicted. Whitey's younger brother Billy Bulger is James Bulger's father, and Billy served on the Thornton Group board of directors. He was formerly a leader in the Massachusetts State Senate.[20] Bulger's partners in the venture included Michael Lin (also known as Lin Junliang), a cofounder of the group. He had considerable connections in Beijing. Originally from Taiwan, Lin moved to Beijing in 2005 and worked as the head of investments for Peking University Founder, a powerful investment vehicle that "has strong connections among the top leaders of the Chinese Communist Party." (As we will see, Founder also has deep commercial ties with Chinese intelligence.) Lin helped give Hunter Biden entrée into the highest levels of Chinese leadership.[21]

Fewer than twelve months after opening Rosemont Seneca, Hunter Biden and Devon Archer were in China with access to those of great financial (and political) influence. The Thornton Group's account of the encounter on their Chinese-language website at the time was revealing: Chinese executives "extended their warm welcome" to the "Thornton Group, with its U.S. partner Rosemont Seneca chairman Hunter Biden (second son of the now Vice President Joe Biden)." The meeting's purpose was to "explore the possibility of commercial cooperation and opportunity."[22]

The meetings were with the largest and most powerful government-backed financial institutions in the country. In April 2010, they met with high-ranking senior Chinese officials, including the head of private equity for the Chinese government's China Investment Corporation.[23]

The timing is important. Hunter's meeting in China occurred just before Vice President Biden met with Chinese President Hu Jintao during the Nuclear Security Summit in Washington.[24]

Joe Biden would emerge as the point person on Obama administration policy on China, so he would be a clear focus of Chinese attention.[25]

Hunter Biden was a centerpiece of these initial meetings—not necessarily for what he brought to the meeting but simply for his participation. The first trip in April was a success. James Bulger wrote to Hunter after, "your presence was a huge boon to us all."[26]

In January 2011, Devon Archer met again with Chinese officials at the highest levels and apparently planned to underscore the partners' exclusive access to the vice president by bringing signed copies of Joe Biden's book, presumably *Promises to Keep* (2007), to hand out. "Any chance I can get 3 Biden books to leave with cic [China Investment Corporation], citic [China International Trust and Investment Corporation] and chairman zong of wahaha [one of China's richest men]?" Devon Archer wrote to Hunter and Eric Schwerin before the trip.[27]

For Beijing, a commercial relationship with the Bidens would offer an opportunity for "elite capture." Joe Biden had already painted a relatively favorable view of the Beijing regime in public statements.[28] Hunter Biden and his team did get meetings with these dominant financial institutions. CITIC reports directly to the PRC State Council, the most powerful governing body in the country, and the China Investment Corporation is one of the government's sovereign wealth funds.[29]

In April 2011, Hunter Biden and his partners returned to Asia, visiting both Taiwan and mainland China. According to internal Rosemont emails, Hunter does not appear to have had a heavy lift in any Rosemont business. "What is the first meeting I HAVE to attend?" he asked Devon Archer in an email.[30] His figurehead presence relative to Rosemont seemed to be enough.

When they returned to Washington, D.C., Hunter's associates emphasized the importance of the vice president's son sending personal notes to Chinese officials. His partners ensured that there should be "a thank you email from Hunter to every meeting contact we met."[31]

And when it came to motivating Chinese nationals to work with Rosemont, Bulger knew to pull the Biden card. "I have [Michael] lin [one of the Chinese partners] all over this he knows he cannot disappoint HB [Hunter Biden]."[32]

On this trip, Hunter and his partners met with someone they dubbed "The Super Chairman," who would play a central role in securing a large deal. The Super Chairman is Che Feng, a Chinese tycoon with close ties to Chinese intelligence. The son of a PLA soldier, Che was a successful businessman and controlled numerous companies.[33] He would become a major player in the relationship between Hunter and Beijing. Described in the Western press as a "shadowy and discreet investor," Che perhaps needed to remain in the shadows and demonstrate extreme discretion because of his very powerful friends and family members.[34] His father-in-law was the governor of the People's Bank of China and was the president of the National Council for Social Security Fund, the government retirement fund in China. The National Council later became an investor in Hunter's private equity deal. But even more important, Che had other disturbing ties: he was business partners with Ma Jian, the vice minister of State Security, essentially China's KGB, at the time.[35] (Ma Jian also had financial ties with Peking Founder, where Michael Lin had worked.) Reportedly, Ma was the director of the ministry's No. 8 Bureau, which targeted foreigners with its counterintelligence apparatus—"Mainly diplomats, businessmen and reporters."[36] French intelligence scholar Roger Faligot said that Ma Jian "oversaw operations in North America."[37]

Ma was a very busy man. Beyond his intelligence work, he reportedly had six mistresses.[38]

The hazard of a Chinese businessman with close ties to the top ranks of Beijing's spy agency conducting financial transactions with the son of the U.S. vice president cannot be overstated. How this did not set off national security or ethics alarm bells in Washington is a wonder in itself.

According to email correspondence, Hunter Biden's relationship with the Super Chairman was warm, and in October 2011, Hunter and his partners returned to Hong Kong as Che's guests. The Super Chairman put them up at the luxurious Four Seasons Hotel in Hong Kong for more discussions about business opportunities.[39]

Hunter Biden was traveling with Secret Service protection, so for the meeting, a Chinese partner instructed Hunter to send the

Secret Service detail to him to check things out. "When secret service wish to call to check things as they always do, pls make them call Jonathan or me."[40]

The plan was to fuse Chinese financial might to those with access to the highest levels of power in the Western world. Together, they formed an entity called Bohai Harvest RST (BHR) to create a pecuniary powerhouse funded by China's biggest government-backed financial institutions. Biden and his partners were enthusiastic about what the Super Chairman was bringing them: an opportunity to work with the largest state-owned financial conglomerates, "or that kind of high power companies." One of Hunter's Chinese partners wrote him in September 2011, "Imagine we will be sitting on the same board with CIC or the other Chinese HUGE investment or fund house(s)!!!"[41]

One of those big "fund houses" was Harvest Fund Management, which was headed by another key figure in the Biden family's deals in China. Zhao Xuejun (aka Henry Zhao) was the chairman of Harvest, and also the company's Chinese Communist Party general secretary. "The mission of our Party is to bring happiness to people," he proclaimed, "and to revive the nation for people."[42]

Zhao, another figure who would steer money to Hunter Biden, also had ties to the very top of Chinese intelligence.

One of Zhao's companies, Harvest Global Investments, was cofounded by Jia Liqing, the daughter of Jia Chunwang, who was a member of the Politburo Standing Committee at the time. Her father is the former minister of state security, which meant he was in "charge of secret service, espionage, and domestic and overseas intelligence work."[43] There is no one more powerful in the world of Chinese intelligence. Beginning in 1985, he ran the foreign espionage section for the Ministry of State Security. He eventually ran the entire intelligence service until 1998, when he became head of public security, which put him in charge of other intelligence operations, the national police, and even the Chinese gulag.[44] He was, in short, the man who ran China's spy apparatus for thirteen years. Jia helped develop China's "deep water fish" (Chendi yü) strategy of developing thousands of special agents "hidden in the deepest strata of society . . . of the enemy" to work with the intelligence services.[45]

Jia Liqing's in-laws were also deeply connected to the Communist Party: her father-in-law, Liu Yunshan, was the head of the Chinese Communist Party's Propaganda Department during early negotiations and up until a year before Harvest secured its deal with Hunter.[46]

The seductive and lucrative deal that Hunter was now putting into place, creating BHR, involved two financiers with ties to the highest levels of Chinese intelligence, a billion-dollar private equity deal that we first exposed in *Secret Empires*.[47] What we now know are the roles played by the spy-connected "Super Chairman" and Zhao.

The deal was negotiated quietly and Hunter's partners wanted to keep his involvement in the agreement private at least until the deal was sealed. "Please remember that I have not informed anyone in my office about the reason for my trip to Hong Kong last week," Jim Bulger wrote to Hunter Biden and others after he returned from Asia. "So no one knows that Hunter was with me last week. . . . I want to keep this effort quiet until we have a contract in place."

"What happens in Hong Kong stays in Hong Kong," replied Eric Schwerin.[48]

According to Michael Lin, another Chinese partner, Hunter's role in the venture was pretty straightforward: "Open as many doors as possible in the western world for this very famous Bohai professional team." There was also the expectation that Hunter and his partners would "join some of the meetings in HK and China they arrange" when communicating with possible financial partners.[49]

Although he would later claim publicly that this private equity deal was not really that lucrative, Hunter's private correspondence shows otherwise.[50] Regarding the "super chairman fund," he wrote in an email in September 2011, "Things are moving rapidly and the percentage he is offering me is much larger than I at first thought." Archer thought the deal made sense—"Not only on it's own merits from an economics standpoint but from the leverage in access it provides with the big boys here in the west who all need China."[51]

Hunter saw dollar signs. "I don't believe in lottery tickets anymore," he wrote to Archer, "but I do believe in the super chairman . . . I think the sky's the limit."[52]

The Bohai negotiations continued over several months. The email correspondence suggests that the Chinese partners did not expect Hunter Biden and the other Americans to be actively involved in the fund; they would do most of the heavy lifting. As Bulger explained to Hunter and Archer, "if all Jonathan needs from us is to sit on the investment committee then it might not be a bad deal. . . . If our involvement is simply to sit on the sidelines and be the 'white face' then I'm personally close to [a] 15% [stake]."[53]

By spring 2013, the Bohai deal was in the final negotiation stage. In June, the principals met in Beijing to go over the terms. Although Biden lawyers have claimed that Hunter was not involved in these final discussions, according to Secret Service travel records, Hunter was in Beijing between June 13 and June 15.[54]

In December 2013, Hunter returned to Beijing, this time arriving on Air Force Two with his father. Vice President Biden was grappling with a multitude of issues between the United States and China. He held high-level meetings with Chinese officials. What Hunter spent his time doing is less clear.[55] However, Hunter later admitted that he had introduced his dad to his business partner Jonathan Li in the lobby of their hotel.[56]

Ten days later, the BHR company was registered in Beijing. Hunter was later offered a 10 percent equity stake in the business and a board seat. The equity stake required him to put in capital, but he apparently did not have enough. Chinese executives gave him a loan, guaranteeing him a stake in the billion-dollar-plus investment firm.[57]

In January 2014, just one month after the finalized BHR deal, Hunter and Devon made plans to meet with the Chinese ambassador in Washington.[58] The purpose of the meeting is unclear.

BHR released a prospectus for investors, noting that Hunter Biden served on the board. They never mentioned Joe Biden per se, but Hunter was listed as "Honorary Co-Chair of the 2009 Presidential Inaugural Committee of the United States." BHR noted that Rosemont brought "extensive political and business networks in America and Europe."[59]

Hunter Biden figured prominently in BHR materials sent to Chinese investors. BHR, in their 2016 annual report, had a graphic titled "Global Network," which included a world map and a photo of Hunter Biden and other BHR partners with an arrow pointing to New York City.[60]

The Super Chairman would fade from the deal after both he and Ma were arrested and charged with money laundering and bribery, respectively. But the partnership between Hunter and Chinese officials was off and running.[61] And Zhao would arrange other deals with Hunter Biden.

Bohai Harvest was not simply an investment fund engaged in ordinary commercial arrangements. Given the intelligence and political ties of those involved in setting up BHR, it should not come as a surprise that Hunter's fund began buying or investing in strategically important companies in China and the United States. One of their early investments was in China General Nuclear Power Corporation (CGN), where Hunter's firm was an "anchor investor." The FBI would later expose that firm as a conduit for nuclear espionage in the West. In April 2016, CGN and a CGN engineer named Allen Ho were charged by the Obama Justice Department with stealing nuclear secrets from the United States—actions prosecutors said could cause "significant damage to our national security."[62]

Hunter's BHR was also contributing to the undermining of our national defense—buying companies in the United States that had clear military application that would benefit Beijing in its strategic competition with the United States. BHR bought an American company called Henniges Automotive, a firm known for anti-vibration technologies with military and civilian applications. The Chinese military interest in the company was obvious, especially given that BHR partnered with the Aviation Industry Corporation of China (AVIC) to close the deal. AVIC is one of China's largest military contractors. U.S. officials have identified AVIC as a major culprit in the theft of U.S. defense technologies.[63]

How much has, and will, Hunter Biden ultimately make on just this one China deal? It is impossible to say. Team Biden has absurdly claimed that his stake in the firm is only $420,000.[64] But recall Hunter Biden's enthusiastic email comparing the deal to winning the lottery. Professor Steven Kaplan from the University of Chicago's Booth School of Business said, "It is difficult to imagine, if not incomprehensible, that a 10% stake in those economics is worth only $420K." Using other similar investment funds as a guide, he estimates Hunter's take on the BHR deal would be closer to $20 million.[65]

The mystery surrounding Hunter Biden's financial ties with Chinese intelligence–connected businessmen is only compounded by a decision he made shortly after those ties began. In July 2014, Hunter Biden took the unusual step of declining Secret Service travel on his future overseas trips. The Secret Service communicated this fact to the Senate Homeland Security and Governance Affairs Committee, but gave no explanation as to why Biden made this move. In 2015, he reportedly requested Secret Service protection on a trip to Europe, but not on any related to China.[66]

***

HOW MUCH DID the Chinese participants make on these deals? Most likely, they do not care. Chinese elites and Communist Party officials who were prospective partners or clients of Hunter were granted off-the-books meetings with Vice President Joe Biden.

On November 5, 2011, Devon Archer forwarded an email from one of his business contacts hinting at a chance to gain "potentially outstanding new clients" by helping to arrange White House meetings for a group of Chinese executives and government officials. The group was the China Entrepreneur Club (CEC) and included Chinese billionaires, Chinese Communist Party loyalists, and at least one "respected diplomat" from Beijing.[67] Despite its seemingly harmless name, CEC has been referred to as "a second foreign ministry" for the People's Republic of China—a communist regime that tightly controls the people and businesses in its country.[68] CEC was founded in 2006 by several Chinese businessmen and diplomats.[69]

"This is China Inc.," the forwarded email claimed, referring to the delegation.[70] This is not only a powerful and prestigious group; it is also fused to the Chinese government. The CEC has been described in U.S. congressional testimony as "the most significant and elite, China government led, cyber-economic command and control entity."[71] CEC's membership includes some senior members of the Chinese Communist Party, including Wang Zhongyu ("vice chairman of the 10th National Committee of the Chinese People's Political Consultative Conference and the deputy secretary of the Party Leadership Group"), Ma Weihua (director of several Chinese Communist Party offices), Jiang Xipei (member of the 16th National Congress), and others.[72]

"I know it is political season and people are hesitant but a group like this does not come along every day," the email stated. "A tour of the white house and a meeting with a member of the chief of staff's office and John Kerry would be great." There was a caveat: "Not sure if one has to be registered to [do] this." The reference here was to the Foreign Agents Registration Act (FARA), which requires registration with the Justice Department when interacting with the federal government on behalf of a foreign entity. No one responded to the query, and no one bothered to register with the Justice Department.[73]

Securing some important meetings in Washington promised Biden and his partners "good access to [the Chinese] for any deal in the future." The email emphasized that the "biggest priority for the CEC group is to see the White House, and have a senior U.S. politician, or senior member of Obama's administration, give them a tour."[74]

Almost a week later, Archer got a follow-up email inquiring how the meeting went with the CEC representatives. It finished, "Do me a favor and ask Hunter [Biden] to call me—I've tried reaching him a couple of times." Archer replied, "Hunter is traveling in the UAE for the week with royalty so probably next week before he will be back in pocket. . . . The meeting with [CEC representative] was good. Seems like there is a lot to do together down the line."[75]

A minute later, Archer followed up after deleting Hunter from his reply, "Couldn't confirm this with Hunter on the line but we got him his meeting at the WH Monday for the Chinese folks."[76] One wonders if Archer was being careful to cloak Hunter's role in acquiring that "WH" access.

Meeting archives from the Obama-Biden administration show that on November 14, 2011, this Chinese delegation visited the White House, and was afforded high-level access. According to White House visitor logs, there were approximately thirty members in the delegation.[77]

Curiously, the White House visitor logs do not mention what

would have been the prize ring for the Chinese delegation: meeting Vice President Joe Biden. But the vice president may well have had such an off-the-books meeting, as one of the core founders of the Chinese group has revealed. In a listing of the CEC members' biographies, CEC secretary-general Maggie Cheng claims that she arranged the CEC delegation meetings in Washington in 2011 and brags of the Washington elites with which the CEC met. The showcase name was Vice President Joe Biden.[78]

Hunter Biden would also personally signal to Chinese officials that a deal he wanted was important to his father when he became involved in another financial venture called Burnham Asset Management. The venture included his friend Devon Archer and a businessman named Jason Galanis. They were in active communication with Henry Zhao, who had helped launch BHR. Zhao was eager to use his company, Harvest Global, in which he was partners with the daughter of the former head of Chinese intelligence, to strike more deals with Hunter.

"Henry we believe, is still interested in doing the JV deal if a fair evaluation of Burnham can be agreed to and if YOU as a deal maker are inside Burnham," wrote James Bulger to Hunter and Schwerin in October 2014. He added, "Henry holds you in very high regard."[79] But even outside of the Burnham deal, Zhao seemed eager to cut deals with the son of the vice president. "Henry remains committed to also making something work with myself and Hunter outside of this Burnham matter as mentioned before," Bulger later wrote to them. "He has a few interesting ideas."[80]

On a previous occasion, Zhao apparently suggested ways to structure a deal "thereby putting money directly into our pockets."[81]

"I look forward to seeing you soon—in Beijing or in U.S.," Zhao wrote to Hunter. "And thank you very much for the picture frame you sent over! I will put our photo in it."[82]

Hunter Biden was all in, happy to be working with Harvest. "I know that we all look forward to participating in the building of Harvest's global platform," he wrote Zhao in April 2016. "Burnham can have no greater partner than Harvest and I am honored that you chose to partner with us on this."[83]

It does appear clear that Hunter solicited a $15 million investment from Zhao, saying as an inducement that the investment was "important to his family," a likely reference to his father.[84]

It is not possible to know the full extent of Hunter Biden's financial ties to Harvest, but court documents indicate that Zhao's firm sent $5 million to Burnham.[85] "Harvest finance has instructed bank to wire the fund to you today," a Harvest executive wrote to Hunter in early 2016. "You should receive it in a day or two."[86] As we will see, several other partners corroborate Hunter's paternal name-dropping in other arrangements involving Chinese firms.

Between these two deals, Hunter had received some $25 million from Chinese businessmen who were tied to the highest levels of Chinese intelligence. There would be more.

Joe Biden regularly met with his son's foreign clients, particularly those from China and Ukraine. Several of these meetings were held "off the books," meaning they do not show up on White House visitor logs. Beyond the gathering in 2011 with Chinese executives in the White House, the email record suggests that Joe Biden also met with Burisma "fixer" Vadym Pozharskyi. (Burisma was paying Hunter $1 million a year at the time.[87]) "Dear Hunter," he wrote to Biden in April 2015, "thank you for inviting me to DC and giving an opportunity to meet your father and spent some time together. It's realty an honor and pleasure."[88] Biden's spokespeople have not denied that Biden may have met Pozharskyi, instead claiming that any such meeting would have been "informal" and "cursory."[89]

Hunter Biden's business associates spoke candidly in emails about Hunter Biden's unique role in the business, tied to his high-level access to the White House. This was particularly the case when it came

to Chinese deals. In an email on November 4, 2014, Jason Galanis discussed a draft pitch he was preparing for possible investors.
"I wanted to focus on the 'other currency' we are bringing to the
table. . . . direct [Obama] administration pipeline."[90]

One important part of that political network was Max Baucus,
who served as U.S. ambassador to China. Baucus, as you recall,
served in the U.S. Senate alongside Joe Biden for many years. We
will learn more about Ambassador Baucus and his financial arrangements with Beijing in chapter 6. As Hunter wrote to his business partners, "On Baucus- we have a very very good relationship
and I can ask anything we need."[91]

***

HUNTER'S NEW CONNECTIONS at the highest levels of power in Beijing
became a calling card for prospective clients and investors for his
firm. John DeLoche, who ran the Hunter-linked firm Rosemont
Seneca Technology Partners, wrote the following in a May 2014
email to a prospective client, copying Hunter. "We have deep relationships in China and could introduce you to a number of potential partners including China Investment Corporation (CIC),
a $400bn sovereign wealth fund as well as several other potential
investors/partners. Hunter and Devon spend a lot of time in the
region and will come back to us with a full list of potential intros
for your thoughts next week."[92]

Stateside, Chinese state-owned conglomerates were soon coming to Hunter's small firm looking for help. Another Chinese
sovereign wealth fund (CITIC) approached Rosemont and asked
Hunter Biden for introductions to U.S. companies, some involving strategic industries where Beijing was looking to expand. In
one instance, Chinese investors wanted to get into the aviation
business. "She [the CITIC executive] kept emphasizing how much

money they have and are willing to commit to these ventures," Schwerin wrote to Hunter in May 2014.[93]

Vice President Joe Biden continued to emphasize in his discussions that China was not a rival or a threat to the United States and that a rising China was good for America. As he said in May 2011, "a rising China is a positive, positive development, not only for China but for America and the world writ large."[94]

Meanwhile, Hunter was becoming involved in an increasing number of Chinese deals that served the national goals of Beijing in its competition with the United States. One deal involved a plan to buy the Greek national railway (TrainOSE), which was being privatized. Hunter Biden and his business partners were planning to do so with Chinese money. Beijing would finance the deal, and he and his partners would make it happen.[95] It would be a strategically important move for the Chinese government, and the involvement of Hunter's firm would probably make the deal more palatable for Western governments who were increasingly concerned about the growing influence of Beijing in Europe.

Who was Hunter's Chinese partner? It was the China Ocean Shipping Corporation (COSCO), a state-controlled firm with deep ties to the Chinese military. Some military strategists call the company the "fifth arm of the Chinese Navy."[96]

China's President Xi was particularly proud of the role COSCO was playing in Europe. "COSCO is the dragon's head for China in Greece," he proclaimed.[97]

COSCO already owned most of a Greek port in Piraeus, and part of their geostrategic plan was to invest in infrastructure projects from the western Balkans leading to the port. The United States had major concerns that Chinese state-linked firms were making inroads in central Europe in a way that would provide Beijing with a strategic advantage. (Harvard's Philippe Le Corre testified before the U.S. Congress that the COSCO-owned port in Greece is a regional "hub" of China's New Silk Road.[98]) Analysts also note that China's "string of pearls" strategy was designed to use ports across the region to "mount a challenge" to the U.S. Navy.[99]

Buying the Greek railroad system would help Beijing even further. The "new route of Chinese products via Piraeus port is 8 days faster than any other route to central Europe," assured Paris Kokorotsikos in an email to Hunter and his business partners.[100] The arrangement was simple: COSCO would pay for everything and finance 100 percent of the purchase price of the rail passenger business.[101] As a result, Hunter Biden and his partners would be able to "make money without any investment."[102] COSCO did not object.[103]

Hunter's Greek partner was an old family friend: Michael Karloutsos, the son of Father Alex Karloutsos, a senior official in the Greek Orthodox Archdiocese of America. The Karloutsoses and the Bidens had a strong friendship going back decades. They first met in 1980. Father Alex's wife serves on the board of directors of the Beau Biden Foundation. When Biden was elected president in 2020, Father Alex had to dispel rumors that he would join the incoming administration.[104]

The deal with COSCO to buy the Greek railroad fell through. The Italian National Railway outbid the Chinese–Hunter Biden partners for the assets.[105] But Hunter's willingness to participate in deals that would benefit Beijing geostrategically was becoming a pattern. And there were other deals with COSCO that would be secured.

***

HUNTER COFOUNDED A real estate company with Devon Archer and other partners called Rosemont Realty.[106] They held commercial real estate properties throughout the United States. Hunter had tried to find investors on his 2011 trip to China and Taiwan, explaining that "some of the United State's wealthiest families have entrusted

Rosemont Realty to manage real estate investments for years."[107] But he apparently got little or no interest.

In 2014, as the deals with Beijing were beginning to bear fruit, Hunter and his partners received an "unsolicited offer" from a Hong Kong–based firm called Gemini Investments to buy the real estate business. According to internal emails, "It's a unique conduit for Chinese investors as well looking to deploy capital in the U.S. in real estate."[108]

Gemini's pedigree was similar to the other companies Hunter was dealing with: they had deep intelligence or military connections. In the case of Gemini, the parent company was then called Sino-Ocean Land (now Sino-Ocean Group), and was "one of the largest real estate companies in Beijing."[109] The chairman of Sino-Ocean Land was also the chairman of COSCO.[110] It is a state-owned entity. According to several governments, including Japan, "Chinese intelligence services are closely linked" to COSCO.[111] This would be yet another large deal that Hunter and his partners secured with Chinese espionage-linked firms.

How much the Chinese firm paid for Rosemont is hard to know. Gemini bought a 75 percent stake in the company. The terms included a $3 billion commitment from the Chinese to inject capital into the company.[112] According to Hunter Biden's emails, he retained his stake in Rosemont even with the new Chinese ownership. It is not clear how much money he made in the deal.[113]

In 2015, Hunter Biden received a $188,616.56 payment from Rosemont Realty. It is not known what other monies might have come his way or whether he still holds a stake in the company.[114]

***

IN DECEMBER 2015, Hunter Biden was approached by Vuk Jeremic, who served as Serbian foreign minister and had worked with Vice

President Joe Biden.[115] Jeremic later became head of the UN General Assembly.[116] He wanted to set up a private meeting with one of China's wealthiest and most connected businessmen. "On Sunday, December 6, I will have a private dinner in DC with an old friend from China - Ye Jiemaing [Jianming] - one of the 10 wealthiest Chinese businessmen. He is the Chairman and majority owner of CEFC China Energy, a second-largest privately owned company on Shanghai stock exchange," Jeremic wrote to Eric Schwerin. "He's very young and dynamic (39), with the top-level connections in his country." This was not the only attempt to connect Ye and Hunter.[117]

Schwerin responded: "It is interesting that you raised the CEFC Chairman. We actually were approached by an acquaintance of Hunter's about setting up a meeting for Hunter with the same gentleman for next week as well. We weren't sure if it was worthwhile but the fact that he is friend's with you makes us feel better about this."[118]

Ye is thin, handsome, and is usually found in a well-tailored suit. Even in Chinese circles, he is an enigma, where there are wild speculations about how he became one of China's biggest financial players at such a young age. As we will see, his "top-level connections" include the Chinese intelligence service and the military.

Hunter Biden developed a close working relationship with Ye on a number of fronts. As Hunter explained to his business partner Tony Bobulinski in text messages, he spoke with Ye on a "regular basis" because "we have a standing once a week call as I am also his personal counsel (we signed an attorney client engagement letter) in the U.S." Hunter also said he was advising Ye "on a number of his personal issues (staff visas and some more sensitive things)."[119]

Hunter also worked with Ye and his associates with the hopes of developing CEFC into a global energy company with vast energy holdings in countries like Oman, Romania, Colombia, and Luxembourg. Hunter was central to this effort and was responsible for "writing to all parties and organizing meetings to continue CEFC promote [*sic*], as well as approving step-by-step strategic and operational elements."[120]

Like Che Feng, Henry Zhao, and companies like COSCO, Ye's strong ties to Chinese intelligence are worth noting.

CEFC was housed in a complex in Shanghai's French Concession section, an area "primarily controlled by China's military."[121] One of Ye's early business partners was the granddaughter of "one of the founders of China's military," Marshal Ye Jianying.[122]

The corporate logo of the company Hunter Biden was now advising, and which would pay him millions, features a star. According to company records on its English website, it represents "civil rights." However, on the company's Chinese-language site, the star signifies that "this organization will play a strong and powerful role for the interests of the Chinese state and nation."[123]

Ye built his business by acquiring assets from Lai Changxing, a former PLA officer closely linked with Chinese military intelligence. Lai reportedly drove a bulletproof Mercedes around Beijing with a license plate adorned with a distinctive Chinese character in red—an indication that his car was owned by the PLA General Staff.[124]

Ye has other connections to the Chinese government's military, intelligence, and political apparatus. He was the deputy secretary-general of either the China Association for International Friendly Contact (CAIFC) or CAIFC's Shanghai branch from 2003 to 2005. CAIFC is funded by Chinese PLA intelligence. Finally, there are Chinese military officers affiliated with Ye's company who are also tied to the PLA National Defense University.[125] Beyond the military and intelligence ties, CEFC has also cosponsored events with neo-Maoist and hard-line nationalists in China who want to radically expand Beijing's global reach.[126] The CEFC funded a related nonprofit think tank called the China Energy Fund Committee.[127] While the Fund Committee sponsored events and research advocating China's territorial claims, another subsidiary, the China Institute of Culture, pledged support for Taiwan's reunification with mainland China.[128] One China Energy Fund Committee analyst, Long Tao, wrote a piece for the government-linked *Global Times* in 2011 titled "The present is a golden opportunity to use force in the South China Sea." The piece was blunt and is worth quoting at length:

> One should not be afraid of small-scale wars, for they are a good way to release fighting potential. By fighting several small wars one can avoid a large war. . . . The South China Sea region has more than 1,000 oil and gas wells, but none of them belong to China. There are four airports in the Spratly Islands, but Mainland China does not have one. China has no other important economic installations. Leaving aside the issue of winning and losing, as soon as war commences the South China Sea will inevitably become a sea of fire. When those towering oil drilling platforms become flaming torches, who will be hurt the most? As soon as the fighting begins, all those Western oil and gas companies will inevitably withdraw, so who will lose the most? . . . As far as China is concerned, this is the best battleground.[129]

In brief, Hunter Biden was now the U.S. representative for an intelligence- and military-linked Chinese company that was supporting voices calling for an aggressive military posture against the United States and its allies.

The red flashing lights blink on.

Ye's companies and affiliates have conducted several joint programs with the People's Liberation Army General Political Department Liaison Department advancing Beijing's political interests around the globe.[130]

Ye was at the center of Beijing's economic strategy. His firm, CEFC, saw itself as playing an important and central role in advancing China's Belt and Road Initiative, which was designed to expand Chinese economic and political influence worldwide.[131] Accordingly, CEFC was also an oil supplier to the People's Liberation Army.[132]

According to CEFC corporate documents sent to Tony Bobulinski and referenced by the office of Senator Charles Grassley in a letter to the Department of Justice, CEFC's corporate mission was to "expand cooperation in the international energy economy and contribute to the national development." Those same documents allow that CEFC is "dedicating itself to serving China's national energy strategy," "developing national strategic reserves [for oil]," and "partnering with centrally-administered and state-owned enterprises." The records leave no doubt that CEFC was part and parcel of the communist Chinese government.[133]

CEFC had large ambitions in the United States and around the world. One plan was to invest in U.S. infrastructure. Two entities, Hudson West IV and SinoHawk, were set up where Ye could invest money to make it happen. Hunter Biden was involved in running those efforts, but because he lacked any expertise, an experienced financial manager was brought in to run the infrastructure fund. Tony Bobulinski, who had managed money for some of the wealthiest people in the world, had plenty of experience managing international deals. He spent time with Hunter Biden and his uncle, James Biden, who was also involved. He even met with Joe Biden.[134]

Bobulinski quickly learned from one associate that the subject of Joe Biden's involvement with these ventures was always a sensitive issue. "Don't mention Joe being involved," James Gilliar wrote to Bobulinski in one message, laying out the ground rules. He continued, "it's only when you are face to face, I know u know but they are paranoid."[135]

Bobulinski soon started clashing with Hunter Biden, who was unhappy with the payment package he was going to receive from the venture. The $850,000 salary and a 20 percent equity stake were not enough. Hunter was to hold another 10 percent of the equity for "the Big Guy" [Joe Biden], according to the correspondence. Hunter wanted more money and pulled the Biden card on Bobulinski. He wrote in blunt, stark terms that Ye and his company are "both coming to be MY partner and to be partners with the Bidens."[136]

Bobulinski could see that Hunter brought little practical experience to the table and that the deal would draw alarm bells from Biden family friends and lawyers. "If you are so worried about your family," Bobulinski wrote him back, "you wouldn't be doing this because as u said, all of your dad's lawyers and any lawyer would advise you and Jim not to touch this with a 100 foot pole."[137]

Touch it they did.

Indeed, Hunter Biden had big plans for his friends at CEFC and his family and sought to simplify matters by fusing CEFC with his family. In 2017, he made plans to house his businesses, the Biden Foundation, one of his father's offices, and CEFC together in an office space in Washington. In an email for signage, Hunter said he had "new office mates: Joe Biden Jill Biden Jim Biden Gongwen Dong (Chairman Ye CEFC emissary)," and that, "I would like the office sign to reflect the following The Biden Foundation Hudson West (CEFC U.S.). The lease will remain under my company's name Rosemont Seneca."[138]

Who exactly is Gongwen Dong, the office mate and business partner of the Bidens, including former Vice President Joe Biden? In addition to being the "emissary" for Chairman Ye of CEFC, he had other notable ties to those embedded in Chinese intelligence and foreign influence operations. At the time he was also the chief financial officer at the Beijing-based Radiance Property Holdings.[139] The firm, now Radiance Holdings, is controlled and run by Lam Ting Keung, a businessman with deep connections to "united front" groups linked to Chinese intelligence. Lam is also a member of the Chinese People's Political Consultative Conference, a high-ranking

Communist Party advisory body that is also a central component of the Chinese government's united front efforts.[140] According to a U.S. federal government commission, united front organizations often serve as covers for Chinese intelligence operations.[141]

It appears that the Bidens and Dong were destined to be office and business partners. Why none of this set off red flags with the Bidens or those in their camp is a complete mystery. Did they not even bother to look because it would prevent them from cashing in? Or did they know and not care?

The money began to flow. Over about a year, CEFC sent Hunter close to $6 million.[142] By July 2017, CEFC began making interest-free, forgivable loans to the Biden family. CEFC executive Zhao Runlong wrote that the $5 million was intended as money "lent to the BD family," not just Hunter.

"This $5 million loan to the BD [Biden] family is interest free," Zhao wrote. "But if the 5M is used up, should CEFC keep lending more to the family?"[143] Interest-free loans provide tremendous leverage because the lender can demand its money back if it is displeased by any action.

In August 2017, CEFC Infrastructure Investment LLC sent Hunter's law firm, Owasco, $100,000. Four days later, the firm wired $5 million to another entity controlled by Ye. That firm then started sending regular payments to Owasco. According to the U.S. Senate report, Hunter then transferred close to $1.4 million of that money to a firm called Lion Hall Group, which was controlled by his uncle James Biden and his wife, Sara Biden.

On September 8, 2017, Hunter Biden and Gongwen Dong, Ye's U.S. operative, applied for a line of credit. Hunter, his uncle James, and his aunt Sara became authorized users for the credit cards on the account. They bought $100,000 in luxury items.[144]

But then suddenly, the FBI intervened—unintentionally—in Hunter's plans.

Patrick Ho was one of Ye's "top lieutenants" and a senior executive with CEFC (Fund). Ho, who had once been the home affairs secretary in Hong Kong, had a chubby face, wore wire-rimmed glasses, and carried a broad smile. In November 2017, the FBI arrested him in New York City on bribery charges. He had reportedly offered money to African officials as part of a "bold operation" involving "channelling illicit payments to UN diplomats—via a network of middlemen, millionaires and suspected spies." While working in New York, he also was a "tireless advocate" for President Xi's "signature venture" at the United Nations.[145]

One of the first phone calls he placed from behind bars was to James Biden; he was searching for Hunter.[146] Despite a lack of a background in criminal defense law, CEFC hired Hunter to provide legal representation in the case. A $1 million retainer was paid to his LLC, Owasco.[147] Hunter Biden would refer to the cherubic-faced Patrick Ho as "the f**king spy chief of China," more intrigued than anxious about that affiliation.[148]

Ho pleaded guilty and went to jail. Hunter Biden later told the *New Yorker* he did not believe that Ye was "a shady character at all" and said the event was only "bad luck."[149]

Before Ho went to jail, Hunter was provided an assistant named JiaQi Bao. Bao received her master's degree from China's Tsinghua University, where her studies were financed by a government scholarship. After graduating, she worked as a research assistant at the Chinese government's National Development and Reform Commission, which is responsible for the management of the country's economy. That employer is under the control of the State Council, the government's ruling body. Next, she moved to OneGate Capital, a Shanghai-based investment firm with ventures funded by Chinese government entities.[150] One of OneGate Capital's partners is Leon Lin (Lin Xuchu), who is closely tied to the CCP.[151]

Bao offered Hunter advice on everything from energy deals to his father's presidential campaign.[152] She also handled a "monthly wire instruction" concerning the transfer of financial payments.[153] When the CEFC infrastructure fund, known as Hudson West, folded, she offered him some curious advice: "Whatever money from Hudson West, please take them, take as much as possible or figure out a way to spend them for your own benefit . . . just take it and keep as much as possible."[154]

***

IN FEBRUARY 2017, the University of Pennsylvania announced that former vice president Joe Biden was appointed to a professorship, and the Biden Center was being launched, to promote the former vice president's vision for global affairs. On the website of the Biden Center, they tout the fact that Biden "has fought to secure American global leadership by defending and advancing a liberal international order."[155] They note the challenge posed by Russia. "In particular, under President Putin, Russia seeks to return to an era when the use of force prevails and the world is carved into spheres of influence." Also mentioned is "climate change," as well as epidemics, terrorism, and cyber attacks.[156]

But there is not a single mention of Beijing as posing any sort of challenge or threat. Instead, in a section called "Advancing the Dialogue of Globalism," there is a featured photo of Vice President Joe Biden with then vice president Xi.[157]

When Joe Biden hit the campaign trail for the presidency, after his family had received that $31 million from Chinese intelligence–linked businessmen, he continued to dismiss the challenges posed by China. "China's going to eat our lunch? C'mon, man," he told a campaign rally in Iowa. He added, "They are not bad folks, folks. But guess what? They are not [unintelligible] competition for us."[158]

From the beginning, the Biden Center was populated with

close aides and allies of the former vice president who would go on to serve in his presidency. This, of course, is not unusual. Steve Ricchetti, a longtime aide, served as the managing director of the Penn Biden Center for a time. Tony Blinken, another close aide, also served as the center's managing director before heading off to work on the presidential campaign in 2019.

When Joe Biden was elected president, Ricchetti became White House counselor, Blinken the U.S. secretary of state.[159]

Tony Blinken, when he served as an advisor to Vice President Biden, reportedly played a central role in denying asylum to a high-ranking Chinese Communist Party official who was hoping to defect. Wang Lijun was the "highest ranking Chinese official to ever offer to defect to the United States." In early February 2012, after being recently fired from his senior post in the Public Security Bureau, Wang snuck into the U.S. consulate in Chengdu dressed in women's clothing. For thirty hours, Wang met with U.S. officials and offered to share everything that he knew—a clear intelligence boon. But Blinken reportedly halted the defection on fears that it would embarrass China on the eve of meetings with the Obama administration. Wang was forced to leave the consulate and face his fate with Beijing authorities—a fifteen-year sentence in prison. Blinken has claimed that he had no involvement in the Wang case.[160]

To run an organization like the Biden Center takes millions of dollars a year, and that money needs to be raised. In this case, there is a lot of mystery about where the funding originates. Under Ricchetti and Blinken, and to this day, the Biden Center does not seem to publish financials separate from the university regarding donations—whether foreign or domestic. In short, there is no obvious disclosure record of who funds the Biden Center.

Yet, the flow of money to the University of Pennsylvania should raise some eyebrows and offer clues as to who is financing the Biden Center's operations.

One trend is unmistakable: after the Biden Center's announcement that it was opening at the University of Pennsylvania, donations
from the Chinese mainland to Penn almost tripled. In the three years
before the announcement, the university received around $15 mil-
lion. In the three years after, the total was close to $40 million. The
latter number is $60 million from China if you include contracts.[161]

Much of the Chinese money that flowed to UPenn after the opening of the Biden Center is anonymous. What we do know about
some of the donors raises important questions. On April 19, 2018, just
weeks after the Biden Center opened, China Merchants Bank sent a
$950,000 contribution to Penn. The bank is a state-owned enterprise
under the direct supervision of the State Council.[162]

On August 2, 2019, a mysterious Chinese firm called Cathay
Fortune sent $1 million. The founder and head of the firm is Yu
Yong, described by the *Australian Financial Review* as a "secretive
Chinese billionaire, who appears to have strong links with the
Communist Party."[163] Cathay itself is the controlling shareholder
of a Chinese company called China Molybdenum.[164] Molybdenum
is a critical mineral for military construction: it helps make steel
more solid. China Molybdenum also happened to be involved in a
joint venture with Hunter Biden's BHR investment fund, investing
in an African copper mine together.[165]

Secretary of State Blinken, while he was running the Biden Center,
also had a private consultancy called WestExec. One of that firm's
roles: helping "U.S. research universities" navigate problems arising
from receiving research grants from the U.S. Department of Defense
while also taking foreign money from China. WestExec listed this
as one of their services on their website—until shortly before Joe
Biden accepted the nomination for the presidency at the Democratic
National Convention in August 2020.

Then they mysteriously deleted it.[166]

During his first nine months as president, Joe Biden toughened his rhetoric toward Beijing. But in keeping with the dictum "big help with a little badmouth," Beijing should certainly be happy with the overall posture of the Biden administration. The talk is tougher, but the main tenets of the foreign policy that Beijing wants Washington to pursue are secure: no radical reduction in the transfer of technology or capital from America to Beijing, no fundamental challenges to the Chinese regime, and mild criticisms over human rights accompanied by excuses for their conduct.

While the administration acknowledges that China is out to replace the United States as the world's convening power, they also insist, in the words of Tony Blinken, that "our purpose is not to contain China."[167] While President Biden criticizes China on human rights, he also makes excuses. He explained on CNN, for example, that human rights abuses were about President Xi trying to "unify" the country.

"If you know anything about Chinese history, it has always been, the time when China has been victimized by the outer world is when they haven't been unified at home," President Biden began. "So the central—it's vastly overstated—the central principle of Xi Jinping is that there must be a united, tightly controlled China, and he uses his rationale for the things he does based on that."[168]

He continued: "And so the idea I'm not going to speak out against what he's doing in Hong Kong, what he's doing with the Uighurs in the western mountains of China . . . Culturally there are different norms in each country, and their leaders are expected to follow."[169]

America's First Family has enjoyed deep financial dealings involving tens of millions of dollars with Chinese entities and businessmen with direct ties to Chinese intelligence. Indeed, every deal the Bidens secured in China involved individuals deeply connected to the CCP spy apparatus. The beneficiaries of these deals include Hunter Biden and James Biden, the son and brother of President Biden. Rosemont Seneca appears to have set up separate phone lines to reach Joe Biden, and paid for that monthly bill, which is not legal. And as we have seen, Hunter Biden and Joe Biden blurred their funds and according to Hunter, he contributed considerably to his dad's financial well-being.

Will the Bidens answer questions about their troubling financial ties to Chinese intelligence-linked officials? Will they explain how and why he was accepting financial support from his son? History shows they have been evasive and changed their story numerous times, and too many members of the media show a lack of curiosity.

When *Secret Empires* was released in March 2018, it soared to number one on the *New York Times* bestseller list, and yet, much of the media ignored it. However, we now know that the FBI formally launched an investigation into Hunter Biden's commercial deals in China later that year. As of this writing, the investigation is still under way.[170]

The initial response from the Biden camp concerning the details in the book was essentially no response. They explained to the *Wall Street Journal*, "We aren't going to engage on a politically motivated hit piece." Attacking the messenger, not the evidence, is a tried-and-true approach in Washington to avoid talking about the facts. The response from Senator Mitch McConnell, who was also featured in the book, was largely the same.[171] But as the story began to get more attention, Team Biden was forced to engage. Their position became simply that Joe Biden did not know about his family's foreign deals, including Hunter's. "I have never discussed with my son or my brother or anyone else anything having to do with their businesses. Period," then-candidate Joe Biden told reporters at a South Carolina campaign stop in August 2019.[172] It was a position he would repeat for months.[173]

Then, as evidence emerged that he had indeed discussed business with his son, and that he had actually met some of Hunter's business partners, the Biden position shifted. The story now became that the

Biden family might have talked about business, and Joe Biden might have even met some of Hunter's business partners, but he never directly benefited from his son's business deals, and he certainly did not help him. "I have not taken a penny from any foreign source, ever, in my life," Biden said at the October 22, 2020, presidential debate.[174]

While technically true, Hunter Biden has declared that he was paying at least some of his father's bills. With that, Hunter's "half [his] salary" complaint, other curious, financial correspondence mentioning "JRB," "the Big Guy," and Joe Biden's mortgage, it is hard to make sense of Hunter's foreign financial arrangements as being completely exempt from Joe's influence—or his benefit.

Clearly, there were deep divisions within the Biden camp and family about how to handle our early revelations regarding their financial deals in China. In one text tirade to a family member, Hunter linked to both a *New York Post* article I cowrote and the Amazon landing page for my book, *Secret Empires*. "[Y]ou see anyone defend me? You don't. You see one word of denial from dad or his staff [?]"[175]

In sum, each deal the Bidens secured in China was via a businessman with deep ties at the highest levels of Chinese intelligence. And in each case there appears to be little discernible business or professional service that was rendered in return for the money.

With their cultivation of a close financial relationship with the Biden family, Beijing has climbed the mountaintop of influence in American politics. Being financially bonded to the First Family provides enormous opportunities for leverage. But Beijing's effort at elite capture is not a one-family problem. Beijing has quietly walked their way through other powerful institutions in Washington, D.C., Wall Street, and Silicon Valley. Let us take a look at who else among the political elite have forged financial ties with Beijing.

3

CAPITOL HILL

They call it a SCIF—pronounced "skiff."

A Sensitive Compartmented Information Facility (SCIF) is among the most exclusive real estate in Washington. Vault-like hardened rooms, they come with heavy steel doors, secured communication lines, protected ventilation systems, and walls lined with a special acoustic material to prevent eavesdropping.[1]

It is here where the U.S. Senate Select Committee on Intelligence convenes when discussing America's deepest national security secrets. With oversight of America's eighteen civilian and military intelligence agencies, the committee has eyes and ears on much of the intelligence America collects overseas.[2] California senator Dianne Feinstein, without a doubt, has spent plenty of time inside a SCIF. She first joined that committee in 2001 and served as chairman starting in 2009.[3]

A SCIF can prevent a foreign government from listening in on sensitive conversations involving America's top decision makers. What all that steel and acoustic material cannot do is halt a foreign government from tempting those meeting inside with financial inducements and persuading them to take favorable actions on that government's behalf.

Since the early 1990s, Senator Feinstein has been extremely influential in American politics; an often-overlooked political force. As a U.S. senator from the largest and arguably most powerful state in the country, she has significant duties and a voice at the most important tables in Washington. She also has deep ties to California's political class. Feinstein conducted Governor Jerry Brown's wedding and hosted a wedding shower for Governor Gavin Newsom in her Pacific Heights home.[4]

Senator Feinstein and others in senior positions on Capitol Hill have profited greatly from the financial largesse of Beijing. Along the way, they have pursued policies beneficial to the regime and verbally supported some of its most brutal actions. Some have even advocated on behalf of Chinese military-linked companies for the right price. As we will see, it is a stunning galaxy of powerful figures on both sides of the political aisle.

China must have begun this campaign with seemingly impossible hopes. Could they get major U.S. politicians to excuse China's crimes as no different than America's? Could they get them to say, "China has a different culture," and that is all there is to it? Could they get them to switch positions or do them favors? That must have seemed too much to wish for.

In Washington, D.C., Senator Feinstein has been at the center of U.S. foreign policy for decades, serving first as a member of the Senate Foreign Relations Committee before joining the intelligence committee.[5]

Beijing speaks favorably of Feinstein. Chinese official media often quotes Feinstein's statements, and they even praise her fashion sense. "Member Dianne Feinstein also caught my attention," Chinese fashion designer Ma Yanli was quoted by a Chinese news network after an official Washington event. "Her crimson coat and lip color perfectly showed her personality and left an impression of stability and trust."[6]

Feinstein admits to having a soft spot for China. "I sometimes say that in my last life maybe I was Chinese."[7] To be more specific, she has a soft spot for the Chinese communist regime. She has claimed that in some respects, China is more democratic than the United States. "Chinese society continues to open up with looser ideological controls, freer access to outside sources of information and increased media reporting. More people in China vote for their leadership on the local level than do Americans."[8] Never mind the Communist Party monopoly on power.

Feinstein's relationship with Chinese officials runs deep. Appointed mayor of San Francisco in 1978, she moved quickly to cultivate a closer relationship with China. In 1979, the United States normalized relations with China. In 1980, she married Richard Blum, an investor with an interest in doing deals in China.[9] With its diverse population and geographic location, the City by the Bay was a logical place to forge early ties with China as it was emerging from the brutal Maoist era. Feinstein developed a "sister city" relationship between San Francisco and Shanghai. That initiative proved particularly fruitful because the mayor of Shanghai then was Jiang Zemin. He would later be elevated to general secretary of the Chinese Communist Party and president of the People's Republic of China. In 1982, she visited Shanghai with her husband. Mayor Feinstein waltzed with Mayor Jiang as he sang, "One Day When We Were Young."[10]

Feinstein made it clear early that her sense of China was a political one more than an ethnic one. She was interested in closer ties with the Chinese mainland—not with the island nation of Taiwan. She even went so far as to press organizers of the city's popular "Chinese New Year Parade" to stop displaying the Taiwanese flag—lest they offend Beijing. "She wanted to encourage trade with China."[11]

Her husband, Richard Blum, had established a merchant banking and money management firm called Richard C. Blum & Associates back around 1975. Publicly, he prided himself on not investing in companies that are "politically or sociologically incorrect, such as those with interests in South Africa, tobacco or gambling."[12] China, despite its massive human rights problems, was apparently not on his list of the morally repugnant. Blum would establish a myriad of firms and partnerships that would do enormous amounts of business with China.

As his wife moved San Francisco to embrace the Chinese regime, Blum began to reap the benefits of the relationship forged with Jiang Zemin. He became one of the earliest American investors in China. In the 1980s, he was vice chairman and director of a company called Shanghai Pacific Partners. That firm created a joint venture with a Chinese government bank called Shanghai Investment and Trust Company. Together they constructed a $30 million complex in that bustling city. The horror of Tiananmen Square came in 1989, and Blum claims that he suspended doing business with Shanghai Investment and Trust. Nevertheless, he remained the Chinese government bank's "foreign advisor," according to corporate records.[13] He also apparently never severed ties to the group's vice president, W. K. Zhang, who ended up joining Blum's Shanghai Pacific Partners also as vice president. Zhang was instrumental in maintaining the fateful sister-city relationship that Feinstein and Jiang fostered, as it was his job to coordinate Jiang's trips to San Francisco.[14]

In 1992, Feinstein ran for the U.S. Senate and won.[15] Her husband had raised substantial amounts of money for the campaign.[16] Feinstein moved to Washington, and Blum mostly stayed in the Bay Area. His deals with China multiplied.[17]

In 1994, he launched a firm called Newbridge Capital with his friend David Bonderman. Zhang joined the firm. An affiliate, Newbridge Asia, set up an office in Shanghai. The fund invested in several state-owned and government-linked firms.[18]

The deals were unusual and groundbreaking. Around 2004, Newbridge bought an 18 percent stake in Shenzhen Development Bank, a Chinese government-controlled lender. It was the first time that a foreign company could buy an equity stake in a bank. The *Wall Street Journal* called it a "landmark deal."[19]

"Newbridge has been a pioneer in turning around and building companies in Asia," Blum later bragged.[20] Chief among the Asian countries was China, where political ties and connections are key.

As the *Los Angeles Times* put it, "Feinstein's longtime friendship with former Chinese political leader Jiang Zemin, dating to the days when they were sister-city mayors in San Francisco and Shanghai, gave Blum, who has investments in China, access to the normally impenetrable Beijing political system."[21]

There were numerous other deals as well.

Blum's firm invested in a Chinese soybean milk company and received $10 million in help from the International Finance Corporation, which is part of the World Bank. According to Rashad Kaldany, who was once head of the IFC's capital market investments in Asia, part of the reason the IFC went along was that "Mr. Blum had some contacts with the Chinese."[22]

While Feinstein's political star was rising, her old friend Jiang Zemin rose to general secretary of the Chinese Communist Party. A few years later, after Feinstein was elected to the Senate, Jiang became president of China. He quickly extended an invitation for Feinstein and Blum to visit Beijing and meet with the party leadership.[23]

Feinstein continued to embrace the regime. In 1994, while the U.S. Senate was considering rescinding most-favored-nation (MFN) trade status with China because of human rights violations in the wake of Tiananmen Square, she argued vigorously against it. Doing so, she said, would only "inflame Beijing's insecurities." As she made those comments, her husband was raising tens of millions of dollars for the Newbridge Asia fund. That fund would later invest in several Chinese companies, including buying nearly one-quarter of the state-linked North Dragon Iron & Steel Works.[24]

The trips that Senator Feinstein and her husband made to Beijing increased in tempo. There were three trips between 1995 and 1997, where they met with top Communist Party officials, including President Jiang Zemin. Once, the couple had the unique opportunity to dine in the Communist Party's inner sanctum, Zhongnanhai, which is part of the old imperial gardens. Mao and his revolutionaries selected it as their seat of government after the revolution. It is generally "forbidden to outsiders."[25]

"We had dinner in Zhongnanhai in Mao Tse-tung's old residence in the room where he died," Feinstein later recalled. "We were told that we were the first foreigners to see his bedroom and swimming pool. It was a very historic moment to see some of these things."[26]

In 1996, President Jiang held a private dinner for three U.S. senators—Feinstein, Senator John Glenn, and Senator Sam Nunn. U.S. intelligence officials believed it was part of Chinese efforts to increase their influence operations in American politics. At the dinner party, Jiang played the piano for Feinstein and talked with Glenn and Nunn. They got the "royal treatment" from Jiang. National Security Agency eavesdroppers later reported overhearing "brave talk about buying access."[27]

Less than a year later, Feinstein undertook a "secret weekend mission" to visit Beijing for a private talk with President Jiang. "I know Jiang well and my purpose was to enable him to see the U.S. position clearly," she said.[28]

Feinstein retained a soft spot for the Chinese leader, overlooking the brutal role he had played in running the Beijing regime. As mayor, Jiang Zemin played a central role in the Tiananmen Square massacre. In the tumult leading up to that event, some in the security services had proposed letting him take over for a leader soft on the agitators. "Comrade Jiang Zemin, the mayor of Shanghai, would make an excellent candidate," said former Shanghai secret service member Chen Yun. "He's a modest man and very respectful of party discipline."[29] While Jiang was supportive of the regime's hard line, Feinstein always spoke fondly of her friend, who, among other things, opened doors for her husband's business ventures. In the 1990s, when the Clinton White House was reluctant to honor him with a state dinner because of his role in Tiananmen Square, Feinstein warmly described Jiang as "the right person to lead China to a very significant destiny."[30]

In later interviews, she made excuses about what happened on that day in June 1989. She explained that the problem was not brutality but a lack of resources. "China had no local police," Feinstein said that Jiang told her. (That would be news to the Beijing municipal public security bureau, who serve as police.) "It was just the PLA. And no local police that had crowd control. So, hence the tanks . . . But that's the past. One learns from the past. You don't repeat it. I think China has learned a lesson."[31]

***

IN NOVEMBER 1995, Jiang Zemin convened a secret meeting of senior officials to create what he called the "Central Working Group to Study the U.S. Congress." They targeted members of Congress with junket trips to China, paid for by the government or government-linked groups.[32]

The Chinese government has focused on recruiting friends—or at least dulling its critics in Congress over the last several decades. In 1995, according to a CIA report declassified in 2006, "Chinese Leaders created the Central Leading Group for U.S. Congressional Affairs to oversee the task of increasing support for Chinese objectives." They recognized the power of Congress and their ability to advance their objectives by working to curry favor on Capitol Hill. One lobbyist explained: "China lobbying has become much more sophisticated; they have a better understanding of how to use our political system. They used to get frustrated when a presidential administration wasn't able to get things done with a snap of their fingers, but now they understand the role of Congress and the President."[33]

Central to their interests in Congress was seeing the passage of most-favored-nation trading status with the United States. He Xin, a foreign policy advisor to two Chinese premiers in the 1990s, allowed at the time, "The question of MFN status between China and the United States is a central issue that will determine the rotation of world history."[34]

***

ON JUNE 9, 1996, Senator Dianne Feinstein and her husband held a swanky fundraiser at their Presidio Terrace home. *Newsweek* described it as "a remarkable gathering of the tribes." Ernest Gallo, the famous wine baron, donated the libations from his private stock. The top dogs of the Bay Area's largest corporations showed up, including Oracle's Larry Ellison and the head of Bank of America. Also present was Xiaoming Dai, described as "chairman and CEO of Asia Securities International, a company involved in real estate development on both sides of the Pacific Rim." That description alone did not do him justice. In fact, he was an executive closely tied to the Chinese government. Apparently, Dai did not yet know Feinstein or her husband. He was at their home because one of the fundraisers for the Feinstein event was John Huang, who was later charged for funneling illegal campaign contributions to American politicians—a controversy known as Chinagate—including Bill Clinton and Dianne Feinstein. (After the 1996 election, the DNC returned $1.6 million of illegal or "murky" donations to Huang.) Less than a week before the dinner, FBI agents had warned the White House about stepped-up efforts by Beijing to sway members of Congress. They were looking at using even "illegal means" to direct campaign cash to politicians. Beijing had even drawn up a list of members that they were targeting for influence operations. One of the names on the list was Dianne Feinstein, in part because her husband had "major investments on the mainland."[35]

The FBI warned Feinstein to be on the lookout, too. However, she dismissed the FBI briefing as unhelpful. "Was I briefed?" Feinstein later said in an exchange with reporters. "Yes. Was it a specific briefing? No. It was a classified briefing. The substance of it was that there were some credible sources that presented the FBI with the view that the Chinese may try and funnel contributions to various candidates. That was it. There were no specifics. How would this happen? When would it be done? Where would it be done?" She added that there was no reason to believe that the Chinese government was trying to fund her campaign. "None whatsoever." Feinstein ended up returning campaign contributions from employees at the Lippo Group, an Indonesian firm associated with Dai and the Chinese that was involved in Chinagate. She dismissed the idea that there was anything wrong with taking the money, returning the contributions "only because they became controversial," she told the *New York Times*.[36]

In 2001, a Chinese fighter jet and a U.S. Navy surveillance plane collided over the Pacific, and the American aircraft made an emergency landing on the Chinese island of Hainan. Chinese officials held the crew of twenty-four for eleven days.[37] Senator Feinstein, who was on the Senate Intelligence Committee at the time, declared that she was "deeply sorry" for what America had done and apologized to Beijing, even though the American plane was in international airspace.[38]

During Senate hearings over China's human rights abuses, she euphemistically referred to the regime's abuses as Beijing's "human rights posture." She went on to explain that Americans criticizing the regime's "posture" would have no effect because they will not respond when "they're preached to by others [that is, Americans] who don't always practice it themselves."[39] Of course, Feinstein has criticized many foreign regimes other than China for their human rights practices, apparently not applying the same standards to China.[40]

The apologetics go on.

Feinstein minimizes the role of the CCP, explaining that the regime is merely "socialist." "There was originally this kind of anti-communist view of China," she explained in 2012. "That's changing . . . China is a socialist country but one that is increasingly becoming capitalistic."[41]

During a Senate hearing, Feinstein compared the Tiananmen Square massacre—which reportedly killed more than ten thousand civilians—to the standoff between federal officials and David Koresh in Waco, Texas. "I was appalled as anyone by the tanks at [Tiananmen] Square, but three tanks of this government went into Waco, (Tex.) and killed 29 children. They weren't criminals. Most of the people in Waco had no criminal record. Now those are not analogous; they are different situations. It was wrong of our government, and it was wrong of the Chinese government."[42]

In another instance, she argued that a human rights panel should be created with both Chinese and American officials impaneled to discuss "the evolution of human rights in both the United States and China," thereby comparing the level of rights abuse in the United States to that of China. She believed the committee should look at "the success and failures [of] both Tiananmen Square and Kent State."[43]

Critics pointed out that Feinstein is not naïve when she announces these proposals. "No one believes Feinstein is sincere in calling for such an inquiry," wrote Ken Silverstein at the time. "Her suggestion, the object of great scorn in Congress, is simply a smokescreen to prevent a serious look at China's awful record."[44]

She has worked hard to protect China's communist leadership

from embarrassment. When members of Congress introduced legislation to name a street in front of the Chinese embassy in Washington for Liu Xiaobo, a Chinese dissident writer who died in state
custody, she blocked it.[45]

Perhaps most important, as we will see, she has been a constant
booster of commercial ties to Beijing. She made the same promises
as many others: greater commercial interaction would make China
more liberal and lead to the fading away of the Communist Party.
It would also benefit the United States economically. These predic-
tions proved wrong. Her wager on China has arguably ended up
hurting the United States. However, her bargain with Beijing did
substantially benefit her and her family.

***

FOR DECADES, SENATOR Feinstein has played a central role in promoting commercial ties with China. Beyond her fond words for
Beijing—or excuses for the regime's behavior—she was an aggressive
supporter of most-favored-nation trade status for China with the
United States and of China's entry into the World Trade Organization (WTO). Her argument was familiar: trade deals would make
the Chinese regime more like us, and would greatly benefit the
U.S. economy. All the while, her husband was a heavy investor in
China, working with Chinese state-backed companies—and becoming enormously wealthy.

A Feinstein spokesman denied there was a connection between
the two. "He's a businessman and he has a right to do business and
he's never done anything wrong," said Kam Kuwata.[46]

Blum is incredulous about the idea that the Chinese government
has benefited his businesses. "I can't think of one single reason why
the Chinese leadership would be wanting to help us with investment opportunities," Blum claimed.[47]

For her part, Feinstein insists that there was no connection be-tween her political position and her husband's deals in Beijing. "He is in San Francisco running his business, I am in Washington being a United States senator, and they are two separate things," Fein-stein told reporters at one point. "I don't know how I can prove it to people like you. Maybe I get divorced. Maybe that is what you want."[48] Of course, she never discussed the fact that her husband had accompanied her during many of her official trips to Beijing.

With controversy swirling, both Feinstein and her husband claimed that he divested himself of his mainland Chinese invest-ments. But her financial disclosures show that was not true.[49]

Blum used another one of his firms, BLUM Capital Partners and its affiliates, to invest in high-tech, aviation, and consumer prod-ucts. His firm is involved in dozens of partnerships, including many deals with mainland China.[50]

One of Richard Blum's most significant holdings is the com-mercial real estate company CB Richard Ellis. The real estate firm began its rapid expansion into China in the 2000s, investing in Shanghai commercial real estate with its Chinese partners. Pur-chasing commercial real estate in China as a foreign investor re-quires the right political connections. By 2007, CB Richard Ellis had more than ten offices on China's mainland.[51]

Blum invested in Francisco Partners, a limited partnership. Fran-cisco Partners acquired a company called Aeroflex in 2007.[52] The company was a supplier of radiation-hardened electronics for space and defense applications.[53] That same year, Aeroflex partnered with a Chinese aircraft maintenance and engineering company called Ameco Beijing.[54] Aeroflex is a company that has a troubled his-tory with China. The company later admitted that between 2003 and 2009, it illegally sent 14,500 rad-chips to China.[55] The com-pany had failed to obtain export licenses for the chip sales, and the advanced chips found their way onto Chinese satellites. The

Obama-era State Department wrote a letter to Aeroflex's CEO accusing the company of 158 Arms Export Control Act and ITAR violations "in connection with unauthorized exports and retransfers, and re-exports of defense articles, to include technical data, to various countries, including proscribed destinations." The letter said the company's actions "caused harm to national security by providing the People's Republic of China a more reliable satellite capability."[56]

According to disclosures, Blum Family Partners LP had some stake in, and shared an address with, AEOW 2000 LP. AEOW was invested in tech firm Agere Systems. Agere was an early and aggressive partner with China's ZTE Corporation and created a joint lab.[57] ZTE is a Chinese government-controlled technology company spun off from the government's Ministry of Aerospace Industry.[58]

The intersection of Feinstein's political position and Blum's ties to Beijing also may have been central in getting him in on a substantial deal involving a Chinese computer company.

Legend was a Chinese company formed by a group of researchers from the government- and military-linked Chinese Academy of Sciences (CAS). They eventually changed the name to Lenovo.[59] In 2005, Lenovo acquired IBM's personal computer business. This was a monumental moment for the company. The acquisition would thrust Lenovo into a major role in the global market.[60] There were, of course, significant security concerns in the United States and other countries. There were vulnerabilities involving backdoor malware reportedly found in some Lenovo devices. In response, government agencies from the United States, Great Britain, Canada, New Zealand, and Australia issued bans on using Lenovo devices for tasks involving sensitive information.[61] Lenovo's plans triggered a federal government review of the transaction. (Recall that Feinstein sat on the Senate Intelligence Committee at the time.) By March 2005, the government approved the deal, and within days, Lenovo announced that it had received a $350 million investment from three U.S. private equity firms, including Blum's Newbridge Capital.[62] In a 2009 interview, Richard Blum claimed that IBM had approached his firm because they wanted an American partner to be part of the new ownership group.[63]

Lenovo, with Senator Feinstein's husband a major owner, would a few years later be accused by U.S. officials of placing spyware on computers sold to the United States military. In 2010, Lee Chieffalo, who managed computer operations centers for the U.S. Marines in Iraq, testified in court: "A large amount of Lenovo laptops were sold to the US military that had a chip encrypted on the motherboard that would record all the data that was being inputted into that laptop and send it back to China. . . . That was a huge security breach. We don't have any idea how much data they got, but we had to take all those systems off the network."[64]

Blum sold his stake in Lenovo in 2011.

A few months after the Lenovo deal, Feinstein and Blum again traveled to Shanghai, along with San Francisco's then mayor Gavin Newsom, whom she introduced to Jiang.[65]

Feinstein's problematic entanglements with Beijing go beyond her personal relationships with Chinese leaders and her husband's deep commercial ties. With Feinstein as a member of the powerful Senate Intelligence Committee, an alleged Chinese spy emerged on her staff. While some news reports claimed that Russell Lowe was Feinstein's driver, he was considerably more important than that. He worked for the senator for twenty years, and was listed as an "office director," serving as a liaison with the Asian American community in California. Lowe attended several events at the Chinese consulate in San Francisco. He was reportedly recruited by China's Ministry of State Security. Feinstein has attempted to minimize the story. "Five years ago the FBI informed me it had concerns that an administrative member of my California staff was potentially being sought out by the Chinese government to provide information," she explained in a 2019 statement. "He was not a mole or a spy, but someone who a foreign intelligence service thought it could recruit."[66]

***

CALIFORNIA POLITICIANS SEEM to be a particular target of Beijing. Intelligence officials note that the interest in California is so great that reportedly China's main foreign intelligence agency, the Ministry of State Security, has a dedicated unit focused exclusively on California, hoping to extract secrets and run political influence operations.[67] Eric Swalwell was a local council member in Dublin City, California, when he first came into contact with a young Chinese woman named Christine Fang (aka Fang Fang). She worked on his campaign, raised money for his elections, and even recruited interns for his office. In 2012, Swalwell was elected to Congress and Speaker of the House Nancy Pelosi later tapped him to join the House Intelligence Committee. In 2014, when he ran for reelection, Fang was a bundler for his campaign.[68] The exact nature of Swalwell's relationship with Fang is not known, but when asked if he had a romantic relationship with her, Swalwell has refused to answer. Swalwell cut ties with her after the FBI raised concerns about her involvement with Beijing. She fled the country shortly thereafter.[69]

Swalwell's tenure on the House Intelligence Committee has led him to issue numerous statements about the challenges and threats posed by Russian intelligence. But critics point out that he has been far softer on the intelligence threat posed by Beijing.[70]

***

DIANNE FEINSTEIN HAS often made excuses for Chinese misdeeds. Generally, the same could not be said for her congressional colleague

Nancy Pelosi. The longtime member of Congress and Speaker of the House was, early in her career, a particularly harsh critic of China's human rights practices. She continues to be vocal about some issues, but her positions have softened as her family has sought and received lucrative commercial opportunities in mainland China.

In 1991, as a junior member of Congress, Pelosi found herself in Tiananmen Square. She was part of a congressional delegation visiting Beijing barely two years after the horrific events had unfolded. Pelosi had been in meetings with Chinese officials, but with a couple of colleagues, she covertly carried a banner into the middle of the square and unfurled it in front of a small crowd and the media. "To those who died for Democracy in China," it read. The Chinese police were furious. They pushed through the crowd to seize the banner. "I started running," Pelosi recalled. "And my colleagues, some of them, got a little roughed up. The press got treated worse because they had cameras, and they were detained." The Foreign Ministry denounced the event as a "premeditated farce."[71]

During her early years in Congress, Pelosi was a vocal critic of China. Unlike Senator Feinstein, she actually fought against most-favored-nation trade status and bringing Beijing into the World Trade Organization. Pelosi expressed skepticism that China would become more democratic.[72] In 2005, she went on the House floor to support an amendment to block the Chinese government-backed Chinese National Overseas Oil Company (CNOOC) from buying the California oil company Unocal.[73]

But her views began to moderate. She was no apologist for the regime, and continued to be critical. "Yet people close to Pelosi see a subtle shift," reported *Politico* in 2009. "She won't back down on her core commitment to democratization in the country, they say, but she's also not looking to pick new fights with China's leaders— or with the Obama Administration as it seeks to strengthen U.S.-China relations."[74] Pelosi explained that the shift was a result, in part, of issues like climate change that the two countries needed to tackle together. "I think this climate crisis is game changing for the U.S.-China relationship," she said at the time. "It is an opportunity we cannot miss."[75]

But there were perhaps other factors at work. Her husband and son started seeking and securing deals on mainland China. Husband Paul became a partner investor in Matthews International Capital Management, a pioneer in the Chinese investment market. Matthews was run by a longtime Pelosi friend and political supporter, William Hambrecht. (Hambrecht has donated millions to Democratic causes.)[76] Hambrecht launched his first China growth fund back in 1995.[77] He was optimistic that investments and technological change would alter China. "The Internet is going to be very difficult to contain within borders," he declared in 1999. "It has a viral effect to it. It spreads whether you like it or not."[78]

Matthews's best-known investment fund is the China Fund. "Under normal market conditions, the Matthews China Fund seeks to achieve its investment objective by investing at least 80% of its net assets, which include borrowings for investment purposes, in the common and preferred stocks of companies located in China," reads the fund's fact sheet.[79]

In addition to Paul serving on the board, the Pelosis had a big chunk of money invested in Matthews. In 2010, the Pelosis held between $5 million and $25 million in a Matthews fund "specializing in Asian investment." Paul Pelosi received partnership income between $100,000 and $1 million.[80]

The Pelosis had previously become involved in other China ventures as well. Paul Pelosi's classmate from Georgetown, Vincent Wolfington, set up a limousine service called Global Ambassador Concierge, which catered to ultra-high net-worth individuals traveling around the world.[81] One big market for Global: the Beijing 2008

Summer Olympics. In Congress, Pelosi had initially been critical of China hosting the games, arguing that its human rights record should prevent it from such an honor.[82] The year after her husband bought shares in Global Ambassador Concierge, she reversed course and opposed a boycott of Beijing's hosting of the games.[83]

The Pelosis also bought a stake in another limousine service, City Car Services (CCS), which Wolfington's son apparently ran. SEC documents show Paul Pelosi as a member of the board of directors of CCS.[84]

Nancy Pelosi's son, Paul Pelosi Jr., was also looking for commercial opportunities on the mainland, and he embarked on a series of ventures that involved Chinese investors and clients. In June 2010, he became the chair of the Universal Energy and Services Group Advisory Board for a company called Tree Top Industries. Upon announcing his appointment, the company declared that Paul Jr. and the company chairman "plan to travel to Vietnam and China to meet potential investors and are attempting to arrange meetings in Washington DC with appropriate federal agencies."[85]

Tree Top eventually changed its name to Global Tech Industries Group, and Paul Pelosi Jr. remains a shareholder in the company.[86] The firm has long sought partnerships in China.[87]

Paul Pelosi Jr. joined the board of another company, International Media Acquisition Corp., with ambitious plans in China. "We believe India and other emerging economics markets, as well as China, represent excellent markets in which to find strong candidates for our initial business combination because of their relatively high growth rates," stated the firm when it filed.[88]

Beginning in 2020 and extending for more than a year, U.S. Speaker of the House Pelosi blocked efforts by Congress to investigate the origins of the COVID-19 virus. With much of the evidence pointing to the possibility of a lab leak of the virus in Wuhan,

Pelosi ordered the Democrats in Congress not to cooperate with any efforts to investigate the matter.[89]

***

IN 1993, MONTHS after Senator Mitch McConnell and his wife, Elaine Chao, were married, the senator from Kentucky found himself in Beijing. But this was no typical honeymoon. He was traveling with his wife and new father-in-law, James Chao, and they had a series of private meetings with senior Chinese officials, including Chinese president Jiang Zemin. Jiang and James Chao had been classmates in China decades earlier.

The meetings were a major publicity coup for Beijing. Tiananmen Square had happened years earlier and few American political figures were visiting the country. McConnell was only the second Republican U.S. senator to do so.[90]

The meetings had a commercial component, too. According to the Chinese government media, McConnell and the Chao family "arrived in Beijing at the invitation of the Chinese State Shipbuilding Corporation."[91] That massive government-owned entity would play a central role in the rise of the McConnell-Chao family's fortunes.

For the next several decades, Foremost Maritime, the Chao family shipping empire, would see its fleet expand and its customers in mainland China grow.

Senator McConnell has been at the pinnacle of American power for decades. He has served as the Senate majority leader and leads the Republicans in that august body. Add the fact that McConnell's wife, Elaine Chao, has served in the cabinets of two U.S. presidents—George W. Bush and Donald Trump—and you have Washington's consummate power couple.

While Senator Feinstein has been remarkably pro-Beijing in her public statements about China, Senator McConnell has been more balanced. But let there be no doubt: the senator from Kentucky and his wife enjoy some of the deepest and most abiding ties to Beijing-linked entities of anyone in Washington, D.C.

"Big help with a little badmouth" seems to be alive and well.

As I recounted in my earlier book *Secret Empires*, McConnell and Chao can count a gift they received from Elaine's father, James Chao, as the single largest contributor to their personal wealth. He built his fortune in the shipping business, and a key ingredient to the success of his company has been good relations with the Beijing government and Chinese state-linked shipping companies.[92]

Chinese human rights activists in the United States have long worried about those ties and how they might be influencing McConnell and Chao's views toward China. "I worry about Elaine Chao's business relationship with communist China," said the late Harry Wu, a scholar at the Hoover Institution at Stanford University.[93]

The ties with the Beijing regime are well known in the small world of international shipping. As the shipping industry publication *Tradewinds* states, "Industry players describe Foremost Maritime as a low-profile shipping company with strong ties to China. They also say it has links with both the U.S. and Chinese governments."[94]

Indeed, the fusion between Foremost, Beijing, and Senator McConnell is perhaps best illustrated with a peek inside the sitting room at the company's headquarters in midtown Manhattan. On the sofa there is a pillow—it features the seal of the United States Senate.[95]

The Chao family first started ordering ships from China in 1990. After that 1993 visit with Senator McConnell, their partnership blossomed. From 2001 to 2011, Foremost received ten mammoth ships from Chinese state-controlled shipbuilders.[96]

When Elaine Chao became transportation secretary in the Trump administration in 2017, the relationship grew even more.

As of July 2018, the Foremost Group signed a series of contracts with the China State Shipbuilding Corporation (CSSC) to build ten more ships, including six of the massive 208,000-ton variety.[97] The financial terms of the deal were not disclosed, but similar transactions with other entities buying these large vessels put the price tag over $50 million each. That puts the total deal in the hundreds of millions of dollars.[98]

In addition to building these ships, the CSSC was financing the construction. Furthermore, their vessels' crews are almost exclusively Chinese. They transport large amounts of raw materials in and out of Chinese ports. Foremost clients include Western companies like Cargill, but they are often moving goods for Chinese government-owned entities like Wuhan Iron and Steel (Wisco) and Rizhao Steel.[99]

In short, the Chinese government is building the Chaos' ships, financing their construction, and providing crews and customers for the family.

Who exactly is CSSC, which plays such a central role in the financial fortunes of the McConnell-Chao family?

CSSC is a state-owned defense conglomerate, and also one of "the world's most prolific builders of large surface combatants and submarines." The Chaos' family business is interested in civilian not military shipping. But in China, the two are deeply intertwined. Daniel Alderman of Defense Group Inc. and Rush Doshi of Harvard University wrote of China's shipbuilding industry generally and CSSC specifically that the Chinese government "views civilian shipbuilding as essential to and intertwined with military shipbuilding." They say, "China's promotion and protection of advanced civilian facilities are likely related to its military purposes."[100]

Beyond the commercial fortunes of the Chao family business, the relationship goes deeper. Beijing openly credits James Chao with helping grow the Chinese shipbuilding industry. Indeed,

Chinese president Hu Jintao praised him "for his years of support to the Chinese shipbuilding industry and his contribution to the shipbuilding industry."[101]

CSSC describes their relationship to Chao as "a business partner and friend of years." Foremost is regarded as "a good client of China State Shipbuilding Corporation," say industry insiders.[102]

How close is the business relationship between the Chinese government and the Chao family? When CSSC was creating a financial offshoot called CSSC Holdings, they actually placed James Chao and Elaine's sister on the board of directors.[103]

When Elaine Chao was secretary of transportation, there was a blurring of the lines between her family's business and her official duties, particularly regarding China. When she visited China in 2017, she included her father and her sister, Angela Chao, as part of the official delegation. Her father and sister attended official bilateral functions between U.S. and Chinese officials. Government ethics officials worried that "if the Secretary were to engage in events . . . at locations closely connected with the Foremost Group, it would provide an inappropriate advantage, in the form of publicity, to Secretary Chao's family's business interests." Some of the events on the trip were canceled because of ethics concerns raised by Department of Transportation (DOT) lawyers.[104]

Secretary Chao also had DOT officials edit chapters of the English-language version of her father's book and create a media strategy for its promotion. She even had DOT officials edit his Wikipedia page.[105]

The McConnell-Chao families' connections to Beijing includes Angela sitting on the board of directors of the government-controlled Bank of China.[106] Angela's husband, Jim Breyer, is a major investor in a host of companies in China, including firms with ties to the Chinese military-industrial complex. Breyer is the co-chairman of IDG Capital, which is headquartered in Beijing, and has offices in Hong Kong, Shanghai, Guangzhou, and Hangzhou.[107] Breyer has done very well in China and enjoys close relations with the political elite in Beijing. Testimony before the U.S.-China Economic and Security Review Commission, which is organized by the U.S. Congress, reveals that "IDG's investment track record in China is legendary." It includes stakes in companies such as Qihoo 360, which the U.S. Department of Commerce dinged for "activities contrary to the national security or foreign policy interests of the United States."[108] Breyer's firm was also an early stakeholder in SenseTime, which works closely with China's Ministry of State Security to monitor the population, especially the Uighurs.[109]

Senator McConnell has spoken out about Beijing's military expansion and human rights, but has been leery of legislation that would restrict commerce with China. He has long supported the view that free trade would mean a freer China.[110] But there can be little doubt that the McConnell-Chao family business fortunes could be disrupted overnight if Beijing looked with too much disfavor at the policy positions he takes toward China.

***

LEAVING CONGRESS AND cashing in as a lobbyist or advisor for special interests has a long and sordid history in Washington. However, those special interests increasingly are not American, but rather the Chinese government and government-linked entities looking to advance their interests in Washington. The Beijing regime and its satellite entities have an embarrassment of riches when it comes to building a roster of former American politicians and officials now on their payroll as lobbyists or advisors.

Indeed, as we shall see, at least twenty former U.S. senators or members of Congress have worked in recent years representing Chinese firms with ties to the military or to intelligence services.

During his tenure as Speaker of the House, John Boehner took positions and actions that were highly beneficial to Beijing. In one particular case, he played the key role in preventing a vote on legislation that would have been catastrophic for the regime.

In 2011, Congress was deliberating over a currency manipulation bill to hold China to account for keeping its currency artificially low. (By doing so, Beijing was making their products cheaper in the United States by some 30 percent and boosting their exports.)[111] Beijing saw the bill as a serious threat—and rightfully so. They mobilized a twelve-member "Congressional Liaison Team" inside the Chinese embassy in Washington and paid the firm Patton Boggs $35,000 a month to help. The firm, one of the most powerful in the United States, has deep and abiding ties to the Chinese government. Back in 1980, the firm became one of the first in the world to be granted a license to set up an office in Beijing. And for decades now, Patton Boggs (later Squire Patton Boggs) has registered with the U.S. Justice Department as a foreign agent of the Chinese embassy in Washington, D.C.[112]

The currency manipulation bill passed through the U.S. Senate 63–35 with strong bipartisan support from Republicans and Democrats. Now attention turned to the House of Representatives, where John Boehner was Speaker. And there it ran smack into a wall.

Boehner would not even allow a vote in the House. Period.[113]

"The only thing standing between business-as-usual and a real shot across the bow to Beijing is House Speaker John Boehner," complained Scott Paul, the executive director of the Alliance for American Manufacturing, on CNBC. "Half of his caucus supports the bill, along with an overwhelming number of Democrats."[114]

Boehner called the bill dangerous. "It's a pretty dangerous thing to be moving legislation through the U.S. Congress forcing someone to deal with the value of a currency," he said, arguing that passing the bill would lead to a trade war.[115] A careful observer might see that his statement compared favorably with statements that Chinese officials were making to the media.[116]

Perhaps it should be no surprise that when Boehner retired from public office in 2015, he signed on as "a strategic advisor to clients in the U.S. and abroad" at Squire Patton Boggs (SPB).[117] The firm continues to advise and help the Beijing government navigate issues that will threaten their interests. According to SPB's 2021 filing with the Justice Department, this has included offering guidance on everything from the U.S. defense budget as well as "the 2020 general elections; actions and potential actions regarding U.S. policy concerning Hong Kong, Taiwan, Xinjiang, and Tibet; and matters pertaining to human rights, immigration, trade, and sanctions legislation."[118]

Beyond representing the Chinese government, Boehner's firm also has a wide array of Chinese government-linked corporate clients that it lobbies for in Washington. These include ChemChina, China Railway Rolling Stock Corporation, Huawei, and Wanhua Chemical Group.[119]

The firm where Boehner now collects large fees has powerful friends—not just in Washington, but in Beijing as well.

In China, SPB has deep ties to the ruling regime. Nick Chan, a senior partner in China, is also a member of the ruling National People's Congress (NPC). "The NPC is the highest organ of state power in People's Republic of China," explained SPB in a recent announcement.[120]

SPB is not just a lobbying shop—it is also a law firm. And here, too, the firm works extensively on projects that benefit the Chinese government. The firm brags that it is "well positioned to support clients on major infrastructure transactions and projects in connection with the 'Belt and Road Initiative.'"[121] Both the Obama and Trump administrations saw Belt and Road as designed to supplant

American influence around the globe and push countries into China's sphere.[122] The massive initiative is also plagued with reports that its projects feature "forced labor."[123]

At the same time, SPB attorneys are regularly quoted in the Chinese state-owned media, criticizing trade and technology restrictions placed on Chinese firms in the United States, while also praising Beijing officials for their welcoming attitude to American companies.[124]

Boehner is not the only former elected official now drawing a paycheck from a firm doing the bidding of Beijing and related companies.

Former U.S. senator Tim Hutchinson of Arkansas, once a member of the Senate Armed Services Committee, lobbies for Alibaba, the Chinese behemoth closely aligned with the Beijing government. Alibaba paid his firm, Greenberg Traurig, $200,000 in 2020, for a team that also included two other former politicians, Congressmen Rodney Frelinghuysen of New Jersey and Albert Wynn of Maryland.[125]

Tencent Holdings is another massive Chinese company. It is closely fused with the Ministry of Public Security and the People's Liberation Army and develops technologies with military application as well as products that monitor and help control the population.[126] In Washington, D.C., the company enjoys the lobbying services of former congressman Ed Royce of California. The Republican was once the chairman of the House Foreign Affairs Committee. Tencent paid his firm $330,000 in 2020 alone.[127]

Another well-known Chinese company in the West is Byte-Dance, which runs TikTok, the social media platform with over one hundred million users in the United States alone.[128] While it pretends to operate like any other company, ByteDance's CEO has been outspoken about the need for the company to follow the guidance of the Communist Party in its business operations. There are Party cells within the corporate structure, and the company admits that it censors political content. Former employees complain that the "content moderation process [is] strongly influenced by Beijing" and that it is used to "downplay subjects Beijing finds sensitive."[129] In Washington, it has two former U.S. senators on the payroll, Democrat John Breaux of Louisiana and Republican Trent Lott of Mississippi. (Breaux once famously said that his vote in the Senate was not for sale, "but it is available for rent.")[130]

Also on the ByteDance payroll are former congressmen Jeff Denham and Bart Gordon, whose firm pocketed $160,000 from the company in 2020.[131]

The military-linked Chinese telecom firm, ZTE Corporation, enjoys the services of former senators Norman Coleman and Joe Lieberman, as well as former congressmen Jon Christensen and Connie Mack IV. Coleman's firm alone raked in a whopping $2.94 million in 2019 representing the company.[132]

Huawei, another Chinese telecom with close ties to the Chinese military, hired Congressmen Don Bonker and Cliff Stearns after their time in office.[133] Back in 2013, the Joint Intelligence Committee, which oversees British intelligence, explained that with a cyber attack, "it would be very difficult to detect or prevent and could enable the Chinese to intercept covertly or disrupt traffic passing through Huawei-supplied networks."[134] Stearns, a conservative Republican from Florida, and Bonker, a liberal Democrat from Washington State, both work at the lobbying firm APCO Worldwide. They have also tag-teamed on a lobbying contract with the aforementioned, PLA navy business buddy COSCO.[135] Who says bipartisanship is dead in our nation's capital?

In 2021, former congressman Lee Terry, from Nebraska, signed up to work for Huawei.[136] Huawei, beyond concerns about its ties to Chinese intelligence, is headed by a colorful and aggressive founder named Ren Zhengfei. A former PLA engineer, he told employees in 2018 to "wage war" on the West and he charged them to "surge forward, killing as you go, to blaze us a trail of blood."[137]

Former congressman Jack Kingston, of Georgia, has lobbied for ChemChina, the state-owned chemical company.[138]

Hikvision is a surveillance company in China, largely owned by a government-controlled defense conglomerate called the China Electronics Technology Group.[139] Hikvision has a particularly odious reputation because its surveillance cameras have been installed by the Chinese government to monitor Uighurs being held in prison camps.[140] But that has not deterred several former politicians from signing up to lobby on their behalf. Hikvision has enjoyed the services of former U.S. senator David Vitter of Louisiana and former congressman Toby Moffett, whose firm they paid $70,000 a month, and former congressman Rick Boucher of Virginia, whose firm pocketed $1.75 million in 2019 for lobbying services.[141] Former California senator Barbara Boxer also signed on to advise the company, registering as a foreign agent with the Department of Justice. She has—no surprise—claimed her motives were altruistic. "When I am asked to provide strategic advice to help a company operate in a more responsible and humane manner consistent with U.S. law in spirit and letter, it is an opportunity to make things better while helping protect and create American jobs." But she later withdrew from the arrangement following a public outcry.[142]

***

INFLUENCING THE HIGHEST spheres of government can come via current members of Congress who enjoy commercial ties as well as ex-politicians who become hired-gun lobbyists. Sometimes Beijing's influence is directed by shadowy nonprofit organizations that work their way through our institutions in Washington, D.C., guided by Americans willing to help—for a fee.

One of the most effective organizations cultivating Chinese interests on Capitol Hill is called the China–United States Exchange Foundation (CUSEF). The nonprofit organization was founded in 2008 by Tung Chee-hwa, a Chinese billionaire with close ties to the party. Tung constructed a massive shipping empire in Hong Kong and was hand-picked by the Communist Party to take over control of the territory in 1997 when it reverted from British rule to Beijing. Tung is vice chairman of the Chinese People's Political Consultative Conference (CPPCC), "one of the united front's most important entities."[143] Tung is a party member and attended the Chinese Communist Party's 19th Congress in October 2017.[144]

Tung takes a hard line when it comes to human rights. During the 2019 protests in Hong Kong, Tung accused Washington of "orchestrating" the events, and defended the actions of the police. In December 2019, he was named by Hong Kong democracy advocates as one of the "top tier perpetrators of human rights and democracy abuse."[145]

He also toes the party line on the matter at hand. "Where democracy is concerned, the West often criticizes China for not practicing a more Western style democracy," says Tung, who is also chairman of CUSEF. "However, history has demonstrated time and again that a country cannot adopt another country's governance system and become successful."[146] Of course, this is precisely what happened in China—the Communist Party seized power and adopted the Soviet Union's model of governance.

Given those views, it is perhaps not surprising that CUSEF has ties to the CCP through the Chinese United Front. The role of the United Front, according to the U.S. Congress's China Security Commission, is to "co-opt and neutralize sources of potential opposition to the policies and authority of its ruling Chinese Communist Party."[147] Both "the number of mainland-based members" of CUSEF's official advisors, and the "easy connections with Chinese government organs" demonstrate how closely tied are CUSEF and the CCP, according to a Stanford University study.[148]

The U.S. congressional commission concurs. CUSEF has involvement "in influence operations" and has spent millions of dollars lobbying in the United States.[149]

In addition, CUSEF works closely with other front organizations, including the PLA-linked group known as the China Association for International Friendly Contact.[150]

Yet, despite these ties, CUSEF enjoys powerful reach and top-shelf friends in Washington. The longtime honorary advisors to this Chinese front organization, listed at the top of the organization's annual report masthead, are former secretary of state Henry Kissinger and Robert Rubin, the former Clinton Treasury secretary.[151]

Both of whom, of course, have a history of considerable commercial interests in China over the years.

Other well-connected individuals are also happy to partner with CUSEF.

In September 2009, the first delegation from the Center for American Progress (CAP) arrived in Beijing for talks with Chinese officials about "issues at the forefront of U.S.-China relations, including climate change."[152] These dialogues between American organizations and Chinese officials were funded by CUSEF and ran through 2016.[153] CAP president John Podesta both facilitated and participated in these dialogues. In 2013, the White House called, and Podesta was appointed counselor to President Barack Obama. His responsibilities "included overseeing climate change and energy policy." Another CAP official, senior fellow Tod Stern, also joined the Obama administration as a lead climate negotiator on the Paris Accords.[154]

While John Podesta and his deputy were helping craft the Paris Climate Accords, his brother, lobbyist Tony Podesta, was working for a Chinese-bankrolled entity called the Coalition for Affordable Solar Energy. In Congress, there were moves afoot to consider legislation to counteract efforts by Chinese solar companies to "dump" panels in the United States at low prices to drive American firms out of business. The coalition was funded by Chinese solar companies Suntech Power Holding, Trina Solar, and Yingli Green Energy Holding. Podesta headed "Team China."[155]

The resulting Paris Climate Accords called for the United States to dramatically reduce its carbon emissions. China, however, had no such requirement. The deal was seen by some as far too favorable for Beijing.[156]

John Podesta has praised China for its commitment to reducing emissions while at the same time going after countries like Australia, claiming that country's approach "is just not going to cut it."[157] This is a bizarre position, given that "in 2020 alone, China brought 38 gigawatts of new coal power online, exceeding Australia's entire remaining capacity of 25 gigawatts (down from 66 gigawatts in 2017)."[158]

Concerns about climate change have become a powerful tool for Beijing to divert attention from human rights and other issues. In September 2021, Speaker of the House Nancy Pelosi delivered a speech at Cambridge University in which she acknowledged China's "genocide" of the Uighurs, while proclaiming that partnering with China on climate change was the "overriding issue."[159] John Kerry, the former U.S. senator and secretary of state, now climate czar for the Biden administration, has said the same.[160] This gives Beijing enormous leverage by granting it a powerful tool with which to silence their critics: talk too harshly about genocide, and we will no longer cooperate with you on climate change policies.

Under the Paris Climate Accords, Beijing, which is the world's largest carbon producer, can continue to grow its carbon emissions up until 2030 (at which point, they are supposed to begin reducing them).[161] The accords also assume that China will honor its commitments—and offer no penalties if they fail to do so. In 2015, President Xi stood with President Barack Obama at the Rose Garden in the White House and promised that he would not militarize islands in the South China Sea. He "lied through his teeth," in the words of the *Economist*, because by 2018, Beijing had military bases there.[162]

China was a big winner in another way, too.

The United States will honor its commitments under the Paris Climate Accords largely by buying solar panels and other green technologies manufactured in China. (Eight out of the ten largest solar companies in the world are Chinese.) "One of the biggest mistakes the West has done on green policies to cut CO_2 emissions and trying to reduce dependence on oil- and gas-producing nations is that the transition to renewable energy puts the West at the mercy of China," says energy industry consultant David Zaikin, founder of London-based Key Elements Group. Eighty percent of the solar panels installed in the United States are made in China. Beijing is positioned to be the "green OPEC."[163] Shortly after the climate deal was concluded, CUSEF hired John Podesta's brother Tony as a lobbyist, paying his firm, the Podesta Group, $880,000 between 2015 and 2017 to lobby on behalf of U.S.-China relations.[164]

CUSEF was not Tony Podesta's only Chinese client. In early 2016, his firm was also hired by ZTE, a Chinese telecom company convicted of selling illegal shipments of telecom equipment to Iran.[165] In 2016 and 2017, ZTE paid Podesta Group over $750,000.[166] The Podesta Group organized specialists to help ZTE in its case against federal agencies. As the British newspaper the *Guardian* reported, ZTE "refused to provide any documents on its activities in Iran, but did provide a list of 19 individuals who serve on the Chinese

Communist Party committee within the company."[167] The U.S. Department of Justice did report that "ZTE's most senior managers constructed an elaborate scheme to evade detection by U.S. authorities."[168]

Tony Podesta more recently signed up as a "consultant" for Huawei, at an annualized rate of $2 million..[169] A posting on Huawei's own corporate message board noted that the hiring was part of an "expanded U.S. influence operation," adding that Podesta had powerful connections in the Biden administration. Huawei employees greeted the news with "thumbs-up" and stars on the message board.[170]

Beyond Podesta, CUSEF has hired an army of lobbyists over the years to push its message. Among them is former Republican congressman Charles Boustany of Louisiana. Boustany, a surgeon by training, served twelve years in Congress and went on to cochair the U.S.-China working group, a bipartisan caucus for members of Congress interested in China matters. As he was leaving office in 2016, he made a play to be a trade representative for the incoming Trump administration.[171] When that did not happen, he went to work at Capitol Counsel, a D.C. lobbying shop. The lobbying firm registered as a foreign agent with the U.S. Department of Justice to represent CUSEF. In its contract with CUSEF, Capitol Counsel's activities included "political intelligence gathering" as well as "substantive advice on China-related legislation," including "arranging meetings" on Capitol Hill.[172]

In 2019, Boustany led a delegation of former members of Congress to China, a trip sponsored by CUSEF.[173]

At the same time, Boustany became a spokesman for an organization called Tariffs Hurt the Heartland, which argued that imposing tariffs on Beijing was damaging to Americans.[174]

Capitol Counsel was also hired by something called the U.S.-China Transpacific Foundation (UCTPF) to lobby on their behalf.

The UCTPF, according to filings with the Justice Department, is funded by the Chinese government with the purpose of sponsoring trips by politicians and their staffs to visit mainland China.[175]

CUSEF also signed the firm founded by Haley Barbour, the former Mississippi governor and former chairman of the Republican National Committee. In 2019, CUSEF paid the firm $370,000, for which Lester Munson, a former Senate Republican staffer and deputy assistant administrator at the U.S. Agency for International Development during the George W. Bush administration, pushed their interests.[176]

***

ONE LONG-TERM CUSEF lobbyist is Claude Fontheim, a fixture in Washington lobbying circles for decades. Fontheim set up his business, Fontheim International, LLC, in 1990. The current location is on Seventeenth Street, just a block from the White House.[177] In 2009, Fontheim started lobbying for CUSEF and registered as a foreign agent with the Department of Justice. Fontheim also did something else. He provided the seed capital for the creation of a consulting firm called Beacon Global Strategies.[178]

It is hard to find a firm in Washington with more insiders than Beacon Global Strategies.

Founded in 2013 by alumni from the Clinton and Bush administrations, Beacon boasts one of the more impressive rosters of ex-military and intelligence officials you could imagine. Cofounders include Philippe Reines, the longtime Hillary Clinton foreign policy advisor, and Mike Allen, a former George W. Bush aide.[179] A list of partners and advisors runs the gamut from former Obama secretary of defense Leon Panetta to former deputy director of the CIA Mike Morell.[180]

"Drawing on our decades of service in the international security arena, we develop strategies that enable companies to achieve their business objectives," the firm says on its website.[181]

Beacon cuts a wide path in official Washington. In 2015, no fewer than three presidential candidates received campaign advice from someone connected to Beacon—Hillary Clinton, who was seeking the Democratic nomination, and GOP senators Marco Rubio and Ted Cruz.[182]

Beacon does much more than simply give advice to political figures. They also use their background and their government experience to help corporate clients navigate the regulatory waters in Washington. This includes companies that are eager to do deals with China. Mike Allen, the firm's managing director, "advises clients on the intersection of business and national security and helps them develop targeted Washington strategies." He also helps clients understand "U.S.-China dynamics, foreign direct investment and CFIUS, national security critical technologies such as AI, as well as trade and challenges arising from geopolitical instability."[183]

When deals involving corporate America and Beijing raise red flags, Beacon jumps in and provides approaches to get around them. At times, Beacon has done this in a manner that ultimately benefits Beijing.

In 2016, the U.S. company Advanced Micro Devices (AMD) announced a new joint venture in China to produce microchips. The venture would utilize the company's own proprietary technology, specifically the X86 processor, the advanced chip produced only by AMD and one other American firm, Intel.[184]

AMD's agreement with Beijing would allow for the direct transfer of technology to a Chinese firm called Sugon Information Industry Company. Sugon, which produced computers for civilian use, also noted on its website that "making contributions to China's national defense and security is a fundamental mission of Sugon."

The deal was a clear attempt by Beijing to create technological independence from the United States.[185]

For these reasons and more, AMD's joint venture in China raised troubling issues in national security circles. "Semiconductors are a space where the U.S. still leads China and the rest of the world," said William Evanina, the U.S. government's paramount counterintelligence official, to the *Wall Street Journal*.

"It's the keys to the kingdom," warned retired Air Force brigadier general Robert Spalding. "Everything today is built on x86."[186]

Pentagon officials also believed that the deal was being structured to possibly "sidestep U.S. regulations" designed to restrict the flow of advanced technologies to China. Defense officials requested that AMD submit the agreement to the federal government's Committee on Foreign Investment in the United States (CFIUS) to review it. (CFIUS is made up of representatives from the Departments of Defense, Treasury, State, and others to review commercial actions involving foreign nations and their implications for national security.) But AMD said it did not require CFIUS review and that the committee did not have jurisdiction. In early 2017, the U.S. Department of Defense unilaterally submitted the proposed deal to CFIUS.[187]

In response, AMD hired Beacon Global Strategies to make the case that the deal would not help China. Beacon, with its roster of former Department of Defense, CIA, and other national security officials, told the Pentagon that the deal presented no national security problems. Never mind that Sun Ninghui, a Chinese official who worked closely with Sugon, actually said that the deal would be beneficial to China and allow the country to get on a better technological footing vis-à-vis the United States. "This gradually advances our ability to comprehend their core technologies," Sun told a Chinese government-affiliated newspaper. "That way, we no longer can be pulled around by our noses."[188]

We do not know how Beacon's advocacy might have swayed the Department of Defense, because in 2019, one of AMD's Chinese partners was put on a restricted list. Sugon was "acting contrary to the national security or foreign policy interests of the United States." That meant the deal was halted.[189]

Beacon played a similar role of running interference on another technology transfer case that would benefit Beijing.[190] When Singapore-based Broadcom announced plans to acquire the American tech firm Qualcomm, some concerns were raised. Broadcom has a close working relationship with China's Huawei. Qualcomm is an advanced technology company very active in the 5G technology sphere, which provides high-speed cellular capabilities. The acquisition of Qualcomm would provide Beijing with a boost in its competition with the United States over 5G technologies.[191]

The fear at the Pentagon was that if the merger went through, China would end up dominating 5G and that within ten years "there would essentially be a dominant player in all of these technologies and that's essentially Huawei."[192]

Broadcom hired Beacon Global Strategies to help fight those concerns.[193]

The Trump administration ultimately blocked the deal on national security grounds.[194]

The intense competition over technology dominance is central to the race between China and the United States. Some of the titans of Silicon Valley have found that coziness with Beijing has its benefits.

4

SILICON VALLEY

In 2015, the CEOs of America's largest tech companies gathered at Microsoft's glass and steel headquarters just outside of Seattle. The leaders from Amazon, Airbnb, Apple, and Facebook were all present to welcome a very special guest. For President Xi, the visit to Seattle was a stopover; he was en route to meetings with President Barack Obama in Washington, D.C. The purpose of visiting Seattle first was to cultivate Beijing's relationship with America's tech titans. The Technorati waited patiently for his arrival. When he entered the room, the titans of Silicon Valley were thunderstruck.

"Did you feel the room shake?" asked Apple CEO Tim Cook.[1]

Days later, some who met privately with Xi had another opportunity to see him in person. This time the venue was an official State Dinner at the White House. The East Room was decorated in peach and pink roses and other flowers. The crowd included two hundred elite guests from the world of government and business. At least a couple of those same tech titans who had met Xi in Seattle were there again, too. Among them was Mark Zuckerberg, the young-looking cofounder of Facebook, and his wife, Priscilla, who is ethnically Chinese. She also happened to be seven months pregnant. When Zuckerberg finally got his chance to see the guest of honor face-to-face again, he made an unusual request: would the communist dictator give his child his Chinese name?

Xi, understandably surprised by the request, declined, saying it was "too great a responsibility."[2]

Silicon Valley's tech giants seem enamored with the Chinese dictatorship's ability to get things done. They are also partly blinded by their technological ambition and are therefore prepared to collaborate with the notorious regime to accomplish their silicon dreams. While they are well known for their wealth and the hubris that comes with it, they often appear to have a euphoric attitude—even giddiness—when dealing with Chinese officials. Yes, they will genuflect for access to the Chinese market. But there is also a sense of personal awe there—and it is not just for President Xi.

Almost a year before this visit, in late 2014, a high-ranking Chinese official named Lu Wei made a trip to Silicon Valley.[3] Lu was a Communist Party hack, the former deputy head of the Propaganda Department of the Communist Party of China. President Xi had recently appointed him to head the "Central Leading Group for Internet Security and Information."[4] In short, Lu was China's internet czar, with the Orwellian job of restricting access to certain ideas and monitoring the flow of information. The Chinese government had given him plenty of tools to do his job. In 2013, they created a law making it a crime to spread rumors online; if a post deemed untrue received more than five hundred reposts, the original poster could be sentenced to up to three years in prison.[5]

"Mr. Lu is basically an old school propagandist," says Paul Mozur, who reports on China for the *New York Times*.[6]

But when Lu visited Facebook's California headquarters in Menlo Park, Zuckerberg treated him like a VIP. The Facebook head gave him a tour of the new Frank Gehry–designed campus, which boasted the "largest open floor plan in the world." Later, the two retreated to Zuckerberg's private office. Lu sat in the CEO's chair, took a few pictures, and then spotted a familiar book sitting on Zuckerberg's desk. *The Governance of China* is a 515-page tome containing the speeches and comments of President Xi. Lu presumably knew the book intimately: it was assembled in part by the Party Literature Research Office of the CPC Central Committee.[7] Why was such a book sitting on a capitalist's desk? Zuckerberg explained to his guest that he bought the book for both himself and his staff as a guide. "I want to make them understand socialism with Chinese characteristics," he said.[8]

During the same visit, Lu stopped by Apple headquarters to meet with Tim Cook. The Chinese media released images of the meeting, which included Cook greeting Lu like "an old friend, beaming while Lu wags a joking finger at him."[9]

Asking the Chinese leader to name your kid or joking around with a censorious propagandist may seem odd or even slightly creepy. But Silicon Valley's hat-tipping to Beijing has an even darker side. For decades, many of the biggest names in tech have made their fortunes thanks to the norms and values of the American system. All the while, they have actively collaborated with the Chinese regime, helping them better control their population. They have even assisted China's attempt to surpass the United States in military capabilities.

Tech executives tend to be optimistic about how engineering progress will lead to societal progress. Perhaps they have such faith in information and the internet that they feel sure technology will bring down a repressive regime. Or, perhaps, they are bowing to their inevitable overlords. It is worth sorting through their actions to figure out which thesis is the better fit.

China, with help from these Silicon Valley elites, hopes to become the world's number one power.

What Chinese leaders seek is "technological supremacy" because that will provide them with economic supremacy, and the ability to match American military capabilities.[10]

President Xi has said, "Science and technology is a national weapon." He goes further: "We should seize the *commanding heights* of technological competition and future development." He believes that "in today's world [science and technology] innovation has become a critical support for increasing comprehensive national strength."[11]

To accomplish this goal, Beijing has created "civilian-military fusion," which means any technological advance in the civilian market must be applied directly to the military sphere.[12] And they have effectively courted and seduced many powerful people in Silicon Valley to willingly, and sometimes enthusiastically, play along.

***

BILL GATES IS one of the world's richest men, rightly recognized as a visionary who helped build a massive technology industry. He has moved into the world of philanthropy to pursue support for some notable causes. He also has a deeply troubling relationship with the Chinese regime.

No one can blame a corporate executive for being enticed by the Chinese market's opportunities. From the earliest days of the internet, China has been seen as a lucrative market for the tech industry. With approximately four times the population of the United States, you can bet Bill Gates saw it, too.

But Gates has cooperated with the regime in ways that other tech titans have not. He has lent credence to the claims of the Chinese Communist Party and been rewarded with access, favors, and titles. He has done the bidding of the regime in the tech world and has apologized or made excuses for its aberrant activities. On top of all that, he has invested in companies attached to Beijing's military-industrial complex.

Gates appears to have always underestimated the repressive nature of the CCP. His relentless techno-optimism has made him an easy mark. He has expressed naïve attitudes about the role of technology in that repression. In 1995, at the dawn of the broader internet age, he suggested that Chinese efforts to censor the web would fail. Gates claimed that Chinese officials would literally need to have someone looking over everyone's shoulder to implement full internet access and maintain censorship.[13]

Of course, Beijing had a censorship system in place just two years later.[14]

Even after China erected what came to be known as the "Great Firewall," Gates still insisted that censorship was too hard to erect and would not work. In 2008, he told students at Stanford University: "I don't see any risk in the world at large that someone will restrict free content flow on the internet," he told them. "You cannot control the internet."[15]

It was a bold statement that proved both inaccurate and disingenuous. At that point, Microsoft had already been helping the regime censor content for several years.

In June 2005, Microsoft launched a blogging software program called MSN Spaces in China, just as blogging was taking off. But the program censored words including "democracy," "human rights," and "freedom of expression." If you typed in those words or phrases, the blogger would receive an error message. The system also blocked or limited results of searches for specific names or phrases like "Tibet independence," "Falun Gong," and "Tiananmen Square." On December 30, 2005, when a Chinese blogger and journalist named Zhao Jing criticized the censorship on his MSN Spaces blog, Microsoft shut him down, "following a request from Chinese authorities," according to Amnesty International.[16] The problem extends even to today.

In early June 2021, users of Microsoft's Bing search engine in the United States, Europe, and Asia reported that they could not pull up images and information concerning the anniversary of the Tiananmen Square massacre on their laptops. Microsoft blamed it on "human error," but did not specify what error would have caused images of "tank man" and others to disappear.[17]

The controversy over the regime's censorship on the internet finally boiled over in 2010 when Google went to battle over search engine restrictions. When the dispute became public, Gates actually sided with Beijing and against Google, arguing that companies need to follow local laws. His position even prompted the Chinese embassy to run an approving story titled, "Bill Gates Bats for China."[18]

Gates tried to sound principled, but this simply did not conform to the realities of his participation in censorship. In 2010, he claimed that China's restrictions were minimal and expressed confidence that technology would overcome it. "Chinese efforts to censor the internet have been very limited," he said. "It's easy to go around it, so I think keeping the internet thriving there is very important." Steve Ballmer, the Microsoft CEO at the time, echoed that sentiment. "If the Chinese government gives us proper legal notice, we'll take that piece of information out of the Bing search engine." Ballmer added that countries like the United States with "extreme" free speech laws also censor some material.[19]

While Gates was attempting to explain away Chinese censorship, he was actively helping the regime accomplish it. Meanwhile, he was critical of any censorship in the United States. Gates was quick to criticize efforts he saw to restrict internet access unnecessarily. One example was his view of legislation that would curb children's access to pornography. As Gates put it:

> Microsoft and others in industry and non-profit organisations were deeply involved in trying to block language that would put chilling restrictions on the use of the Internet for the free publication of information. The language, ostensibly aimed at keeping pornography out of the hands of children, goes much too far in restricting freedom of expression. . . . Let's

not undermine the world-wide trend toward free expression by setting a bad example when it comes to free speech on a computer network.

Clearly, Gates did not want children to have easy access to pornography. Yet, while the vagueness of language concerning that law bothered him, China's censorship apparently did not, given his frequent defense of it.[20]

Beyond the issue of apologizing for Beijing's censorship, Gates continued to appease the Chinese government. Microsoft promised Beijing that it would begin outsourcing jobs from the United States to China—it was an explicit promise. By the early 2000s, Microsoft was on track to have outsourced a thousand jobs. When the Chinese government criticized the company for not keeping pace, Microsoft said they would work harder to ship more jobs more quickly to the Chinese mainland.[21]

Gates's efforts to support the regime's policies have been rewarded over the years. In 2006, the state-run *People's Daily Online* named Gates among "50 foreigners shaping China's modern development." Joining him on the list were Karl Marx, Vladimir Lenin, Albert Einstein, Charles Darwin, and Joseph Stalin. Gates was the only person from the world of technology on the list.[22] Earlier that year, when Chinese president Hu Jintao made his first official visit to the United States, he too stopped in Seattle for a visit with Gates at his "palatial home" before heading to Washington, D.C. ABC News declared, "Chinese President Meets Bill Gates First."[23]

The relationship between Microsoft and Beijing improved. By 2010, Microsoft had taken another step in its tightening association with the Chinese government. The company set up a research laboratory in China to work on artificial intelligence (AI) with a Chinese military university, an essential area of research that would have huge implications for the economy and on the battlefield. Microsoft even started taking in interns from the People's Liberation Army at its Asian research facility.[24]

Microsoft worked with the Beijing regime in other ways. The company allowed the PLA to access communications on Skype, the company's online videoconferencing platform. Communist officials were monitoring chats that might include organizing protests or other activities that might displease the regime. When asked about it, Microsoft simply said, "Skype's mission is to break down barriers to communications and enable conversations worldwide."[25]

Microsoft later formed a partnership with the state-owned military conglomerate China Electronics Technology Group (CETC) to make Windows available to government officials in Beijing. The agreement would provide "operating system technology and services for Chinese users in specialized fields in government institutions and critical infrastructure state-owned enterprises." The decision by Microsoft to work with CETC raised plenty of eyebrows in the tech world. As *Computerworld* noted, "CETC manages scores of research institutes and more than 180 commercial subsidiaries, most of them involved in defense-related research and development, the production of defense and dual-use electronics, or supplying the People's Liberation Army (PLA) and government agencies and state-run companies with technology products." CETC's labs designed the electronic guts for China's first nuclear bomb, as well as its guided missiles and satellites. There are "very blurred lines" between what is civilian and military at CETC, the publication noted. The specifics of the deal were mysterious. Microsoft said that it made "changes" to Windows for the Chinese government but would not explain what they were.[26]

Gates appeared unconcerned.

Gates's budding relationship with the Chinese government opened the door to other opportunities. In 2014, when Gates stepped down as chairman of Microsoft, he remained on the board as a technical advisor. He wanted to spend time on his nonprofit foundation, but it is clear that he still had other interests related to technology. With a fascination with nuclear power, he had cofounded a company called TerraPower in 2008, with hopes to build nuclear reactors in China. He started working with Beijing on a project in 2011.[27]

As TerraPower chief technical adviser Roger Reynolds explained during an interview, they were collaborating with the Chinese National Nuclear Corporation (CNNC) to build a "next-generation" reactor. The technology involves something called a "traveling wave reactor," which is based on a molten-salt reactor conceived initially by American scientists more than fifty years earlier.[28]

Gates seemed oblivious to national security concerns about the project. By working with the communist regime, he was providing the government a strategic leg up in its competition with the United States for control over global nuclear markets. As the U.S. State Department has repeatedly explained, China uses "its large, rapidly-growing, state-sponsored nuclear industry as a strategic tool with which to augment China's 'comprehensive national power'— both through development in the civilian sector *and* in support of a military buildup." Furthermore, his partner, CNNC, has also come under fire from the Nuclear Threat Initiative because it is "involved in the development of China's nuclear energy program, both civilian and military."[29]

Gates's project also helped the communist regime in its military competition with the United States. These "new generation" reactors are incredibly effective at propelling ships at sea, including military vessels. Beijing already had an active thorium molten-salt reactor program itself, and the PLA is planning to use the technology to propel aircraft carriers and military drones.[30]

In 2018, Gates's plans to build nuclear reactors with the Chinese government came to a halt when "policy changes" in Washington made the project difficult to achieve. Later, the U.S. Department of Defense released a list of twenty Chinese companies linked to the PLA. His Chinese partner was on the list. This forced Gates to shelve his joint deal with CNNC.[31] But it was not for a lack of trying.

He has pledged to continue seeking efforts to cooperate with Beijing on nuclear power projects. "The TerraPower thing, that was a setback, but there are ways to come back and engage China in a fairly deep way later in the project," he told Chinese state media.[32]

Gates is also an investor in a Chinese electric vehicle company with the uplifting name Build Your Dreams (BYD) and has praised the company's product. (His good friend Warren Buffett also owns a stake.)[33] BYD also has deep ties to, and cooperates with, the Chinese military. According to a study sponsored by the Alliance for American Manufacturing, BYD grants military enterprises access to its technologies and research data. In 2018, for example, BYD announced that it would conduct "strategic cooperation" with the China Academy of Launch Vehicle Technology—a PLA entity—which is the "largest research and production base of missile weapons and launch vehicles in China." At the same time, BYD works with military institutions to shape its products. For good measure, the company's founder and CEO is a Communist Party official.[34]

Beyond the deals, Gates has gone out of his way to personally praise President Xi. During an interview with the Communist Party's *People's Daily* in 2017, Gates talked about his relationship with Xi and the fact that the Chinese leader took so much time to speak with him. They discussed "the area of science, where China is now leading a lot of ways and willing to invest, that's been something I discussed with President Xi." He added: "And I am impressed of how hard President Xi works. Now he is involved in the committee that are looking at this problem and that problem. He's quite amazing that he's able to contribute in a number of ways."[35]

What does this mean? It means that one of the richest men in the world was praising the leadership of a man who runs ethno-political prison camps.

This is more than idle chatter. Gates is now an advisor of sorts to the Chinese government. In 2017, the Chinese Academy of Engineering (CAE) honored Gates with a lifetime membership. The CAE is under the direct supervision of the Chinese State Council, Beijing's top governing body. This elite body, whose name sounds relatively harmless, is actually at the center of Chinese government power and plays a central role in the Chinese military-industrial complex.[36]

Membership in the CAE requires "strict political clearance." Foreigners can join only if they have contributed to China's development. As the state-run *People's Daily* reported, "Election as a foreign member of CAE is a lifelong honor that is expected to build up the institution, promote international cooperation and exchanges, and improve CAE's status in the field of engineering."[37]

The CAE has a formal responsibility to advise the government, and on its website, it has numerous political articles extolling Xi and the Chinese Communist Party:

Enshrining Xi's thought into the Party Constitution has proved the main highlight of the congress, signifying a leap forward in the Sinicization of Marxism.

The resolution on the amendment to the Constitution states that with the integration of theory and practice, Chinese communists, with Xi as their chief representative, have given shape to the new thought since the 18th CPC National Congress.

This year marks the 150th anniversary of the publication of Karl Marx's iconic book "Das Kapital," while 2018 marks the 170th anniversary of the Communist Manifesto as well as the 40th anniversary of socialist China's launch of the reform and opening-up drive.

Xi believes that the new era of socialism with Chinese characteristics means "scientific socialism is full of vitality in 21st century China, and that the banner of socialism with Chinese characteristics is now flying high and proud for all to see."[38]

The founder of the Chinese Academy of Engineering was Zhu Guangya, China's "leading scientist in the country's research and development of nuclear weaponry." On the anniversary of his death in 2011, the current academy president, Zhou Ji, "pledged to follow his example and urged all Chinese scientists to contribute to 'the great rejuvenation of the Chinese nation.'"[39]

None of this seems to have bothered or concerned Gates as he joined the organization.

Indeed, it was Zhou Ji who granted Gates his membership in the academy.[40]

One of the most critical roles for the CAE is to adapt civilian technologies to military use. These are so-called "dual-use" technologies. Zhou Ji has noted on other occasions that artificial intelligence "will be the most important dual-use technology in the coming decades."[41] The Chinese Academy of Engineering sees that AI has a role in boosting the Chinese military. In October 2012, the CAE signed a partnership agreement with the People's Liberation Army Navy (PLAN) "to strengthen cooperation and push forward the military-civilian integration and innovative development of the PLA Navy and the CAE."[42]

Microsoft continues to work closely with military researchers in China, particularly in the area of AI. In 2018, Microsoft researchers wrote three research papers on AI in cooperation with China's National University of Defense Technology (NUDT). The Central Military Commission has authority over the school. Microsoft research enjoys "long-running links to Chinese military-funded academia." This includes running "tech clubs" at several universities known to have military connections.[43]

Microsoft, despite this close work with Beijing, is not immune to cyberattacks launched with the support of the Chinese government. In 2021, the Biden administration pointed a finger at Beijing regarding a massive breach of Microsoft. But Microsoft has given no indication that they will be scaling back their work with the government that is targeting them.[44]

Gates has continued to praise Beijing—even its handling of the coronavirus outbreak. Gates, ignoring the fact that the regime has "disappeared" Chinese doctors, journalists, and others trying to alert the world about the virus, has misrepresented what they knew about it, and falsely blamed the U.S. military for the virus, explains that Beijing "did a lot of things right."[45]

The Bill and Melinda Gates Foundation is where Gates spends much of his time these days, working on health care issues around the world. They do considerable work in Africa, where the foundation has worked to expand Chinese government influence. According to emails obtained through the Freedom of Information Act, the foundation helped "raise China's voice of governance by placing representatives from China on important international counsels as high-level commitment from China."[46]

***

SADLY, BILL GATES is not alone in his embrace of the Beijing regime.

Google has a similar but more complex history with China. The company was founded in 1998 and quickly saw the Chinese market's value and worked hard to succeed there. The hope was to bring the search engine into the hands of one billion Chinese consumers. Google quickly found itself the target of pressure to censor information available to Chinese users. At first, the company accommodated

Beijing, working to restrict certain words in a search. YouTube, a subsidiary, also adjusted its algorithm to remove phrases critical of the Communist Party. (It was "accidental," the company later explained.)[47]

Eric Schmidt, the CEO, tried to turn cooperation with the communist regime into a virtue. "I think it's arrogant for us to walk into a country where we are just beginning to operate and tell that country how to operate," he explained when Google set up its offices in Beijing.[48]

But there was division at the top of Google about how to deal with China. While Schmidt and cofounder Larry Page favored continued cooperation with the Chinese regime, cofounder Sergei Brin, a child refugee from the Soviet Union, was skeptical that the strategy would work. By 2008, he was arguing for Google to stop censoring in China.[49]

Eventually, Google made a public announcement that it was exiting the Chinese market after human rights campaigners pressured the company. The reality was more complex.

Indeed, Google has continued to work with the communist regime and even the military.[50] At the heart of the company is an unquenchable thirst for data, and their dealings in China show they cannot resist tapping any vast resource offered to them.

In 2017, Google announced the opening of an AI research facility in Beijing. The Google AI China Center would include "a small group of researchers supported by several hundred China-based engineers."[51] The head of the venture for Google, Fei-Fei Li, explained, "I believe AI and its benefits have no borders."[52] The research at the Google AI China Center includes machine learning that would classify, perceive, and predict outcomes based on massive amounts of data. This is precisely the sort of work that military and intelligence officials would want from AI.

Google's cooperation with China on AI research occurred the

same year that the Chinese Communist Party and government laid out its "artificial intelligence development plan." A report issued by the Chinese government explains that "AI has become a new focus of international competition," mastering that technology enhances "comprehensive national power," and that it would lead to the "great rejuvenation of the Chinese nation." It was quite clear that the plan was to "promote two-way conversion and application for military and civilian scientific" collaboration.[53]

Beijing has declared that passing the United States in artificial intelligence is a "national priority."[54]

Peter Thiel, cofounder of PayPal and the first outside investor in Facebook, is a major player in the tech world, and criticized Google for the decision, explaining that "A.I. is a military technology." He quoted President Obama's defense secretary Ash Carter: "If you're working in China, you don't know whether you're working on a project for the military or not."[55]

Thiel was not alone in his concerns.

"The work that Google is doing in China is indirectly benefiting the Chinese military," marine general James Dunford, then chairman of the Joint Chiefs of Staff, told a U.S. Senate committee. Then he corrected himself. "Frankly, 'indirect' may not be a full characterization of the way it really is, it is more of a direct benefit to the Chinese military." It is immaterial that Google might say that the research work is intended for civilian application. "The technology that has developed in the civil world transfers to the military world," explained then acting secretary of defense Patrick Shanahan. "It's a direct pipeline."[56] Google executives know and admit that they cannot control all "downstream use" of their [cloud and AI] technology, Diane Greene, CEO of Google Cloud, allowed in a June 2018 blog post.[57]

Collaboration between American tech companies and Chinese military-linked research labs has enormous implications for our national security. What makes that collaboration even more gall-ing is the fact that China has very different anticipated uses for the technologies than the United States. As the National Security Commission on Artificial Intelligence announced in its final report, "Authoritarian regimes will continue to use AI-powered face rec-ognition, biometrics, predictive analytics, and data fusion as instru-ments of surveillance, influence, and political control."[58]

The chair of that commission? Former Google CEO Eric Schmidt. He remained as executive chairman until 2015, then took that same role at Alphabet, the new parent company, until 2018. Schmidt was a "technical adviser" there until 2020.[59]

In short, Schmidt favors continued AI joint work with Beijing, knowing that they will be using it to make Orwell's dystopian *1984* a reality.

The very real prospect of benefiting the Chinese military has not deterred Google. In 2018, the tech giant announced that it was going to fund research in artificial intelligence at China's Tsinghua University. The school, often called "China's MIT," is a tech-heavy institution with close ties to the Chinese military.[60] What kind of university is Tsinghua? The school is intimately involved in the de-velopment of military tools that will be pointed against Beijing's rivals, including the United States.

"The university's research portfolio targets defense and military capabilities," explains scholar Roslyn Layton. "At least one labora-tory at Tsinghua University has been approved by the state as a key national defense discipline lab with other labs dedicated to advanced military technology development."[61]

The university runs a subsidiary called Tsinghua Tongfang, which "supplies military communications control equipment and electronic countermeasures and satellite navigation equipment to the People's Liberation Army."[62] Indeed, the school has been quite vocal about its commitment to the "military-civil fusion" program outlined by the government. You Zheng, the vice president of the university, explains that "Tsinghua University will closely integrate the national strategy of military-civilian integration and the AI superpower strategy." It does not get any more clear-cut. Indeed, the school is the headquarters for the "High-End Laboratory for Military Intelligence." When it comes to artificial intelligence, the focus of Google's work at Tsinghua, the university's vice president explained that cooperation was necessary "especially in actually supporting military applications of AI. Only in this way can we ensure that our country becomes a veritable AI superpower."[63]

Google was not done.

In June 2018, the company signed yet another research agreement, this time with Fudan University, an elite multicampus school in northeastern Shanghai. Google was setting up another joint artificial intelligence research lab on campus. (That same day, Beijing authorities graciously allowed Google to release its second mobile app in the country.[64]) Fudan, like Tsinghua, is deeply wedded to the Chinese military. Indeed, shortly after signing the two-year deal with Google, Fudan set up the Science and Technology Research Institute, incorporating the schools' former Military Projects R&D Office.[65] Elsa Kania, a fellow at the Australian Strategic Policy Institute's International Cyber Centre, explained, "This Fudan S&T Research Institute includes the Military-Civil Fusion Research Office, and there was also a Military Project Confidentiality Office (军工保密办公室) opened at that time."[66]

In 2019, Fudan University changed its school charter under the direction of the Ministry of Education. You might say it was truth in advertising, making completely clear where the school is focused. They removed "free thinking" (which was never really allowed) from the charter and replaced it with "patriotic devotion." And while the original charter proclaimed that the university was to be run by the "teaching staff and students" (again, never really true), the new charter declares "leadership by the Communist Party in the spirit of Marxism and socialism" is in charge.[67]

Google also supports Chinese military research in other ways.

In January 2019, a research paper was published on the subject of "non-negative matrix factorization," an algorithm used in machine learning. Five coauthors contributed to the report, including a researcher at Google. What was unusual was that the lead author was Professor Guan Naiyang, an associate professor at the People's Liberation Army NUDT—again, a school controlled by the Central Military Commission, the country's top military body. Guan's doctoral thesis earned him top prizes from the PLA. In the past, he had worked on three projects focused on online surveillance and information gathering. Guan was quite open in China about the purpose of his research: "I want to hasten the software development and application of high-performance computers, comprehensively propelling artificial intelligence toward the battlefield."[68]

There were two other papers the same year where Google employees conducted joint work with Chinese military researchers in artificial intelligence. Apparently, no one at Google saw a problem with this.

In 2019, the *South China Morning Post* revealed that a Google researcher named Shumin Zhai wrote a research paper with Chinese researchers that helped to enhance the military capabilities of Beijing's Stealth fighter aircraft. (Zhai's collaborators on the piece worked at China's State Key Laboratory of Computer Science.) The J-20 (Weilong or "powerful dragon") is designed to challenge America's F-22 Raptor. The paper in question was about a technology to "speed up on-screen mobile target selection by more than 50 percent and improve accuracy by nearly 80 percent."[69]

An anonymous PLA researcher asserted that such collaborative projects could be used for military applications without necessarily letting the Google contributors know. "What we need is their brain. For instance, they can be asked to develop an algorithm but not briefed on the details of how the algorithm would be used."[70]

When his claim was initially published, the Chinese Academy of Sciences described the paper as having "broad application prospects in military, medical, education and digital entertainment." After the *South China Morning Post* exposed it, the academy deleted the reference to military applications from the paper's description.[71]

Google responded by denying that the research helped the military: "There is nothing in this paper that refers to a military application."[72] Can they truly be that naïve?

***

AMERICAN TECH GIANT Intel is also investing in Chinese artificial intelligence companies that have links to the Chinese military. Intel is an investor, along with Sequoia Capital China, in something called Horizon Robotics. "Horizon had early ties with the People's Liberation Army (PLA)," notes the industry-leading corporate intelligence service Intelligence Online. "CEO Yu Kai served as deputy secretary-general of the Chinese Association for Artificial Intelligence (CAAI), an industry group headed by Major-General Li Deyi, in 2016. Li was previously deputy director of the [People's Liberation Army] General Staff Department's 61st research institute, which is responsible for information systems."[73]

What could possibly go wrong?

***

IT IS CLEAR why Beijing wants to work with Silicon Valley firms. But why are America's technological gurus so eager to work with Beijing? The short answer: data is king. "More data helps you more than any other algorithm," explains Dr. Kai-fu Lee, a tech investor and author of *AI Superpowers: China, Silicon Valley, the New World Order.* "Therefore, in the era of AI, if data is the new oil, then China is the new OPEC."[74] China has so much more data than the United States because Chinese consumers are more data-connected, but even more importantly because the Chinese government collects so much more data on people than Western governments do. You can collect all sorts of data in China that you cannot access in the United States or in other Western countries. The secret attraction to AI research in China is the fact that they have more data, not so much that they have greater technical talent.

More data beats a better algorithm.[75]

Google's parent company, Alphabet, works with Chinese military-connected institutions in other ways. The company owns a $550 million stake in JD.com, which is the second-largest e-commerce platform in China. That may sound innocent enough, but JD.com is not just some Chinese version of eBay. The company has deep ties to the Chinese military, including an agreement to help update the logistics for the Chinese air force.[76]

The founder and CEO of JD.com, Liu Qiangdong, is a controversial figure and an outspoken, true believer in the Chinese communist system. He declared in 2017 that technological advancements were making communism a reality. "Throughout the past, many people believed that communism is something that can't be achieved, but with the technologies we have laid out in the last two or three years, I have come to recognize that communism can indeed be achieved in our generation," he claims. Robots, he explained, could do most of the work, so the government could distribute the wealth to everyone, and "there will be no more poor or rich people and all the companies will be nationalized."[77] It appears that Liu believes that artificial intelligence offers some utopian promise. Does Google?

***

JOHN CHAMBERS, THE CEO and executive chairman of Cisco Systems, was at the 2015 Seattle meeting with President Xi.[78] That same month, Cisco forged a $100 million joint venture with Inspur, a Chinese computer company focused on developing advanced information technology infrastructure, among other initiatives. Inspur is linked to the Chinese military. The military uses Inspur technologies, including communications systems, mobile mapping systems, and networking equipment. Inspur also counts among its clients the Chinese military's Air-to-Air Research Academy and the China Academy of Engineering Physics.[79]

Most of Cisco's business in China comes from the central government; as the Chinese media put it, "The majority of Cisco's customers in China have ties with the central government—including State-owned enterprises." The *Global Times* observed, "Losing the good graces of Beijing could cost Cisco dearly."[80] So Cisco stays in line.

Cisco Systems has been a regular partner with the Chinese military-industrial complex. The company has a long history of working with the Chinese Public Security Ministry, providing the technological tools to develop the PoliceNet as well as upgrade their "Golden Shield" surveillance database project (and its subset web-filtering project—the "Great Firewall").[81] Golden Shield is a decades-long ambitious program to create an "all-encompassing surveillance network" to monitor the Chinese people.[82]

Huawei pitched Iranian officials on the fact that their equipment "makes it easier to spy on potential troublemakers." Cisco seems to have followed suit in China.[83]

Leaked presentation materials indicate that Cisco executives knew that the Chinese would use their technology against dissidents in the country. One religious group that received the government's ire was a Buddhist offshoot spiritual group called Falun Gong. A Cisco corporate slide on its work on Golden Shield said China's motives for the project were to "combat 'Falun Gong' evil religion and other hostiles."[84]

Cisco provided technology for the project, and company engineers were deeply involved in enabling keywords to be blocked online. The company was also commissioned to provide continued technical support. "Cisco is very pleased to play another critical role in the latest ChinaNet backbone network expansion," one company vice president proclaimed.[85]

Cisco CEO John Chambers appeared uninterested in how the government would use Cisco's technology—and clearly does not want to pass judgment on the totalitarian regime. As he said, "One thing a technology company should never do is fall in love with one political party or one form of government. We don't provide any unique capabilities to any government, we will not enable any organization uniquely, including our own U.S. government."[86]

After all, falling in love with a free, representative government can be bad for business.

Desperate to sell its products in China and get access to the massive market, Cisco actually sold its products cheaply to Beijing in the hopes of winning favor. For example, they sold firewall boxes to the government-run China Telecom for just $20,000 apiece; they sold the same product to Western customers for up to $50,000 each.[87]

As a result, Cisco won plaudits from the government for its work in China. It was voted the title "China's Best Corporate Citizen" by the Chinese 21st Century News Group for four consecutive years.[88] State-run media was apt to quote Chambers for his positive comments about China, including his declaration that "China is becoming *the* center of innovation and creativity"[89] (emphasis added).

Chambers was also quite open about seeing the company's future more anchored in Beijing than in Boston. After all, hiring engineers in China was far cheaper than hiring engineers in the United States. "My workforce has to be five times as productive in this country than [in] the rest of the world," he explained during a lecture at the Massachusetts Institute of Technology. Engineers in China were paid about $40,000 a year, he explained, compared to U.S. tech workers who made up to $250,000.[90]

However, Cisco's embrace of Beijing was not perpetually reciprocated. The government came to support the rise of a significant homegrown competitor—Huawei. With a suitable Chinese alternative, the communist government leaned on local governments and businesses to start buying computer networking technologies from Chinese companies like Huawei rather than American firms like Cisco. For sensitive government entities, authorities declared, 100 percent must come from Chinese firms. For less critical projects, 70 percent should be from Chinese companies. Cisco was suddenly feeling the squeeze of unrequited love.[91]

Three years earlier, Cisco and Chambers, and other tech firms had encouraged U.S. officials to investigate Huawei.[92] The Chinese government responded, in part, with the restrictions we have just shown. Cisco caved and negotiated with the Chinese government, agreeing to invest $10 billion in mainland China for job creation. Like Microsoft, Chambers was committing to export jobs from the United States in order to get back into the good graces of the Beijing regime.[93]

***

TWITTER WAS FOUNDED in 2006.

In 2010, Jack Dorsey was stunned to learn that Twitter was banned in China—something he did not know as the CEO of the company.[94] The response from the company was to propose a censored form of Twitter that would conform with the "local laws" of authoritarian governments. Reporters Without Borders, a free speech organization, wrote to Dorsey: "By finally choosing to align itself with the censors, Twitter is depriving cyberdissidents in repressive countries of a crucial tool for information and organization." Critics noted that the policy move was made shortly after Twitter received a $300 million investment from billionaire Saudi prince Alwaleed.[95]

Twitter pursued deals with the Chinese government and touted its services. It signed up the official Xinhua News Agency and helped it beam its message to the globe.[96]

Twitter founder and CEO Jack Dorsey has long coveted expanding his business into China. The social media app is banned there, but Dorsey figured the way to entry was in hiring the right person. So, in April 2016, the first managing director of China for Twitter came on board. Kathy Chen had an unusual pedigree. Dorsey's choice had previously served in the PLA for seven years, where she focused on missile defense technology research. She was also involved in a technology joint venture partly owned by China's Ministry of Public Security.[97]

China's official news agency, Xinhua, sent her a "congratulations" upon her appointment. Chen immediately wrote back: "Thanks and look forward to closer partnership in the future!"

"Let's work together to tell great China story to the world!" she tweeted to another news service, CCTV.[98]

Twitter's unusual hire sent shock waves through Chinese human rights organizations concerned about where the company was going. It did not take long for them to see that she was friendly with the regime. Shortly after joining Twitter, she tweeted that message of cooperation with CCTV, the government-controlled television and media outlet. Chen also prompted Twitter to start working with advertisers for Xinhua and the *People's Daily* (the Chinese Communist Party's newspaper).[99] After only seven months, Chen stepped down—ostensibly to rest and investigate "more international business opportunities."[100]

Twitter, which touts a commitment to free speech, appears happy to bow to Beijing's wishes. Professor Anne-Marie Brady from the University of Canterbury in New Zealand is a world-renowned expert on China. When she tweeted criticisms of Beijing on the one hundredth anniversary of the founding of the Chinese Communist Party, Twitter blocked her account. Even the temporary stifling of speech—as was the case here—in defense of the CCP is baffling.[101] In 2019, in the days before the thirtieth anniversary of the Tiananmen Square massacre in Beijing, Twitter removed the accounts of several Chinese dissidents. The company claimed they were not actually censoring, but that it was merely a "routine effort to stop inauthentic and spam accounts." Of course, they apply those rules inconsistently, and only seem to use them against those who oppose the regime.[102]

In the 2020 election and the run-up to the riot at the U.S. Capitol, more than four hundred Chinese government–linked Twitter accounts spread anti-U.S. propaganda. The Crime and Security Research Institute (CSRI) at Cardiff University in Great Britain conducted a major study monitoring the activity. Calling the operation "sophisticated and disciplined," they found that it "played a key role in spreading disinformation during and after the U.S. election."[103] The theme of the effort was presenting America as a "chaotic nation on the verge of political collapse and major disorder," and had a notable anti-Trump sentiment. "It is unlikely that the network operates without some official awareness and/or guidance," noted Professor Martin Innes, director of the CSRI. "This is significant given the levels of influence and interference in U.S. politics that the accounts have engaged in."[104]

Regardless, Dorsey has continued his courtship of Beijing. He has granted Chinese government entities a wide latitude on Twitter—wider than he has given U.S.-based users, including former president Donald J. Trump.[105] When Chinese party officials accused the U.S. military of being behind the coronavirus in Wuhan, Dorsey defended the decision to leave the tweet up for two months with no label as to its lack of veracity.[106]

Likewise, when Chinese officials went on Twitter to deny Uighur abuse, they were not removed.[107] More than that, Twitter promoted tweets by the state-run *Global Times* furthering the propaganda.[108]

In May 2020, Twitter announced that it was putting Fei-Fei Li on the company's board of directors. Li, a professor at Stanford University, is a controversial figure in tech circles because of her bond to Beijing. She has multiple ties to Chinese Communist Party–linked United Front groups. Li, as we saw earlier, opened Google's artificial intelligence center in China and does considerable work with military-related entities.[109] At that time, she was quoted in Chinese state media as using the Chinese Communist Party slogans "stay true to our founding mission" and "China has awakened."[110] While Google's China lab was working with military-linked researchers, she became involved in a controversy at Google over their cooperation with the Pentagon. Initially ambivalent, in a later response, she emphasized that she believed that artificial intelligence research should be designed for the "social good."[111]

Chinese dissidents complained that shortly after her appointment, their Twitter accounts were unceremoniously shut down. One complained that at her arrival, Twitter was "dyed red."[112]

***

ELON MUSK IS one of the richest men in the world, and perhaps the most followed tech visionary on the planet. An early investor in PayPal, he has gone on to launch a variety of cutting-edge companies, including SpaceX, Tesla, and the Boring Company, among others.[113] Musk has a knack for riding the technology waves of the future and does so with an eccentric and at times flamboyant style. His gigantic ambitions include sending one million people to Mars by 2050.[114]

Whether tech rebel or iconoclast, Musk has increasingly tied his commercial fortunes to Beijing. Once outspoken and open about the challenges presented by Beijing, he has, following a series of favors, heaped praise on the government and the Communist Party.

In 2016, he announced his plans to blanket the skies with satellites to provide high-speed internet around the globe. Unlike with fiber-optic cables, it is much harder to block satellite transmissions. The plan was to free the internet around the globe. But he was open about how the Beijing regime censored communications. "If they [Beijing] get upset with us, they can blow our satellites up, which wouldn't be good," said Musk. "China can do that. So probably we shouldn't broadcast there."[115]

In 2018, with his company Tesla producing popular electric vehicles for export, he voiced his frustrations about Beijing's high tariffs on imported cars, including his own. "Do you think the US & China should have equal & fair rules for cars?" he asked. "Meaning, same import duties, ownership constraints & other factors." He went on: "For example, an American car going to China pays 25%

import duty, but a Chinese car coming to the US only pays 2.5%, a tenfold difference." He likened China's tariffs to "competing in an Olympic race wearing lead shoes."[116]

Musk was also well aware that his companies, especially SpaceX, were being probed by Chinese intelligence. SpaceX is a "prime target" for Chinese espionage, and Beijing seems to have successfully stolen designs related to the company's Starship rocket design. Musk himself acknowledges that Chinese entities stole software code from his company Tesla. That is not just a competitive problem, it is a national security one: that same software is used by Musk's SpaceX, which launches payloads and works closely with the U.S. military.[117]

But Musk has clearly changed his tune. Perhaps part of it has to do with the fact that Beijing built him a massive factory in China.

Musk had for several years denied that he was going to build a facility in China, claiming that he was quite happy with his production in the United States. In 2015, when transcripts of a meeting in China were leaked, indicating he had plans to build a factory there, he quickly declared that the transcripts were not accurate, refuting them on Twitter. "My comments in China weren't transcribed correctly. Tesla will keep making cars & batteries in CA & NV as far into future as I can imagine."[118]

Beijing still courted him. In March 2017, China's government-linked Tencent Holdings bought a 5 percent stake in Tesla. Musk explained on Twitter that Tencent would be both "an investor and advisor." (What advisory role the company would play was never explained.)[119] Then Beijing rolled out the red carpet: Chinese government–backed banks coughed up $1.6 billion in subsidized loans. And the regulatory red tape to build in China was eliminated by government authorities. "What surprised me is how little time it took for the regulatory process to get approved by the Chinese government," explained Ivan Su, an analyst at Morningstar Inc. The enormous plant was built in less than a year.[120]

Musk arrived in the country for the groundbreaking ceremony and met with top-ranking officials. Two days later, he was meeting with Vice Premier Li Keqiang in the private compound reserved for high-ranking visitors. "I love China very much and I am willing to come here more," Musk reportedly told Li. The vice premier offered to make him a permanent resident in the country. He also clearly wanted Musk's help in the wake of the Trump administration's pushback on some of Beijing's technology and export policies. "We hope your company can become an in-depth participant of China's opening and a promoter of the stability of China-U.S. relations," he told Musk.[121]

Musk says they discussed "history, philosophy, and luck" at the meeting. He later tweeted, "Excellent meetings with senior leaders in China. Very thoughtful about the long-term future."[122]

The Tesla factory was up and running in a year, producing cars for sale in China and for export. The next step in the movement of the company toward China came when it was soon announced that Tesla was not only putting manufacturing in China, but also creating design facilities there. China's social media company WeChat alerted people, noting, "In order to achieve a shift of 'Made in China' to 'Designed in China,' Tesla's CEO Elon Musk has proposed a very cool thing—set up a design and research center in China."[123]

Several politically connected executives were put in charge of Tesla's China operations. Tom Zhu took control of operations, and, according to employees, started insisting that, when possible, emails should be written in Chinese. Direct contact with the U.S. headquarters of the company was "sharply limited." Employees were punished for directly reaching out to Musk. (The Tesla founder had historically encouraged employees to reach out directly with problems.) Grace Tao, a former television personality for China Central Television, was brought on to head up communications and government affairs. She explained to fellow employees that she was linked to the highest levels of government and could communicate with President Xi through a single intermediary if she needed to.[124]

In addition to producing cars (and apparently designing them), Tesla has taken other actions as well. Tesla China has "aligned itself explicitly with President Xi Jinping's economic policy goals."[125]

Musk has since become a Beijing booster. In January 2021, he explained in one interview how the unelected Beijing regime was possibly "more responsible" toward its people than the democratically elected U.S. government. "When I meet with Chinese government officials, they're always very concerned about this. Are people going to be happy about a thing? Is this going to actually serve the benefit of the people? It seems ironic, but even though you have sort of a single-party system, they really actually seem to care a lot about the well-being of the people. In fact, they're maybe even more sensitive to public opinion than what I see in the US."[126]

The Chinese foreign minister praised Musk for his wisdom, and the government-backed *Global Times* added, "Anyone who is unbiased and hopes to understand the real China objectively will come to such a conclusion."[127]

A few months earlier, Musk had effused, "China rocks in my opinion. The energy in China is great. People there—there's like a lot of smart, hardworking people." He went on to criticize his adopted home country the United States. "I see in the United States increasingly much more complacency and entitlement especially in places like the Bay Area, and LA and New York."[128]

In March 2021, Musk went on Chinese state television and touted China's leadership, explaining, "I'd like to strike an optimistic note and I'm very confident that the future of China is going to be great and that China is headed towards being the biggest economy in the world and a lot of prosperity in the future."[129] Beijing obviously loved the vote of confidence and reported his comments widely.[130]

His most explicit endorsement of the regime came on the one hundredth anniversary of the founding of the Communist Party of China. The state-controlled Xinhua News tweeted a quote from President Xi Jinping, stating that the party had achieved its "first centenary goal of building a moderately prosperous society" and was heading toward accomplishing its goal of building China into a "great modern socialist country."

Musk replied on Twitter: "The economic prosperity that China has achieved is truly amazing, especially in infrastructure! I encourage people to visit and see for themselves." For good measure, he also posted on his Weibo social media account in China.[131]

Musk is not as effusive in his praise as some of his compatriots. (He did not ask President Xi to provide a Chinese name for his child.) But Musk's shift has been obvious. Experienced observers see Musk as having perhaps placed himself in a compromised position.

Musk's company SpaceX has numerous military- and intelligence-related contracts with the U.S. government. His company launches rockets for the U.S. Space Force, builds satellites that track missiles for the Department of Defense, and deploys spy satellites for the National Reconnaissance Office, among other things. This is, obviously, very sensitive work.[132]

Tesla and SpaceX are disparate companies but they share key personnel and some technologies. Elon Musk; his brother, Kimbal Musk; as well as investor Antonio J. Gracias serve on the board of directors for both companies. Charles Kuehmann, an engineer, is vice president of materials engineering—also for both. In 2020, Tesla even "temporarily" assigned twenty employees to "support SpaceX." Musk views the two companies as collaborators to some extent. "That's cross-fertilization of knowledge from the rocket and space industry to auto back and forth, as I think it's really been quite valuable," Musk explained in one 2017 call with investors.[133]

When legislation was introduced in Congress that would require determination whether Chinese entities might be leveraging U.S. companies that do work with NASA, SpaceX lobbied against the legislation.[134]

Some national security experts are very concerned about Beijing's ability to leverage Musk and possibly SpaceX. Miles Yu, a professor at the U.S. Naval Academy, says that Beijing lured Tesla "into China with initial preferential tax and regulatory treatments. Once you are hooked in China, and have gained initial success, the CCP would not hesitate to use your investments in China as a leverage to force you to comply with a whole list of demands, outright or subtle, including sharing proprietary technologies and knowledge, prohibiting transfer of funds out of China, curtailing your market share inside China and possibly divulging critical national security secrets in your company's other operations with the U.S. government such as the SpaceX project."[135]

In 2021, the Chinese government became critical of Tesla. Complaints about the quality of their cars by some of the public were boosted by criticisms from Chinese government officials. Tesla quickly issued an apology that could have come out of the Maoist era, vowing to "carry out strict self-examination and self-correction."[136]

***

REID HOFFMAN, THE founder of LinkedIn, may be less well known than Bill Gates, Elon Musk, Google, or Jack Dorsey, but he is at the center of the tech elite, known as "the most connected man in Silicon Valley."[137] Outspoken about politics in the United States and what he regards as the rising authoritarianism in America, he has mastered the art of cooperation with authoritarian Beijing.

Hoffman has had great success in China because he is quite willing to give the Beijing government the control that it demands. As one report puts it, "U.S. companies considering a China move often talk about the 'LinkedIn model'—a model that means close local ties and full cooperation with the government."[138] Hoffman also appears at government-backed events that are denounced by many in the tech industry as sham events designed to bolster the reputation of the regime.[139]

Back in 2014, LinkedIn had only four million users in China. Today that number has soared to fifty-two million, a testament to the company's success through cooperation with the regime.[140] LinkedIn has agreed to store data about Chinese citizens on servers hosted in China, making them accessible to authorities. LinkedIn allows the Chinese government to censor what gets posted, with relative impunity.[141] (LinkedIn says it will leave China in 2022.)

This arrangement has led to the censorship of Chinese human rights activists like Zhou Fengsuo, one of the student leaders of the prodemocracy demonstrations in Tiananmen Square in 1989. LinkedIn blocked his account without explaining why. Eventually, LinkedIn reversed the decision after news reports drew attention to the ban.[142]

Reid Hoffman sits on the board of directors of Microsoft, having sold LinkedIn to the company in 2016.[143] He presumably has no objections to Microsoft's close work with Beijing.

When Peter Humphrey, a British journalist and corporate investigator, criticized Beijing on his LinkedIn account in Great Britain, he found his account frozen and his critical comments removed by LinkedIn. His sin? He called China a "repressive dictatorship." Though the account was reinstated upon appeal, this shows how quickly dissent is quashed in support of what is, objectively, a dictatorship that is repressive.[144]

Hoffman, like so many other tech leaders, is a Beijing booster. He meets regularly with Chinese government officials and participates in official events geared to legitimize the government's control of its people. When he met with President Xi in 2015, he explained that Chinese tech companies have an advantage over Silicon Valley firms because "they work much harder and will do anything to win."[145]

When asked in the United States who the United States should look to and emulate, he said, "I think China, it's super impressive. . . . And I think there's a bunch of things that they are actually in fact practically investing in; everything from infrastructure, to technology, to government, that we should also be doing as a society. There's things we should be learning from how China invests."[146]

It is hard to find anything critical he has said about Beijing. Presumably, he is up on events in the country—including its massive human rights problem, abuses of power, and its increasing military challenge to the United States. After all, President Barack Obama's secretary of defense, Ash Carter, appointed Hoffman to the Pentagon's Defense Innovation Advisory Board in 2016.[147]

Hoffman wants Silicon Valley firms working in Beijing. "The biggest opportunity is for Silicon Valley and China to work together and combine their respective strengths," he says in a book he cowrote called *Blitzscaling*.[148]

Hoffman has also been a consistent participant in a Chinese government-sponsored sham event called the "World Internet Conference." Held in the city of Wuzhen, known for its ancient canals, the event is sponsored by the Chinese government's chief censorship body, the Cyberspace Administration. Foreign governments from around the world shun the event; those who do show up include Russia, Pakistan, Tajikistan, and a few others known for supporting internet censorship. Chinese Communist Party cyber expert Lu Wei explained in promoting the conference: "Freedom is our goal and order is our means. . . . Controlling the Internet is necessary in order to correct rumours. . . . [It] protects the rights and interests of Internet users." The glossy program put out for the event features cover photos of President Xi. *Fortune* magazine described the event as "farcical . . . The World Internet Conference was really a soapbox for Xi to outline China's Internet vision." In 2015, President Xi addressed the conference and called for countries to respect each other's "cyber sovereignty." *New York Times* reporters attempted to attend the conference but were denied press credentials.[149]

Yet Reid Hoffman spoke at the event for several years running—strangely, the only Westerner who appears to have done so. He appeared on the podium at the event in 2014, 2015, and 2016. In 2016, the conference featured a member of the Standing Committee of the Political Bureau of the Communist Party of China (CPC) Central Committee, Liu Yunshan, who talked about "innovation in internet development."[150] Hoffman spoke that same year and praised the communist government's "One Belt, One Road" infrastructure plan.[151]

Curiously, his speeches are not publicly available. He speaks before the assembled guests, including Chinese internet censors, behind closed doors.

Hoffman's participation is notable, particularly in light of the fact that the human rights group Freedom House continues to name China as the "worst abuser of internet freedom."[152]

The irony of Hoffman's involvement in these sham, government-supported events is thick, given his claims about President Donald Trump's authoritarianism. "LinkedIn CEO Reid Hoffman is there (he's passionately opposed to Donald Trump's blustery authoritarianism, but apparently fine with Chinese authoritarianism)," noted TechInAsia.com.[153]

Few other tech execs have joined Hoffman at the propaganda event. In 2017, Google CEO Sundar Pichai made a surprise appearance, heralding Google's return to China. Apple CEO Tim Cook was there the same year, too. Apple had agreed to block apps to the iPhone that allow Chinese citizens to bypass government censors.[154]

Jim Breyer, brother-in-law to Senator Mitch McConnell and an investor in China, has attended the event as well.[155] Indeed, he told Chinese state media he was "amazed at the long term strategic view President Xi Jinping has articulated." He noted that "we don't often see leaders articulate a 10 to 20 year plan."[156]

***

AMERICA'S TECH TITANS have seen the shifting public sentiment against the Beijing regime. But they do not want to give up their cooperation agreements with the government. Many have balked at policies that would hold China to greater account—arguing as always that we need to be "engaged" with China and not "decoupling," which in their minds is the worst thing that could happen. "We are enabling the decoupling," former Google CEO Eric Schmidt, a frequent voice on China and technology, warned *Wired*. Decoupling, particularly in tech, "splinters the internet platforms, reduces revenue for our companies, and produces few opportunities for our tech firms to succeed," he believes.[157]

Never mind that Beijing has already made plans to either control or split the internet.

Schmidt and others want more U.S. taxpayer money to go for tech. But what they do not want is restrictions on selling rope to Beijing. They do not favor disengaging from research projects with China, which is the main source of concern. How can we win the tech race if U.S. firms are effectively helping Beijing run faster? Why continue to subsidize and cooperate with the Beijing regime?

Some Silicon Valley tech titans are capable of speaking honestly about Beijing. Tech investors such as Peter Thiel have been critical of those cooperating with the regime, calling them "useful idiots."[158]

That is certainly the view that China's President Xi has. In January 2017, he delivered a speech explaining that the "power to control the internet" is the "new focal point of [China's] national strategic contest." The kicker: he expected to use American tech companies to help him do it. He did not elaborate.[159]

In 2019, Mark Zuckerberg spoke honestly about censorship in China and pledged that Facebook would never set up a data center in the country. His criticisms were not well received in Beijing.[160] Facebook currently sells more than $5 billion worth of ad space to Chinese businesses and government agencies looking to promote their messages abroad.[161]

Zuckerberg's Facebook teamed with Google in 2016 to build an undersea cable that would link San Francisco (and therefore the United States) with Hong Kong, China, and other locations in Asia. The so-called Pacific Light Cable Network would provide better internet and data services to their customers in Asia. But the two American tech superpowers chose to partner with a Chinese company called Dr. Peng Telecom & Media Group to provide the link to Hong Kong.

The U.S. Federal Communications Commission in 2020 took the unprecedented step of blocking the project. The Facebook-Google cable presented "'unprecedented opportunities' for Chinese government espionage," according to the U.S. Justice Department.[162]

Dr. Peng was financially backed by the Chinese government's China Securities Finance Corporation, and worked closely with Huawei and military defense contractors in China.[163]

How the tech giants did not see the obvious espionage risk to their plans is a mystery. Or maybe they saw it and did not care.

Why do already fabulously wealthy tech titans kowtow to such a brutal regime? Why do they lay such obsequious comments at their feet? Why do they seemingly shrug their shoulders to the reality that they are boosting the Chinese military in its mortal competition with us?

Thiel believes that there is something more at work here than simply money. He said at the Nixon Forum in 2021: "There's something about the woke politics inside these companies, the way they think of themselves as not really American companies. And it's somehow very, very difficult to, for them to have a sharp anti-China edge of any sort whatsoever."

He went on:

"You have this almost magical thinking that by pretending that everything is fine, that's how you engage and have a conversation. And you make the world better. And it's some combination of wishful thinking. It's useful idiots, you know, it's CCP fifth columnist collaborators."[164]

The attraction may also be the power that tech giants can feel in an authoritarian society. It is what writer Noam Cohen calls tech's interest in "the veneer of ultimate control."[165] He quotes computer science trailblazer Joseph Weizenbaum of the Massachusetts Institute of Technology, who wrote in the 1970s about the lure of power through technology. "No playwright, no stage director, no emperor, however powerful, has ever exercised such absolute authority to arrange a stage or a field of battle and to command such unswervingly dutiful actors or troops. The computer programmer is a creator of universes for which he alone is the lawgiver."[166]

Dictatorships in the real world work nicely with dictatorships in the digital world.

Power—along with market access—can indeed be intoxicating. And authoritarian regimes are capable of granting both without the sort of ethical restraints that apply in a free country like the United States.

If Silicon Valley is America's innovation center, Wall Street is the financial engine. And many of the financial masters of the universe, the ultimate beneficiaries of the capitalist free market system, have equally troubling links with the authoritarian leaders in Beijing.

5

WALL STREET

In February 2017, dozens of guests arrived at a palatial Palm Beach estate for an elaborate and opulent extravaganza. One of Wall Street's titans was celebrating his seventieth birthday. The party theme was the "Silk Road," and the entertainment included Mongolian soldiers, acrobats—even a couple of camels. Attending guests included the super-rich from finance as well as newly minted Trump cabinet members Steve Mnuchin and Elaine Chao, the soon-to-be-confirmed commerce secretary Wilbur Ross, and Ivanka Trump and Jared Kushner.[1]

Stephen Schwarzman certainly knows how to throw a party. He is also one of the most powerful people on Wall Street. Dubbed the "King of Wall Street" by *Fortune* magazine, he cofounded Blackstone Group and built it into a global financial titan.[2] He has engaged in many audacious deals during his career, but perhaps most troubling is his partnership with the Chinese communist regime. The Chinese government has invested both financial and political capital into the Yale-trained financier's business success. Simultaneously, Schwarzman has served as a goodwill ambassador of sorts for Beijing, blunting criticisms and cheerleading the regime's policies. As he jokingly explains it, he is the middleman between the two superpowers, serving as both the "unofficial U.S. ambassador to China" as well as the "unofficial Chinese ambassador to the U.S."[3]

Thus, the theme of his 2017 blowout.

Beijing has benefited enormously from its close relationship to Wall Street, in ways that are similar but also different from the ties it enjoys in Washington and Silicon Valley. Wall Street titans clamoring for opportunities in China have been seduced with financial riches, accolades, and appeals to their self-importance. It has worked fabulously well for Beijing, leading America's top capitalists to praise the dictatorial regime, help finance its operations, and even fund some of its propaganda efforts.

But why China? Can the wealthiest Americans not find other ways to be enriched and enabled? China offers several things that other countries cannot. First, financiers tend to see the vast majority of people as drones and obstacles preventing innovation. The appeal of dictatorship is significant. Second, Wall Streeters constantly talk as if their jobs were life-and-death—making a killing, scorched earth, raiders—and China allows them to be close to genuine peril (without being in peril themselves). Finally, there is no more appealing word than "growth," and China has provided it reliably for decades.

Schwarzman's enormous financial successes, in part, result from his close working relationship with Chinese Communist Party officials in Beijing. This capitalist has deep and enduring ties with top Chinese communists. By his own account, he knows "many of the members of the Standing Committee and the State Council." He first met current Chinese president Xi back in 2007. As Schwarzman puts it, "If you want to get anything done [in China], the strength of your relationships means everything."[4]

China's economic climb has been the result of many factors, but what must not be underestimated is the role played by Wall Street finance and people like Schwarzman. Capital investments by major players on Wall Street have fueled both China's economic rise and its military buildup. Influential Wall Street figures have played an enormously important role in China's efforts to challenge the United States—and they have been paid handsomely for their efforts.

In 2007, Blackstone was going public, and Schwarzman found an unusual new partner. The Chinese government and Communist Party bought a 9.9 percent stake in the fledgling firm for $3 billion. It was a sudden and surprising move—done through the government's sovereign wealth fund known as the China Investment Corporation (CIC).[5] The 9.9 percent stake was precise and specific: it was just below the threshold of 10 percent that would have triggered a U.S. federal government national security review in Washington.[6]

Beyond the investment of money, however, the deal was a clear signal of confidence from Beijing that they would work to make Blackstone a success. "It is a double victory for Blackstone because you have to assume that the deal will be good for their expansion plans in China," one Hong Kong banker explained at the time. "Beijing now has a vested interest in the firm performing well."[7] And Schwarzman now had an apparent interest in Beijing doing well, too.

The Chinese government transaction with Blackstone yielded Schwarzman some powerful allies. Lou Jiwei, head of CIC when it made that initial investment, later became Beijing's finance minister.[8]

Further deals between Blackstone and Beijing followed. Schwarzman's firm bought and sold companies with the Chinese state, and he quickly became the "go-to man for Chinese buyers."[9] Today, Schwarzman is a regular fixture at high-level meetings and events organized by CIC.[10]

Blackstone's profits, courtesy of the Beijing regime, have come with a certain quid pro quo. Blackstone-owned entities censor stories that might anger the Beijing regime. With a partner, Thomson

Reuters, the firm owns a large chunk of Refinitiv, a financial news and data analysis service. In June 2019, the thirtieth anniversary of the Tiananmen Square massacre, Refinitiv censored and suppressed stories about the event at the request of the Cyberspace Administration of China.[11]

But more important, Schwarzman has also been a cheerleader for Beijing, deflecting criticisms or painting the regime in a stunningly benign light.

When some voice criticisms of China's economic policies, Schwarzman defends them: "It should not be surprising that as China goes through an evolution mistakes will be made. The developed world makes mistakes too. No group has a monopoly on good policy."[12] He has characterized China's rampant theft of America's intellectual property as "other approaches to intellectual property."[13]

While officials from both the Obama and Trump administrations have characterized China's Belt and Road Initiative as a challenge to America's global position, Schwarzman has actually praised it as a wonderful program.[14]

When pressed on China's economic power and the rising suppression of its own population, Schwarzman punts about any role that he could play in pushing for reforms. "Well, you know, we're not a one-person reform bureau."[15] He appears to have little negative to say about how Beijing conducts its affairs.

Chinese government news outlets quote Schwarzman to show Western approval of the Beijing regime. "The words of U.S. financier Stephen Schwarzman may serve as a straightforward interpretation of the CPC's core mission," explained the official government news agency after the Communist Party Congress in 2012.[16]

When China state television quotes him, they also give him the moniker "King of Wall Street."[17]

Schwarzman's attachment to China is so great that in 2013, he launched an audacious $100 million plan to create a global education scholarship program in China to rival the Rhodes Scholarships offered at Oxford University.[18] Cecil Rhodes, who was South African, said he established his famous program at Oxford to provide a British education for people worldwide so they could learn the merits of British civilization. Schwarzman was turned down for a Rhodes scholarship as a young man, so perhaps that has given him added motivation.[19]

The Schwarzman Scholars do not study at an independent university like Oxford, but instead at Tsinghua University, a training ground for the Chinese Communist Party and government elite.[20] (The school has an "Institute for Xi Jinping Thought on Socialism with Chinese Characteristics for a New Era," established with the cooperation of the Central Committee of the Communist Party of China.)[21]

Students from around the world—but especially the United States—would come and be exposed to the Chinese communist system. Schwarzman explains that his goal in setting up the program is that "recipients would return to their countries able to interpret the massive change in China in a way that calmed fears and misunderstanding about the country."[22]

Chinese officials have the same vision for the program. "Through interactive learning at lectures and intensive deep-dive travel seminars, they will gain deep insights in China's society and culture. Once they return to their motherland upon graduation, they will become influential leaders in politics, economics, culture, education and other fields, contributing to human civilization and progress as well as world peace and development."[23]

Government and Communist Party officials are very happy with the program. Indeed, as the Associated Press notes, "[Schwarzman's program has] drawn support from the top ranks of the ruling communist party."[24] Madame Chen Xu, secretary of the CPC Tsinghua University Committee, was a big supporter of the project.[25]

In the beginning, a committee was put together to ensure a "scientific and fair" admission process for Schwarzman's program. The committee met on September 20, 2015, and included an interesting mixture of experts. Along with academics, those present included officials from the Chinese Communist Party Youth League, the Central Party School (which imposes ideological discipline), and the United Front Work Department, which runs political influence operations.[26]

The program's founding dean, David Daokui Li, was viewed by the government's propaganda arm "as an especially reliable ally."[27]

Who runs the program? Who establishes the curriculum for American students and others from around the world to study? That would be Professor Daniel Bell, the Schwarzman Scholar program chair professor. A Canadian, Bell is a Chinese government apologist, explaining the superiority of the Chinese system of government over those of his own country or the United States. In his book *The China Model: Political Meritocracy and the Limits of Democracy*, he praises the Chinese communist system as a "meritocracy" in comparison to the failing Western system of one person, one vote.[28] The Chinese system is so much better because Communist Party "cadres are put through a grueling process of talent selection, and only those with an excellent record of past performance are likely to make it to the highest levels of government."[29] (Never mind that China admits to a corruption problem and is known to have the resident abuses of any authoritarian state.)[30] Bell also praises the Chinese media, which is, of course, controlled by the Communist Party and government. He considers it superior to the free press in the West. "When Chinese journalists interview their subjects, they try to put forward a balanced account of what the interviewees have to say, with emphasis on what can be learned and communicated as something new and interesting," he said. "They rarely engage in muckracking [*sic*], public character assassination, or put on a smiling face then betray their interviewees in print."[31]

Of course they do not. Journalists in China investigating the cover-up of the COVID-19 outbreak were arrested or disappeared by government officials.

Bell, with his warm views of the dictatorial regime, is, again, "chair professor" in Schwarzman's program.[32]

Chinese government and party officials regularly interact with students in the program. When the inaugural class of Schwarzman Scholars held their convocation ceremony, the vice premier of the State Council of China, Liu Yandong, attended. The State Council is one of the top decision-making bodies in the country.[33]

Schwarzman Scholars studying at Tsinghua are also required to take a course titled "Theory and Practice of Socialism with Chinese Characteristics," which is taught by He Jianyu, associate professor in the School of Marxism at Tsinghua University. The curriculum notes: "There will also be group discussions based on the course literature, a mid-term paper aimed at teaching how to read and analyze the official text of CCP documents and files, and a final paper aimed at providing an opportunity to communicate with a policy maker who is engaged in the decision-making process or an ordinary Chinese citizen who is experiencing the change of China."[34]

The convocation of the first class for Schwarzman Scholars brought congratulatory messages from both President Xi and President Barack Obama. Xi explained the program's value "to foster the global vision and stronger sense of cooperation to strive together a better future for mankind." The American president lauded the program for meeting the need to "instill in [the next generation] the same spirit of cooperation that drives our community of nations towards peace and progress."[35] It is unclear whether or not the Obama White House was aware of the program's curriculum.

The university highlighted one of the Chinese students participating in the Schwarzman program, noting that the architectural
student "also has a great record in terms of social work experience. He was the secretary of the Communist Youth League in the
School of Architecture."[36]

So what does this mean? A Wall Street financier worth billions,
courtesy of the free market system, is funding courses in Marxism-
Leninism and a program that preaches the superiority of Chinese
communism over American capitalism.

In 2017, Chinese president Xi addressed a group of American
corporate executives at Tsinghua, which happens to be his alma
mater. Among those present were Facebook's Mark Zuckerberg,
Apple's Tim Cook, and Stephen Schwarzman. They met in the
Great Hall of the People, where Xi spoke to them, explaining
that the recent 19th Communist Party National Congress was of
"great significance, and has enhanced China's confidence on the
path of socialism with Chinese characteristics." He went on to present in stark terms his views concerning who should be educated
in China: "constructors and successors of socialism with Chinese
characteristics, rather than bystanders or opponents, should be
trained through education." It was a pointed endorsement of party
rule and party control, even over education. The Chinese media
said that Schwarzman and the others "were deeply impressed by
President Xi's report."[37]

Schwarzman's embrace of the regime's agenda was also reported
by the Western media. Schwarzman was among those present who
"praised Mr. Xi's leadership of China," according to the *Wall Street
Journal.*[38]

In 2019, when the Schwarzman Scholars held their commence-
ment ceremony, the speaker for the event chosen by school officials was a notorious figure to human rights officials worldwide,
Tang Xiao'ou. He is the founder of the Chinese high-tech com-

pany SenseTime, which created facial recognition software able to identify racial minority groups within larger crowds. The Beijing regime has used the technology to identify and target Muslim minorities in Xinjiang province. Four months after his speech, SenseTime was placed on the U.S. government's "entity list," prohibiting American companies from working with the firm because of its involvement in human rights violations.[39]

Schwarzman had nothing public to say about the controversy, or about the myriad of human rights problems in China. However, he has spoken out about far less brutal and widespread racial matters in the United States.[40]

When Washington and Beijing have diplomatic or strategic disagreements, Schwarzman has characterized the two as feuding parents who cannot get along, both seemingly equally responsible.[41] During the Trump administration, he played an important role serving as a go-between for the two powers. (The *Washington Post* dubbed him the "China Whisperer.")[42] Jim Breyer, brother-in-law of Senator Mitch McConnell and Elaine Chao, sits on the Blackstone board of directors.[43] But Schwarzman's written account of his shuttle diplomacy appears more critical of Washington than it does of Beijing, accusing the Trump administration of "ratcheting up the rhetoric" at one point, but not criticizing Beijing in a similar fashion.[44]

In 2021, Blackstone took an early and substantial stake in a Chinese company called JD Logistics, a spinoff of the tech giant JD. The Wall Street firm became one of the company's largest shareholders.[45] JD Logistics is no ordinary logistics company. In 2017, the firm signed a "strategic cooperation" agreement with the People's Liberation Army Air Force, which included plans to "jointly build an information sharing platform" as well as providing "personnel training and support services for the Air Force Logistics Department." This will allow China to further project air power into the Pacific, challenging U.S. military forces.[46]

Schwarzman explained to President Trump that "President Xi is a great guy."[47] It is common to see such praise for Xi on Wall Street, ignoring the widespread and brutal suppression of dissent in the country.

Hank Paulson, the former head of Goldman Sachs and U.S. Treasury secretary under President George W. Bush, once described Xi as "a guy who really knows how to get over the goal line."[48] Dictators often appear to have such a gift. Billionaire Michael Bloomberg has proclaimed that the unelected Xi is "not a dictator."[49] In January 2021, Schwarzman took the podium at a New York City black-tie dinner hosted by the China General Chamber of Commerce. It was the Chinese Lunar New Year of the Dog Gala, and after brief remarks by the Chinese ambassador to the United States, businessman Tung Chee-hwa took the stage. Tung, you may recall, runs a united front organization called CUSEF, which pushes influence operations in Washington. Tung sang Schwarzman's praises and then presented him with the "Goodwill Ambassador for China-U.S. Exchange Award."[50]

* * *

SCHWARZMAN AND BLACKSTONE are not the only players on Wall Street who have enjoyed a warm and cozy, mutually beneficial relationship with the communist regime in Beijing. Carl Walter and Fraser Howie, in their book *Red Capitalism*, explain, "The New China of the twenty-first century is a creation of the Goldman Sachs . . . of the world."[51] In the 1990s, the venerable Wall Street investment house picked up the moniker "Government Sachs" because of its close ties in Washington, D.C.[52] But it is the embrace of the Beijing regime that is more notable and troubling.

Like Schwarzman and Blackstone, Goldman has enjoyed great success through its partnerships with the Chinese government

and state-owned enterprises. In 1993, they were lead managers
when the China International Trust and Investment Corporation
(CITIC) issued its first bond offering in the United States. The
following year, the firm opened its first China office (in Beijing,
of course) and was granted a "special seat" on the Shanghai Stock
Exchange, the first American investment bank with such an honor.
Goldman profited enormously in the following years advising on
the privatization of state-owned firms, including China Telecom
and PetroChina.[53] Goldman found eager partners among China's
political and military elite. It launched a venture capital fund with
the son of a former health minister.[54] Another critical ally for Goldman's entry into the Chinese market was Fang Fenglei, the son of
a former senior official in the People's Liberation Army. Goldman,
desperate to further expand its footprint in China, bailed out a
business with which Fang was involved and set up a joint venture
with him.[55]

Chinese regional governments were also hiring the firm to help
with their debt restructuring.[56]

The deals accumulated and proved to be enormously lucrative.
In just six months of 2006, Goldman saw a nearly $4 billion in-
crease in value on a single investment in China.[57]

Goldman became a trusted partner to Beijing because it advised
officials on how to incorporate Communist Party leadership structures into Chinese corporations. John Thornton, a former head of
Goldman Sachs Asia, explained it this way when discussing the par-
tial privatization of China's national telecom company, Netcom:

In Netcom's case we focused on putting in place the right
structures, processes, and interactions. We defined specific
roles for the Communist Party and left the rest to the board—
for example, the party participates and votes on key matters
through nominated directors on the Netcom board, but fewer

than half of the board members are party designees. We clearly defined the boundaries of party mandates for senior-executive appointments, company strategy development, and key investments. We gave authority to nominate and approve CEO and CFO candidates back to the board. The CEO now owns the strategy-setting process and is supported by a newly created strategy department.

Thornton explained that there was no contradiction between the interests of the Chinese Communist Party and corporate investors.[58]

Perhaps no one figure at Goldman is more responsible for the cozy ties the firm enjoys in Beijing than Thornton, who has become fabulously wealthy in part because of those ties. Thornton received some unwanted attention for his oversized way of living when it was revealed that during an extended drought in South Florida, his Palm Beach home and property consumed 8,698,492 gallons of water in a single year, well above the 108,000 gallons for the average resident.[59]

The son of two "well-born Manhattan lawyers," he attended prep school at Hotchkiss before heading to Harvard, Oxford, and Yale. He joined Goldman in 1980 and became a veteran mergers and acquisitions banker (called "fiercely ambitious" by *Fortune* magazine) and in 1996 took charge of Goldman's Asia office based out of Hong Kong.[60] That same year he gathered a group of Chinese bureaucrats and government officials on the Chinese island resort of Hainan, where they were "fed, cosseted, and given a primer on how to privatize their vast state-owned corporations."[61] Of course, Goldman was positioned, courtesy of Chinese Communist Party officials, to collect hefty fees to help them do so. They were also set to become early investors in Chinese state-owned companies.

Thornton worked hard to cultivate working relationships with the Chinese political elite and Communist Party officials. Thornton became friends with Jiang Zemin when he was mayor of Shanghai in the 1980s.[62] Since he later became president of China, it would seem that Goldman was in the driver's seat to make deals. He met regularly with the mayors of large cities and members of the Political Bureau of the Communist Party of China.[63]

Through those relationships, Thornton gave Goldman the opportunity to be the lead underwriters for major Chinese state-owned companies going public, including China Telecom and PetroChina.[64]

"The Chinese government views Goldman as a very important and reliable business partner," said Fang Zheng, a partner in Neon Capital Management at the time.[65]

Thornton is an odd commodity, an unabashed defender of his Gordon Gekko–like attitudes about business. "What we have in New York," he told one reporter, "is unfettered capitalism, and that involves killing each other. A lot fall by the wayside. When I look at the tombstones of the last 15 years! It's a Darwinian model and the survivors are very fit." He went on: "Money is the ultimate commodity. So if what you want is the cheapest funds as fast as possible, then there are global institutions such as ourselves who can find you the money. If you're operating at our level, you've got to be big, mean and intelligent, and it's at that end of the business where we shine. We've handled any number of big Chinese privatizations—Chinese Telecom in Hong Kong, Bank of China, the big oil company PetroChina—all in the last five years. All of them were in billions and all of them were complicated."[66]

At the same time, as we will see, he has been happy to work with the Beijing regime as a trusted friend and perhaps even ally.

In 2003, Thornton abruptly left Goldman and took a professorship at the elite Tsinghua University, the same institution where Schwarzman would later set up his Schwarzman Scholars program.

It seemed a strange move. He was the first foreign full professor at
the school since the communist revolution in 1949. Thornton said
he would commute to Tsinghua from his New York home.[67]

Perhaps Thornton did not give up finance for the idyllic life in
academe. Rather, maybe he took the position because he saw China
as the center of gravity on the planet. "The single most important
thing to happen in our lifetime will be the emergence of China,"
he said in taking the job.[68] And by joining the faculty of the most
elite institution of higher learning in China, he became "one of
the most important contacts for any businessman with thoughts
of investing in the People's Republic."[69] As the Japanese business
media stated, "His presence in China, where personal connections
are a key factor in business success, is likely to give Goldman Sachs
a great deal of leverage for its future expansion in the country, people familiar with the matter say."[70]

Thornton continued to advise investment firms on deals with
Beijing, relying on his network of close ties. He also established
a center to study China at the venerable Brookings Institution in
Washington, D.C., and served as the think tank's chairman for
several years.[71] In October 2008, the Chinese government con-
ferred upon him the highest civilian award it grants to foreigners:
the Friendship Award. China's premier, Wen Jiabao, personally
presented the award, which had been established to "thank and
commend outstanding foreign experts annually for their contributions to China's social development and economic, scientific,
technological, educational and cultural construction."[72] Months
later, Thornton spoke about Premier Wen and the Chinese government in glowing terms. In Washington, he explained to the
Congressional-Executive Commission on China that China was
moving toward democracy. Thornton claimed then that party
leader and premier Wen Jiabao often advocated for the values of

democracy. He spoke of it in ways similar to many in the West. "When we talk about democracy," said Wen, "we usually refer to the three most important components: elections, judicial independence, and supervision based on checks and balances."

> Premier Wen's emphasis on universal values of democracy reflects new thinking in the liberal wing of the Chinese political establishment.
>
> Political participation through institutional means remains very limited. Yet, the ongoing political and intellectual discourse about democracy in the country, the existence of a middle class, commercialization of the media, the rise of civil society groups, the development of the legal profession, and checks and balances within the leadership are all important, contributing factors for democratic change in any society. In all these aspects, China was making significant progress.[73]

Of course, those universal values never really gained traction in the Communist Party.

Beyond glossing over Beijing's human rights record, Thornton has in more recent years cooperated with them in ways that benefit the government and help the regime accomplish its geostrategic goals, which are aimed squarely at the United States. These deals also stand to make him even more money. Thornton serves as the chairman of the board for the Silk Road Finance Corporation, an investment firm funded by the Chinese government and designed to support the government's Belt and Road Initiative.[74]

As Thornton's firm explains on its website, "SRFC is commercially driven, while complementing [Chinese] Government policy."[75] The firm's strategic partner is the Silk Road Planning Research Center, which advises and helps guide government policy on

One Belt/One Road. A "core shareholder" in Thornton's firm is "a financial services conglomerate under the direct supervision of the State Council of the People's Republic of China."[76]

The CEO of Thornton's Silk Road Finance Corporation, Li Shan, is a member of the powerful China People's Political Consultative Conference, a top-level decision-making body.[77]

Belt and Road, also known as One Belt One Road, and sometimes dubbed the "new silk road," is an attempt by the Chinese government to create development projects around the world spanning Europe, the Middle East, Asia, Southeast Asia, and Africa and link them with China. Supporters of the project believe that it will "seriously affect the dollar's previous dominance and with it the ability of the United States to exercise economic and political influence throughout the world."[78] The United States government certainly sees it as a geopolitical play by Beijing to supplant U.S. power around the world.

A wide array of officials call Belt and Road a strategic program to enhance Beijing's position. Belt and Road is "boosting China's ability to project its power across the region and the world," said Jack Lew, who was Barack Obama's Treasury secretary.[79]

The project is not good for everyone in China. "The entire *Belt and Road initiative* is based on *forced labor*," said Li Qiang, director of China Labor Watch, a human rights organization.[80]

At the same time, Thornton continues to be a funder of the U.S. policy debate in Washington, D.C. He has served as the chairman of the prestigious Brookings Institution and currently serves on its board of directors. The institution's China policy centers, one housed in Washington, the other in Beijing, are named after him. President Xi Jinping's nephew reportedly interned at Brookings.[81]

The big Wall Street firms actively bring the children of Beijing's party bosses into their companies. It was reported that in 2013 Goldman had more than two dozen sons and daughters of

high-ranking officials at the firm, including the grandson of Jiang
Zemin, the former Chinese premier and longtime friend of John
Thornton. Merrill Lynch, J.P. Morgan, and other firms have done
the same. Merrill managed to snag the son-in-law of the second-
highest-ranking Communist Party official at the time.[82]

Today, Goldman Sachs offers derivative products on the Hong
Kong stock exchange directly linked to the Chinese military companies. They only stopped trading them after the Trump administration limited financial firms from doing business with Chinese
military entities.[83] Goldman also issues U.S. dollar bonds for Chinese military-linked companies as identified by the Pentagon.[84]
Trump's declaration led Goldman Sachs, Morgan Stanley, and J.P.
Morgan to delist about five hundred warrants they had outstanding
on PLA-linked companies.[85]

* * *

ONE OF THE most powerful people on Wall Street is Ray Dalio,
founder of Bridgewater, the world's largest hedge fund. Dalio, who
by his own account started investing in the stock market when he
was twelve years old, has made billions running his investment
funds. In 2018 alone, his compensation from Bridgewater was said
to be $2 billion.[86]

But he is troubled by American capitalism. Capitalism is the
world's best system, he says, but it has not worked well for ordinary
Americans.[87]

On the other hand, the capitalist has only warm words for China
and its dictatorial leadership. He has called Wang Qishan, the second
most powerful man in the Chinese Communist Party, a "personal
hero."[88] In his book, *Principles*, published in 2017, Dalio goes further,
describing him as "a remarkable force for good for decades." Spending time with Wang is a religious-like experience, Dalio explains.

"Every time I speak with Wang, I feel like I get closer to cracking the unifying code that unlocks the laws of the universe."[89]

Following the release of his book in the United States, Dalio toured China promoting it. (At the same time, he was trying to get government approval for a hedge fund in China.) State television later reported that his tome was one of the most popular translated books in the country that year.[90]

So who exactly is Wang, to warrant such high praise from the world's largest hedge fund head?

Wang is President's Xi's enforcer. The *Economist* calls him "perhaps the most feared" leader in China.[91] He oversees party discipline and has waged an anticorruption campaign in the country, which many observers point out is really a thinly veiled tool to help Xi purge his political opponents and consolidate political power.[92] Ironically, Wang and his family are said to have received "gifts" from Deutsche Bank as part of their strategy of using bribes to gain access in China, yet no one from his family has been charged.[93]

Under Wang ("a remarkable force for good"), the anticorruption campaign uses techniques like beatings and torture to elicit confessions, according to Human Rights Watch and other organizations.[94] And of course, Wang (a "personal hero") is a Communist Party man, bluntly declaring, "there is no such thing as the separation of powers between the party and the government."[95]

By 2010, Bridgewater was doing big business with China. The Chinese government's State Administration of Foreign Exchange (SAFE) was investing billions of dollars in a number of hedge funds in the United States, including Bridgewater.[96] Dalio's relationship within the highest ranks of the government was becoming more direct, including a personal meeting with the Chinese foreign minister.[97] As Dalio built his powerful ties in Beijing, he also hired those with relationships in Washington to work for the firm. Dalio tapped James Comey, former associate attorney general of the United States, to serve as Bridgewater's top lawyer in 2010. (Comey left in 2013, when he was appointed FBI director by President Barack Obama.) "He's [Dalio is] tough and he's demanding and sometimes he talks too much, but, God, is he a smart bastard," Comey told the *New Yorker*.[98]

Comey indicated that he learned a lot from Dalio, including his creating a culture of speaking truth to power. Unless you are talking to dictators, of course.

In 2018, just a year after the publication of his book with the wonderful words about Beijing's number two, Dalio's firm became a significant player in China, having been granted the first license to provide hedge fund investments to locals in China.[99] And beyond his love letter to Wang, Dalio has been a consistent apologist for the communist system in China. His troubling views about China are worth quoting at length:

> One of China's leaders who explained this concept to me told that the word "country" consists of two characters, state and family, which influences how they view their role in looking after their state/family. One might say that the Chinese government is paternal.
>
> For example, it regulates what types of video games are watched by children and how many hours a day they play them. As a broad generalization, when the interest of the country (like the family) is at odds with the interest of the individual, the interest of the country (like the interest of the family) should be favored over the interest of the individual.
>
> Individuals are parts of a greater machine. As a result of this perspective, the system seeks to develop, promote and

reward good character and good citizenship. For example it gives people a social credit score that rates the quality of their citizenship. And each person is expected to view themselves as parts of the greater whole.

He concludes: "I'm not saying which system is better."[100]

In addition to stating his appreciation for the virtues of Beijing's authoritarian rule, Dalio has backed other Chinese government actions. In November 2020, the Chinese government went after billionaire Jack Ma for voicing criticisms of Chinese regulators and canceled his Ant IPO. Ma also disappeared for almost ninety days. Ray Dalio, however, sided with the government against Jack Ma. The billionaire described Chinese regulators as, among other things, "caring."[101]

Dalio is a Beijing regime booster. "Whatever criticisms you may have about Chinese 'state capitalism,' you cannot say it hasn't worked," he wrote in the *Financial Times* and on his LinkedIn page. He is also quick to echo Beijing's claims about human rights violations in America being similar. Dalio, from the comforts of his Greenwich, Connecticut, estate, calmly restates Beijing's argument: "China's rejoinder is that a strong hand is needed to maintain order, what happens inside its borders is its business, and the U.S. has its own human rights problems."[102] He does not refute Beijing's claim. (Remember, their rule is "paternal.") But he does add that many in the West possess a "persistent anti-China bias"—one of many China-defending points happily relayed by Chinese state media. They should "clear their mind," he says.[103]

Dalio believes in Beijing's dictatorial model, because the leadership is smart. He is skeptical that having leaders democratically accountable would be better. "The Chinese leadership is extremely knowledgeable in the lessons of its history and how things work," he said in 2020. "What I would convey to you and my fellow

Americans is that they have a lot of internal disagreement and processes for dealing with it well within the government, so it does exist. Whether or not it is more productive to have the entire population in those discussions is a matter of opinion."[104] Dalio is what one might call a Freedom Skeptic.

Dalio defends his bullish views of China, saying, "people have accused me of being biased, naïve, and in some cases unpatriotic. I think I'm just being objective."[105]

Dalio's defense of the Beijing regime and his efforts to invest in the country are even more appalling because he believes that America is already effectively at "war" with Beijing. As he explained in 2020, "In terms of China, we will—we are in a conflict with China. You can call it a war, like the 1930s, so that there is a—there is a trade war, there is a technology war, there is a geopolitical war, and there could be a capital war. And so that's the reality."[106]

Dalio enjoys a "rock-star investor status" in China, and his business is booming, thanks to the assist from the Beijing government.[107] In 2020, the government granted him the right to launch a second investment fund.[108]

* * *

THE BIGGEST ASSET manager in the world is BlackRock. Built from the ground up by Larry Fink (the CEO) and his partners, the firm has transformed finance. Beyond the amount of money that it manages, BlackRock also provides analytical tools that other investment firms use to assess their investment decisions, such that "those who oversee many of the world's biggest pools of money are looking at the financial world, at least in part, through a lens crafted by BlackRock."[109] So how Fink and BlackRock interact with China and, perhaps even more important, view China, will have an enormous effect in the world of finance.

Fink has been outspoken for years on the need for greater "social responsibility" in investing, especially on environmental, social, and governance (ESG) issues.[110] He wants investors to focus not just on profits but on doing social good through companies.

But those standards do not apply to investments in China. Indeed, as we will see, Fink sings the praises of the regime and avoids criticizing some of the more abhorrent actions in the country.

Fink was raised in Van Nuys, California, graduated from the University of California, Los Angeles, and headed to Wall Street after college. He was a young, aggressive financial professional at First Boston when his career seemingly went up in flames: the department he was running lost $100 million in a single quarter because of a bad bet. Fink was asked to leave, and he kicked around for a few years, working at Schwarzman's Blackstone. Ultimately, he went on to form his own firm, BlackRock.[111]

During the financial crisis in 2008–9, he made a series of decisions that would transform BlackRock into a Wall Street monster. Most important, his firm bought Barclays Global Investors, which ran the collection of iShare index funds. That segment of the investment industry exploded, and Fink found himself as one of the biggest players on Wall Street. Fink, known for his direct talk and financial acumen, not only became fabulously wealthy, but also became known as a "Wall Street Wise Man." Today, he serves as not only the head of BlackRock but also as an advisor to CEOs, officials at the U.S. Federal Reserve, Treasury secretaries, and U.S. presidents. BlackRock has become so large and powerful that some bankers regard it as "almost a shadow government."[112] Others have called it the "fourth branch of government."[113]

Fink has sought to use that size and muscle to push for causes he believes in. His biggest is what he calls "corporate responsibility."

Businesses should not just focus on the bottom line; they should also factor environmental and social concerns into determining whether they are successful.

In 2018, Fink called on corporate CEOs to make big changes in how they operate. "Society is demanding that companies, both public and private, serve a social purpose," he wrote in a letter. "To prosper over time, every company must not only deliver financial performance, but also show how it makes a positive contribution to society."[114] In another letter to corporate executives he insisted: "A company cannot achieve long-term profits without embracing purpose and considering the needs of a broad range of stakeholders. A pharmaceutical company that hikes prices ruthlessly, a mining company that shortchanges safety, a bank that fails to respect its clients . . . these actions that damage society will catch up with a company and destroy shareholder value."[115]

What about a financial firm that partners with a repressive regime?

In 2018, Fink applied that approach when it came to Saudi Arabia. A Saudi journalist named Jamal Khashoggi had been murdered and brutally dismembered, and there was evidence that the Saudi government was behind the killing. Fink went on CNBC and explained why he was boycotting the Saudi government's investment conference in protest. "We have an incident now that we need to be mindful of. You know, there's an unexplainable death or murder. It could impact relations worldwide. We have to be sympathetic to this. This was a big issue with BlackRock's employees. This was a big issue with many clients who reached out and called."[116]

When it comes to China, Fink does not have much criticism, despite the widespread and persistent nature of its abuses. Indeed, Fink actually praises the conduct of the Beijing regime and misrepresents what is going on in the country.

"If Xi's benevolent it's a good thing, if he's not benevolent it's a bad thing," he told the *Australian Financial Review.* "But I don't see any reason to fear." The mounting evidence of abuses against Uighurs, Hong Kongers, or other minorities did not faze him. He went on, declaring that the suppression of rights that was taking place was theoretical and on balance, not so bad. "I think his first five years have shown that the Xi government has done very well in terms of navigating the economy and improving the quality of life for more Chinese. *In theory, some elements of the society may have less rights, but on the other hand I would say the majority of society in China have done very well*" (emphasis added).[117]

This apparent excuse for repression is quite remarkable coming from someone who wants to push corporations to be more "responsible," and make "positive contributions to society."

Fink went on in the interview to offer a ringing endorsement of Xi's regime. "I would qualify the Chinese leadership as one of the best leadership teams in the world."[118]

Fink has apparently made clear to Chinese officials not to expect any high-minded talk about human rights, social issues, or the role of corporations as reformers. In November 2019, he reportedly told officials in Beijing that "BlackRock should be a Chinese company in China."[119] In fact, in 2021, while Beijing was crushing the pro-democracy movement in Hong Kong, BlackRock was actually expanding its presence in that city. Repression, apparently, is not bad for business.[120]

China's sovereign wealth funds, like the China Investment Corporation (CIC), have hired BlackRock and others "to manage large portions of their portfolios," according to a U.S. congressional report.[121] CIC is no ordinary investment firm and is "expected to pursue government objectives."[122] It also is a "central feature of China's technology acquisition strategy."[123] So BlackRock collects fees while its client works to advance Chinese interests at the expense of the United States.

BlackRock also manages the assets of "a lot of high-net-worth clients in China," presumably including members of the politically connected corporate elite.[124] Fink clearly sees China at the center of BlackRock's future. "We are here to work with China," he says. "We firmly believe China will be one of the biggest opportunities for BlackRock."[125] And indeed, recently BlackRock struck up a partnership with China Construction Bank Corporation to form a joint venture.[126] China Construction Bank is a financial titan backed by the Chinese government.

But the governance standards he applies to American companies do not apply in China. Chinese companies listed on American stock exchanges were exempt from normal regulatory and accounting rules that applied to American and other foreign companies listed. In 2020, Congress passed by overwhelming majorities the Holding Foreign Companies Accountable Act. The law was straightforward. BlackRock, for all its bluster about better governance, was weirdly silent about the bill.[127]

When seventeen students were killed by a gunman at a Parkland, Florida, high school, BlackRock was quick to argue for corporate responsibility. The financial giant pledged to use its ownership in several gun manufacturers through index funds to push for change. China state television reported on the story and quoted a Black-Rock spokesman: "We focus on engaging with the company and understanding how they are responding to society's expectations of them."[128]

So, BlackRock takes extra care to speak to providers of weapons to law-abiding American citizens. In China, they own shares in companies directly linked to the People's Liberation Army. The companies in which BlackRock owns shares directly support Xi's "Military-Civil Fusion."[129] One wonders who might suffer at the wrong end of those weapons and technologies. There is no evidence that BlackRock has spoken to these Chinese companies asking them how *they* are "responding to society's expectations of them."

Longtime global investor George Soros has called out BlackRock for its financial efforts in China, declaring that it is on the "wrong side" of the struggle between Beijing and the West, and noted that BlackRock's efforts "will damage the national security interests of the U.S. and other democracies."[130]

One of Fink's great passions is climate change, and he often speaks of the necessity of fighting it. He has been critical of fossil fuel producers and companies resisting climate goals.[131] But those criticisms seem to stop at China's border. Beijing is by far the greatest contributor to greenhouse gas emissions in the world. China continues to dive into coal-fueled power; the use of coal in the country is "soaring." In 2020 alone, local governments in China approved forty-six gigawatts of new coal power plants in the country. More than half of the coal power in the world is now generated in China.[132]

Fink has not taken the regime to task here, either.

While Fink has pushed for better governance of companies in the United States and the Western world, he has done the opposite in China. Indeed, in China, Fink has used BlackRock's muscle to help the Communist Party consolidate control over companies.

In 2017, the CCP pushed for companies listed on the Hong Kong stock exchange to change their corporate charters to make it explicitly clear that the corporate boards would be required to "seek advice on major decisions from Communist Party committees" in Beijing.[133] The proposed changes would give the Communist Party more powers—allowing "China's communist party writing itself into company law." The reforms established "internal party committees to be consulted on important decisions." Some made clear that corporate executives were also to serve as heads of internal Communist Party committees in their companies.[134]

It was a clear power grab by Beijing.

The investment giant Vanguard voted against the measure.

And BlackRock? They voted in *favor*.[135]

Observers called the move by BlackRock and others "bizarre," likening it to "turkeys voting for Christmas."[136]

The fact that BlackRock went along and voted for greater Communist Party control is, as Tamar Groswald Ozery at Harvard Law School's Program on Corporate Governance puts it, "suggestive of their support or at least indifference."[137]

Fink and those like him know that by cooperating and doing what the party and regime want, they will get greater access to the Chinese market and become even richer.

BlackRock's reach extends beyond the purviews of financial markets, and now includes the highest reaches of the White House. No less than three executives from the firm, who were central to the firm's push into China, are in senior roles in the Biden administration. Brian Deese, the former global head of sustainable investing at BlackRock, is the head of the National Economic Council.[138] Deese had served in the Obama administration, where he helped negotiate the climate change deal that allowed China to avoid curtailing carbon emissions for more than a decade.[139]

Beijing was bullish on his appointment. Former trade official He Weiwen told the *Global Times*, a party-run paper, that Deese represented the interests of large corporations at BlackRock who "have tasted the sweetness of doing business with China."[140]

Fink's kowtowing to the regime means BlackRock gets a special seat at the table in Beijing.

In March 2021, Beijing authorities approved BlackRock's bid to sell wealth management products on the Chinese mainland.[141]

Wall Street thoroughly bought into the idea that as China grew more prosperous, it would become less militaristic and more democratic. Of course, that has not happened. And money is fungible—making China more prosperous helps them build their military. That means that even if financial deals with the Beijing regime may not be directly related to military activity, they still pose a serious security risk. As two scholars declared: "In today's interconnected financial world, transactions that pass formal legal muster may in fact still engender substantial diplomatic and security consequences."[142]

Wall Street ignored the consequences of its financial dealings with Beijing. They subsidized and helped construct the Chinese military, which is ultimately aimed at our men and women in uniform. It has helped the Chinese Communist Party grow wealthier and even more powerful.

"Why are we sending American capital to a country and supporting a defense industry that's popping out a couple destroyers and frigates a month and threatening to have total overmatch against us in the Pacific?" asked White House national security advisor Robert O'Brien. "I don't see why we should be underwriting the Chinese defense industry."[143]

O'Brien went on to call out the California Public Employees' Retirement System (CalPERS), the largest public retirement system in the United States, for its investments in China. "Some of the CalPERS investment policies are incredibly concerning," he went on. "If someone told me I had to invest my 401(k) in Chinese state-owned enterprises or partially state-owned enterprises, where they don't follow the generally accepted accounting principles, and they don't have to report to independent regulatory bodies, I'd be pretty worried about that."[144]

CalPERS, the notoriously underfunded and overcommitted pension system, responded that the Chinese investments were "necessary for the pension fund to meet its 7% investment return target to pay retirement benefits for our members for the long term." In other words, because the California state government hopelessly underfunds the state pension system, it is now necessary to pour capital into Chinese state-owned companies connected with the Chinese military-security state.[145]

Chinese officials are well aware of the power they have over Wall Street and the willingness of financiers to do their bidding.

On November 28, 2020, Di Dongsheng, the vice dean at Renmin University, spoke candidly about the power that Beijing enjoys through its relationships with Wall Street firms. As we saw in chapter 2, he referenced Beijing's links to the financial activities of Hunter Biden. In that same speech, he explained, "Since the 1970s, Wall Street had a very strong influence on the domestic and foreign affairs of the United States. So we had a channel to rely on." He went on to note that Wall Street had pushed hard against Donald Trump's tariffs on Beijing. "So during the U.S.-China trade war, they [Wall Street] tried to help, and I know that my friends on the U.S. side told me that they tried to help, but they couldn't do much."[146]

Indeed, Wall Street has been a go-to weapon for Beijing to deploy against Washington. As Clive Hamilton and Mareike Ohlberg write in their book on Chinese global influence operations, *Hidden Hand*, "Whenever presidents Clinton, Bush or Obama threatened to take a tougher stance on China's trade protectionism, currency manipulation or technology theft, Wall Street chiefs used their influence to persuade them to back off."[147]

They conclude, "Financial institutions have been Beijing's most powerful advocates in Washington."[148]

Too many of America's financial titans, who prospered under a free market system and benefited from American rule of law, are now actively cheerleading for Beijing and profiting from the regime's actions.

We have looked at Washington, Silicon Valley, and Wall Street. Now let us peek behind the curtain to see what some of America's most esteemed public servants and diplomats have been doing with Beijing.

6

DIPLOMATS

In 1861, shortly after becoming the sixteenth president of the United States, Abraham Lincoln nominated a former Massachusetts congressman named Anson Burlingame to be the American minister to China's Qing Imperial Court. Burlingame was a respected abolitionist and considered a highly principled figure. He was well liked by Chinese officials. In fact, he was so good that Prince Gong of the royal family approached him with a proposition: Could they hire him away from the U.S. government? Would he come to work for them, representing Chinese interests in the West? Burlingame accepted, and served the Chinese Royal Court until he died in 1870 in St. Petersburg, Russia.[1]

Burlingame's switching sides in the nineteenth century was perhaps not such a big deal. China was then a weak and decaying dynasty representing no threat or challenge to the United States—and with no apparent aspirations beyond "upholding [the] nation's sovereignty and territorial integrity."[2]

Today, however, the consequences of playing for the other team are far more troubling.

America assigns its diplomats to protect and expand American interests abroad. Diplomats actually swear an oath to defend the Constitution and protect the country from "enemies, foreign and domestic."[3] But all too often, when they leave government service, they end up serving the interests of foreign governments and entities in the host countries where they were paid to represent us. They make a perfect target for influence. Diplomats become diplomats because they believe they can make slow and steady cultural progress. More cooperation is an end in itself. They see more trade as better, no matter what it does to the economies trading. They see international infrastructure in the Belt and Road gambit as a worthwhile goal, no matter how it changes the playing field. They see human rights violations as events to be handled quietly, no matter how many there are or have been.

The greatest assets they possess—and the key point of advantage for their clients—are the relationships they have forged with both foreign and U.S. officials. When they leave office, in order to maintain those relationships, they need to speak nice about Beijing or risk losing their access. Their relationships with Chinese government officials give them the power to make money. That money grants the regime leverage over these former diplomats involved in deals.

At the same time, many of these retired American officials appear on national television, write for publications, testify before Congress, and give paid speeches ladling out advice on how to deal with China. Rarely—if ever—are the financial realities of their dependence on access to Beijing revealed or made clear.

Some of the officials featured here will talk critically about China, but they will never cause concern in Beijing because they restate the necessity of engagement, and the accompanying access to American capital and technology. The spirit of "big help with a little badmouth" thrives. But speak too critically of Beijing and these officials risk losing their moneymaking opportunities.

Today a long stream of former American diplomats and defense officials have launched businesses that are dependent on being in the good graces of the Beijing regime and create a conflict that is far less innocent than that of Ambassador Burlingame. Some have become wealthy courtesy of the Chinese government while advancing China's interests.

Henry Kissinger, the dean of American diplomats, once confided in a colleague his concerns about the challenge that Beijing would present to the United States. "When [the Chinese] don't need us," he reportedly said, "they are going to be very difficult to deal with."[4]

Apparently, until that time comes, there is no reason not to cash in.

Kissinger pioneered the idea of cashing in by using the relationships he had forged serving as America's chief diplomat. Kissinger was the national security advisor to President Richard Nixon, and later secretary of state under Nixon and later President Gerald Ford. Most important, he had impeccable ties in the country that he had helped open in 1972: China. It was Kissinger, after all, who had conducted the secret diplomacy with Chinese officials beginning in 1971 that led to the restoration of diplomatic ties between the two countries in 1972.[5] As a result, he is revered in Chinese government circles. Kissinger, in return, was awed by Chinese leaders. "No other world leaders have the sweep and imagination of Mao and Chou [Zhou] nor the capacity and will to pursue a long-range policy," he marveled to Nixon after one meeting in Beijing.[6] Chairman Mao was apparently less impressed. He reportedly told British prime minister Edward Heath that Kissinger was "just a funny little man. He is shuddering all over with nerves every time he comes to see me."[7]

When he left government service in 1977, Kissinger had spent his entire career in academe and government. Now it was time to make some money. "Making money is actually boring, even if it is necessary," he reportedly told Soviet foreign minister Andrei Gromyko in their last meeting.[8]

In July 1982, he launched Kissinger Associates as an active business. Kissinger had no legal training and no background in finance, so the prospect of joining a high-powered law firm or investment bank was not an option. But he had something more important than both of those qualities: he had unparalleled relationships overseas—especially important were impeccable ties in Beijing.

Kissinger was clearly a regime favorite. As a private citizen, he repeatedly visited Beijing at the invitation of the Chinese government, often meeting with Deng Xiaoping and other Chinese leaders.[9]

China in the early 1980s was still off the beaten path for many Western corporations. There can be little doubt, though, that many corporate leaders saw the massive potential in a market of one billion people. The work of Kissinger Associates included opening doors for foreign clients, but his most important and lucrative role was cutting through government regulations in Beijing. To do business in China, for example, you needed government endorsement and approval. As one Indian scholar allows, for Kissinger, this "often involved making a few well-placed phone calls to friends in top government positions."[10]

At the same time, Kissinger was a widely cited spokesman and commentator on foreign affairs, appearing on network television, in America's leading newspapers, and of course in America's bookstores. Kissinger seemed to ride these two horses at once until the tragic events of June 1989 put him in an awkward position. That was when the People's Liberation Army marched into Tiananmen Square. The conflict resulted in the deaths of thousands of peaceful protestors.[11] As events unfolded, Kissinger went on ABC News, where anchor Peter Jennings asked him: "What should America do?" Kissinger was calm and noted that we needed to maintain close relations and "I wouldn't do any sanctions." ABC News was paying him $100,000 a year at the time to provide insight and commentary on world events. In his newspaper columns, Kissinger took the same line, explaining that while he was "shocked by the brutality" of what had happened, we needed to view it as "an internal matter."[12]

Kissinger defended the Chinese government's actions, strangely arguing, "No government in the world would have tolerated having the main square of its capital occupied for eight weeks," and that "a crackdown was therefore inevitable." How the United States responded was key, he argued, rejecting economic sanctions and suggesting that we could not do much. Doing little was "a test of our political maturity." Above all, he maintained, it was "too important for American national security to risk the relationship on the emotions of the moment."[13]

What Kissinger did not disclose at the time was that while he was discussing China matters seemingly as a detached scholar or analyst, he was simultaneously neck-deep in commercial deals involving the Chinese government. Kissinger had worked with Atlantic Richfield, the energy company, to negotiate a deal with the Chinese government. When International Telephone and Telegraph (ITT) wanted to hold a board meeting in Beijing, he found a government agency that would act as their host. H. J. Heinz executives were trying to set up a baby food factory in China, and Kissinger helped the company navigate through the cobwebs of the Chinese bureaucracy. American International Group (AIG), where he was chairman of the international advisory board, wanted licenses in Shanghai while constructing an office tower. Bottom line, Kissinger had a reputation for being able to bring clients to Beijing and get them meetings with the top Chinese officials.[14] Condemning the Tiananmen Square massacre too much would cost him access.

In fact, in December 1988, just six months before the horrific event, Kissinger launched a limited investment partnership called China Ventures. It was supposed to be a vehicle for U.S. corporations to invest in joint ventures with the Chinese government.

Kissinger was the firm's chairman, CEO, and general partner. The deal promised to be enormously lucrative for Kissinger: he was to receive management fees topping more than $1 million a year and 20 percent of profits after investors got an 8 percent return on their investment.[15]

As Kissinger went on network television urging inaction in the face of the massacre, word got out about his deals in Beijing. Rather than address them, he described the criticisms as "McCarthyism," insisting there was no link between his views on China and his business ventures.[16]

Kissinger's reputation survived the substantial conflict of interest. And he continued to work hard shaping and steering America's approach to China over the course of the next several decades. And more deals came.

In February 1995, Speaker of the House Newt Gingrich visited Taipei and argued that Taiwan should be admitted to the United Nations. Beijing, of course, was outraged. They viewed Taiwan as a province of China, not as an independent country. Kissinger "personally admonished" Gingrich for suggesting such a thing.[17]

In 1997, Kissinger became a crucial advisor to a corporate lobbying group that wanted better U.S.-China relations and was eager for China's admission into the World Trade Organization. At the time, Justice Department officials argued that his activity "strains the limits of lobbying disclosure laws and possibly violates the Foreign Agents Registration Act."[18]

Still, he continued to appear before the public as an impartial analyst on U.S.-China relations. At various times, he was a paid media commentator by ABC News, CBS, and CNN.[19] In a few instances, he was forced to disclose his commercial links to Beijing. In a 2005 piece for the *Washington Post*, he explained that containment of China was not needed and would not work. He added: "Before dealing with the need of keeping the relationship from becoming hostage to reciprocal pinpricks, I must point out that the consulting company I chair advises clients with business interests around the world, including China. Also, in early May I spent a week in China, much of it as a guest of the government."[20]

In the corridors of official Washington, he remained a voice that had the ear of America's top policy makers. During her tenure as secretary of state, even Hillary Clinton called on him for advice.[21]

The election of Donald J. Trump as president of the United States in November 2016 threatened to upend U.S.-China relations in a manner that would be detrimental to Beijing. Trump had publicly said that he was going to renegotiate trade deals, challenge China's military expansion into the South China Sea, and deal with a myriad of other issues far more assertively than his predecessors. In a demonstration of his tougher approach, the president-elect had even accepted a congratulatory call from Taiwan's President Tsai Ing-wen, infuriating Beijing.[22]

China's President Xi wanted to know more about Trump, so he turned to Kissinger, who flew to Beijing to meet with him. Kissinger was reassuring: "Overall, we hope to see the China-U.S. relationship moving ahead in a sustained and stable manner."[23]

Kissinger's relationship with the Beijing regime includes more than just informal consultations and help with his clients. The Chinese government appointed Kissinger to the international advisory council of the China Development Bank (CDB), a government-backed bank erected to compete with Western financial institutions like the World Bank.[24]

Kissinger has helped in other ways, too. He has used his prestige as an added gloss to Chinese government-backed events. In 2009, the Chinese government established the China Center for International Economic Exchange (CCIEE), which the government's central planning agency oversees. Indeed, Chinese premier Wen Jiabao created the organization by directive. The organization's personnel office also serves as the office of its Party Committee's Discipline Inspection Committee—which should tell you everything you need to know about who controls the organization. CCIEE organized "a major international conference" with Bloomberg, and Henry Kissinger served as the conference's advisory board chair. In his words, the purpose of the meetings was "making the national goals of China and the United States compatible."[25]

As we saw earlier, he also agreed to serve as an honorary co-chairman of the China–U.S. Exchange Foundation, the united front group linked to the government. Kissinger was also given the honored title of "an old friend" of China, as one who has "rendered great help to China." He is in a rarefied group.[26]

When the Chinese government set up a think tank in Washington, D.C., called the Institute for China-America Studies, it did so in part to be "'sending a clear message' about Beijing's claims on the South China Sea." Beijing asserts territorial control over vast portions of the ocean, a claim rejected by the Philippines, Japan, Vietnam, and the United States. But Kissinger sent the organization a video message welcoming the new program.[27]

Kissinger's legacy as a major friend of China is well established in Beijing. As authors Clive Hamilton and Mareike Ohlberg put it, "Kissinger is a revered figure in CCP circles. It's said that at the Central Party School in Beijing there is only one picture of a foreigner adorning the walls, that of Kissinger."[28]

Kissinger Associates has grown to include an array of other well-known and powerful members of the American political class. John Brennan, who served as CIA director during Barack Obama's tenure, is a "senior advisor" at the firm.[29] Brennan has some familiarity with consulting work in China. Brennan's previous stint in international consulting work, from 2005 to 2009, was serving as the president and CEO of The Analysis Corporation (TAC), which was controlled by Global Strategies Group (GSG), a British-based security company. GSG had an office in Beijing, housed in the seventeen-story glass, curtain-walled Towercrest International Plaza in the Chaoyang District of the capital city. This was in the hopes of winning "security contracts from Chinese state-owned corporations." A plan was discussed to sell TAC's sensitive intelligence software to the Chinese government, but GSG eventually gave up because "it was covered by military secrecy export restrictions." They did manage to secure one deal with Beijing—a security contract with the government-run China National Petroleum Corporation. A former employee remarked, "It was all a massive conflict of interest, and it was all a bit weird."[30]

* * *

BEYOND KISSINGER ASSOCIATES, other senior American diplomats from secretaries of state to U.S. ambassadors have cashed in with a similar business model. They have all collected large fees because of their access to the highest reaches of government, while at the same time speaking as elder statesmen, allegedly offering objective advice on American foreign policy. It represents a troubling conflict of interest that clouds our national conversation about the China threat.

Alexander Haig had a long, illustrious career as a military officer and government official. He served as the Supreme Allied Commander of NATO forces, later in the Nixon White House, and briefly as President Ronald Reagan's secretary of state.[31] Once Haig left public service, he joined the ranks of those working for Chinese government-backed companies. He served as an "honorary senior advisor" to the Chinese "government-controlled maritime operation, the China Ocean Shipping Co., or Cosco."[32] We met this military-linked company back in chapter 2.

* * *

IN MAY 1998, Secretary of State Madeleine Albright was in China tilling the ground for a later visit by President Bill Clinton. One of the highlights of her trip was a planned speech in Beijing on the rule of law. Just after she arrived, the government-controlled *China Daily* ran a story about what China needed to do to improve the rule of law. When Albright took the podium to give her speech, she held up the newspaper and, with a big smile, declared that it was a sign that China was getting better when it came to bringing the rule of law to Beijing. "Clearly, both your leaders and your citizens recognize the need to strengthen the rule of law," she told the audience. James Mann, who was the *Los Angeles Times* Beijing bureau chief, recalled, "She did not seem to grasp that the newspaper story was not some random, independent bit of journalism, but had been timed specifically to influence her and her trip."[33]

When Bill Clinton appointed Madeleine Albright as secretary of state, he made history: she was the first woman to serve as America's top diplomat. Once she left office, she would prove as equally adept as Kissinger at cashing in on her time of service. And she would look to Beijing as a place for the biggest payday.

As secretary of state, Albright was an essential player in the effort to bring China into the WTO. She echoed the themes that "engagement" with China was the key to both American prosperity and a more open China. In her memoirs, Albright declared, "By entering the WTO, China committed to free itself from the 'House that Mao Built,' including state-run enterprises, central planning institutes, massive agricultural communes, and parasitic bureaucracies" as well as "more institutions and associations free from Communist Party control."[34]

Albright was rosy in her assessment of the deal. "[China's membership] would give the United States more access to China's market, boost our exports, reduce our trade deficit, and create new well-paying jobs," she claimed.

Albright was entirely wrong. There was no massive movement away from Communist Party control. And America's annual trade imbalance with China was $70 billion in 2000 when China joined the WTO and ballooned to $200 billion by the end of 2005.[35]

American exports to China may not have blossomed as she promised. But the consultancy she opened in China after she left the State Department certainly did.

Albright launched the Albright Group—later Albright Stonebridge Group—a "strategic consulting" practice that would profit from the relationships she had forged while America's chief diplomat. Like Kissinger, she touted the fact that many of her clients were American firms looking for help or a hookup in foreign countries. As in the Kissinger case, this obscured the primary tenet: her commercial opportunities rested on staying in the good graces of foreign governments, particularly Beijing. American firms wanting help in China would only pay her if she had access to the highest levels of government in the Chinese capital. As author Sarah Chayes puts it, "Its business model consists mostly in leveraging Albright's reputation and the relationships with developing country leaders she gained as secretary of state to win favors for large corporations."[36]

Albright also established a hedge fund, Albright Capital, despite a lack of experience in the finance world. Her son-in-law, Gregory Bowes, runs this business.[37]

Albright eventually joined forces with Sandy Berger, the former

Bill Clinton national security advisor, who had started a consulting firm called Stonebridge with deals in Beijing. By his own account, Berger was a frequent fixture in China's capital. He would meet with government officials and make appearances on Chinese state media. "I'm a consultant to government and to business, in the political and economic spheres," he told the government's Xinhua News during one visit. "My two identities are like two hats, but they both play the role of bridge in the development of U.S.-China relations."[38]

While Albright's firm—rechristened as Albright Stonebridge Group (ASG)—does business in Europe, it is in China where she has truly cashed in. As the ASG website puts it, "ASG's China practice is the firm's largest single country practice. With full-time senior-level professionals based in Beijing, Shanghai, and Washington, DC, our team of over 30 professionals supports clients across a wide variety of sectors." The firm even boasts that its senior leadership includes both former U.S. officials as well as "former high-level" Chinese government officials. ASG leverages its relationships within the Chinese government: "We work to create allies within the Chinese system," according to the website.[39]

The chairman of the ASG China operation is a former senior Chinese official named Jin Ligang, who spent twenty years in the Chinese Ministry of Commerce.[40] His American counterpart at ASG is Amy Celico, who worked in the State Department and as senior director for China affairs in the U.S. Trade Representative Office. Celico's job there was "developing negotiating positions" on policies related to intellectual property rights.[41]

Celico was critical of President Trump's hard line toward China, arguing that we needed to "rightsize" the threat posed by China. Indeed, she argues, we should not view China as a "threat" but as a "challenge." When the Trump administration and other foreign governments took actions against Huawei because of its ties to the Chinese security services, Celico argued that this was a "very dangerous trend," creating the impression that we wanted to "keep China down" rather than compete with them.[42] The list of countries that have identified Huawei as a security threat include Japan, Taiwan, France, Great Britain, the United States, Australia, and Germany, among others.[43]

When Celico made these comments before the prestigious Aspen Institute, it was never disclosed how her firm made their fees courtesy of their access to high-ranking Chinese government officials.

Celico is not alone at ASG in her relatively rose-colored view of the Beijing regime.

Those views were echoed by Linda Thomas-Greenfield, who headed up ASG's Africa practice until she was appointed by President Joe Biden as the U.S. ambassador to the United Nations in 2021. In 2019, Thomas-Greenfield gave a speech at the Chinese government-funded Confucius Institute at Savannah State University in Georgia. She praised China's commitment to values and the role that the regime was playing in Africa. She declared that the United States and China could work in Africa together on "shared values of peace, prosperity, sustained economic growth and development, and a firm commitment to good governance, and gender equity, and the rule of law."

She added, "China is in a unique position to spread these ideals given its strong footprint on the continent."[44]

For good measure, Thomas-Greenfield even threw in a few good words for Beijing's Belt and Road Initiative on the continent of Africa. Never mind that Chinese officials, such as Major General Wang Weixing, consider Belt and Road part of the military's plan to "go global."[45]

When the speech came up during her U.S. Senate confirmation hearings for her appointment as UN ambassador, Thomas-Greenfield explained that she now regretted having given it.

* * *

ANOTHER ALUMNUS FROM the Clinton administration set up a lucrative consulting service following his tenure running the Pentagon. William Cohen, the former Republican senator from Maine, established the Cohen Group in 2001 to advise on everything from the defense industry to international trade. But China has played a central role: two of the four offices the Cohen Group has overseas are in China.[46] Cohen's background of more than thirty years in public life—first as a member of Congress and the U.S. Senate, then as secretary of defense—makes him an ideal candidate to work with Beijing. The Cohen Group actually touts his deep ties to Beijing, noting that he first visited China as a congressman in 1978 when he met Deng Xiaoping. "Since then, he has been a constant presence in the U.S.-China relationship, including commercial development and security cooperation," reads the Cohen Group website.[47]

During his tenure as secretary of defense, Cohen pushed policies for greater cooperation with China.[48] Near the end of the Cold War, Beijing was trying to emerge from international isolation in the years following the Tiananmen Square massacre. In July 2000, he paid his final visit as SecDef to meet with Chinese leader Jiang Zemin.[49]

Within a year, he had opened his consulting firm.

The Cohen Group has grown over the years to include a pantheon of former military officers and government officials, including former secretary of defense James Mattis, and former vice chairman of the Joint Chiefs of Staff General Joseph Ralston. The roster of professionals runs the gamut from the Department of Defense, State Department, the White House, the Department of Homeland Security, to the intelligence community.[50]

On the other side of the Pacific, Cohen enjoys access to the highest levels of the Chinese government, personally meeting with the vice premier of the State Council and members of the Chinese Communist Party Central Committee.[51]

Cohen Group executives have met with Chinese officials in the hopes of working on Beijing's Belt and Road projects, by which China will fuse itself internationally to other countries via large-scale infrastructure projects. While both the Obama and Trump administrations raised serious strategic concerns about the Belt and Road Initiative, the Cohen Group views it differently—and in a very positive light, extolling the virtues of the Chinese strategic development plan, which also employs forced labor. "I think it's a very important project," Marc Grossman, the vice chairman of the Cohen Group, told the official Chinese news agency Xinhua in an interview. "Because if you look at the area, especially in South Asia, this is a part of the world where, unlike many other parts of the world, there are very few connections really."[52]

China Daily, the government news site, quoted Grossman, the former undersecretary of state in the Obama administration, under the banner "Belt and Road Receives Global Backing."[53]

"The Belt and Road Initiative is a very positive project that helps boost sustainable economic development in the world, especially in ill-connected Asia," he told them.[54]

The Cohen Group goes further than Kissinger or Albright in that it not only works with U.S. companies seeking access in China; it also has pledged to work with the Chinese government to help "Chinese companies go global and conduct investment in the U.S., Europe and other regions."[55] Indeed, the Cohen Group is "eager" to help Chinese companies by "leveraging our regional expertise in the United States" and elsewhere, Cohen said on a 2020 visit to China.[56]

The Cohen Group even extends its support to help Chinese state-owned enterprises, often used as tools of the Chinese state.

In 2018, as the United States and other Western countries were grappling with a myriad of contentious economic issues with Beijing, William Cohen sat down in Switzerland with the man who heads up China's state-owned enterprises and "expressed willingness to support and assist Chinese central SOEs' [state-owned enterprises] international operations, especially their business expansion in Europe and the United States, with his company's global resources."[57]

Like Kissinger and Albright, Cohen is a regular—even frequent—voice on national security matters, including China. In addition to his lucrative consulting business, Cohen has also served as the vice chairman of the U.S.-China Business Council, a lobbying group. He also sits on the board of the network CBS and is a trustee at the Center for Strategic and International Studies, a prestigious Washington-based think tank.[58] In 2006, he even penned a China-themed thriller called *Dragon Fire*. The plot: a "rogue faction in the Chinese government plots the end of U.S.-Sino cooperation, and only the Secretary of Defense can stop the madness."[59]

Cohen gives dozens of interviews on television networks such as CNN, MSNBC, and elsewhere. But the fact that he is reliant on access to Beijing officials for his business, and even works on behalf of Chinese state-owned enterprises, does not seem to get mentioned when he offers advice on how to deal with China.

Cohen also works as a government advisor in China—specifically to the mayor of Tianjin Municipal Government. He also serves as an honorary professor at Nankai University.[60]

When Huawei was deemed a security threat because of its close ties to the Beijing regime and the Chinese intelligence apparatus, the company hired the Cohen Group to negotiate with the U.S. director of national intelligence to find a way to sell equipment in the United States. Those efforts ultimately failed.[61]

Beyond Kissinger, Albright, and Cohen, plenty of other diplomats and trade officials have set up shop and have done deals in

China. Carla Hills, the former U.S. trade representative, created Hills & Company. There is the Scowcroft Group, headed by former George H. W. Bush national security advisor Brent Scowcroft. Mickey Kantor, the trade representative and commerce secretary during the Clinton administration, negotiated a series of deals with Beijing and then joined the law firm Mayer, Brown, Rowe, & Maw. For good measure, he took two experts in China from the Trade Office with him. Charlene Barshefsky, who had negotiated China's entry into the World Trade Organization on behalf of the Clinton administration, returned to private practice in 2001, joining the law firm WilmerHale, where she headed up—of course—the firm's China team.[62]

* * *

FOLLOWING IN MADELEINE Albright's footsteps, Condoleezza Rice became the second woman to serve as secretary of state, appointed by President George W. Bush in 2005. During the Bush administration, the policies of engagement with China, meaning greater trade, capital investment, and technology transfer, were the order of the day. Indeed, steps were taken to streamline regulations and controls on the export of critical technologies to China. The new rules, ultimately issued through the U.S. Commerce Department, promised "exports for civilian use while denying items that would support China's military modernization."[63]

Robert Gates, who served as secretary of defense during both the Bush and Obama administrations, supported this export of U.S. technologies under the Export Control Reform Initiative.[64]

Those rule changes streamlined efforts to export technologies to China. It also offered these former government officials a business opportunity.

In 2009, after leaving public service, Rice formed a strategic consulting firm that would be eventually called Rice, Hadley, Gates, and Manuel (RHGM). As the name shows, she has powerful partners, including former George W. Bush national security advisor Stephen J. Hadley, as well as Anja Manuel, who held positions in the Bush State Department. Robert Gates added his name to the company placard after he left the Pentagon in 2011.[65]

According to the firm's website, an important component of the business is helping guide companies through those new technology export rules and to "navigate the political, policy, and regulatory problems related to their expansion into China."[66]

These include "technology transfer" issues.[67]

Elsewhere, RHGM says that it "assists in dealing with national security and foreign policy challenges associated with offering sophisticated technologies, products, and services in these overseas markets."[68]

RHGM's client list is secret. We do know that beginning in 2009 the firm established a close relationship with a Swiss-based investor named Marko Dimitrijevic and his investment firm Everest Partners. Dimitrijevic himself managed elements of the George Soros fortune. When Everest failed, its executives created RWC Partners, a new London-based firm. RHGM continued to advise them.[69]

"We . . . have a unique consulting arrangement with Rice, Hadley, Gates and Manuel," explained John M. Malloy, an executive with RWC, in a December 2020 interview. "Condoleezza Rice, the former Secretary of State under Bush, started a consulting firm, and they speak to world leaders, they have contacts, they have very good access."[70]

RWC specializes in emerging market investments, including China. The firm's investments included controversial companies like Hikvision.[71] Hikvision partners with the PRC government to carry out citizen surveillance both in Tibet and upon Uighurs in Xinjiang, acts for which the U.S. government sanctioned it in October 2019.[72]

Hikvision's involvement with Orwellian monitoring of minority populations in China was not a secret. RWC and RHGM had to have an awareness of what the company was doing. Hikvision's role in the surveillance was first raised as early as 2013 in outlets as mundane as *USA Today*.[73] Meanwhile, RWC Partners was happily reporting the profitability of its Hikvision investment at least as late as May 2019. They note that the company has "proven to be a leader in the surveillance theme" of the booming market in China.[74]

Han's Laser is another investment in China.[75] The company is "the Chinese national laser industry's flagship" and produces lasers with a military manufacturing application.[76]

RHGM casts a much smaller shadow than the other consulting firms. Rice and Gates have been critical of China. But their commercial interests—and the necessities of access in Beijing—create powerful incentives to limit their criticisms of the regime and to avoid recommending restrictions of technologies transfers and capital investments in military-linked Chinese firms.

RHGM partner Anja Manuel has been particularly outspoken on tech issues relating to China. While arguing that the United States needs to spend more on research and development to stay ahead of China in the tech race, she generally opposes efforts to restrict cooperation between American firms and Chinese tech companies. When the U.S. government and several allies, including Australia and Great Britain, were working to restrict the flow of technology to Huawei because of its ties to the Chinese military and intelligence services, she criticized the move as "really quite draconian."[77]

"Chinese Tech Isn't the Enemy," was the title of an *Atlantic* article she wrote on the theme. "America needs to work with China to get ahead in tech."[78]

Manuel has additional motives beyond RHGM to see greater tech cooperation between the two countries. She sits on the board of directors of MoneyGram, a money transfer company. When a Chinese finance company tried to buy it in January 2018, the deal was blocked by the U.S. government on national security grounds.[79]

* * *

WHEN ANSON BURLINGAME was appointed minister to the Qing Imperial Court in the nineteenth century, China was considered a diplomatic backwater. Better to be posted in London, Paris, or Tokyo. Today, the post of U.S. ambassador to the People's Republic of China is an important position because of the rivalry and commercial links between the two countries. While ambassadors do not quite have the prestige of the secretary of state, they do sit at the crossroads of enormously important relationships that can help make or break major deals.

Unfortunately, recent U.S. ambassadors to China have used that position to go to work on behalf of Chinese entities after leaving the diplomatic service.

Gary Locke was a rising star in American politics. The son of Chinese immigrants, he had received an Ivy League education and entered politics in Washington State early. He served as a prosecutor, then as a member of the state legislature. In 1996, he was elected governor, the first Chinese-American elected to that office in the United States.[80] But during his gubernatorial run, he received the financial support and aggressive backing of several donors implicated in the "Chinagate" fundraising scandal that rocked Washington, D.C. John Huang, who pleaded guilty to violating federal election laws in connection with fundraising for the Clinton campaign, organized two fundraisers for Locke in Washington, D.C., three more in Los Angeles, and yet another in Universal

City, California. He also donated to Locke's campaign personally, as did Ted Sioeng, an Indonesian business mogul. The U.S. Justice Department believed that Sioeng was acting on behalf of the Chinese government in his donation activities during Chinagate. In 1998, Locke also took nearly $14,000 in donations from monks and nuns who were members of a Buddhist temple in Redmond, Washington. That was a surprise given that they had taken vows of poverty, spoke little English, and when asked, did not recall donating to Locke's campaign.[81]

After leaving the Washington State governorship in 2005, Locke joined the Seattle-based law firm Davis Wright Tremaine, which did significant business in China. Indeed, that would be central to Locke's work at the firm. His focus was on lobbying and trade deals. Locke boasted that he had high-level access in Beijing, helping clients navigate certain regulatory requirements. As the *Seattle Times* stated at the time, "Locke has parlayed his experience and ancestry to an elevated perch at the apex of power in a country where politicians still have a heavy hand in business." Indeed, Locke met the second most powerful man in China, where they convened in the walled compound of the central government's inner sanctum. He said he hoped to demonstrate to people that "China's growth doesn't harm Americans." Joseph Borich, president of the Washington State China Relations Council, said Locke was "extremely well-liked" by the Chinese leadership. They had an "appreciation" for him.[82]

Locke also did legal work for politically connected Chinese firms. He had financial ties to the HNA Group, a controversial Chinese company with a reputation for courting American political figures.[83]

"They trust Gary, and they trust him not to bring up the most difficult issues in the relationship, or to keep them in a very compartmentalized part of the dialogue," said Professor David Bachman of the University of Washington.[84]

In 2009, Locke was tapped to join the Obama administration as the commerce secretary, where his portfolio included handling commercial ties with Beijing.[85] He met with the Chinese foreign minister in Washington, and traveled to China.[86]

In 2011, President Obama gave him another assignment, appointing him U.S. ambassador to Beijing. He was quickly confirmed by the U.S. Senate. The move meant that he needed to sell his six-bedroom, five-bathroom house in Bethesda, Maryland. But the home sat on the market for more than two years, until September 2013, when a Chinese couple paid the asking price for it. Huaidan Chen, an executive with American Pacific International Capital (APIC), paid $1.68 million for it—more than $150,000 over what Locke had paid. APIC had deep ties to China. In the next chapter we will see how she was involved in the illegal transfer of $1.3 million in campaign contributions to the Jeb Bush presidential campaign.[87]

As U.S. ambassador, Locke listed the sale on his federal financial disclosure, but curiously, he listed it under "rents and royalties" instead of capital gains. When a reporter asked the U.S. State Department about whether ethics officials reviewed such transactions, the astonishing answer was no. "There is no requirement for any State Department official to clear the sale of his or her personal residence with ethics officials at the department, regardless of the value of the property. The department does not review or approve the terms of sale for an employee's private residence."[88]

It emerged later that the purchase of the home was not a random event. Locke had first met APIC's president Gordon Tang (Huaidan Chen's husband) in 2008 during a ribbon-cutting ceremony for a Chinese factory owned by APIC. In fact, Locke had provided legal services to APIC before heading to Washington, D.C., to become commerce secretary in 2009. Just before the home purchase, Locke had met a man named Wilson Chen in Beijing, who happened to be Huaidan Chen's brother and who sat on the board of APIC.

According to Wilson Chen, Locke complained at the time that his house was sitting on the market for months and he was disappointed with his real estate agent.

Locke was "desperate to sell," Chen recalled.[89]

Soon after, Chen and Tang bought it.

In short, wealthy foreign nationals from a country where Locke represented the United States bought his home after he had told of his desperation to someone well known to them.

Curiously, three months after the home purchase, Wilson Chen got a choice invitation to an exclusive meeting with Ambassador Locke at the U.S. Embassy. The meeting was to discuss real estate opportunities in the United States. Others attended the conclave, but APIC was by far the smallest player in the room.[90]

The fact that Ambassador Locke saw no problem in receiving a financial favor from a Chinese business couple while he was representing the United States in that country is quite astonishing.

Locke's biggest test as U.S. ambassador emerged in 2012 when a famed Chinese dissident named Chen Guangcheng showed up at the U.S. Embassy seeking help. Known affectionately as "the barefoot lawyer," Chen is legally blind and active in human rights issues in China—a courageous man and a considerable thorn in the government's side. Having made an amazing escape from communist captivity, slipping past a police cordon around his small farmhouse, spending nineteen hours on the run, he arrived at the U.S. Embassy.[91]

Chen's life was on the line, and he wanted political asylum in the United States. His presence at the embassy, however, stood to be a major embarrassment to the Chinese Communist Party.

Ambassador Locke was in the middle of it, and as Chen would later recall, the American embassy team left a lot to be desired when it came to standing up for basic freedoms. Heated negotiations took place between the Chinese and the Americans about Chen's fate. Remarkably, the Americans were proposing that he stay in China and study at New York University's Shanghai campus. Beijing demurred, but promised to protect his rights. Chen said that he felt pressured by the Americans to accede to Chinese demands. He was mystified by American approval only of options that kept him in China and at risk.

"If it weren't a question of my safety, then why would I have come here?" he asked. "If there were anywhere else in China I could go where I felt safe, why would I have come to the American Embassy?"[92] The dissident was perplexed.

"I wondered if the Americans fully understood the power Chinese officials have over ordinary citizens," he later wrote. He found himself "exasperated at having to defend the idea of basic freedoms to American officials."

After a series of negotiations, Chen emerged from the U.S. Embassy with Ambassador Gary Locke holding his left arm. They were headed to a Beijing hospital to receive medical attention for his injured foot.[93] "Senior U.S. officials in Beijing who helped negotiate Chen's case say the activist left the diplomatic compound of his own free will," reported Voice of America. "In a background briefing with reporters, the officials said Chen consistently stated his desire to stay and work in China."

Chen, however, had a very different account of what had transpired. He said he felt "pressured" by U.S. officials to leave the embassy.[94]

Chen eventually was able to leave China and settle in the United States to continue his fight for human rights.[95]

But Locke's efforts to defuse the situation with Chen no doubt

won him new friends in Beijing. After he finished his tenure as
U.S. ambassador in 2014, he rejoined Davis Wright Tremaine,
which was still handling major deals in China. "We are delighted
with Gary's decision to join us as a leader in our China and government relations group," explained the firm's chairman.

Locke also set up his own advisory firm called Locke Global
Strategies.

The Chinese executives who had purchased his house also hired
him as a "senior advisor."[96] Locke began giving frequent speeches
at conferences "as an expert on the ways Chinese business interests
can invest in the United States."[97]

Locke was eager to note his deep ties with Chinese officials. "I
have good contacts and good relationships with high-ranking government officials throughout China," he declared.[98] No surprise:
many of his opportunities would come from Chinese government-
connected firms.

Now back in private life, he was unrestrained in his praise for
the regime and President Xi. He touted China as "the world's most
modern civilization" in an interview with state media, ignoring, of
course, the myriad of human rights abuses in the country.

"President Xi Jinping has done an excellent job as president,"
he proclaimed, while praising initiatives designed to challenge
America's position globally. "He has great presence and visibility
around the world. The Belt and Road Initiative is receiving positive reviews around the world, especially in those undeveloped
countries that will benefit. He is doing very well in talking about
the needs of global cooperation and avoiding protectionism. He
has done much to help bring stability and prosperity to the people
of China."[99]

It was a ringing endorsement of the authoritarian leader, one
who heads a country in which he hoped to do a lot of business.

In 2016, Locke was invited to join the board of AMC Entertainment, a Chinese-owned theater chain. He replaced board member Jian Wang.[100] China's Wanda Group had bought AMC in 2012.[101] The founder and chairman of Wanda Group was Wang Jianlin, who has also served as a deputy to the National Congress of the Communist Party.[102] A wide array of observers, from Republicans in Congress to the *Washington Post* editorial board, expressed alarm at the company possibly using its power to censor film content that would be critical of Beijing.[103] And now Locke was on the board and would receive handsome stock options.[104]

In December 2016, Locke became the chairman of the advisory board for something called the NW Innovation Works (NWIW). The name was innocuous-sounding enough. The business planned to develop one of the most "environmentally responsible, advance manufacturing plants ever built," by constructing a methane gas plant in Washington State, with the products exported to China.[105] The project even enjoyed support from the highest levels of the Chinese government, including President Xi.[106]

Who was behind the project? That would be a company called Chinese Academy of Sciences Holdings, or appropriately CASH. The company is an investment vehicle run by the Chinese government.[107] Wu Lebin is the chairman of CASH, and prides his entity's operation for following the "national strategy" as laid out by the government.[108] A look at the organizational structure of CASH shows the "State" at the top of the pyramid, followed by the Chinese Academy of Sciences (CAS), which in turn runs CASH. The government's role and the tight relationship between CAS and CASH is unmistakable.[109] CAS has deep ties to the Chinese military, developing weapons systems for cyber warfare, the navy, and other branches of the armed forces.[110]

As the U.S. Department of Defense reveals, CAS "reports directly to the State Council . . . with much of its work contributing to products for military use."[111]

With all of these commercial bonds with Beijing, Locke contin-ues to appear on U.S. national television opining on China rela-tions. His posture is generally soft and uncritical of Beijing. When the Biden administration pushed back on China over human rights violations, Locke argued on CNN: "That's a subject matter they're very, very sensitive to because they think it's other countries med-dling in their internal affairs and they're trying to push back and say basically: who are you, the United States, to lecture us on hu-man rights and civil rights and so forth when you have your own problems?"

His financial links to Beijing were never discussed. He was sim-ply identified as "a former U.S. Ambassador to China."[112]

* * *

THE MAN WHO succeeded Gary Locke as U.S. ambassador was an-other politician, Senator Max Baucus of Montana. Baucus was one of the most powerful people on Capitol Hill. And like Locke, he would find ways to translate his service at the embassy into a lucra-tive career helping Chinese firms, while at the same time taking Beijing's side in its trade dispute with the United States.

Baucus had long been a booster of closer ties with Beijing. For decades, Baucus sat on the Senate Finance Committee, which handles trade issues with China. He played an essential role in the U.S.-China Bilateral Investment Treaty, "which sets the rules for U.S. investments in China and vice versa."[113] That treaty has been roundly criticized for empowering Chinese efforts to force Amer-ican firms to turn over their technology in order to do business in the country.[114]

Former staffers from his Senate years remember Baucus was of-ten fascinated about business opportunities in China. "There were times when I said, Senator, I know you love China, but we need to allocate appropriate time vis-à-vis the time you spend on China and trade issues versus what you spend on [other issues]," recalled Russ Sullivan, a former staff director of the Senate Finance Committee that Baucus chaired. "If you were in the multinational business community interested in China, you knew Max Baucus was going over there."[115]

As a senator, Baucus was a strong supporter of retaining China's most-favored-nation (MFN) trading status and not letting concerns about human rights get in the way. "Nothing can set freedom back farther than revoking M.F.N.," he claimed, to the benefit of Beijing.[116]

Baucus also championed China's membership in the WTO and made the same well-worn arguments of so many others featured in this book: embracing China would liberalize the country and help American manufacturing. During the opening hearings of the Senate Finance Committee concerning the WTO, he explained that letting Beijing join "should contribute to the development of a more open, market-oriented society in which not only are people bound by the laws and regulations, but so will be the government."[117]

Of course, history did not turn out that way.

As a U.S. senator, Baucus never wanted to use America's economic leverage with China to address sensitive issues including military activities in the South China Sea or human rights violations. In short, he took off the table the most important form of influence the United States had over China.[118]

When Baucus became ambassador, tensions were rising between the Obama administration and Beijing. But his tenure in Beijing was largely noneventful.

Shortly after he left as ambassador, Baucus started lining up Chinese clients. In 2017, along with his wife, Melodee Hanes (a former Senate staffer), he founded the Baucus Group. The firm specializes in advising Chinese firms as well as American firms looking to do business in China. Like so many others, he made a point of marketing his close ties to Beijing's gatekeepers and his ability to make things happen with Chinese officials.[119]

Two Chinese firms quickly signed him up. A firm called Ingram Micro put him on the board of directors. Based in Irvine, California, Ingram Micro had been acquired in 2016 by China's HNA Group, which had strong connections to the Chinese government. HNA director Chen Feng openly declared that the company would "consciously safeguard the Communist Party's central authority with General Secretary Xi Jinping as the core" and "unswervingly follow the party."[120]

Alibaba, the Chinese tech giant closely linked to the Chinese government and Communist Party, placed Baucus on their board of advisors. Baucus served the company until May 2019.[121]

In his home state of Montana, the former ambassador set up the Max S. Baucus Institute at the University of Montana Law School, with a "China Summer Study Abroad" component to its programs.[122] He was also an enthusiastic supporter of the Confucius Institute established at the University of Montana, participating in their activities.[123] UM history professor Steven Levin, who is fluent in Chinese, was partly responsible for bringing the Chinese government-backed institute to the state. "Frankly, now I regret it because the Confucius Institute . . . is in fact an instrument of Chinese soft power." He went on: "The teachers are very carefully vetted to make sure that they don't differ one syllable from any of the official lines in Beijing."[124]

Back in China, Baucus also became a featured guest on Chinese state-owned television, where he quickly established a tone that was far more critical of Washington than Beijing. He appeared on China Global Television Network (CGTN), a mouthpiece for the communist regime, in 2020. During the height of the coronavirus, there were deep concerns about Beijing's lack of transparency about the origins of the disease and the disappearance and arrest of doctors who were trying to alert the public.

Baucus went on the attack—but not against Beijing. Instead, he went after those in Washington desiring to hold China accountable.[125]

The segment was about how "President Trump is continuing to blame China for the coronavirus outbreak" and how "China is fighting back."[126]

"Joe McCarthy [and] Adolf Hitler . . . rallied people up, making people believe things that were really not true," he said on May 12, 2020. "The White House and some in Congress are making statements against China that are so over the top and so hypercritical, they are based not on the fact, or if they are based on fact, sheer demagoguery, and that's what McCarthy did in the 1950s."[127]

A few days later, Baucus chatted to the government-run *Global Times*. The United States is entering "a kind of an era which is similar to Joe McCarthy," he told Chinese writers, and "a little bit like Hitler in the '30s." He added, "Today people kind of like to see China get criticized, which is unfortunate, because I think, basically, the American people like the Chinese people, just like Chinese people . . . like American people."[128]

China's propaganda outfits were quick to echo his sentiments. Party-controlled media like the Xinhua News Agency, *Global Times*, and *People's Daily* all enthusiastically reported Baucus's comments.[129]

On May 15, he appeared on CGTN again, claiming that the concerns raised about China were problematic. "There are a lot of pretty smart people in the United States who are not speaking up," he claimed. "People in office, moderates, especially moderates on the Republican side. They are afraid to speak up, they are intimidated, intimidated by President Trump. And it's kind of sliding toward a form of McCarthyism—how it is politically incorrect to speak the truth, speak the truth to power."[130]

There was no mention, of course, of Chinese medical professionals who were afraid of being arrested for speaking up.

It was not the first time Baucus was quoted in Chinese government news outlets. In March 2018, he had an interview with the *People's Daily.* On this occasion, he criticized the U.S. position on tariffs on Chinese goods, which he said were the "wrong policy" and "too confrontational."[131]

As the Trump administration sought increasing oversight of Chinese companies, particularly those linked to the Chinese military, Baucus advised Chinese firms to hang tough.

"Hang in there," he coached them in a webinar with the China General Chamber of Commerce, and "keep building those relationships as much as you can," since "this too shall pass," and the enmity with China will eventually "die down."[132]

When the United States and other countries began to impose sanctions on individual Chinese government officials over their involvement in genocide against the Uighurs, Baucus went on CNBC and dismissed it as causing more problems than it solves.[133]

His commercial ventures in China were never mentioned.

Baucus also linked up with the Chinese government's united front organization China United States Exchange Foundation (CUSEF), which as we saw in chapter 3, is so active on Capitol Hill making Beijing's case before U.S. lawmakers.[134] His wife and business partner lists the foundation as one of her interests on her LinkedIn account.[135]

In March 2021, Baucus was hired by the Chinese-owned cryptocurrency exchange company Binance as a "policy and government relations advisor."[136] The firm was launched by Changpeng Zhao in China in 2017. Shortly after Baucus joined the company, it was announced that Binance was being investigated by the U.S. government for money laundering and tax charges.[137]

* * *

THE ELECTION OF Donald Trump in 2016 set off a global earthquake, especially in China, where Trump's rhetoric about the country's trade and financial practices was alarming.

The man whom Trump appointed to follow Locke and Baucus to the ambassadorship was yet another politician.

Terry Branstad was a political institution in Iowa: he had served as the Republican governor of the state throughout the 1980s and '90s and again from 2011 to 2017. At first glance, he might appear to be an unusual choice for U.S. ambassador to Beijing. But Iowa does big business with China, especially with selling farm commodities like pork and soybeans. Branstad had an important personal connection as well: he was officially an "old friend of the Chinese People," in the words of China's President Xi, because the governor and president were quite literally "old friends." The two had first met back in 1985 when Xi was visiting Iowa as part of an official delegation representing Hebei province, Iowa's "sister state" in China.[138]

Trump's election as president came with a promise to get tougher on China. Beijing was flexing its muscle in the South China Sea, but there was also growing resentment about China's economic and technology policies.[139] With Branstad's appointment as U.S. ambassador, the Trump transition team emphasized that the governor "supports President-elect Trump's mission to negotiate trade deals that put America's interests first."[140]

For that reason, Branstad was a curious choice for Trump. For most of his career, he had been a champion of closer commercial ties to China. Indeed, members of his family would directly benefit from increasing commerce. For this reason, publications like the *Economist* said his appointment was a "conciliatory signal to Beijing."[141]

Beijing clearly saw it that way.

Branstad's friendship with Xi was not necessarily a bad thing. Personal bonds can be enormously helpful in resolving a diplomatic impasse. But such friendships can also cloud judgments. Branstad, who had known Xi for decades, appears to have seriously underestimated what the Chinese leader would be like when he assumed the top spot in China. In 2012, Xi made a return visit to Iowa, shortly after Branstad reclaimed the Iowa governorship. During the visit, the governor gave his assessment of Xi. Branstad told China Central Television (CCTV) that Xi was a "progressive" who was trying to "open China." He went on: "He's very personal. When we had the state dinner in Des Moines, about half or maybe even over half of his remarks were personal, off-script. I was impressed with that, and I think it was very sincere and very genuine."[142]

Branstad's assessment of Xi's easy manner proved to be correct and a much-commented-on feature of the leader's style. But his views about his desires to "open China" proved to be completely wrong.

As U.S. ambassador, Branstad pushed Trump to back down on restrictions on goods and services trading despite the ongoing trade disputes, while leaving unaddressed "the more fundamental complaints of the American side."[143]

Branstad may have been partially blinded by his friendship with Xi. More troubling were the strong financial ties that his family enjoyed with Chinese entities that would provide powerful incentives for him to be soft on Beijing.

One Branstad son, Marcus, is a registered lobbyist for the American Chemistry Council (ACC).[144] The ACC was adamantly opposed to Trump's actions on China, arguing that "[we] deeply value our trade relationship with China and believe it is critical to the continued expansion and success of our industry." They wanted the Trump administration to "return to the negotiating table and rescind these destructive tariffs."[145] Despite its name, the American Chemistry Council also includes Chinese companies as members, including the Wanhua Chemical Group, one of the world's largest chemical producers. While one can buy stock in the company, the "ultimate controlling shareholder of the firm is a division of the Assets Supervision and Administration Commission of China, the government entity that oversees state-owned enterprises."[146]

Another son, Eric, joined the Trump campaign and served as the Iowa director during the 2016 election.[147] Like his father, he was rewarded with a federal job once Trump entered the Oval Office. In 2017, he became the U.S. Commerce Department's liaison to the White House.[148]

He was at the epicenter of the looming trade dispute between Washington and Beijing, and he immediately began making the rounds. He attended a Chinese-government-backed China General Chamber of Commerce Gala in Chicago. According to Chinese state media, the organization's gala is designed to highlight those who have "contributed significantly to increasing Chinese industry and relations" in the United States.

"The U.S.-China relationship is simply too important not to get right," he told the government's Xinhua News Agency.[149]

The younger Branstad was not a faceless political appointee. He traveled with President Trump for a November 2017 trade mission to China. According to documents obtained by the Intercept, he also seemed to use his tenure at Commerce to cultivate opportunities in the lobbying game. While still there, he met with a friend, Bryan Lanza, who worked at the lobbying firm Mercury and represented Chinese companies. One meeting he took included Chinese executives.[150]

In June 2018, shortly after he left the Trump administration,

Eric Branstad made a trip to Shanghai, traveling with Lanza and Li Zhao, an Iowa-based business consultant. (Zhao was investigated by the FBI in connection with a case involving the theft of intellectual property for the benefit of Beijing but was never charged.) Young Branstad was now working for Mercury. (His father, of course, was still U.S. ambassador.) According to the Intercept, which broke the news of this trip, Lanza was directly representing the Chinese telecom ZTE, which was paying Mercury $75,000 a month.[151]

ZTE was in the crosshairs of the Trump administration because of its close ties to the Chinese military and concerns that it might be surveilling global telecommunications networks.

While in China, Branstad and Lanza had "meetings with Chinese government groups," according to the Intercept. One of them, the China Development Research Foundation, had links to the Ministry of State Security.

Branstad told the Intercept that he did not lobby for ZTE on the trip and had no "business or policy discussions" with the Chinese entities. He was in China, he claimed, to "culturally connect and show good feelings."[152]

According to Chinese officials in their accounts of the meetings posted online, they did in fact discuss issues and policies, some of which were close to concerns about ZTE. During the trip, Eric also delivered an odd but self-serving speech. Speaking before a government-backed group on the topic "How to React to (Potential) U.S.-China Trade War?" he announced before more than one hundred lawyers, bankers, and advisors that he had joined Mercury. He was clearly fishing for clients. Attendees noted that Branstad "highlighted his personal relationship with Mr. Trump and plans for his firm to open a China office."[153]

Weeks after the trip to Beijing, the U.S. Commerce Department announced that it had come to terms with ZTE.[154]

The firm that Branstad joined had a myriad of Chinese clients beyond ZTE, including Hikvision, who, as we noted previously, works with the Chinese government to monitor its citizens.[155]

America's diplomats are hired and paid to look out for our national interests. They take an oath to do exactly so. But how effective can they be at their jobs if they are looking down the road and seeing fat fees by doing business deals in Beijing? The revolving door is a permanent fixture in Washington, D.C. Usually, it spins between the U.S. government and American businesses. Diplomats have globalized it—and far too often gone into business with our chief rival on the global stage. Beijing knows this, and through seduction and perhaps even cajoling, manages to put many of America's national security and diplomatic figures on the payroll.

Gathering favor with Beijing is not just profitable for former diplomats; it is also transferrable to others within political families. Let us explore two of the most prominent political families in North America and dissect how they were enriched. And how favorable ties with Beijing can be transferred from generation to generation, which makes those relationships all the more tantalizing.

7

THE BUSH AND
TRUDEAU DYNASTIES

In 2019, Neil Bush, son of one American president and brother of another, took the stage at an event in Hong Kong. Tensions were rising as people in Hong Kong were protesting the increasing restrictions on their rights by Chinese government authorities. Bush had stern words—not for Beijing, but for politicians back in Washington. "I'd advise my American friends not to meddle in the internal affairs of China," he declared. Bush went on with a bizarre claim that the dictatorial regime would be restricted when it came to repression. "If the Chinese government gets carried away with denying basic rights, then there will be a pushback from within," he claimed, without offering any evidence. "Once people enjoy the taste of freedom, there is no turning back."[1]

Neil Bush, who has a cluster of financial ties to Chinese political elites in Beijing, is a frequent voice on Chinese state television. He has nice things to say about the government—just not politicians in Washington. In 2019, when the U.S. Congress passed the "Hong Kong Human Rights and Democracy Act," calling out Beijing for a massive and violent crackdown in the city, Bush shot back that those who voted for the bill were not "well enough informed" about the true state of "freedom and democracy."

"I don't understand what freedoms are not enjoyed by Hong Kong people," Neil declared.[2]

Sometimes, Beijing finds influential Westerners who are true be-
lievers. They believe they are being given lucrative opportunities in
industries they know about because China is the new land of opportunity. They believe the Chinese system is creating unparalleled economic justice. They believe China will eventually become a force for
good in the world. When China finds people like that, they shower
their families with economic and political rewards.

In 2013, the son of a Canadian prime minister—and future prime
minister himself—was standing in front of a small group of political
donors. He was fielding questions, and someone asked him about
which country's "administration he most admired." Justin Trudeau,
then a young member of parliament (MP), thought for a moment,
smiled, and responded: "There is a level of admiration I actually have
for China . . . because their basic dictatorship is allowing them to
actually turn their economy around on a dime and say 'we need to
go greenest, fastest—we need to invest in solar.' I mean, there is flex-
ibility that I know Stephen Harper [the Canadian prime minister at
the time] must dream about of having a dictatorship that he can do
everything he wanted, and I find that quite interesting."[3]

It might be easy to dismiss Bush's comments as unimportant. He
was, after all, the Bush son who always seems to get into trouble.
Or one could dismiss Justin Trudeau's admiration for a "basic dictatorship" as an error or simply youthful daydreaming. But in both
instances, these sons of notable political families enjoy deep and
complex histories with Beijing that have benefited both of them.
Their families became wealthier courtesy of Beijing's largesse, and in
the case of Trudeau, his political fortunes have bloomed as a result
of those ties.

As we have seen in previous chapters, Beijing's courtship and seduction of elites can happen quickly—the result of a single deal with
a powerful American figure. At other times, the relationship and ties
grow over the course of years. In this particular case, those bonds

have been strengthened over decades, as the Beijing regime has quietly and steadily worked to cultivate opportunities to get "the foreign
to serve China."[4]

Let us explore these two prominent political families and trace
how Beijing has worked to cultivate warm relations, helping these
families become wealthier and more sympathetic to the Beijing
regime.

George H. W. Bush was a Texas oilman and former congressman
with an Ivy League pedigree when, in 1974, he was appointed chief
of the U.S. Liaison Office to the People's Republic of China. (The
United States did not have full diplomatic relations at the time so he
was the senior U.S. representative in the country.) His job was to
be the face of the United States in a communist country that was just
slightly opening up to the outside world.[5] Those duties also created
opportunities for him to develop meaningful relationships with Chinese government officials that would serve his family for generations.
"My hyper-adrenaline, political instincts tell me that the fun of this
job is going to be to try to do more, make more contacts," he wrote in
his first diary entry while in China. "And it is my hope that I will be
able to meet the next generation of China's leaders—whomever they
may prove to be." Bush served in Beijing for just over fourteen months
before heading back to Washington to head the Central Intelligence
Agency.[6] On the eve of his departure, Chinese leader Deng Xiaoping
threw him a going-away party. "You are our old friends," said Deng.
"You are welcome to come back anytime in the future."[7]

And return to China they did.

In 1981, George H. W. Bush was sworn in as vice president
of the United States. Within a year, his older brother, Prescott
Bush Jr., made his first visit to China.[8] Prescott, who lived in
Greenwich, Connecticut, and worked in the insurance brokerage
business, started making deals in China.[9]

As George H. W. Bush continued his political climb, the deals continued to roll in for his brother. By February 1989, George was in the Oval Office, and Prescott was off for a series of meetings in Beijing. The timing of Prescott's trip was precise: his brother, the president, was scheduled for an official visit just ten days later. Prescott closed a deal to build a golf club in Shanghai for foreign business executives. It was one of the few golf courses in China that received government approvals required for construction. Etched out of the ground along the Huangpu River, the exclusive club later hosted the China LPGA "Shanghai Classic." The mayor of Shanghai during negotiations for the golf course, Jiang Zemin, became a Bush family friend who later became the premier of China. The Bush family had collected another powerful ally.[10]

During that same trip, Prescott met with Chinese officials to discuss another business venture, which included the creation of an international satellite communications network in the country. At the time, a New York financial firm called Asset Management International Financing and Settlement Ltd., which was hoping to finance the deal, was paying Prescott.[11]

In June 1989, the horrific events of Tiananmen Square happened. The Western world significantly curtailed its commercial ties to Beijing in protest. But Prescott Bush continued working. Shortly after the massacre, he visited mainland China. "We aren't a bunch of carrion birds coming to pick the carcass," he insisted to the *Wall Street Journal*. "But there are big opportunities in China, and Americans can't afford to be shut out."[12]

In December 1989, President Bush was grappling with a decision concerning existing sanctions against China that had been erected only months earlier. He was considering lifting restrictions on the export of civilian satellite technologies to China. Beijing was hoping to launch three communications satellites built by Hughes Aircraft. The problem was that his brother Prescott was being paid $250,000 a year as a business consultant for Asset Management, which was financing the deal. President Bush did eventually grant the waiver for the satellite exports to Beijing. The Bushes denied that the lifting of sanctions and Prescott's involvement in the deal were related.[13]

President Bush was concerned about appearances and had Secretary of State James A. Baker send a cable to every U.S. embassy telling them not to have "any appearance of preferential treatment" for any deals involving his brother or other members of his family.[14] But the move clearly had little, if any, effect on the Bush family's mounting deals in China. Any restrictions applied only to the U.S. embassy— not the Beijing government or the Bush family.

In 1993, after President Bush left office, Prescott helped start the U.S.-China Chamber of Commerce (USCCC), to serve as a lobby for deeper commercial ties. "My brother, George, has been instrumental in the development of U.S. and China relations since 1974," he wrote in a pitch letter.[15] The organization touts the perks of membership including "access to important contacts," "opportunities to host delegations from China," and more.[16] Prescott Bush's USCCC client list included Chinese state-owned companies with military links, including COSCO.[17]

Chinese officials no doubt hoped that deals done with the Bush family would redound to their benefit by bonding the family to their success. So, when George W. Bush was elected president in 2000, more commercial opportunities arose. Beijing valued its ties to the Bushes and sent as its new ambassador to Washington an old Bush family friend. Ambassador Yang Jiechi was an experienced diplomat who had first made contact with the Bushes in 1977, when George H. W. Bush had made a return visit to China. Yang served as his interpreter and host. The Bush family even had a nickname for the new ambassador: they called him "Tiger" Yang.[18]

Shortly after George W. Bush became America's commander in chief, a Hong Kong–based company called Plus Holdings hired Prescott Bush as a special advisor. In 2003, they made him honorary chairman.[19] "He has many friends in China," said the company's website at the time.[20]

Prescott collected an impressive array of financial partners in China, including a "close working relationship" with Rong Yiren, a former Chinese government trade minister and vice president. He was known as the "Red Capitalist."[21]

When the issue of his commercial deals with politically connected businesspeople in China would come up, Prescott claimed that they had nothing to do with his family's political power. "I don't get a lot of business because my nephew is president or my brother was president," he boldly claimed. Still, he conceded, "You can meet a lot of people because of it."[22]

He did go on to admit that the family was well liked in Beijing. "We are regarded well, if I may say so myself, by the Chinese."[23]

With George W. Bush as president, Beijing officials were banking on his father influencing his views on China. Jiang Zemin, friends with both former President Bush and his brother Prescott, explained, "The father of President [George W.] Bush, Bush Sr., came over to China many, many times and had many meetings with me in the seat you are now occupying," he told one reporter. "We believe Bush Sr. will definitely push Bush Jr. to bring U.S.-China relations to a new level."[24]

During the George W. Bush presidency, a new generation of Bushes began securing deals with Chinese officials. Neil Bush, brother of the president, signed a contract with a Chinese company called Grace Semiconductor Manufacturing. Bush had no background in computing, but the firm paid him $400,000 a year. The company's cofounder just happened to be Chinese premier Jiang Zemin's son.[25] Neil also set up a firm called Interlink Management Corporation, which would work with Chinese-linked firms like Charoen Pokphand Group, which is based out of Thailand and was then run by a CEO of Chinese descent.[26]

Doors swung wide open for Neil Bush in China. In 2009, he helped Chinese state-controlled oil giant Sinopec bid on an oil contract in Africa.[27]

In 2016, Neil helped launch still yet another firm, Asia and America (A&A) Consultants, "which focuses on cross border business development, mergers and acquisitions, fund management and financial advisory."[28] Neil founded the firm with "a former senior government PRC official," according to the company website, and provides advice for dealing with "large-scale enterprises under the administration of the PRC central government, local state-owned enterprises, and private enterprises." To top it off, the firm even included a reference to Neil's father, explaining A&A is "the sole institution founded by direct member of [a] U.S. presidential legacy in China."[29]

Today, Neil remains firmly wedded to Chinese companies. He serves as the chairman of SingHaiyi Group Ltd., a real estate holding company.[30] He is also the cochairman of CIIC, a real estate company in Beijing, and deputy chairman of Hong Kong Finance Investment Holding Group (HKFI) Ltd. Hui Chi Ming, a politically active member of the Chinese People's Political Consultative Conference (CPPCC), leads this shadowy firm. The CPPCC meets regularly in Beijing to advise the Chinese government. In 2019, the firm paid Neil about $77,000, according to the corporate annual report. It is unclear whether he has secured stock options.[31]

Neil Bush is not just involved in Chinese business deals. His value to Beijing includes the work he does through an organization called the George H. W. Bush Foundation for U.S.-China Relations. He is a frequent fixture on Chinese state media and makes appearances before government-linked think tanks where he has made dubious and troubling comments about the nature of the Beijing regime.

In July 2019, he appeared at an event arranged by the aforementioned government-linked front organization China-U.S. Exchange Foundation (CUSEF). The former member of the First

Family lashed out at the "America first" rhetoric of the Trump administration and generally argued that Washington needed to stop seeing China as an existential threat. "China is not an economic enemy or existential national security threat to the United States. . . . The demonization of China is being fueled by a rising nationalism in the U.S. that is manifested in anti-immigrant, anti-Chinese, pro-America-first rhetoric," he proclaimed. He had nothing to say about rising nationalism in China, nor Xi's stated ambitions. Naturally, the Beijing government loved what he had to say.[32]

It has recently come to light that beginning in 2019, CUSEF became a major donor to the Bush China Foundation. The pledge was to contribute $1 million per year for five years beginning in 2019. This amount would constitute a large portion of the nonprofit's income. While a spokesperson claimed that the gift would not influence the foundation's efforts, it is hard to imagine that Neil Bush would find cause to be critical of Beijing in the future, given his defense of bad behavior as described above.[33]

***

JEB BUSH, A very successful two-term governor of Florida, traveled to the Chinese province of Hainan in search of opportunities after he left office. An island off the southern coast, often called the Hawaii of China, Hainan had been a place of drama under his brother George's tenure in the White House, when that Chinese fighter jet collided with the U.S. Navy surveillance plane over the South China Sea. You will recall that the American plane made an emergency landing in Hainan, and that the Chinese held the twenty-four crew members of the aircraft for eleven days.[34]

When Jeb visited Hainan a decade later, he was treated as a visiting dignitary. Bush wore a necklace of flowers, and according to the

Chinese media, the former governor lauded "Hainan's environmental and economic development and spoke hopefully of establishing stronger ties between Hainan and Florida."[35]

Jeb set up a consulting business along with several investment funds. In January 2012, he made a return trip to China. This time he enjoyed the company of the highest-ranking officials in Beijing, including a private meeting in the Great Hall of the People with then Chinese vice president Xi Jinping. (Xi would become president just over a year later.) Xi noted the Bush family's close history with China. "The Bush family has made great contributions to promoting relations between China and the United States, 'which the two nations and the two peoples will not forget,' the Chinese vice president said." In response, Jeb Bush pledged that he would "continue making contributions to the development of bilateral ties and economic cooperation between the two nations."[36]

Seven months after that meeting, Xu Erwen, an ambassador for the People's Republic of China, was in Miami to meet with Jeb Bush.[37]

Doors continued to open in China.

In February 2013, Jeb Bush met with Tan Xiangdong, the president of the HNA Group. The HNA Group has been described as a "mysterious company" with close ties to Beijing's "red aristocracy." According to the HNA website, the purpose of Jeb Bush's meeting was to talk about "cooperation in the broad market between China and the United States."[38]

But it was more than a discussion. It was an opportunity for this red aristocrat to develop a business relationship with a probable candidate for the presidency of the United States. Three months after that meeting, Jeb set up something called Britton Hill Holdings, and brought in several partners with Wall Street experience. However, some of the largest investors in his new venture would be Chinese entities. Britton Hill created an entity called BH Logistics, which raised $26 million to invest in a liquid petroleum shipping company. Among the investors was the HNA Group.[39]

The relationship benefited Bush, but it also helped the politically linked HNA Group avoid public scrutiny. "This is a classic example of the way sophisticated Chinese firms work," explained American Enterprise Institute scholar Derek Scissors at the time. "They don't want to get involved directly in a U.S. startup that's involved in shale, so they'll take a minority stake to keep a lower profile. They're looking for political protection, and the Bush name legitimizes the investment and makes him the perfect partner."[40]

Jeb Bush was not done. His next investment fund was BH Global Aviation, which again found Chinese politically connected investors ready to participate. According to SEC filings, 98 percent of BH Global Aviation's funding came from "non-U.S. persons." Aviation was, of course, an HNA Group strong suit. They already ran a regional airline in China. Among the other investors in Jeb's venture was Guang Yang, CEO of a Beijing-based finance firm called Finergy Capital.[41]

Jeb Bush's prescription for American foreign policy was generally to engage with China but expect them to cheat. "So total engagement with the Chinese is important, and recognizing that they're going to cheat. They're going to push. They're going to constantly probe. And when they see weakness they will move forward."[42]

Engagement was the key—there was no discussion of restricting Beijing's access to American capital and technology. Again, big help with a little badmouth.

In the previous chapter, we met a Chinese couple named Gordon Tang and Huaidan Chen, who had purchased U.S. ambassador Gary Locke's house near D.C. and later put him on the payroll. In 2013, they appointed Neil Bush to the board of their real estate company, SingHaiyi, as chairman.[43] In 2016, with Jeb's presidential

campaign launched, they sent $1.3 million to a SuperPAC support-
ing his candidacy.[44]

A report by the Intercept exposed the donations, and at the behest
of the Campaign Legal Center, the Federal Election Commission
(FEC) investigated. The FEC eventually charged Tang and Chen
with funneling their contributions through their American-based
company, American Pacific International Capital (APIC), to avoid
detection. (Donations from foreign nationals to American political
campaigns are illegal. Both Tang and Chen are Chinese citizens.)
APIC was fined $550,000 and the Right to Rise PAC agreed to pay
$390,000 for "soliciting a foreign national contribution." Jeb Bush
had raised money for Right to Rise but was never directly implicated
in the Chinese donations.[45]

And there was more money coming.

At least nine Chinese nationals linked to Chinese government-
connected front groups became actively involved with the Jeb
Bush 2016 presidential run, and later the Donald Trump campaign.
Cindy Yang attended Jeb Bush's presidential campaign kickoff
event in Miami on June 15, 2015. She had never been politically
active before—but she was firmly linked to Chinese government-
run groups. She served as the vice president of an organization
called the "Florida Association for the Reunification of China,"
which is tied to a Beijing-based entity run by the government.
According to John Dotson, who tracks the organization, it is "directly under the Chinese government and has chapters in several
countries." The president of that Florida group, Xianqin Qu, also
attended the 2015 Bush presidential campaign launch, as did another
board member.[46]

Yet another Chinese national involved with the Bush campaign
was Zhonggang Li, who lived in Boca Raton. He started the South
Florida chapter of a group called the "China Association for Science
and Technology," whose main headquarters is in Beijing. "It's known

as an intermediary for establishing contact with and cultivating ethnic Chinese overseas to encourage them to return knowledge to China," says John Dotson of the Jamestown Foundation.

Li dismissed the idea that he was linked with the Chinese government as "absurd."[47]

"It fits in perfectly with what we know about United Front," says Teufel Dreyer, a professor at the University of Miami. "They try to mobilize all available segments that might be sympathetic to their cause and draw them to their side."[48]

When Bush dropped out of the 2016 Republican primary, Yang and her compatriots started donating to the Trump campaign. Yang gave $37,000 to political action committees linked to Trump, and her husband and parents kicked in another $32,400. None had contributed to any campaigns before 2015.[49]

The Bushes have seen Beijing ties redound to their benefit over decades, profiting multiple generations of the family. George H. W. Bush was viewed in a favorable light by Beijing's leaders, a figure who took positions that were beneficial to China. His family members were rewarded with access to the highest levels of government as well as lucrative business deals.

***

IN CANADA, PERHAPS the most prominent political dynasty in modern times are the Trudeaus. Pierre Trudeau was a flamboyant and passionate labor lawyer who went on to serve as prime minister of Canada for more than a decade. He was philosophically attracted to Communist China and would later cash in on the relationship he enjoyed with the Beijing ruling elite. The torch in the family would be passed to his sons, one of whom, Justin, would enter parliament in 2008 and later ascend to the prime minister's office. As we will see, the family's warm ties to China and China-linked entities play an essential role in their personal fortunes and influence how they govern.

Before the story is told, it is important to note that it is impossible to know the full extent of the Trudeau family's commercial and other ties with Beijing because in 2019 it was revealed that Canada's top spy agency had destroyed its files on Pierre Trudeau thirty years earlier. Trudeau died in 2000, and the documents had been expected to be released in 2020. The move was audacious and denounced by historians as both "outrageous" and a "crime against Canadian history."[50]

Pierre Trudeau was a French Canadian with a "lifelong fixation on China."[51] The interest was initially about ideology. Trudeau was influenced in his early years by socialism. "The party of the people— socialism, communism—will eventually come out the winner," he wrote as a young man.[52]

He first visited China in 1949, as the country was engulfed in the revolutionary violence between the communist forces led by Mao and the nationalist forces of Chiang Kai-shek.[53] He traveled again in 1960 with his friend Jacques Hébert, this time at the request of the communist government. The invitation was unusual; few Westerners were invited to visit the country and Trudeau was hardly a prominent figure at the time. He had yet to enter parliament.[54]

Trudeau and Hébert traveled the country with official guides during the height of the Great Leap Forward, when millions of Chinese were confined, arrested, or killed by the regime. Trudeau later wrote about the trip in a book he coauthored called *Two Innocents in Red China*.[55]

He was enormously sympathetic to the regime and failed to take note of anything involving repression, violence, and death around him. "Goals have no more reality than the means that are devised to reach them. . . . Indeed, the experience of that superb strategist, Mao Tse-tung, might lead us to conclude that in a vast and heterogeneous country, the possibility of establishing socialist strongholds in certain regions is the very best thing," the two wrote.[56] This travelogue of his visit to China is filled with naïveté and revolutionary sloganeering. Trudeau and Hébert posed for pictures with the members of Young Pioneers, the Communist Party Youth Group rich in indoctrination, and proclaimed, "It is these red-scarfed kids who in twenty years will be the New Men of a country which at that time will have a billion inhabitants." While making no mention of the Red Terror that was taking place, they claimed, "The Chinese revolutionaries influence adults, they even give some attention to the old, but it is on the young that they found all their hopes."[57]

The trip afforded Trudeau the rare opportunity to meet with both Chairman Mao and Chou En-lai, his right hand. Why the two young French Canadians were granted such a meeting is unclear.[58] Trudeau was awed by the two brutal leaders. He would regard Mao as "The Great Helmsman," steering the Chinese state as a benevolent leader. Chou En-lai, who helped Mao carry out the Cultural Revolution and the Great Leap Forward, resulting in the estimated deaths of fifty million or more people, he described in warm, congenial terms:

Our firm impression was of a simple person, deeply committed to the communist cause, but not at all with the aim of achieving personal power, one who was almost deferential to all those around him, whether Chinese villagers or foreign guests, a decent human being who attracted respect because of his person, not his position.[59]

Trudeau's book was openly supportive of the communist regime. One friendly reviewer stated, "Observing and conversing with local farmers, Trudeau discovers Chairman Mao Zedong's logic in fomenting his Communist Revolution amongst peasants rather than industrial workers, and gains an understanding into why the 1960s

Cultural Revolution was deemed necessary for communism to triumph."[60]

Trudeau would retain his sympathies for the communist regime, even as the horrors of the Maoist era became well known in the West. Throughout his career, Trudeau was much harsher on the nationalist government in Taiwan than on the communist dictatorship on the mainland. Later, in retirement, he described the nationalists as "dictatorial and brutal," but argued that when it came to mainland China, "To fail to recognize the undoubted successes of the communist regime would be foolhardy."[61]

Beijing authorities were no doubt thrilled with Trudeau's account of Maoist China. On the eve of his son Justin's rise into national politics, a Chinese government-controlled publishing house released a Chinese-language version of the book. (What the Chinese government paid the Trudeaus for the rights to the book is unknown.) The book was launched at a lavish press conference in Shanghai with coauthor Jacques Hébert and Alexandre Trudeau, Justin's younger brother, fielding questions from fifty Chinese journalists. Hébert called the republication of the forty-five-year-old book a "miracle." Alexandre reflects, "Indeed, one must truly ask why it is that, almost half a century after its publication in Canada, a big Chinese publishing house would decide to launch a Chinese edition of this relatively obscure little book."[62]

Why, indeed? Perhaps because it was an opportunity to put some money in the pocket of a powerful political family in Canada and cultivate the relationship further.

Pierre Trudeau was elected to parliament in 1965 and, within a couple of years, decided to seek the leadership of the Liberal Party.[63] He became prime minister in 1968. One of his first acts was to seek and achieve diplomatic relations with Beijing, which occurred in 1970. For good measure, Trudeau dropped diplomatic ties with Taiwan, something that the United States did not do when Richard

Nixon established relations with China in 1972.[64] Mao saw the move by Trudeau as a significant victory, and reportedly said, "Now we have a friend in the US' backyard."[65]

Trudeau continued with his enthusiastic courtship of Beijing. In 1973, the prime minister and his wife made a landmark trip to China and officials pulled out all the stops. His wife, Margaret, recalled about the arrival ceremony, "There were maybe 10,000 children out on the tarmac with ribbons. Some of them were as small as three and four, dancing in perfect symmetry," singing, "Long live the friendship between the peoples of China and Canada!" Margaret Trudeau explained, "The children were very, very disciplined and very courteous."[66] During the visit, her husband, the prime minister, held extensive talks with Chinese officials, with his "most valued memory" of the visit discussing politics with Chou En-lai "far into the night."[67]

When the Trudeaus returned home, the prime minister spoke in parliament in glowing terms about China. He extolled members on the importance of recognizing "the magnitude of one of the most significant revolutions in the history of the world and the extension of basic human amenities to hundreds of millions of persons to whom they had been denied for millennia."[68]

Pierre Trudeau had close ties in Beijing. But critical to his rise in national politics was his alliance with a powerful corporation that wanted to do business with China.

Aptly named, the Power Corporation was headed by a fellow Quebecker, Paul Desmarais, a highly connected businessman who cozied up to political figures and enriched them. His company had supported Trudeau for a long time, beginning in the 1960s when Trudeau sought the leadership of the Liberal Party. "Paul Desmarais collects prime ministers and senior politicians like rare butterflies," said journalist Peter Newman. He adds, "One of his favourite collectibles was Pierre Trudeau."[69]

Desmarais was a forceful advocate for business deals with Beijing.

Like Trudeau, he ignored the repressive nature of the Chinese regime and embraced the brutal leaders as friends. Later, one of the prized paintings displayed on the wall in his palatial home was given to him "by his good friend Li Peng," who gave the infamous orders to declare martial law in China leading to the massacre at Tiananmen Square.[70]

In 1978, the Power Corporation formed the Canada-China Business Council with Prime Minister Trudeau's support. The organization included Canadian business firms, but also the Chinese government-run China International Trust and Investment Corporation (CITIC). The purpose of the Council was not just to help Canadian businesses get access to China, but also to help CITIC invest in Canada.[71] Desmarais, and his role in starting the venture, helped the council "set in motion the beginnings of investment in Canada by Chinese state-owned companies."[72]

Jonathan Manthorpe, a longtime journalist and author of a book about Chinese influence in Canada, calls the Canada-China Business Council "the CCP's principal channel for influence in Canada."[73]

Trudeau and Desmarais guided Canada's relationship with Beijing, with Trudeau as prime minister pushing closer relations with the regime while Desmarais cashed in on significant deals with Beijing's elite. When Trudeau retired from politics, he went to work at Power Corporation, further nurturing those deals and becoming wealthy in the process. The legacy of these arrangements would provide a robust base of support when his son Justin would run for prime minister decades later.

Trudeau continued to be a booster of China throughout his tenure. When he left office in 1984, he remained close to the Chinese regime. Trudeau's fidelity to China financially benefited the family as he exploited his cozy relationships in Beijing. The former prime minister became a consultant for Canadian businesses looking to access the Chinese market. Trudeau could use his ties with Chinese officials to help—for a price. Beijing had long used commercial market access to reward friends, and Canadian companies looking for access to Chinese leaders paid Trudeau handsomely.

Much of his work was for the Power Corporation. He signed on as an "international advisor" to the firm.[74] During his tenure, "Power Corp. has been building its connections at the highest levels of the Chinese government . . . the result has been a series of investments across China in industries as diverse as real estate, rail cars and high technology." There were also joint ventures in Canada with CITIC investing capital along with the company.[75]

Trudeau also became a lawyer at a Montreal firm, where he was paid to help even more companies score meetings with Chinese leaders, including a business delegation to China in 1985.[76] He returned the following year with another group of clients, and officials at the highest levels of the communist government greeted them, including Deng Xiaoping, in the Great Hall of the People.[77]

During the summer of 1989, Trudeau received an invitation from Beijing to visit with two of his sons (including future prime minister Justin Trudeau). Unfortunately, horrific events intervened when the People's Liberation Army sent tanks into Tiananmen Square to attack student protestors. According to Alexandre Trudeau, the family debated: should they still go? Eventually, the Canadian government asked them to stay home—settling the matter. But the following year, the opportunity arose again, and former prime minister Pierre Trudeau brushed aside any qualms about going, aside from the optics. "My father was still a little concerned about appearances," Alexandre recalled.[78]

On the trip, according to Alexandre, his father danced around the subject of Tiananmen Square with government officials. "When called to speak, my father would invariably refer very delicately to the sad difficulties that China had recently faced." "Sad difficulties" almost implied that some external disaster rather than a brutal crackdown had occurred. But Pierre Trudeau would tell his government hosts, "Outsiders simply cannot know what is best for China nor how it need travel down its chosen paths." Trudeau added softly, "It is hard to know how China needs to move forward."[79]

The events of Tiananmen Square appeared to be little more than a nuisance, or a speed bump, in Trudeau's race to work with Beijing.

According to Alexandre, "This awe, this suspension of judgement toward China, never left him."[80] And there is plenty of evidence that those sympathies were passed along to his sons.

In 2008, Justin Trudeau ran for parliament. His father had died eight years earlier, but his name, good looks, and charming demeanor helped him rise quickly through the ranks of the Liberal Party. His views on China were similar to those of his father. Recall that during a 2013 Liberal Party fundraiser in Toronto, he had expressed his admiration for the "basic dictatorship" of China.[81]

It was not just Trudeau's words of admiration for the regime in Beijing—the young MP also endorsed policies that benefited the Chinese state. In 2012, he outlined his support for a controversial energy deal involving the Chinese National Offshore Oil Corporation, which was seeking to acquire the Canadian energy company Nexen. There were concerns about the significant implications to national security and possible damage to "Canadian interests and values." Trudeau's attitude seemed to allow for considerably expanding China's investments in Canada, a view he said stemmed in part because "obviously, my family has historical ties with China."[82]

When Justin Trudeau became prime minister in 2015, Beijing greeted the news with great enthusiasm. The Chinese ambassador to Canada declared his election meant "real change," a move away from the previous government's skepticism about Beijing. He also noted the "extraordinary political vision" of Justin's father.[83] Chinese officials appreciated that his father had not let matters like human rights or geopolitical issues cloud trade. "[Pierre] Trudeau didn't allow much politics to color Canada-China relations," recalled the executive deputy director for the Centre for Canadian Studies at the Guangzhou Institute of Foreign Languages, Tang Xiaosong. "He took politics out of economic and trade relations. . . . The younger Trudeau, I think, will very much follow in the footsteps of his father. Because his father had a very positive stance toward China."[84]

Indeed, in 2016 the state-owned Yilin Press published a Chinese edition of Justin's memoirs retitled as *The Legend Continues*. Beijing's ambassador to Canada proclaimed that he "strongly" recommended the book. Curiously, some of Trudeau's national security aides were not even aware that the rights to his memoir had been sold to Beijing, not finding out until 2021, after being contacted by the media. "I think what gets me is that this is all being sponsored by the propaganda department," said Richard McFadden, a former Trudeau advisor who also served as the head of the Canadian intelligence service. Trudeau's aides would later explain that all profits from the book were going to the Red Cross. But the *Globe and Mail* newspaper could not confirm that claim with either the publisher or the Red Cross.[85]

The Communist Party publication *Global Times* looked at the younger Trudeau's soft spot for Beijing and added, "Junior Trudeau has obviously been influenced by his family's political opinions."[86]

In May 2016, Justin Trudeau was in a beautiful mansion in Toronto for a political fundraiser. At a cost of $1,500 a head, it was a small, elite affair with only thirty-two people in attendance—perhaps not so unusual for a politician. In this case, however, the host of the event and some of the guests coughing up donations would raise eyebrows. Benson Wong, the chairman of the Chinese Business Chamber of Commerce, had opened up his mansion for the gala and several other Chinese billionaires attended. One of them, Zhang Bin, was no ordinary businessman. He was a political advisor to the Beijing government and head of something called the China Cultural Industry Association, which the communist government supervised.[87]

One attendee at the fundraiser was controversial Chinese businessman Wei Wei, a real estate developer who actively worked to foster
closer relations between China and Canada. Among multiple meetings, Wei had a private discussion with Prime Minister Trudeau, along
with three other representatives of a Chinese government-endorsed
industry group. In 2020, police raided Wei's ornate 20,000-square-
foot home near Toronto for running an illegal gambling operation.
There were allegations of trafficking women, too. "The money
moving through these underground casinos leads to huge profits for
criminals that fund other ventures such as prostitution and drug trafficking," said the York Regional Police in a statement.[88]

Trudeau raised a good amount of money that day.

Shortly after that fundraiser, the Trudeau Foundation announced
that Zhang had made another contribution, this time a $200,000 do-
nation "to honor the memory and leadership" of Justin Trudeau's
father. Also chipping in was Niu Gensheng, another wealthy Chinese businessman. The Trudeau Foundation, which was seeded with
Canadian taxpayer money, had been established to memorialize the
late prime minister and his political views. The family was naturally
involved. Justin Trudeau had been a member of the board of directors
and brother Alexandre was still on the board, as was another member
of the family. Additional funds were also donated for a statue of Pierre
Trudeau.[89]

Alexandre Trudeau, in accepting the gifts, promised they would
"strengthen the Sino-Canadian friendship developed by his father,"
according to the Chinese government's *China Daily*.[90]

In 2016, Justin Trudeau flew to China for a series of high-level
meetings. Chinese social media took a liking to Trudeau, calling him
"Little Potato" shortly after he visited the country.[91] Trudeau directly
linked Canada's fate to China. During a visit to Shanghai on that trip,
he told the Canada-China Business Council that "the success of the
world is inexorably linked to China's success." He never precisely de-

fined what a successful China would look like, but he called for more trade and closer economic ties.[92]

When he finally raised the issue of human rights, he was quick to point out that Canada is bad, too. "[I] talked about the challenges, but also talked about the fact that Canada is not immune to criticisms on human rights, either," he said during an onstage interview at a Canadian Chamber of Commerce event in Hong Kong.[93]

The lack of any candor about the repressive nature of the communist regime runs deep in the Trudeaus. Brother Alexandre Trudeau says that both he and his brother inherited much of their thinking about China from their father. When asked about the human rights situation in China, Alexandre responded: "I could be very harsh, and you could find stories that are disgusting, but in a way I'm harsher on Canada, or way more on the United States, which I think have every reason to be better."[94]

The Trudeau family clearly has a soft spot for strongman tyrants. Alexandre Trudeau described Fidel Castro, whose government killed, tortured, and imprisoned thousands of Cubans, this way in a eulogy: "His intellect is one of the most broad and complete that can be found. He is an expert on genetics, on automobile combustion engines, on stock markets, on everything. . . . Combined with a Herculean physique and extraordinary personal courage, this monumental intellect makes Fidel the giant that he is."[95]

Pierre Trudeau and his family have justified their silence on matters of human rights because they do not want to "judge Chinese values by western standards." This is a naïve and absurd position. It also happens to be a favorite line of argument pushed by the CCP.[96]

The suppression of rights and the brutality of the regime in China is not a function of "Chinese values." Marxism–Leninism is not a Chinese idea—it is a profoundly Western idea. Repression in the country is a function of a Leninist dictatorship run by the Chinese Communist Party. The brutality that occurs in China is similar to that of every Marxist-Leninist regime: the Soviet Union, East Germany, and Cuba, to name a few.

But as we have seen, the ties are more than ideological.

Alexandre Trudeau is more than the brother of Prime Minister Trudeau; he has also served as his foreign policy advisor when Justin ran for the leadership of the Liberal Party. He wrote a book about China—retracing his father's steps taken during that 1960 visit. The book was, in Alexandre's words, commissioned by the Beijing government.[97] (How much he was paid has not been disclosed.) When he released the book, Alexandre explained: "I now look at our own freedoms with a little more circumspection and consider some of the irresponsible nature of some of the freedoms we enjoy."[98] He also praised the communist dictatorship in Beijing, explaining that China could not "have come so far so quickly without the unity and organizational power" of the dictatorial government.[99]

His brother read the book as prime minister before making his first official trip to China. "He read it a week before he left for China and he told me it helped him get up to speed in what to think and feel about China," recalled Alexandre.[100]

The Trudeaus' apologetics for the Beijing regime have become increasingly unpopular in Canada. Mounting concerns among the Canadian public about Beijing's growing influence in their country prompted Trudeau's government to become involved in a two-year effort to persuade Canadians that China is not so bad. The initiative, funded by major Canadian corporations, was titled "Public Policy Forum: Consultative Forum in China." The goal was to push Canadian public opinion to favor more trade with China.[101] It does not appear to have worked.

Trudeau's government took other steps to accede to Beijing's wishes.

In March 2017, the administration overturned a previous order pushed by the Canadian Security Intelligence Service to bar a Chinese company called O-Net from taking over a Canadian research company called ITF Technologies. The Beijing government partly owned O-Net, and ITF was developing technology related to fiber-laser-directed energy weapons.[102] Not too much later, Trudeau's administration permitted another Chinese firm, Hytera, to buy Norsat International, a Canadian firm that provides military satellite communication systems to the U.S. Department of Defense and the government of Taiwan. Reportedly, Trudeau's government agreed to allow the purchase without even "doing an in-depth security review."[103]

As prime minister, Trudeau joined forces with Beijing and took a stake in the Asian Infrastructure Investment Bank, which was being hailed as China's competition for the World Bank. This happened despite Canadian diplomats' warnings that the bank was going to be used to "leverage its economic prowess to gain regional influence and export its model of governance around the world." They argued, "[China] promotes perspectives on governance, economic security, and human rights that diverge in fundamental ways from Canada's." The Trudeau government ignored the warnings.[104]

When Prime Minister Trudeau was reelected in October 2019, he made some changes. Among them was the appointment of a new foreign minister, François-Philippe Champagne. The new foreign minister was almost gushy in his praise of the Beijing regime. In a 2017 interview with Chinese state television (CGTN), he explained how wonderful President Xi and the government were because they "stand out as [a] beacon of stability, predictability, a rule-based system, a very inclusive society."[105] Champagne also happened to have borrowed more than $1 million from the Bank of China to buy two apartments in London. When the loan was exposed, he changed banks.[106]

Relations between China and Canada have deteriorated. After Canadian officials arrested a Huawei executive in 2018 for extradition to the United States on criminal charges, Beijing retaliated

by detaining two Canadians on spy charges.[107] The Canadian public became increasingly suspicious of the Chinese regime given its
aggressive conduct. When the Canadian government joined the
United States and the European Union in sanctioning Chinese officials involved in the suppression of the Uighurs, some turned an-
grily on Trudeau. "Boy, your greatest achievement is to have ruined
the friendly relations between China and Canada, and have turned
Canada into a running dog of the U.S.," tweeted Li Yang, a Chinese diplomat posted to the embassy in Brazil.[108] But Trudeau was
hardly leading the parade. He gave all indications of being a reluctant
participant. Just two months earlier, on February 22, 2021, the Canadian House of Commons voted 266–0 in support of a resolution
calling China's actions against the Uighurs "genocide." Trudeau and
his cabinet abstained from the vote.[109]

Critics note that during the height of the pandemic, the Trudeau
administration granted lucrative contracts to a Chinese company to
produce personal protective equipment to fight the COVID virus
over Canadian firms that had the same capacity.[110] And when the
prominent Canadian Halifax International Security Forum invited
Taiwan's president Tsai Ing-wen to receive the John McCain Prize
for Leadership in Public Service, the Trudeau government tried to
pressure it to disinvite her.[111]

When Prime Minister Trudeau leaves office, he will no doubt
be looking for financial opportunities just as his father and so many
other politicians have. Will he mimic his father and brother, building
on his own network of government contacts in China? His family's
history seems to indicate that he will. And, of course, he will conduct the balance of his tenure in office precisely with that in mind.

8

HIGHER EDUCATION

Nathan Law has lived a remarkable and impactful life even though he has not yet reached the age of thirty. It was for good reason that *Time* magazine named him one of "The 100 Most Influential People of 2020."[1]

Born in Shenzhen, China, he moved to Hong Kong with his family at age six. At the age of twenty-one, with Beijing clamping down on the city's citizens, Law became involved in the so-called Umbrella Movement, a peaceful protest organization standing up for the individual rights the regime had once promised to Hong Kong. Protesting in the streets and leading petition drives, Law founded a prodemocracy group called Demosisto. By 2016, Law was elected to the Hong Kong legislature at the ripe age of twenty-three—the youngest ever. But Beijing took a disliking to his advocacy and forcibly removed him from office. Law went to jail for eight months, beginning in August 2017. Eventually, he found his way to Yale University for graduate school.[2]

Yale was perhaps an obvious choice for a young man from China. The school has a long history of ties to his country. The first Chinese student to graduate from an American university—in 1850—went to Yale.[3]

But arriving in New Haven, Law did not receive what one might call a rousing welcome. He found himself subject to harassment and abuse by other students from mainland China who were supportive of the regime. And while some other students and faculty reached out to him offering encouragement, the university administration essentially abandoned him, "remaining silent against this attack on free speech and the safety of a student."[4]

The plight of Nathan Law is emblematic of the growing problem of Chinese communist influence at America's elite universities. It is not simply an issue of pro-Beijing Chinese students attending elite American schools and becoming politically active on campus. Entire institutions of higher learning in the United States are being influenced by the flow of money from China via large gifts from wealthy alumni linked to the mainland's power structure. We never know how large this flow is because it is chronically (and illegally) underreported. It appears that the talking points originated at American universities: criticizing the CCP is racist against Asians and critics of Beijing are sadly "misinformed" or uneducated. At Yale, it has been particularly pronounced, and as we will see, this university and other schools have worked to cover up the origins of these funds.

Given Nathan Law's extensive background and central role in historic events unfolding in Hong Kong, one might think he would be a popular speaker on the Yale campus. And he did speak at the Schell Center for International Human Rights, albeit with hecklers confronting him.[5] One place where he never spoke was the Paul Tsai China Center, at the heart of Yale Law School. At first blush, it would seem to be a perfect fit. The Tsai Center's mission is to study the Chinese legal system and encourage U.S.-China relations. Law, as a young activist and legislator, would have some valuable insights on both of those subjects and more.[6] However, when you dissect who is behind the Tsai Center—with apparent strings attached—it becomes quite clear why Law did not have many New Haven allies.

It was, without a doubt, a generous gift. Joe Tsai, a billionaire tech entrepreneur and Yale graduate, donated $30 million to the China

Center at Yale Law School to honor his father. In recognition of the donation, it was rechristened the Paul Tsai China Center.[7]

Yale president Peter Salovey naturally hailed the donor as "one of Yale's great citizens."[8]

Tsai is a huge donor to colleges around the United States and the owner of the National Basketball Association's Brooklyn Nets. But he also has strong and troubling views about and ties to the dictatorial regime in Beijing. These positions and relationships are important to understand in light of his remarkable influence in shaping the national conversation about China.

The source of Tsai's enormous wealth, estimated at over $10 billion, is his involvement with the Chinese tech giant Alibaba. Tsai joined the nascent company back in 1999 when company founder Jack Ma was still working out of his apartment with twenty employees.[9] Alibaba staffers were expected to work sixteen-hour days, seven days a week. Ma even insisted that employees live within ten minutes of work to minimize commuting.[10]

Tsai, who was then working for a Swedish investment firm, quit his job and threw in with Ma. In some respects, the two men were opposites. While Jack Ma came from a poor family in mainland China, Tsai came from a prominent family in Taiwan. While Ma had a big vision of what he wanted Alibaba to be, Tsai brought a financial acumen and understanding of Western financial markets that Ma simply did not possess. Tsai became Ma's "right-hand man," eventually rising to serve as Alibaba's chief financial officer and later executive vice chairman.[11]

"Alibaba wouldn't be where it is today without Joe Tsai," explained Porter Erisman, who worked at Alibaba in the early days. "Joe is the international lens for the whole group."[12]

Alibaba also had key allies in the Chinese government that were critical to the company's rise. While Alibaba is listed on the New York Stock Exchange, the company has heavy ownership from the

Communist Party elite. Indeed, their significant investors include the sons and grandsons of the most influential members of the ruling Communist Party. As the *New York Times* has reported, "For Alibaba, the connections go to the highest levels of government."[13]

Indeed, Alibaba's fortunes grew because of these Beijing ties. "Since the early days, Alibaba has been supported by the Chinese government which used Alibaba's Taobao and Tmall sites to do billions of dollars of transactions between various government agencies which allowed Alibaba to post eye-popping revenues and growth in the early days," reports *Forbes* magazine. It continued to do so "to ensure the continued scorching growth rates that Alibaba has been able to post year in and year out."[14]

Alibaba is organized in a way that resembles the governance of the Communist Party of China. "The Alibaba governance structure is probably inspired by the Chinese political structure," says former banker David Webb. The firm is organized to be run by a "Partnership"—not the shareholders. "The shareholders are equivalent to the People, who have no say in how their country is run."[15]

It was Joe Tsai who was behind that "partnership governance model," which gave a limited number of individuals much control in creating the board of directors.[16]

This design makes it harder for shareholders to actually influence how the company is run. When MSCI, a financial firm controlled by Morgan Stanley, looked at the corporate "Governance," including "Ownership & Control," it gave Alibaba a "worst in class" designation.[17]

Understanding Alibaba requires more than recognizing how it is structured and how it prospered with government help. It helps to know the loyalties of the corporate leaders, which in turn will help explain why Tsai's philanthropy deserves serious attention.

Jack Ma has remained a longtime and loyal member of the CCP. Along the way, he defended the regime's decision to send tanks and soldiers into Tiananmen Square, killing thousands. It was, he declared, "the correct decision."[18] While Ma mysteriously "disappeared" in 2020 for his outspoken expressions of frustration about Chinese regulators, the Alibaba founder has over the years been a "vocal backer" of President Xi's policies. He speaks favorably about the "stability" provided by a one-party dictatorship and endorses his country's "strict online censorship." He is even supportive of constructing a comprehensive online surveillance system to monitor the general public.[19]

The corporate culture that Tsai has built with Ma reflects the founders' attitudes related to the government and Chinese nationalism. Military analogies are used to highlight well-regarded employees. High fliers in the company are called "King of Soldiers," and corporate leaders use the fictional character Xu Sanduo as a model. Xu, a character from the Chinese TV show *Soldiers Sortie*, rose from a village boy to become an elite fighter in the People's Liberation Army (PLA).[20]

Ma's favorite books "by far" are those in a series of novels that contains "strong elements of Chinese patriotism," as Chinese villagers fight off invaders from the north.[21] He has been known to compare his challenges at Alibaba with those of Mao and has sought guidance from his example.[22]

Beyond verbally supporting the regime, Alibaba also helps the CCP dispense propaganda. Recently, Alibaba developed for the Chinese government a propaganda app called Xuexi Qiangguo, which means "Study to make China strong." It includes quotes and comments from President Xi, and Communist Party members were told to download it.[23]

Alibaba also has close ties to the Chinese military. Alibaba Cloud Computing, for example, has a strategic cooperation agreement with military-linked firms to create a platform called "'Cybersecurity Feitian' for military customers." Several other Alibaba research projects are being carried out jointly with industry and university labs and will benefit the military and intelligence services.[24] The company even partnered with China's biggest defense company to create a location-based navigational system.[25]

Joe Tsai has also been outspoken in his defense of the Beijing regime and its corporate cohorts and has attacked their critics. Unlike Ma, who remains more reserved, Tsai addresses the issues openly. In 2019, for example, the United States and several allied governments began expressing concerns about Huawei and its close ties to the Ministry of State Security and the PLA. The firm is widely seen as posing a serious security risk. In his public comments, Tsai never actually disputed Huawei had such ties but instead slammed the United States and Western allies who raised them as "extremely unfair." The issue was "very politically motivated," he told one conference.[26]

One notices that Tsai often deflects rather than dealing with the underlying facts.

When speaking on college campuses, Tsai presents a remarkably rosy view of the communist regime. He explained to students at the University of California, San Diego, for example, that the Chinese government does not see the relationship with the United States as competitive. (Never mind that Beijing *itself* has said it is competing with the United States.) Tsai contends that the Chinese Communist Party is simply trying to improve the country's economy and the life of the average citizen.[27]

In 2018, Senator Mark Warner, then vice chairman of the Senate Intelligence Committee, spoke at a tech conference and observed that Chinese companies are "penetrated deeply by the Communist Party," thereby creating a security risk. (Few people dispute these facts.) Tsai later took the same stage and simply dodged, claiming the problem was really that some Americans wanted to "stop China" from innovating. Tsai again painted a benign portrait of the Communist Party. "Communist Party, per se, seems like a dirty word here, but in China, that's the form of government."[28]

On other occasions, Yale's big benefactor has expressed his support for China's Orwellian social credit system. The communist government is constructing a giant technological web in which ordinary citizens will be monitored, tracked, and graded concerning what they say and do. The better they "behave," as defined by the Beijing regime, the higher their scores. The higher the score, the better opportunities an individual will have in society. Tsai believes this is a great development. "Especially for young people, your online behavior goes toward building up your online credit profile, and we want people to be aware of that so they know to behave themselves better," he said.[29]

Tsai's children, of course, won't have to worry about their social credit score. While Alibaba is based in China, Tsai's family lives in California.[30]

Tsai has been involved in other efforts to obscure China's role in suppression. Under the guidance of Joe Tsai and Jack Ma, Alibaba bought a prestigious Hong Kong English-language publication called the *South China Morning Post* (SCMP) in 2016.[31] The newspaper had a stellar reputation for serious and fair reporting. That started to change under the new ownership. When the SCMP covered protests in Hong Kong in the summer of 2019, reporters sent a draft article describing in detail the "chaotic and shocking scenes" of police officers attacking "cowering commuters" on a subway train. But *South China Morning Post* editors altered the story. The final version described instead how masked "radical protesters" fled into the subway from "elite Hong Kong police." The newspaper, according to observers, has "exemplified the type of heavy-handed, slanted editing that became common" during the demonstrations.[32]

When Alibaba took over the *Morning Post*, Tsai certainly had coverage of China in mind. He argued at the time, "A lot of journalists working with these Western media organisations may not agree with the system of governance in China, and that taints their view of coverage."[33]

In 2017, Joe Tsai bought a stake in the Brooklyn Nets NBA franchise. (He became the sole owner in 2019.[34]) Tsai is a lifelong sports fan, so his purchase certainly made sense given the wealth he had accumulated. From the perspective of NBA management and owners, it served their purposes as well. Tsai could be enormously helpful in expanding the league's presence in China, where it was quickly becoming professional basketball's best burgeoning market. In fact, Tsai served as the league's ambassador to China.[35]

A few months after Tsai became a full-fledged NBA owner, Houston Rockets general manager Daryl Morey set off a firestorm with a simple tweet about ongoing protests in Hong Kong. "Fight for Freedom, Stand with Hong Kong," he tweeted.[36]

The Chinese government in Beijing was furious and immediately asked for Morey to be fired.[37]

Much more controversial statements had been issued by NBA players over the past few years on other subjects. Comments about the police, racism, social justice, and civil liberties are common. But Tsai jumped in after Morey's tweet and immediately declared that expressions about China and civil rights were entirely out of bounds. In a long, passionate, and frankly intolerant letter, Tsai mischaracterized the Hong Kong protestors—declaring that they were a "separatist movement." (Most protestors were not calling for separation from China, they were merely asking for the rights that they had been promised would be respected.) Tsai also falsely claimed that the protests were threatening the "territorial integrity" of China. (No one was asking for borders to be altered.) In his letter, of course, Tsai ignored the abuse of Uighurs in Chinese government concentration camps, Tibetan activists harassed or imprisoned, and Christian churches shut down by authorities.[38]

Tsai went even further, proclaiming that foreigners did not have a right to even talk about human rights in China. "When the topic of any separatist movement comes up," he declared, "Chinese people feel a strong sense of shame and anger because of this history of foreign occupation."[39]

Tsai was, in short, trying to erect "boundaries for acceptable speech about China," as the *Economist* put it.[40]

Tsai's efforts to end any debate or discussion of human rights in China were not a clumsy mistake. Indeed, as many observers pointed out, his line of argument echoed the Chinese Communist Party's line.[41]

But Tsai's public letter was only the beginning. Soon after Morey made his statement, Taobao, a massive online sales website owned by Tsai's Alibaba, took almost all Houston Rockets jerseys and products off the platform.[42] The Houston Rockets, the most popular NBA team in China because basketball great Yao Ming once played center for the team, were shut out of the Chinese market.[43]

Others with ties in China piled on.

NBA superstar LeBron James rebuked Morey for his tweet. "You know, when you're misinformed, or you're not educated about something, and I'm just talking about the tweet itself, you never know the ramifications that can happen," said James.[44] "So many people could have been harmed, not only financially, but physically, emotionally [and] spiritually." James never explained how Morey was "misinformed." But the part about being financially harmed was no doubt correct—and demonstrated the limits of his activism. James, who is outspoken on numerous social issues, and has said that he wants to speak the truth regardless of the cost, suddenly went silent on the issue of justice in Hong Kong—and even appeared to defend the regime.[45]

James actually has quite a long history of doing just that.

Since early in his professional career, James has coveted the Chinese market. Early on, he mulled learning Mandarin before a trip to China—perhaps to make himself more marketable.[46] Back in 2006, James explained, "I say all the time, and I tell my friends and teammates, that you have to go global—in basketball and business."[47] That meant, of course, avoiding criticisms of Beijing.

Morey's tweet was not the first time the normally outspoken James has remained silent about Chinese abusive actions. In 2007, black Sudanese Christians were being slaughtered in Darfur by a regime backed by the Chinese government. In all, an estimated 200,000 to 400,000 were killed. Beijing provided the regime with political support and was the Sudanese government's chief trading partner. The unfolding atrocities gave rise to a movement calling on Beijing to stop supporting Sudan. A letter to the Chinese government was written by one of James's teammates on the Cleveland Cavaliers. Every player on the team signed the letter, save two. One, a backup guard, had a shoe contract with a Chinese company. The other was superstar LeBron James.[48] After howls of protest, James eventually did come out with a muted statement about human rights.[49]

James has a sizable contract with the sports apparel company Nike. While based in the United States, it does huge business in China and views itself as a Chinese company. (Nike's then CEO Mark Parker startled investors on a 2019 earnings call when he declared that Nike "is a brand of China, for China."[50]) Beyond selling his jersey in China, James also has an exclusive arrangement that caters to the Chinese elite. The superstar releases some of his coveted shoes in China first, before fans in the United States can get access to them. At the same time, he has a line of Chinese-themed shoes that are available only in China, called "China" editions. They are "inspirations from deep within Chinese history and culture ingrained into the design of the shoe."[51]

James also has an enormous presence in the country, courtesy of Chinese media companies. James starred in a movie called *More than a Game*, which was coproduced by a Chinese company called Xinhua Sports and Entertainment, and was distributed by the state-owned China Film Group Corporation.[52] How much they paid James for the movie is not clear. Similarly, he works as a spokesman for a variety of companies selling their products in China.[53] During the off-season, James travels the Chinese mainland playing games. He even dedicated a basketball court in the People's Republic.[54]

Morey eventually lost his job in Houston because of the angry reaction in China. So, too, did David Levy, a new executive brought in by the Brooklyn Nets to help run the team, when Joe Tsai became an owner. Levy's sin? As the NBA controversy regarding the Hong Kong tweet swirled, Levy had the character to declare in an interview, "Whatever corporation you're in or country you live in, you should remain loyal to the values you have. Period." He was fired shortly after, with the Nets assuring the press it was "not based solely on his comments."[55]

Tsai's vigorous defense of the Beijing regime amid the NBA controversy quickly spilled over onto the campus at Yale because he was a substantial donor to the university. Nathan Law was on the Yale campus at the time and sounded a warning about what he saw happening on campus. "Undoubtedly, China is a huge country with a lot of talent and funding that universities here want," he told the *Yale Daily News*. "But we need to understand money coming from China is colored; it comes with purpose, with influence, and with aims that may not be stated when the relationships are built. There is a balance between forming relationships with China and not making concessions on core values of academic freedom."[56]

Chinese donors often do attach strings to their donations. C. J. Menard, a development consultant who has worked for Harvard and Boston Universities, says that in China, "donors tend to be more transactional. . . . There is an expectation of a quid pro quo."[57]

Some students were appalled that Yale remained silent as Tsai worked to squelch any discussion about human rights in China. Kelsang Dolma, a student who is ethnically Tibetan, told the *Yale Daily News*: "This may be a little naïve but I used to have this idea that universities could be a beacon of freedom of speech, morality, and education. I learned very quickly that ideas, such as freedom of speech, could be used as shields for University administrators from speaking out against people like Joseph Tsai. If people like Tsai have freedom of speech, surely so do Yale administrators. For a University that sells itself on its quest for light and truth, it is appalling that it would consistently turn a blind eye to disinformation in order to appease a foreign nation."[58]

We will discuss how Tsai's financial largesse to Yale has shifted the debate about China on campus and even in the United States as a whole. However, it is important to note first the byzantine structure that he has set up for his charities to distribute his vast fortune—and how Yale has tried to hide the source of those funds.

Tsai's contributions to Yale and other institutions in the United States come through an international network of charitable nonprofits he established that spans four countries. We can only guess his motives for the complexities of the arrangement, but it raises a cloud of doubt over where they came from. The origin of the funds is important because of federal law.

The charities were set up outside of China because of the challenges for each of the two types of Chinese charities. Chinese foundations, who do not pay taxes on gifts and whose gifts are tax-deductible for the giver, have higher financial thresholds when setting them up, higher operating costs, and stricter rules on expenditures. Chinese charitable trusts have different benefits and setbacks. They are far more flexible but do not have the tax advantages and can hold only cash—no stocks or bonds.[59] Therefore, Alibaba decided to set up Symasia Foundation Limited in Singapore, to hold shares for Jack Ma and Joe Tsai to distribute to charities they would establish. In his initial agreement with Alibaba, Tsai was entitled to steer fifteen million shares of Alibaba stock to a charity he created.[60]

Tsai did not just establish a single charity; he created three corporate entities in three different countries (the United States, Hong Kong, and Guernsey, a British tax shelter island in the English Channel) to hand out money originating from China.[61] Why establish three charities instead of just one?

There may very well be tax reasons for doing so. But one notable effect of this structure is that it makes it much easier to obscure the actual source of the money. For example, Tsai donated $30 million to rename Yale University's Law School China Center after his father, Paul Tsai.[62] The Joe and Clara Tsai Foundation is the single United States charity, which he set up in La Jolla, California. As we will soon see, Yale would have been required to disclose that the donation came from Tsai directly, or from the Hong Kong or Guernsey entities—and there were no such disclosures at the time. We must assume, then, that the donation came from the Joe and Clara Tsai Foundation, based in California.

That is a problem: a review of that charity's filings with the Internal Revenue Service (the 990-tax filing) reveals that the La Jolla–based Tsai Foundation has almost *no assets* and *never donated* funds to any organization, including Yale. Indeed, there is not a single directed donation that has appeared on their Form 990.[63] This means that the funds that Tsai sent to Yale must have come from Tsai foundations located in Hong Kong or Guernsey—or from Tsai himself—a noncitizen of the United States.

Why is this important?

Federal law requires American universities to disclose any foreign donations to the U.S. Department of Education (DOE). Section

117 of the Higher Education Act of 1965 demands "accurate and transparent disclosures of sources and amounts to the Department." The requirement was explicitly added to the law in 1998. More recently, a U.S. Senate committee directed the DOE to communicate to universities that the department was "prohibiting the use of domestic conduits and intermediaries to avoid the disclosures of foreign gifts."[64]

That means a considerable gift Yale received—likely from the Tsais' Hong Kong or Guernsey foundations—would need to be disclosed to the federal government. Only if the donation came from the La Jolla, California–based charity, would no disclosure be required. When you check Yale's disclosures to the DOE concerning foreign donations, the university never listed a contribution from Tsai foundations in either of those foreign locations. But of course, they should have because the California-based foundation, as we demonstrated above, had no assets and gave no grants.

Because of this type of maneuver, the DOE launched an investigation into the Tsais' gift and foreign gifts Yale received from 2014 to 2017. What officials discovered was that Yale—over and above the Tsai donations—was not listing hundreds of millions of dollars of overseas gifts they had received, many of them from mainland China.[65]

There are other sidesteps in which the Tsai Foundation engaged. According to Alibaba's filings with the Securities and Exchange Commission (SEC), Joe Tsai's La Jolla–based foundation seems to own the foundation he established in Guernsey. It is hard to tell because the Guernsey entity (Joe and Clara Tsai Foundation *Limited*) is "wholly-owned by Joe and Clara Tsai Foundation." Not *the* Joe and Clara Tsai Foundation (La Jolla). And not the Joe and Clara Tsai *Charitable* Foundation (Hong Kong).[66] (What the hell?) Why is this important? Because U.S.-based charities are required to disclose to the IRS any close connections or affiliations with other organizations.[67] But if the La Jolla–based Tsai Foundation owns the Guernsey foundation and never revealed any such relationships, it would be lying for consistently answering "no" when asked if it had any affiliations with or links to other organizations.

This is a pattern that has been repeated over and over again by the Joe and Clara Tsai Foundation based in La Jolla. The charity has "donated" hundreds of millions of dollars to institutions like Yale, Stanford, and the Smithsonian Institution in Washington. In every case, these institutions issued press releases proclaiming that the donation came from either the La Jolla–based foundation or some bastardization of the three foundation names. In its tax filings, the La Jolla–based foundation lists no such contributions, so the funds must have come from the foreign foundations.

* * *

HOW HAS THE Tsai money influenced the situation at Yale? How have Yale scholars guided the debate in the United States when it comes to China policy?

The Paul Tsai China Center often echoes the positive views that the funder has of the Beijing regime. This happens partly because the Tsai Center often hosts visiting scholars and former government officials from Beijing, connected to both the Chinese Communist Party and the Chinese military.[68]

Even Western scholars running the Tsai Center have had positive things to say about Beijing that run contrary to reality.[69] Such positions could at best be regarded as hopelessly naïve about the increasingly autocratic regime under President Xi.

Over the past decade, Xi has concentrated further power in his own hands and exerted the authority of the Chinese Communist

Party into every phase of Chinese life. Few Western scholars dispute this. But Paul Gewirtz, director of the Paul Tsai Center, explained in a 2014 piece for the *New York Times* that the "current regime led by Mr. Xi has already signed onto many reforms and even adjustments in ideology that represent positive steps toward a modern system of rule of law. These changes aren't just window dressing; they reflect the leadership's recognition that it needs to improve governance, address widespread public grievances, and respond to public opinion." Xi and other Chinese leaders, he claimed, recognized the need for the Communist Party to "constrain some of its power." Gewirtz added, "A sea change has taken place in government transparency, with important requirements of open government information changing the relationship between the state and citizens."[70]

Of course, the trend has been entirely the opposite; greater power by Xi and the Communist Party, more incarcerations, Uighur camps, the arrest and detention of protestors in Hong Kong, and more.

Scholars at the Tsai Center have, like Tsai himself, also minimized the totalitarian nature of the "social credit" system being developed by the Beijing regime. In an article titled "China's Orwellian Social Credit Score Isn't Real," Tsai Center senior fellow and former executive director Jamie Horsley explained, "Its essence is compliance with legally prescribed social and economic obligations and performing contractual commitments." Contrary to all the evidence, she says the tight public oversight is mainly about dealing with fraud and counterfeiting.[71]

In 2016, despite the crackdown on free speech and increasing arrests in China, Horsley noted that "the Chinese Party-state continues to press forward with putting in place and improving new governance mechanisms to achieve 'open government' as part of its broader goal of more innovative, clean, service-oriented and law-based government."[72]

In yet another article, she was complimentary of the Beijing government's so-called Belt and Road Initiative (BRI), which, as we have noted earlier, is part of Beijing's geostrategic ambitions and also makes use of forced labor. Horsley suggests some improvements for the program and writes:

> Such good governance improvements can help ensure that the BRI will genuinely contribute to, rather than complicate, China's drive to achieve common development, connectivity and prosperity, while at the same time advance better global and local governance, thus also enhancing China's reputational influence. This would truly be a "win–win" situation for all.[73]

Apparently, China's global ambitions are not a threat to anyone.

Those linked to and being paid by the Tsai Center are not simply ivory tower academics. The influence of the Tsai Center extends into the highest reaches of Washington. Jake Sullivan, appointed Joe Biden's national security advisor, was a paid fellow at the Tsai Center before he headed to the White House. Jeff Prescott, the deputy director of the Tsai Center, was nominated by Biden as deputy U.S. ambassador to the United Nations. Tsai Center senior fellow Mira Rapp-Hooper landed a senior position at the U.S. State Department.[74]

The fact that Tsai has donated funds to charities in congruence with the interests of the Chinese government has drawn scrutiny from experienced China watchers. During the COVID crisis in 2020, Alibaba cofounders Joe Tsai and Jack Ma made a gesture by promising to deliver one thousand ventilators to the state of New York. Scholars saw this for what it was. "Prominent Chinese entrepreneurs would not make these gestures without permission from the Communist Party," explained Joseph Nye, professor emeritus at Harvard. "China has used a government-sponsored propaganda campaign and aid programs to promote the theme that China's behavior had been benign, and to restore its soft power." Steve Tsang, the director of the China Institute at the SOAS University of London, went even further. The philanthropy was tied to what he called a "highly orchestrated propaganda operation."[75]

Tsai may want to limit and control debate about injustices in China. Here in the United States, though, he stands atop his fortune to speak out about the wrongs he sees here. While Tsai has little criticism for how the CCP governs the mainland, he has lots to say about what he sees as the widespread injustice in the United States. Again, this echoes the strategy Beijing has employed in dealing with its critics.

Tsai's philanthropic interests appear to operate in congruence with what Chinese authorities are doing: widely repressing individual freedom in their own country while equating them with American civil rights issues. In August 2020, Joe Tsai donated $50 million through the Joe and Clara Tsai Foundation to various activist groups in the United States to "advance social justice and economic mobility for Blacks, Indigenous people, and people of color." His Brooklyn Nets gave $10 million more to the NBA Foundation to carry out similar work.[76] The "Social Justice Commitment Statement" accompanying the donations explained the need for "antiracist" training.[77] His wife, Clara, remarked: "When it comes to dismantling systemic racism and economic inequality in our communities, we want to lead by example."[78] Joe Tsai even set up "a gathering space for Black Lives Matter" in the plaza of the Barclays Center, where the Brooklyn Nets play.[79]

Recall earlier how Tsai implied that we should support the communist dictator in China because that is the "system of governance." In other words, we should simply accept that system and move on. A vastly different standard seems to apply here, where the Tsais believe systematic change is necessary.[80]

China has a deplorable, farcical system of "justice," which features incarceration without trial, torture, and other issues. Curiously, we could not find a single statement by Tsai criticizing the Chinese regime.

Meanwhile, his wife is one of the founding partners of REFORM Alliance, a U.S. nonprofit focused on reducing the prison population and helping criminals reenter society. This may be a very worthy organization, but the Tsais ignore the imprisonment of Chinese Uighurs by Beijing while working on fairer treatment of those on probation or parole in what is, without question, a much fairer judicial system in the United States.[81]

When Tsai appeared on CNBC in June 2021, Andrew Ross Sorkin asked Tsai a very direct question: "How do you think about your role as a leader here in the United States on issues around Asian Americans, Black Lives Matter, voting rights, all of that. And whether and how you can speak out about for example, human rights abuses in China?"

Tsai, as always, deflected, and suddenly things like voting rights now did not matter. "You have to be specific on what human rights abuse you're talking about because the China that I see the, the large number of the population, I'm talking about 80 percent, 90 percent of the population are very, very happy with the fact that their lives are improving every year."

He added that dictatorships had their advantages, like, well, good infrastructure. He noted, "You also have a very different political system, in that one single party dominates the governance of the country which, you know, whether you like it or not, there are some great benefits, like, China has managed to build a terrific infrastructure."[82]

The yawning gap between Tsai's stated interest in "social justice"

in the United States and his support for the brutal and unjust regime in Beijing is further evidenced by the fact that Tsai's company
holds patents "for tools that can detect, track and monitor Uighurs
in a move human rights groups fear could entrench oppression of
the Muslim minority."[83] The technology can determine if a subject
is "ethnic" and notably, "Is it Uighur?"[84] Moreover, Alibaba is a
big backer of Megvii, which developed software that the *New York
Times* reported is a vital part of the "vast, secret system of advanced
facial recognition technology to track and control the Uighurs."[85]

* * *

YALE'S STRONG TIES to China, particularly China's elite who govern
the country, are not by happenstance. Yale, as we noted earlier, has
deep historical ties to the country. Today, more than eight hundred
Chinese students and about eight hundred Chinese scholars are in
residence at Yale.[86]

Yale made a conscious decision decades ago to cultivate ties in
China, both academic and financial. "Part of the strategic thinking
was to make China a real priority," recalled President Rick Levin
of his tenure back in the 1990s. "It was emerging as a global power
even then, and it seemed to us that the new century would be a
China century."[87]

Levin seemed to embrace the idea peddled by so many that what
was good for the Beijing regime was good for the world. When
congressional members from both political parties argued for trade
restrictions to deal with China's ballooning trade surplus back in 2006,
he claimed that free trade was the best policy for both nations.[88]

As Yale embraced Beijing, some faculty members began to express concerns about the drift in thinking at the university because
of the growing financial ties. "What would happen if there were
another Tiananmen?" asked the Yale Council of East Asian Studies

chair, Mimi Hall Yiengpruksawan, back in 2005. "Where would Yale stand?"[89] She did not answer her own question, but clearly, she was doubtful that Yale would stand against the regime.

Collaborations began to mount, particularly with institutions linked to the ruling government and the Communist Party.

In 2006, Yale University announced an agreement with the Foreign Language Bureau of the CCP to produce joint publications. As the name implies, this is not a scholarly body but an organization run by the Party. Using the publisher's name, China International Publishing Group, the collaboration was officially launched at an event in the Great Hall of the People. Yale scholars sat with senior officials from the Communist Party's Propaganda Department at the ceremony.[90]

In 2013, Yale expanded its partnership with the All-China Youth Federation for training programs at Yale. What exactly is the All-China Youth Federation? It is a CCP-controlled organization that trains cadre leaders for the Party. In announcing the program, Yale glossed over the disturbing details, saying, "ACYF is a training organization for China's future leaders; members have included former president of China Hu Jintao and the current premier, Li Keqiang, and vice premier, Liu Yandong." President Xi, in a recent speech, explained ACYF's role as "organising and mobilising a large number of young people and students to follow the party."[91]

Yale University also operates a series of joint research centers with Chinese universities, including the University of Science and Technology of China (USTC). The joint work is in software engineering. What exactly is USTC? It is a prestigious university set up to "serve national objectives in science and technology." It also "has recently sought to deepen its contributions to military research." Along those lines, it established a "military-civil fusion" center to make sure civilian technology advances can be integrated into the PLA.[92]

The university's alumni are linked to something called the Yale-China Association. David Youtz, president of the association, said that when it comes to operating in China, "We try to follow rules, we don't want to get in trouble and have things closed off."[93]

Getting in trouble with Beijing seems to explain quite a bit of Yale's behavior these days. In February 2019, Yale president Peter Salovey traveled to China to meet with officials to discuss research ties. (He is said to average three professional trips to China every year.[94]) During this trip, he also met with alumni, just shortly after it was revealed that a Yale University geneticist had provided data to the Chinese government used to track and control Uighurs.[95]

Several months earlier, at a forum on China, Salovey was asked by a *Financial Times* reporter whether the school would invite the Dalai Lama to speak on campus. The Tibetan leader, of course, is exiled by Beijing ostensibly because he had previously called for independence from China. According to the *Yale Daily News* account, the Yale president was unenthusiastic about the idea of having the Dalai Lama speak on campus. "Salovey answered that while Yale's policies of free speech would prevent them from barring a speaker, the administration would still recognize the action as being offensive to the Chinese Communist Party and would have to manage protests to prevent any voices from being smothered."[96]

Not all university presidents operate with such complete caution toward Beijing. When Harvard president Lawrence Bacow delivered a speech at Peking University in March 2019, he raised the issue of Uighur suppression occurring in Xinjiang province. He even quoted a Uighur verse to make his point.[97]

Yale's financial dependence on Chinese elites goes beyond Joe Tsai. The Yale University endowment has a large amount of money tied up in investments in mainland China. In 2005, Yale gave $20 million in "seed funding" to a Beijing-based investment firm called Hillhouse Capital to manage money for the endowment, and sent another $10 million shortly after. The fund was established by a 2003 Yale graduate named Zhang Lei. It is important to note that Zhang did not locate Hillhouse in Shanghai, China's financial capital, but in Beijing, the seat of government power. Today, Hillhouse manages billions of dollars for Yale and other university endowments and investors.[98]

Yale was an early entrant in trading stocks in China. It was the first foreign university allowed to trade in its "heavily regulated stock market" back in 2006.[99] Having the right connections is always helpful.

Zhang has enjoyed enormous financial success. Much of the economic success for Hillhouse (and therefore Yale) has been Zhang's ability to spot and gain access to big deals in China.

He got in on the ground floor of Tencent and other major companies before their public offerings. Hillhouse also invests in controversial companies like Yitu Technology, blacklisted in the United States for providing facial recognition technology to the Chinese government.[100]

In recent years, Yale has taken an unconventional investment approach to its endowment. The Yale Endowment has less than 10 percent of its money in U.S. stocks. Instead, the endowment has gravitated toward alternative investments, including a significant commitment to emerging markets. This means that Yale's financial interests are increasingly decoupled from American markets and more closely tied to markets overseas, including China.[101]

Zhang not only makes Yale richer; he also now helps steer the university as he was appointed to the Yale board of trustees.[102]

What other ties does Zhang have?

He is also closely aligned with the Chinese government and involved with United Front organizations. He sits on the board of directors of the China-U.S. Exchange Foundation, the front organization we highlighted in chapter 3.[103]

Zhang has used his money to support programs aggressively pushed by President Xi and his regime. Zhang donated $45 million to the Renmin University Gaoling School of Artificial Intelligence, an AI development program operated jointly with the CCP's China Association for Science and Technology.[104] During the ceremony announcing the project, the association's party secretary, Huai Jinpeng, a member of the 19th Central Committee of the Communist Party, said that the center would follow the guidance offered by President Xi Jinping "to develop an AI system that is suitable for the government to provide services and make policy decisions."[105]

Another partner in Zhang's lab is China International Publishing Group, run by the CCP Propaganda Department. At the opening ceremony for the AI center, officials from the Group explained that the purpose of the Zhang-funded lab would be to "'breed new AI broadcasting projects' by working with the government's international propaganda 'big data service platform.'"[106]

* * *

UNFORTUNATELY, YALE IS not the only university that has significant and entangling financial ties with Beijing and works to obscure them. A U.S. Senate subcommittee investigation found that numerous universities were systematically underreporting donations from China and were inaccurately disclosing them to the federal government.[107] As the general counsel of the U.S. Department of Education noted in a 2019 report, these are not likely to be mistakes. "Most foreign funds flow to large, wealthy, and sophisticated institutions with highly credentialed administrators and ready access to the very best accountants and attorneys," he wrote in the report. The general counsel further noted that universities are very good at tracking any expenses owed to them by students. How is it that they cannot track large foreign gifts from China?[108]

Chinese officials seek influence on American universities to steer the debate in a way more favorable to themselves. They also want research partnerships in science and technology to enhance their ability to steal technological and intellectual property. This has been known by universities for quite some time but largely ignored. In 2011, the FBI Counterintelligence Strategic Partnership Unit issued a white paper called "Higher Education and National Security: The Targeting of Sensitive, Proprietary, and Classified Information on Campuses of Higher Education." The report warned that "foreign adversaries and competitors take advantage of" the openness of American higher education to "improve their economies and militaries by stealing intellectual property from a world technology leader like the United States. There are also foreign adversaries that seek to gain advantages over the United States."[109] China clearly seems to be the leading culprit.[110]

The U.S. Justice Department has charged individual scholars in the United States for taking money from China for research and failing to disclose it. It happened to the chair of the Chemistry Department at Harvard University in June 2020. The next month, a visiting researcher at Stanford University was charged "with visa fraud in connection with a scheme to lie about her status as an active member of the People's Republic of China's military forces while in the United States conducting research at Stanford University."[111]

The Senate report also noted that Beijing is seeking to use its financial support "to change the impression in the United States and around the world that China is an economic and security threat."[112]

In 2020, the DOE's general counsel referenced that Senate subcommittee investigation from the previous year, noting that 70 percent of colleges and universities in the United States "fail to comply with the law, and those that do substantially underreport" foreign donations, primarily from China. As a result of this finding, the DOE initiated twelve civil investigations targeting universities seeking greater disclosure about the flow of undisclosed money from Chinese sources. Yale University was among the twelve schools targeted. The investigations resulted in the schools reporting $6.5 billion in previously undisclosed foreign gifts and contracts. The sums of money involved are staggering. Yale alone had "failed to comply with federal reporting obligations" by some $375 million.[113]

* * *

WHAT HAPPENS ON college campuses does not stay on college campuses. Students are influenced by what they learn and hear; some will become the leaders of tomorrow. But colleges are often a holding tank for those who are heading to Washington to shape our policy.

America is in a grim position. Beijing's effort at "elite capture" appears to be working spectacularly. We have exposed how elites, from Washington to Wall Street, from Silicon Valley to academe, have been coopted and are helping the regime while in some cases even bolstering China's military and intelligence complex.

But there are very real things we can do to fight back. There are people who are committed to counteracting Beijing. And there are changes we can make to turn the tide. We will explore that next.

9

FIGHTING BACK

From the White House to Capitol Hill, from the diplomatic corps to the national security establishment to the executive suites of Wall Street and Silicon Valley, American elites have sold the rope that will hang us to Beijing. That rope has many strands, but the end result is that these elites have helped strengthen and embolden a government that sees us as their rival—or even as their enemy.

Elite capture by Beijing is a reality we must firmly counter. Many of those profiled in this book know that the clock is ticking, and time is in Beijing's favor. Recall Kissinger's sage quote, "When [the Chinese] don't need us, they are going to be very difficult to deal with."[1]

Clearly, we are approaching that point now.

There is still hope if we take action.

From the beginning of our country, there have been deep concerns that foreign money and corruption would be used to buy off America's aristocracy. Alexander Hamilton, writing in Federalist 22, argued, "One of the weak sides of republics, among their numerous advantages, is that they afford too easy an inlet to foreign corruption."[2] The Founders assumed that foreign rivals—especially Great Britain—would look for opportunities to weaken and divide us by striking deals with members of American high society.

George Washington echoed those concerns in his farewell address, speaking of the "insidious wiles of foreign influence," which he considered "the most baneful foes of republican government."[3]

Likewise, James Madison was wary of foreign influence operating in the corridors of American politics and the business elite. "The public attention has been much employed for some time, on the danger of foreign influence," he wrote in 1799. "To be honorable to our character, and adequate to our safety, it [attention] ought to be pointed to every quarter where danger lurks, and most awake to that, from which danger is most to be feared."[4]

Madison believed the business elite were vulnerable because the British Crown had money to throw around: "Being an absolute monarchy in its executive department, [Britain] can distribute its money for secret services with every advantage of safety and success."

Sound familiar today?

Madison noted that the lure of money would tempt people to seek informal alliances with foreign rivals like London; the "great flood-gate of British Influence" was "British Commerce." As he allowed: "Money in all its shapes is influence; our monied institutions consequently form another great engine of British influence."[5]

America has tried to address the problems of hostile foreign powers capturing the interests of the American elite. But the attempts have been feeble at best. Part of the problem is that many of the needed reforms have to be implemented by members of the establishment, including the very people who benefit financially from the reforms *not* being enacted.

The first modern attempt came amid the rising concerns about fascism in Europe. In 1938 Congress passed, and President Roosevelt signed into law, the Foreign Agents Registration Act (FARA). The law required individuals in the United States acting on behalf of foreign governments or entities to register and describe their work to the U.S. Department of Justice.

But the law has been inconsistently enforced. While some people have been charged with FARA violations, many have not, including many of the people featured in this book who seem to have clearly violated that law.

The law was not perfect when it was set in place. Foreign powers could still try to influence our political leaders by donating to political campaigns. So in 1966, a law was passed effectively banning all foreign nationals from making political contributions to U.S. elections. The ban was also added to the Federal Election Campaign Act in 1974. Like FARA, this law is certainly not airtight, and there is a loophole. Foreign companies can set up U.S. affiliates and still donate to campaigns through their U.S.-based corporate offices. So long as the campaign funds do not come directly from the foreign entity, they can still make contributions.[6]

These laws are a good start, but they do not go nearly far enough. Here are some clearly needed protections to hold America's elites to account.

Ban lobbying on behalf of Chinese military- and intelligence-linked companies. Lobbying has developed a bad reputation—for good reasons. The U.S. Constitution does guarantee citizens the right to petition their government—not all lobbying is bad. But that right does not extend to foreign companies, especially those linked to the Chinese military-intelligence apparatus. Too many former politicians and diplomats are making bundles of money representing these interests in the corridors of Washington power.

Ban Chinese military- and intelligence-linked companies from appearing on American stock exchanges. Chinese military- and intelligence-linked companies receive dollars from American investors, pension funds, and investment firms, who then use that capital to enhance Beijing's military capabilities. How on earth is this a good idea? We need to ban Chinese companies from raising capital in our markets to strengthen their military and intelligence capabilities. There are financial professionals who will argue that this is draconian, but they are probably being paid to say so.

Ban joint research by American universities, investors, and corporations with Chinese military and intelligence projects. It is shocking to discover that we actually have to pass a law preventing American tech firms and universities from working with and aiding Chinese companies that are part of Beijing's military-industrial complex. That is precisely what we must do.

Why exactly does anyone in a corporate office or a college campus believe it is a good idea to help strengthen Beijing's military capabilities?

It is very popular in Washington right now to push for greater federal spending on American science and technology so we can compete more effectively with Beijing. But that is not enough. If we continue to provide Beijing with access to technologies that will help them run faster in the race against us, how do we expect to compete?

Critics of this proposal will argue that part of the problem is that in China it is impossible to know whether the military or intelligence community is involved in research projects. That is precisely the point: Beijing has formalized the fusion of civilian and military technology. They are responsible for this problem; we should not encourage them.

Beyond passing laws, there are actions that corporate America and the media can take to bring these problems further into the light.

Journalists need to openly ask questions about links to China. Wall Street heads and Silicon Valley titans who collaborate with China should be asked to give an account of their activities. Rather than adoring interviews with corporate heads asking for their insights about markets or technology, why not ask them about the remarkable statements they have made about Beijing? How about asking them about their technology cooperation agreements with military-linked companies?

Media companies need to insist on truth and transparency when it comes to their experts. Retired politicians, diplomats, and intelligence officials are regular fixtures on cable news, opinion pages, and Sunday morning news programs. They offer all sorts of wisdom and advice on how to deal with China. But should we not know if they are dependent on the Beijing regime for their businesses to work? Media companies should ask experts whether they do business in China and the nature of those relationships when they are pontificating about how to handle Beijing. When financial advisors appear on business television programs offering stock picks, they are often required to disclose their own investment holdings to reveal possible conflicts of interest. Why shouldn't diplomats and ex–public officials disclose their financial ties to China if they are offering sage advice about China?

Wall Street firms need to consistently apply Environmental, Social, and Governance (ESG) standards to Chinese companies. ESG investing is all the rage, particularly among large financial firms like BlackRock. But why do they only apply those standards to American and European companies while ignoring Chinese firms? Financial firms, if they insist on pushing conformity at home, and they want us to take them seriously on these matters, need to apply these standards to Chinese firms that are often engaged in much more serious problems relating to ESG. And financial titans like Larry Fink, who want to profess their commitment to making the world a better place, can begin by speaking honestly about the Beijing regime, not communicating how impressed they are by them. Otherwise, it makes a mockery of ESG investing.

Use shareholder activism to hold corporate executives to account. Many of the largest Wall Street and Big Tech companies exposed in this book are publicly traded, which means you can buy stock in the company and attend shareholder meetings. Shareholders should ask questions of corporate leaders about their craven attitudes toward China. The Free Enterprise Project does exactly this sort of thing. (The project is an offshoot of the National Center for Public Policy Research, where I sit on the board of directors.) The Free Enterprise Project is already challenging corporate executives when it comes to China. This sort of shareholder activism is a highly effective tool because corporate executives do not like to appear stupid in front of their shareholders.

We also need to reject the entire outlook regarding China, which has enriched the elite and emboldened China.

For decades the mantra from Washington, D.C., is that "engagement" with China is our only hope for a peaceful world. Engagement was supposed to help the American trade balance with China, reduce Beijing's ambitions, and help them embrace the international community of nations. But by every single measure, that policy has failed.

Trade balances did not get better with engagement—they have become worse. Beijing has become more ambitious around the world, not less. And they have explicitly said they reject the international community of nations erected after World War II. They want to create their own community—with Beijing at the top.

James Mann is the former Beijing bureau chief of the *Los Angeles Times* and is now a scholar at Johns Hopkins University.[7] He argues that "engagement" is essentially a strategic fraud. He writes:

> "Engagement" became the principal catchword used to describe and justify American policy toward China's one-party state, and it has endured to the present day. The suggestion was that sheer contact would serve to moderate or alter China's political system. Yet the policy of engagement is simply a process, one that merely prescribes continued contacts;

if China's repression becomes more severe, then under the logic of engagement, the solution is to have more meetings. Engagement says nothing about results. It does not require any changes in policy on the part of the "engagee." The implication is that the "engager" will not let the behavior of the Chinese regime, however reprehensible, get in the way of continued business with China.[8]

In short, this policy has been good for China, and it has been great for American elites who continue to profit from their special access in China. Never mind that they are contributing to their own—and more important, our—possible demise.

It is time for us to change our approach to China—to see them as the competitor and rival that they are.

Clyde Prestowitz, a longtime observer and author on China matters, believes we should replace engagement with reciprocity.

If the *New York Times* cannot be distributed in China, the CCP should not be allowed to own newspapers in America. If Amazon is limited in China's market, Alibaba should be similarly limited in the U.S. market. If GE will have to move its avionics division into a joint venture with state owned Avic, Washington will halt the move unless Avic drops state ownership and enters into joint development, production, and sales ventures with Boeing and Airbus for its planned new aircraft. Just as U.S. universities, nonprofits, and religious organizations are restricted in China, so Confucius Institutes and Chinese Student and Scholars Associations will be restricted or banned in the United States.[9]

Beijing always wants rules applied inconsistently. We need to demand that change.

This book paints a grim portrait of the American elite. I am often accused of creating despair because I expose the corruption of America's leaders but fail to highlight those who are doing some good. When it comes to China, there are some individuals in Washington, Silicon Valley, and Wall Street who do take a superior approach to Beijing, are prepared to resist the temptations being offered, and are willing to confront the challenges we face.

Let me offer some names.

President Donald J. Trump took strong positions against Beijing that have helped to reshape the debate in the United States. Whether the reader likes him or not, there can be little doubt that he saw the challenge posed by China clearly and moved America in a positive direction to confront it.

Along the way, Trump received assistance from a political rival who agreed with him on little else but clearly sees the threat posed by Beijing. During one particularly bruising battle with Beijing, Trump received an encouraging word of support from Senate leader Chuck Schumer, Democrat of New York. "Hang tough on China," he told him in May 2019. "Strength is the only way to win."[10] Like Schumer or not, he has been quite good when it comes to China.

We need to see this sort of bipartisan cooperation if we are going to successfully navigate the perilous waters ahead of us.

There are others in the United States—from both political parties—who have been solid on China. Republican senators Ted Cruz, Rand Paul, and Marco Rubio have been consistently tough, as have Democratic senators Mark Warner, Chris Coons, and Joe Manchin.

Our political leaders need to focus their criticisms on the dictatorial regime, identifying the CCP, not the Chinese people, as our adversary. This was the approach President Ronald Reagan took during the Cold War to call out the "evil empire."

In the business world, there are executives who are resisting the siren call of Beijing, which promises access to the Chinese market in exchange for strengthening the regime. In the tech world, legendary investor Peter Thiel has not only been outspoken about the need to recognize the China threat; he is also running his businesses that way. Thiel, who was an early investor in Facebook and still sits on the company's board, is the founder of a new data company called Palantir. One of the company's principles is that it will not conduct business with adversarial countries to the United States. That includes China.

Keith Krach, the former chairman and CEO of Docusign, has been equally outspoken about the need to see the China threat for what it is, and for high-tech firms to avoid aiding and abetting Beijing.[11]

"For our friends we produce fine wine. Jackals, we welcome with shotguns."

The aggressive statement came from Chinese ambassador Gui Congyou in 2019. The ambassador was not talking tough to the United States or Russia; the warning was not directed at a terrorist organization. Instead, his words were fired directly at small, neutral Sweden. A free-speech organization in that country had honored a Chinese-imprisoned Swedish citizen with a human rights award. Hence, his angry threat.[12]

The bold and belligerent challenge presented by Beijing is visible, open, and clear to see. Verbal wrath directed at a country offering a human rights award halfway around the world is indicative of where a bolder China is headed.

One can only assume that those who refuse to accurately see it have other motives.

As muckraker and novelist Upton Sinclair reminds us, "It is difficult to get a man to understand something when his salary depends on his not understanding it."[13]

ACKNOWLEDGMENTS

This is without a doubt the most troubling book that I have written—and one of the most challenging. The author alone is responsible for the contents of this book. However, this work would not have been possible without the contributions of numerous people.

First, the board of the Government Accountability Institute is fearless and is prepared to go wherever the truth takes us. For that I am grateful. Our chairman, Rebekah Mercer, provides thoughtful and courageous leadership and, along with her family, great encouragement. The other members of the board of directors, including Ron Robinson and Thomas W. Smith, also share that spirit and provide sage leadership and guidance. I am grateful to all of them for their insightful guidance.

For this particular book, I have been blessed to have a research team that is second to none: research directors Seamus Bruner, Jedd McFatter, and Jacob McLeod did a superb job guiding the effort. The research efforts of Brian Baugus, Hunter Pease, Maggie Dowd, Steven Richards, Mark Hoekenga, Keegan Connolly, Christina Hunter, Corey Adamyk, Price Sukhia, Peter Aagaard, and Caleb Stephens made an enormous difference in following the most important research trails. I also appreciate Matthew Tyrmand for his help in securing the Bevan Cooney emails.

Working with a manuscript that includes masses of complex information requires a deft and steady hand. To that, I owe Steve Post, GAI's vice president for content, for his tremendous help in the preparation and editing of the manuscript, with considerable support from Tarik Noriega and Joe Duffus.

Running an organization like GAI requires great leadership, and I am blessed to have the help of our executive vice president and general counsel, Stuart Christmas, as well as vice presidents Eric Eggers and Steve Stewart, executive vice president Peter Boyer, and our operations/IT manager, Catherine Baer. Thanks also go to Grace Overholt.

Navigating the world of media can be frustrating and complex. But it is made much easier with the guidance of our media team, Sandy Schulz, Faith Bruner, and Maggie Clemmons.

Thanks also go to Glenn Hartley and Lynn Chu for their expert representation, and to Eric Nelson for his thoughtful comments and guidance on this difficult project. It is a blessing to have such a terrific editor to work with.

My wonderful wife, Rhonda, has been so supportive and patient. Thank you—I love you. To my family, my children, my sister, and my mother, I can only say the same.

NOTES

1: The Rope

1. Quoted in Rush Doshi, *The Long Game: China's Grand Strategy to Displace American Order* (Oxford: Oxford University Press, 2021), 261.
2. "Lenin 1870–1924," in Susan Ratcliffe, ed., *Oxford Essential Quotations*, 5th ed. (Oxford: Oxford University Press, 2017) accessed July 14, 2021, https://www.oxfordreference.com/view/10.1093/acref/9780191843730.001.0001/q-oro-ed5-00006613.
3. William Safire, "On Language," *New York Times Magazine*, April 12, 1987, https://www.nytimes.com/1987/04/12/magazine/on-language.html.
4. Anne-Marie S. Brady, "Making the Foreign Serve China: Managing Foreigners in the People's Republic of China" (thesis, 2000), 1.
5. Anne-Marie Brady, "China's Foreign Propaganda Machine," Wilson Center, October 26, 2015, https://www.wilsoncenter.org/article/chinas-foreign-propaganda-machine.
6. Clive Hamilton and Mareike Ohlberg, *Hidden Hand: Exposing How the Chinese Communist Party Is Reshaping the World* (London: Oneworld Publications, 2020), 26.
7. Tobias Hoonhout, "Chinese Government Assigning Han Men to Live and Sleep with Uighur Women Whose Husbands Have Been Detained: Report," Yahoo News, November 4, 2019, https://news.yahoo.com/chinese-government-assigning-han-men-194535189.html.
8. Austin Ramzy and Chris Buckley, "'Absolutely No Mercy': Leaked Files Expose How China Organized Mass Detentions of Muslims," *New York Times*, November 16, 2019, https://www.nytimes.com/interactive/2019/11/16/world/asia/china-xinjiang-documents.html.
9. Emma Graham-Harrison and Juliette Garside, "'Allow No Escapes': Leak Exposes Reality of China's Vast Prison Camp Network," *Guardian*, November 24, 2019, https://www.theguardian.com/world/2019/nov/24/china-cables-leak-no-escapes-reality-china-uighur-prison-camp.
10. Professor Sir Geoffrey Nice and Professor Martin Elliott, "Organ Transplants and Human Rights Abuses in China," Gresham College, October 10, 2019, https://s3-eu-west-1.amazonaws.com/content.gresham.ac.uk/data/binary/3121/2019-10-10_GeoffreyNice_OrganTransplants_T.pdf.
11. "Li Wenliang: Coronavirus Kills Chinese Whistleblower Doctor," BBC News, February 7, 2020, https://www.bbc.com/news/world-asia-china-51403795.
12. Clyde Prestowitz, *The World Turned Upside Down: America, China, and the Struggle for Global Leadership* (New Haven, CT: Yale University Press, 2021), 9–10.
13. Elsa B. Kania and Wilson Vorndick, "Weaponizing Biotech: How China's Military Is Preparing for a 'New Domain of Warfare,'" Defense One,

August 14, 2019, https://www.defenseone.com/ideas/2019/08/chinas
-military-pursuing-biotech/159167/.

14.   Maya Angelou (@DrMayaAngelou), "When someone shows you who they
      are . . . ," Twitter post, 11:18 a.m., August 20, 2020, https://twitter.com
      /drmayaangelou/status/1296466556856291329?lang=en.

15.   Lu Hui, ed., "Commentary: Milestone Congress Points to New Era for
      China, the World," Xinhua Net, October 24, 2017, http://www.xinhuanet
      .com/english/2017-10/24/c_136702090.htm; Michael Pillsbury, *The Hundred
      Year Marathon: China's Secret Strategy to Replace America as the Global Superpower*
      (New York: Henry Holt, 2015), 27.

16.   Yang Yi, ed., "Commentary: Enlightened Chinese Democracy Puts the West
      in the Shade," Xinhua Net, October 17, 2017, http://www.xinhuanet.com
      /english/2017-10/17/c_136685546.htm.

17.   Pillsbury, *The Hundred Year Marathon*, 27–29.

18.   Walter Russell Mead, "Why Foreign Influence Is on the Rise," *Wall Street
      Journal*, September 30, 2019, https://www.wsj.com/articles/why-foreign
      -influence-is-on-the-rise-11569885340.

2: The Bidens

1.   Di Dongsheng, "Will China's Opening Up in the Financial Sector Attract
      Wall Street Wolves?," *The Answers* television program, November 28, 2020,
      transcript provided by *Washington Times*, https://media.washtimes.com
      /media/misc/2020/12/06/Di_Dongsheng_trasncript.pdf.

2.   "China Censors Boast About Influence on Biden, Wall Street After It Goes
      Viral," Bloomberg, December 9, 2020, https://www.bloomberg.com/news
      /articles/2020-12-10/china-censors-viral-boast-of-influence-over-wall
      -street-biden.

3.   CV for Di Dongsheng, Renmin University of China website, September 4,
      2017, http://sis.ruc.edu.cn/html/1/m/258/260/427.html.

4.   Ling Yun, "Beijing Has Enormous Sway over Wall Street, Hopes for Biden
      Win: Chinese Professor," *Epoch Times*, December 8, 2020, https://www
      .theepochtimes.com/beijing-has-enormous-sway-over-wall-street-hopes
      -for-biden-win-chinese-professor_3604038.html.

5.   "China Censors Boast About Influence on Biden, Wall Street After It Goes
      Viral"; Dongsheng, "Will China's Opening Up in the Financial Sector
      Attract Wall Street Wolves?"

6.   "China Censors Boast About Influence on Biden, Wall Street After It Goes
      Viral."

7.   James Kynge, Lucy Hornby, and Jamil Anderlini, "Inside China's Secret
      'Magic Weapon' for Worldwide Influence," *Financial Times*, October 26, 2017,
      https://www.ft.com/content/fb2b3934-b004-11e7-beba-5521c713abf4.

8.   Text message from Hunter Biden to Naomi Biden, January 3, 2019.

9.   Email From: SMancinelli, To: Rebekah J. H. Sullivan, Subject: Biden Matter,
      December 9, 2016, shows that Hunter Biden was paying a multitude for
      family members including a $260 monthly phone bill for Joe R. Biden. In
      numerous communications and corporate documents, there are indications

that Rosemont Seneca Advisors paid or reimbursed Hunter for the AT&T cell phone bills.

10. Ibid.

11. "Gift Rules for the Executive Branch," Public Citizen, June 2011, accessed June 10, 2021, https://www.citizen.org/wp-content/uploads/migration/gift-rules-executive-branch.pdf.

12. Email From: Joan Mayer, To: Hunter Biden, Subject: ATT, February 8, 2017. (Emphasis added.)

13. Email From: Eric Schwerin, To: Hunter Biden, Subject: JRB Bills, June 5, 2010; Email From: Eric Schwerin, To: Hunter Biden, Subject: JRB Bills, June 8, 2010; Miranda Devine, "Hunter Biden Engaged in Some Daddy Pay Care: Devine," *New York Post*, July 4, 2021, https://nypost.com/2021/07/04/hunter-biden-engaged-in-some-daddy-pay-care-devine/.

14. My team and I do not have direct access to the Hunter Biden laptop, but we do have an exact copy of the laptop's hard drive. How did we verify the authenticity of the content? We checked the material against the verified evidence we already had. When the Hunter Biden emails referenced travel, did they correspond with the Secret Service travel logs? When the Hunter Biden emails indicated that an email was sent to Bevan Cooney or Tony Bobulinski, did those collections possess the exact same email and content? In each and every case, we found them to be a correct match. We found no inconsistences or contradictions between the collections. Note: Except where we wish to show emphasis to highlight specific information, or add bracketed information for clarity, all quoted email or other correspondence is *exactly* as it appeared in the original—in context. This may make for more difficult reading, but we did not want to edit them in any other sense.

15. Peter Schweizer, *Secret Empires: How the American Political Class Hides Corruption and Enriches Family and Friends* (New York: Harper, 2019), 24–26.

16. "President Obama Announces More Key Administration Posts," White House Office of the Press Secretary, March 10, 2015, https://obamawhitehouse.archives.gov/the-press-office/2015/03/10/president-obama-announces-more-key-administration-posts; Email From: Eric Schwerin, To: Hunter Biden, Subject: Equity Interests for Mediation, March 10, 2017.

17. Email From: Eric Schwerin, To: Hunter Biden, Subject: JRB Future Memo, July 6, 2010.

18. Email From: Hunter Biden, To: Miguel Aleman, BCC: Jeff Cooper, Subject: Me and Jeff, February 24, 2016.

19. Rachel Deason, "How Did China Really Get Its Name?," Culture Trip, December 21, 2017, https://theculturetrip.com/asia/china/articles/how-did-china-really-get-its-name/.

20. Schweizer, *Secret Empires*, 28.

21. "Lin Junliang, the Original Matchmaker, Moved to Beijing for Many Years and Served as an Important Position in Chinese State-owned Enterprises," *Apple Daily*, October 17, 2020, https://tw.appledaily.com/headline/20201017/U4XZ4PRGLBD6JIV2HMWJX5IK4I/.

22. Schweizer, *Secret Empires*, 29.

23. Email From: Hunter Biden, To: Gao Xiqing, and reply by Hu Bing, Subject: Rosemont Realty, July 22, 2011; George Chen, "UPDATE 1-China Sovereign Fund CIC Names New Private Equity Head," Reuters, April 29, 2009, https://www.reuters.com/article/china-cic-privateequity/update-1-china -sovereign-fund-cic-names-new-private-equity-head -idUKHKG18815820090429.

24. Schweizer, *Secret Empires*, 29.

25. Steve Clemons, "Biden Gets China," *Atlantic*, January 2, 2012, https://www .theatlantic.com/politics/archive/2012/01/biden-gets-china/250747/.

26. Email From: James Bulger, To: Hunter Biden, Subject: AES Sparrows Point, April 12, 2010.

27. Email From: Eric Schwerin, To: Devon Archer, Hunter Biden, Subject: Biden Books, January 8, 2011.

28. "Remarks by the Vice President at Sichuan University," White House Office of the Vice President, August 21, 2011, https://obamawhitehouse.archives .gov/the-press-office/2011/08/21/remarks-vice-president-sichuan-university; "Remarks by Vice President Joe Biden to the Opening Session of the U.S.- China Strategic & Economic Dialogue," White House Office of the Vice President, May 9, 2011, https://obamawhitehouse.archives.gov/the-press -office/2011/05/09/remarks-vice-president-joe-biden-opening-session-us -china-strategic-econ.

29. *Report of the Select Committee on U.S. National Security and Military/Commercial Concerns with the People's Republic of China*, H. Rept. 105–851, 105th Cong. (Washington, D.C.: Government Printing Office, 1999), https://www. govinfo.gov/content/pkg/GPO-CRPT-105hrpt851/html/ch1bod.html; Bloomberg, "Bridgewater Booming in China," Pensions & Investments, November 10, 2020, https://www.pionline.com/money-management /bridgewater-booming-china; Allen T. Cheng, "How Ray Dalio Broke into China," *Institutional Investor*, December 18, 2017, https://www.institutional investor.com/article/b15yw0fcgtz1l8/how-ray-dalio-broke-into-china.

30. Email From: Hunter Biden, To: Devon Archer, Subject: Yo, April 20, 2011.

31. Email From: Devon Archer, To: Caryn Suffredini, Dan Burrell, Person Marie Anne, Hunter Biden, and Hermes Chang, Subject: RREAF Syndicate schedule and follow-up, April 25, 2011.

32. Email From: James Bulger, To: Devon Archer, Subject: Hey, June 20, 2011.

33. Email From: Devon Archer, To: Hunter Biden, Subject: Re: Super Chairman, November 13, 2011; Yu Ning, Wang Duan, and Cui Xiankang, "Che Feng, the Actual Controller of the Digital Kingdom, Was Investigated," Caixin.com, June 4, 2015, https://companies.caixin.com/2015-06 -04/100816165.html.

34. Scott Johnson and Carolyn Giardina, "Accusations of Fraud, Nonexistent Companies and Shadowy Chinese Billionaires: The Very Strange Saga of Digital Domain," *Hollywood Reporter*, July 27, 2016, https://www.holly woodreporter.com/news/digital-domain-legal-dispute-chinese-915004.

35. "Xi Jinping Aims Crosshairs at Moutai Private Club Members," Financial Services Monitor Worldwide, July 2, 2015 (Lexis); "The Day After Tomorrow,"

Week in China, February 17, 2017, https://www.weekinchina.com/2017/02
/the-day-after-tomorrow/; Snehesh Alex Philip, "Ministries of Security,
Strategic Support Force–China's Intel Agencies & How They Operate," The-
Print, July 18, 2020, https://theprint.in/defence/ministries-of-security
-strategic-support-force-chinas-intel-agencies-how-they-operate/463697/;
Dai Xianglong, biography, China Vitae, accessed June 10, 2021, https://
www.chinavitae.com/biography/Dai_Xianglong; BHR Cross-Border Investment Fund Private Placement Pitchbook, BHR Partners, June 2014, 15.

36. "China to Prosecute Former Senior Spy Catcher for Graft," Reuters, December 29, 2016, https://www.reuters.com/article/uk-china-corruption-security
-idUKKBN14J09T.

37. Roger Faligot, *Chinese Spies: From Chairman Mao to Xi Jinping* (London: Hurst,
2019), 391.

38. Edward Wong, "Chinese Security Official Ma Jian Had Six Mistresses: Reports," *Sydney Morning Herald*, April 1, 2015, https://www.smh.com.au/world
/chinese-security-official-ma-jian-had-six-mistresses-reports-20150331
-1mc8ks.html.

39. Email From: Michael Lin, To: Jimmy Bulger, Hunter Biden, Subject: Four
Seasons Hotel, October 8, 2011.

40. Email From: Michael Lin, To: Hunter Biden, James Bulger, Jonathan Li,
Subject: Hong Kong Trip, October 8, 2011.

41. Email From: Michael Lin, To: Hunter Biden, Jim Bulger, Subject: Heads up-
Fund, September 22, 2011.

42. Frank Fang, "Chinese Firm's Role in Takeover of Japanese LCD Maker
Raises Security Concerns," *Epoch Times*, April 4, 2019, https://www
.theepochtimes.com/possible-chinese-takeover-of-japanese-lcd-maker-raises
-security-concerns_2866772.html.

43. Faligot, *Chinese Spies*, 228; "Liu Yunshan's Daughter-in-law Lives in Bel-Air
to Open a BVI Company for Asset Management," *Hong Kong News*, May 3,
2016, https://www.hk01.com/社會新聞/18866/巴拿馬文件-劉雲山媳豪住貝
沙灣-開bvi公司做資產管理.

44. Faligot, *Chinese Spies*, 180, 226.

45. Ibid., 141.

46. Michael Forsythe, "Panama Papers Tie More of China's Elite to Secret Accounts," *New York Times*, April 6, 2016, https://www.nytimes.com/2016
/04/07/world/asia/china-panama-papers.html.

47. Schweizer, *Secret Empires*, 33–34.

48. Email From: Jim Bulger, To: Eric Schwerin, Hunter Biden, Subject: Super
Chairman, October 24, 2011.

49. Email From: Michael Lin, To: Jimmy Bulger, Hunter Biden, Subject: Heads
up-Fund, September 20, 2011.

50. Steven Nelson, "Hunter Biden Reportedly Still Owns 10 Percent Stake in
Chinese Firm," *New York Post*, December 24, 2020, https://nypost.com/2020
/12/24/hunter-biden-still-owns-10-percent-stake-in-china-firm-report/.

51. Email From: Devon Archer, To: Hunter Biden, Subject: Checking in, September 21, 2011.

52. Email From: Hunter Biden, To: Devon Archer, Subject: Heads up–Fund, September 22, 2011.

53. Email From: James Bulger, To: Hunter Biden, Devon Archer, and Michael Leonard, Subject: Response to Jonathan, March 8, 2013.

54. Secret Service, "Protectee Visits Detail Report," for Hunter Biden, January 1, 2008–January 31, 2017, obtained via FOIA by Judicial Watch.

55. Schweizer, *Secret Empires*, 30.

56. Adam Entous, "Will Hunter Biden Jeopardize His Father's Campaign?," *New Yorker*, July 1, 2019, https://www.newyorker.com/magazine/2019/07/08 /ill-hunter-biden-jeopardize-his-fathers-campaign.

57. Nelson, "Hunter Biden Reportedly Still Owns 10 Percent Stake in Chinese Firm"; Russell Flannery, "Hunter Biden Listed as Director At China State-Backed Company, SCMP Says," *Forbes*, October 5, 2019; Email From: Eric Schwerin, To: Robert Hunter (Biden), CC: George Mesires, Subject: Year End, December 20, 2018.

58. Email From: Devon Archer, To: Jonathan Lee, CC: Hunter Biden, et al., Subject: My visit to U.S., January 23, 2014.

59. Bohai Harvest RST Private Equity Fund, March 2014, 2.

60. Bohai Harvest RST (Shanghai) Equity Investment Fund, BHR Partners, 2016, 11.

61. "China to Prosecute Former Senior Spy Catcher for Graft"; Johnson, "Accusations of Fraud, Nonexistent Companies and Shadowy Chinese Billionaires."

62. Schweizer, *Secret Empires*, 48–49.

63. "BHR and AVIC Auto Acquire Henniges Automotive," PR Newswire, September 15, 2015, http://www.prnewswire.com/news-releases/bhr-and-avic -auto-acquire-henniges-automotive-300143072.html; Schweizer, *Secret Empires*, 46–49.

64. Nelson, "Hunter Biden Reportedly Still Owns 10 Percent Stake in Chinese Firm."

65. Robert Farley, "Trump's Claims About Hunter Biden in China," Factcheck. org, October 10, 2019, https://www.factcheck.org/2019/10/trumps-claims -about-hunter-biden-in-china/.

66. "Hunter Biden, Burisma, and Corruption: The Impact on U.S. Government Policy and Related Concerns," U.S. Senate Committee on Homeland Security and Governmental Affairs and U.S. Senate Committee on Finance Majority Staff Report, 31–34, https://www.hsgac.senate.gov/mo /media/doc/HSGAC_Finance_Report_FINAL.pdf; Senator Chuck Grassley, "Johnson, Grassley Use Secret Service Records to Verify Content from Alleged Hunter Biden Laptop, Request More Travel Records," press release, October 20, 2020, https://www.grassley.senate.gov/news /news-releases/johnson-grassley-use-secret-service-records-verify-content -alleged-hunter-biden.

67. Email From: Devon Archer, To: Gary Fears, Bevan Cooney, and Mohamed Khashoggi, Subject: China Entrepreneurs Club, November 5, 2011.

68. Nathan Vanderklippe, "Economic, Political Plans at Play as Ma Sells Trudeau on a Modern China," *Globe and Mail*, September 2, 2016, https://www

.theglobeandmail.com/news/world/eonomic-and-political-plans-will-be-at
-play-during-trudeau-ma-meeting/article31703382/.
69. "About Us," China Entrepreneur Club, accessed June 10, 2021, http://www
.daonong.com/english/About/.
70. Ibid.
71. Statement of Jeffrey Z. Johnson, president and CEO of SquirrelWerkz,
U.S.-China Economic and Security Review Commission, Hearing on
"Chinese Investment in the United States: Impacts and Issues for Policy
Makers," 115th Cong., January 26, 2017, https://www.uscc.gov/sites
/default/files/Johnson_USCC%20Hearing%20Testimony012617.pdf.
72. Wang Zhongyu, biography, China Enterprise Confederation/China
Enterprise Directors Association website, accessed June 15, 2021, http://
www.cec1979.org.cn/view_nbqt.php?id=129; "Ma Weihua," Cofortune
Information Technology Co., Ltd., on Internet Archive, March 18, 2019,
https://web.archive.org/web/20201101010914/http://english.boaoforum
.org/2019jb1/43940.jhtml (the screenshot of the site was captured on November 1, 2020); "Profile of Chairman of the Board of Directors," Far East
Holding Group Co. Ltd., accessed June 11, 2021, https://www.fegroup
.com.cn/ydkg-en/349545/349549/index.html.
73. Email From: Devon Archer, To: Gary Fears, Bevan Cooney, and Mohamed
Khashoggi, Subject: China Entrepreneurs Club, November 5, 2011.
74. Ibid.
75. Email From: Devon Archer, To: Gary Fears, Hunter Biden, and Bevan
Cooney, Subject: Potash, November 11, 2011.
76. Email From: Devon Archer, To: Gary Fears and Bevan Cooney, Subject:
Potash, November 11, 2011.
77. White House Visitor's Logs (downloaded), November 14, 2011, https://
obamawhitehouse.archives.gov/goodgovernment/tools/visitor-records.
78. "About Us," China Entrepreneur Club, accessed June 15, 2021, http://www
.confindustria.pu.it/allegati/notizie/n20150590_01b.pdf.
79. Email From: James Bulger, To: Hunter Biden, Subject: Henry Call, October
23, 2014.
80. Email From: James Bulger, To: Eric Schwerin, CC: Hunter Biden, Subject:
Harvest, January 19, 2016.
81. Email From: James Bulger, To: Hunter Biden, Subject: BHR, June 13, 2014.
82. Email From: Henry Zhao, To: Hunter Biden, Subject: Introduction, May 10,
2016.
83. Email From: Hunter Biden, To: Henry Zhao, Subject: Burnham, April 22,
2016.
84. United States Court of Appeals, Second Circuit, Case 19–619, Document
89–1, March 4, 2020, 2792967, 103.
85. Ibid.
86. Email From: Jiang Ming, To: Devon Archer, CC: Hunter Biden, James
Bulger et al., March 18, 2016.
87. Ariel Zilber, "Hunter Biden 'Was Paid $83,333 a Month by Ukrainian Gas
Company to Be a "Ceremonial Figure" with a "Powerful Name" While His

Firm Got a Total of $3.4 Million,'" *Daily Mail*, last updated October 20, 2019, https://www.dailymail.co.uk/news/article-7592235/Hunter-Biden-paid-83 -333-month-Ukrainian-gas-company-ceremonial-figure.html.

88. Email From: Vady Pozharskyi, To: Hunter Biden, Subject: Meeting for Coffee, April 17, 2015; Dana Kennedy, "Hunter Biden's Ukraine Contact Allegedly a 'Fixer' for Shady Oligarchs," *New York Post*, October 31, 2020, https://nypost.com/2020/10/31/hunter-bidens-ukraine-contact-allegedly -fixer-for-rulers/.

89. Kyle Cheney and Natasha Bertrand, "Biden Campaign Lashes Out at New York Post," *Politico*, October 14, 2020, https://www.politico.com/news /2020/10/14/biden-campaign-lashes-out-new-york-post-429486.

90. Email From: Jason Galanis, To: Devon Archer and Bevan Cooney, Subject: No Subject, November 4, 2014.

91. Email From: Hunter Biden, To: Devon Archer, Subject: Burisma, April 21, 2014.

92. Email From: John DeLoche, To: Ramji Srinivasan, Eric Evans, Hunter Biden, and Devon Archer, Subject: China, May 28, 2014.

93. Email From: Eric Schwerin, To: Hunter Biden, Subject: CITIC, May 29, 2014.

94. "Remarks by Vice President Joe Biden to the Opening Session of the U.S.-China Strategic & Economic Dialogue."

95. Email From: David Wittig, To: Hunter Biden and Michael Karloutsos, March 24, 2015.

96. Ibid.; Schweizer, *Secret Empires*, 40.

97. Anthee Carassava, "Greek Port Is Our 'Dragon's Head' in the Mediterranean, Says Xi Jinping," *Times* (London), November 12, 2019, https://www.thetimes .co.uk/article/greek-port-is-our-dragons-head-in-the-mediterranean-says-xi -jinping-xrd5nll0r.

98. Hearing Before the Subcommittee on Europe, Eurasia, and Emerging Threats of the Committee on Foreign Affairs, 115th Cong. (2018), https:// www.govinfo.gov/content/pkg/CHRG-115hhrg30178/html/CHRG -115hhrg30178.htm.

99. Carassava, "Greek Port Is Our 'Dragon's Head' in the Mediterranean, Says Xi Jinping."

100. Philippe Le Corre, Harvard University, Testimony Before the Subcommittee on Europe, Eurasia, and Emerging Threats, "Chinese Investment and Influence in Europe," 115th Cong. (2018), https://www.govinfo.gov/content/ pkg/CHRG-115hhrg30178/html/CHRG-115hhrg30178.htm; Email From: Paris Kokorotsikos, To: Hunter Biden et al., Subject: GR politics, December 30, 2014.

101. Email From: David C. Wittig, To: Hunter Biden and Michael Karloutsos, March 24, 2015.

102. Email From: David C. Wittig, To: Hunter Biden and Michael Karloutsos, March 11, 2015.

103. Email From: David C. Wittig, To: Hunter Biden and Michael Karloutsos, March 24, 2015.

104. Joseph P. Shaw, "Q&A: Father Alex Karloutsos on His Close Connection with the President-Elect," 27East.com, November 11, 2020, https://www .27east.com/southampton-press/qa-father-alex-karloutsos-on-his-close -connection-with-the-president-elect-1736335/; Tasos Kokkinidis, "Father Karloutsos: Biden Considers Himself Part of the Cultural Heritage of Greece," Greek Reporter, January 19, 2021, https://greekreporter.com/2021 /01/19/father-karloutsos-interview-joe-biden-greece/.
105. "FS Completes Acquisition of Greek National Operator Trainose," *Railway Gazette International*, September 14, 2017, https://www.railwaygazette.com /europe/fs-completes-acquisition-of-greek-national-operator-trainose/45168 .article.
106. Schweizer, *Secret Empires*, 38.
107. Email From: Hunter Biden, To: Thomas Tsao, Subject: Thank You, April 29, 2011.
108. Email From: Devon Archer, To: Jonathan Lee, James Bulger, Michael Lin, and Hunter Biden, Subject: Pipeline-RR, August 26, 2014.
109. As quoted in Schweizer, *Secret Empires*, 39.
110. Ibid., 40.
111. "The Role of Chinese Institutions in the Acquisition of Business Intelligence," Institute of Developing Economies, Japan External Trade Organization, accessed June 12, 2021, https://www.ide.go.jp/English/Data/Africa_file /Manualreport/cia_06.html.
112. Bruce Krasnow, "Global Development Firm Purchases Rosemont Realty," *Santa Fe New Mexican*, last updated August 25, 2015, https://www.santa enewmexican.com/news/business/global-development-firm-purchases -rosemont-realty/article_2fa9787e-350d-5d44–83e3-b24b1300978f.html; Rosemont Realty, LLC, "Gemini Investments and Rosemont Realty Form Joint Venture," PR Newswire, August 24, 2015, https://www.prnewswire .com/news-releases/gemini-investments-and-rosemont-realty-form-joint -venture-300132117.html.
113. Email From: Eric Schwerin, To: Hunter Biden, Subject: Re: Equity interests for Mediation, March 10, 2017.
114. Email From: Eric Schwerin. To: William Morgan, Subject: Taxes, April 14, 2016.
115. "U.S. Vice President Biden to Visit Balkans," BalkanInsight, April 28, 2009, https://balkaninsight.com/2009/04/28/us-vice-president-biden-to-visit -balkans/.
116. "Past Presidents: 67th Session—Vuk Jeremić," United Nations, General Assembly of the United Nations, accessed June 12, 2021, https://www.un.org /en/ga/president/67/index.shtml.
117. Email From: Vuk Jeremic, To: Eric Schwerin, Hunter Biden, Devon Archer, and Joan Mayer, Subject: Dinner in DC, December 1, 2015.
118. Ibid.
119. Hunter Biden and Tony Bobulinski October 14, 2017, text message exchange, uploaded by the *Epoch Times*, https://www.scribd.com/document /481679945/2017-10-14-Biden-Bobulinski-Texts.

120. "Hunter Biden, Burisma, and Corruption: The Impact on U.S. Government Policy and Related Concerns: Majority Staff Report Supplemental," U.S. Senate Committee on Homeland Security and Governmental Affairs, November 18, 2020, 5, https://www.finance.senate.gov/download/hsgac_ -finance-joint-report-supplemental.

121. "Top Chinese Oilman Falls Out of Favor and a $9 Billion Russian Deal Is at Risk," *Wall Street Journal*, March 14, 2018, https://www.wsj.com/articles /top-chinese-oilman-is-struck-down-and-a-9-billion-russian-deal-is-at-risk -1521025204.

122. "The Secretive China Energy Giant That Faces Scrutiny: QuickTake," Bloomberg, last updated April 3, 2018, https://www.bloombergquint.com /quicktakes/the-secretive-china-energy-giant-that-faces-scrutiny-quicktake.

123. Andrew Chubb and John Garnaut, "The Enigma of CEFC's Chairman Ye," Southseaconversations, June 7, 2013, https://southseaconversations.wordpress .com/2013/06/07/the-enigma-of-cefcs-chairman-ye.

124. Sam Cooper, *Wilful Blindness: How a Network of Narcos, Tycoons and CCP Agents Infiltrated the West* (Ottawa: Optimum Publishing International, 2021), 125, 126.

125. See for example Professor Dai Xu, who both worked at the PLA National Defense University and was affiliated with CEFC's Beijing Office; "Top Chinese Oilman Falls Out of Favor and a $9 Billion Russian Deal Is At Risk"; Mark Stokes and Russell Hsiao, "The People's Liberation Army General Political Department: Political Warfare with Chinese Characteristics," Project 2049, October 14, 2013, 26, https://project2049.net/wp-content/uploads/2018/04 /P2049_Stokes_Hsiao_PLA_General_Political_Department_Liaison_101413 .pdf; Michael Raska, "China and the 'Three Warfares,'" *Diplomat*, December 18, 2015, https://thediplomat.com/2015/12/hybrid-warfare-with-chinese -characteristics-2/.

126. Stokes and Hsiao, "The People's Liberation Army General Political Department: Political Warfare with Chinese Characteristics," 28.

127. Alexandra Stevenson, "U.S. Bribery Case Sheds Light on Mysterious Chinese Company," *Minneapolis/St.Paul Business Journal*, November 22, 2017, https:// www.bizjournals.com/twincities/news/2017/11/22/u-s-bribery-case-sheds -light-on-mysterious-chinese.html.

128. J. Michael Cole, "Unstoppable: China's Secret Plan to Subvert Taiwan," *National Interest*, March 23, 2015, https://nationalinterest.org/feature /unstoppable-chinas-secret-plan-subvert-taiwan-12463.

129. Andrew Chubb, "'A Golden Opportunity to Use Force': Mysterious China Energy Fund Committee Attack-Dog," Southseaconversations, September 29, 2011, https://southseaconversations.wordpress.com/2011/09/29/golden -opportunity-to-use-force-says-china-energy-fund-committee/; Long Tao, "Time to Teach Those Around South China Sea a Lesson," *Global Times*, on Internet Archive, September 29, 2011, https://web.archive.org/web/ 20111001222727/http://www.globaltimes.cn/NEWS/tabid/99/ID/677717 /Time-to-teach-those-around-South-China-Sea-a-lesson.aspx (the screenshot of the site was captured on October 1, 2011).

130. Cole, "Unstoppable: China's Secret Plan to Subvert Taiwan."
131. "Chairman of the Board of Directors of CEFC China Ye Jianming Bestows the Distinguished Alumni Award by East China University of Political Science and Law," M2 PressWIRE, November 20, 2017 (Lexis).
132. "Top Chinese Oilman Falls Out of Favor and a $9 Billion Russian Deal Is at Risk."
133. "Grassley Questions DOJ on Biden Family FARA Compliance Stemming from Business Deals with Chinese Communist-Backed Energy Tycoons," Chuck Grassley's Senate page, November 10, 2020, https://www.grassley .senate.gov/news/news-releases/grassley-questions-doj-biden-family-fara -compliance-stemming-business-deals; Email From: James Gilliar, To: Tony Bobulinski, Subject: Ye Jianming & CEFC updated profile, Attachment: "Ye Jianming & CEFC China Energy Company Limited: An Introduction," March 5, 2017.
134. Emma-Jo Morris, Ebony Bowden, and Bruce Golding, "Hunter Biden's Ex-Business Partner Told 'Don't Mention Joe' in Text Message," New York Post, October 22, 2020, https://nypost.com/2020/10/22/hunter-biden-ex -business-partner-told-dont-mention-joe-in-text/.
135. Ibid.
136. This comes from access we were given to text messages and emails on Tony Bobulinski's phone. While we were unable to corroborate this with other sources as we were with many of the emails, this information comports with our body of research on the Biden MO, and comes from Bobulinski himself, who had nothing to gain personally by divulging this correspondence. He gave this same correspondence to the Senate and the FBI.
137. Ibid.
138. Email From: Hunter Biden, To: Cecilia Browning, Subject: 507, September 21, 2017.
139. Fang Block, "Chinese Buyer Snaps Up Second Manhattan Trophy Apartment," Mansion Global, July 28, 2017, https://www.mansionglobal.com /articles/chinese-buyer-snaps-up-second-manhattan-trophy-apartment -70060; E. B. Solomont, "New York's Top 10 Residential Sales of 2017," Real Deal, December 20, 2017, https://therealdeal.com/2017/12/20/price-matters-in -2017s-top-residential-sales/; Radiance Holdings (Group) Company Limited, "Global Offering," October 16, 2020, I-12, https://www1.hkexnews.hk /listedco/listconews/sehk/2020/1016/2020101600015.pdf.
140. "Chinese People's Political Consultative Conference," National People's Congress, Chinese People's Political Consultative Conference, accessed September 4, 2021, http://www.china.org.cn/english/27750.htm; Eleanor Huang and Wu Yufei, "Civic Leaders Slam US Sanctions as Barbarous, Hegemonic," China Daily, August 8, 2020, https://www.chinadailyasia.com /article/139448; Radiance Holdings (Group) Company Limited, "Global Offering," 6, 297.
141. Alexander Bowe, "China's Overseas United Front Work: Background and Implications for the United States," U.S.-China Economic and Security Review Commission, August 24, 2018, https://www.uscc.gov/sites/default

/files/Research/China's%20Overseas%20United%20Front%20Work%20
-%20Background%20and%20Implications%20for%20US_final_0.pdf.

142. Daniel Bates, "Revealed: Hunter Biden Raked in $6M in Just Nine Months
from Chinese Business Dealings–and That Doesn't Include the 2.8 Carat-
Diamond He Got as a Gift," *Daily Mail*, December 10, 2020, https://www
.dailymail.co.uk/news/article-9040381/Hunter-Biden-raked-6m-nine
-month-Chinese-business-dealings.html.

143. Morris, Bowden, and Golding, "Hunter Biden's Ex-Business Partner Told
'Don't Mention Joe' in Text Message."

144. "Hunter Biden, Burisma, and Corruption: The Impact on U.S. Government Policy and Related Concerns," U.S. Senate Committee on Homeland
Security and Governmental Affairs and U.S. Senate Committee on Finance
Majority Staff Report, accessed June 12, 2021, 76–78, https://www.hsgac
.senate.gov/imo/media/doc/HSGAC_Finance_Report_FINAL.pdf.

145. "Top Chinese Oilman Falls Out of Favor and a $9 Billion Russian Deal Is at
Risk"; "Patrick Ho, Former Head of Organization Backed by Chinese En-
ergy Conglomerate, Sentenced to 3 Years in Prison for International Bribery
and 'Money Laundering Offenses,'" U.S. Department of Justice, press release,
March 25, 2019, https://www.justice.gov/usao-sdny/pr/patrick-ho-former-
head-organization-backed-chinese-energy-conglomerate-sentenced-3; Chris
Lau, "Jailed Ex–Hong Kong Official Patrick Ho Released After Finishing
U.S. Sentence for Bribery and Money Laundering," *South China Morning Post*,
June 9, 2020, https://www.scmp.com/news/hong-kong/law-and-crime
/article/3088112/jailed-ex-hong-kong-official-patrick-ho-set-be; Nick Mc-
Kenzie and Bethany Allen-Ebrahimian, and Zach Dorfman and Fergus Hunter,
"Beijing's Secret Plot to Infiltrate UN Used Australian Insider," *Sydney Morn-
ing Herald* (Australia), November 11, 2018, https://www.smh.com.au/world
/asia/beijing-s-secret-plot-to-infiltrate-un-used-australian-insider-20181031
-p50d2e.html.

146. Alexandra Stevenson, David Barboza, Matthew Goldstein, and Paul Mozur,
"A Chinese Tycoon Sought Power and Influence. Washington Responded,"
New York Times, December 12, 2018, https://www.nytimes.com/2018/12
/12/business/cefc-biden-china-washington-ye-jianming.html.

147. Hunter Biden, revised letter to Kevin re Ho representation, March 19, 2018;
"Hunter Biden, Burisma, and Corruption: The Impact on U.S. Government
Policy and Related Concerns."

148. Tim Hains, "Leaked Audio: Hunter Biden Discussing Business Deals with the
'Spy Chief of China,'" RealClearPolitics, October 28, 2020, https://www
.realclearpolitics.com/video/2020/10/28/leaked_audio_hunter_biden
_discussing_business_deals_with_the_spy_chief_of_china.html.

149. Chris Lau, Lilian Cheng, and Gigi Choy, "Back in Hong Kong After Serving
U.S. Prison Term for Bribery, a 'Very Tired' Patrick Ho Begins Quarantine
After Testing Negative for Covid-19," *South China Morning Post*, June 10,
2020, https://www.scmp.com/news/hong-kong/politics/article/3088464
/back-hong-kong-after-serving-us-prison-term-bribery-very; Entous, "Will
Hunter Biden Jeopardize His Father's Campaign?"

150. "JiaQi Bao," LinkedIn profile, accessed June 15, 2021, https://www.linkedin.com/in/jiaqibao/?miniProfileUrn=urn%3Ali%3Afs_miniProfile%3AACoAAANJjdcBKckUwWg83TrlcBlkeASgPskQc90.

151. Lin Xuchu, profile, World Economic Forum, accessed June 12, 2021, https://www.weforum.org/people/lin-xuchu.

152. Email From: JiaQi Bao, To: Hunter Biden, Subject: LNG News, February 12, 2018; Email From: JiaQi Bao, To: Hunter Biden, Subject: Letter to Hunter, March 14, 2019.

153. Email From: JiaQi Bao, To: Hunter Biden, Subject: Fitzgerald Hotel Lease, December 2, 2017.

154. Email From: JiaQi Bao, To: Hunter Biden, Subject: confidential—howdy and items to wrap up, March 26, 2018.

155. "Our Mission Statement," Penn Biden Center for Diplomacy & Global Engagement, accessed June 12, 2021, http://global.upenn.edu/penn-biden-center/our-mission-statement.

156. "Addressing Threats to the Liberal International Order," Penn Biden Center for Diplomacy & Global Engagement, accessed June 12, 2021, https://global.upenn.edu/penn-biden-center/addressing-threats-liberal-international-order.

157. Ibid.

158. "Biden: China Not Economic Threat to U.S.," campaign stop in Iowa City, IA, May 2, 2019, uploaded to YouTube by AP Archive, May 7, 2019, https://www.youtube.com/watch?v=dew9qqoAM9A.

159. Pia Singh, "After Joe's Election Win, Penn Biden Center Faces Calls to Become a Public Policy Hub," *Daily Pennsylvanian*, November 29, 2020, https://www.thedp.com/article/2020/11/penn-biden-center-future-public-policy-demand-students-professors.

160. Bill Gertz, *Deceiving the Sky: Inside Communist China's Drive for Global Supremacy* (New York: Encounter Books, 2019), 29–33.

161. "Foreign Schools Gift and Contracts Report with Date Range 01/01/2014 to 12/31/2019," Studentaid.gov, March 30, 2020, https://web.archive.org/web/20210113061739/https://studentaid.gov/sites/default/files/fsawg/datacenter/library/ForeignGifts.xls (the screenshot of the spreadsheet was captured on January 13, 2021).

162. "About Us," China Merchants Group, accessed September 4, 2021, https://www.cmhk.com/main/a/2016/a26/a30448_30530.shtml.

163. Angus Grigg, Lucy Gao, and Michael Hobbs, "Rio's Northparkes Sold for $886m," *Australian Financial Review*, July 30, 2013.

164. Yixiang Zeng, "China Molybdenum Has New Controlling Shareholder," *SNL Metals and Mining Daily*, January 14, 2014.

165. "China Moly to Help BHR Acquire Stake in Congo's Tenke Copper Mine," Reuters, January 22, 2017, https://www.reuters.com/article/us-congo-mining/china-moly-to-help-bhr-acquire-stake-in-congos-tenke-copper-mine-idUSKBN1560OP.

166. Yuichiro Kakutani, "Biden-Linked Firm WestExec Scrubs China Work from Website," *Washington Free Beacon*, December 2, 2020, https://freebeacon.com/elections/biden-linked-firm-westexec-scrubs-china-work-from-website/;

home page, WestExec Advisors, accessed June 12, 2021, https://web.archive
.org/web/20200726175137/http:/westexec.com/ (the screenshot of the site
was captured on July 26, 2020); Note: for archived WestExec site, see "Managing China-Related Risk in an Era of Strategic Competition," home page,
WestExec Advisors, on Internet Archive, accessed June 15, 2021, https://web
.archive.org/web/20200802014748/http:/westexec.com/ (the screenshot of
the site was captured on August 2, 2020).

167. Norah O'Donnell, "Secretary of State Antony Blinken on the Threat Posed
by China," CBS News, May 2, 2021, https://www.cbsnews.com/news
/antony-blinken-60-minutes-2021-05-02/.

168. Frank Chung, "Joe Biden Suggests China's Uighur Genocide Is Part of 'Different Cultural Norms,'" News.com.au, February 18, 2021, https://www
.news.com.au/finance/work/leaders/joe-biden-suggests-chinas-uighur
-genocide-is-part-of-different-cultural-norms/news-story/86a85d79ca830f6
b7601a3638798c5ab.

169. Ibid.

170. Danya Hajjaji, "As Hunter Biden FBI Probe Rolls On, Laptop Story Resur-
faces After U.S. Claims About Russia," *Newsweek*, March 19, 2021, https://
www.newsweek.com/hunter-biden-fbi-probe-rolls-laptop-story-resurfaces
-after-us-claims-about-russia-1577438.

171. Aruna Viswanatha, "Author Alleges China Used Business Deals to Influence
Families of Mitch McConnell, Joe Biden," *Wall Street Journal*, March 15, 2018,
https://www.wsj.com/articles/author-alleges-china-used-business-deals-to
-influence-families-of-mitch-mcconnell-joe-biden-1521141489.

172. Bill Barrow, "Biden Pledges 'Absolute Wall' Between Job, Family Business,"
Associated Press, August 28, 2019, https://apnews.com/article/7e50648e9d
0040e096ccc3ec65bd72fb.

173. For example, he told *60 Minutes* in October 2019: "I've never discussed my
business or their business, my sons' or daughter's. And I've never discussed
them because they know where I have to do my job and that's it and they have
to make their own judgments." There are numerous other examples; Norah
O'Donnell, "Joe Biden Defends His Son Hunter's Ukraine Dealings, Answers
for His Gaffes in 60 Minutes Interview," CBS News, October 27, 2019,
https://www.cbsnews.com/news/joe-biden-interview-full-transcript-watch
-video-norah-odonnell-60-minutes-exclusive-2019-10-27/.

174. Brett Samuels, "Biden Denies Unethical Behavior Involving His Son Hunter
During Questioning at Debate," *Hill*, October 22, 2020, https://thehill.com
/homenews/campaign/522377-biden-denies-unethical-behavior-involving
-his-son-hunter-during-questioning.

175. Text message exchange between Hunter Biden and Hallie Biden, Beau
Biden's widow, on February 24, 2019.

3: Capitol Hill

1. Elliot Carter, "Check Out the Government's Spy-Proof Conference Rooms,"
Architect of the Capital, December 11, 2016, https://architectofthecapital.
org/posts/2016/12/9/scif-conference-rooms.

2. "Members of the IC," Office of the Director of National Intelligence, accessed June 15, 2021, https://www.dni.gov/index.php/what-we-do/members-of-the-ic.

3. "The Intelligence Committee," Dianne Feinstein's senator page, accessed June 15, 2021, https://www.feinstein.senate.gov/public/index.cfm/the-intelligence-committee.

4. Leah Garchik, "Oakland's Royal Wedding/Nearly 600 Attend Jerry Brown's Nuptials," *San Francisco Chronicle*, last updated January 19, 2012, https://www.sfgate.com/entertainment/garchik/article/Oakland-s-royal-wedding-Nearly-600-attend-Jerry-2627405.php; Laurence H. Shoup, "Richard C. Blum and Dianne Feinstein: The Power Couple of California," FoundSF, accessed June 15, 2021, https://www.foundsf.org/index.php?title=Richard_C._Blum_and_Dianne_Feinstein:_The_Power_Couple_of_California.

5. Committee on Foreign Relations, United States Senate, Millennium Edition 1816–2000, 105th Cong. (2000), https://www.foreign.senate.gov/download/history-of-the-committee.

6. "Ma Yanli Commented on Obama's Inauguration Dress to Disappoint," Sina, January 22, 2009, https://translate.google.com/translate?hl=en&sl=zh-CN&u=http://ent.sina.com.cn/s/m/2009-01-22/15352353740.shtml&prev=search&pto=aue.

7. Edwin Chen, "Feinstein Plays Unbilled Role in Taiwan Dispute," *Los Angeles Times*, March 22, 1996, https://www.latimes.com/archives/la-xpm-1996-03-22-mn-50059-story.html.

8. Dianne Feinstein, "Most-Favored Status Is Not a Perk," *Los Angeles Times*, May 19, 1996, https://www.latimes.com/archives/la-xpm-1996-05-19-op-5907-story.html.

9. Bill Van Niekerken, "Sen. Dianne Feinstein: Tracing Her Career, from S.F. to D.C.," *San Francisco Chronicle*, November 2, 2018, https://projects.sfchronicle.com/2018/dianne-feinstein-timeline/; "U.S. Relations with China," Council on Foreign Relations, accessed June 15, 2021, https://www.cfr.org/timeline/us-relations-china.

10. James Areddy, "A Conversation with Dianne Feinstein," *Wall Street Journal*, last updated June 6, 2010, https://www.wsj.com/articles/BL-CJB-8981; Wu Yan, "The Artistic Talents of Chinese Leaders," *China Daily*, last updated September 16, 2015, https://www.chinadaily.com.cn/china/2015-09/16/content_21895472_4.htm; Qidong Zhang, "Cultivator for U.S.-China Relations," *China Daily*, last updated April 11, 2014, http://usa.chinadaily.com.cn/a/201404/11/WS5a2e14dba310eefe3e9a2763.html.

11. Ben Weingarten, "Feinstein's Real Insider Trading Scandal Is Selling America Out to China," Federalist, March 23, 2020, https://thefederalist.com/2020/03/23/feinsteins-real-insider-trading-scandal-is-selling-america-out-to-china/.

12. Martha Groves, "The Man Behind the Woman Who Would Be Governor," *Los Angeles Times*, May 27, 1990, https://www.latimes.com/archives/la-xpm-1990-05-27-fi-426-story.html.

13. Lance Williams, "Husband Invested in China as Feinstein Pushed Trade," *San*

Francisco Chronicle, last updated February 5, 2012, https://www.sfgate.com /news/article/Husband-invested-in-China-as-Feinstein-pushed-3051244.php.

14. "Shanghai Pacific Partners, L.P.," OpenCorporates, accessed June 15, 2021, https://opencorporates.com/companies/us_ca/198931300014; "WK Zhang," profile, Crunchbase, accessed June 15, 2021, https://www.crunchbase.com /person/wk-zhang; Glenn F. Bunting, "Feinstein, Husband Hold Strong China Connections," *Los Angeles Times*, March 28, 1997, https://www .latimes.com/archives/la-xpm-1997-03-28-mn-43046-story.html.

15. Niekerken, "Sen. Dianne Feinstein: Tracing Her Career, from S.F. to D.C."

16. Glenn F. Bunting and Dwight Morris, "Husband's Business Ties Pose Dilemma for Feinstein: Politics: She Says His Myriad Investments Do Not Influence Her Votes and She Is Aware of Potential Conflicts," *Los Angeles Times*, October 28, 1994, https://www.latimes.com/archives/la-xpm-1994 -10-28-mn-55837-story.html.

17. Lee Smith, "China Queen Dianne Feinstein Used Her Senate Power to Push Most-Favored-Nation Status for the CCP's Corrupt Dictatorship. Why?," *Tablet Magazine*, April 20, 2020, https://www.tabletmag.com/sections/news /articles/lee-smith-china-coronavirus-1.

18. Williams, "Husband Invested in China as Feinstein Pushed Trade"; "Newbridge Offices," Newbridge Capital, on Internet Archive, accessed June 16, 2021, https://web.archive.org/web/20050207195211/http://newbridgecapital .com/offices.html (the screenshot of the site was captured on February 7, 2005).

19. Smith, "China Queen Dianne Feinstein Used Her Senate Power to Push Most-Favored-Nation Status for the CCP's Corrupt Dictatorship. Why?"; Jane Lanhee Lee, "Newbridge Capital of U.S. Gets Control of Shenzhen," *Wall Street Journal*, October 9, 2002, https://www.wsj.com/articles /SB1034198572968249876.

20. "Steven J. Schneider Joins Texas Pacific Group and Newbridge Capital as Partner; Former GE Executive Will Lead Operations Group in Asia," Business Wire India, December 14, 2005, https://www.businesswireindia.com /steven-j-schneider-joins-texas-pacific-group-newbridge-capital-as-partner -former-ge-executive-will-lead-operations-group-asia-8627.html.

21. Rone Tempest, "Deal-Maker's Worlds Mesh at Party in S.F.," *Los Angeles Times*, November 18, 2005, https://www.latimes.com/archives/la-xpm -2005-nov-18-me-blum18-story.html.

22. Bunting, "Feinstein, Husband Hold Strong China Connections."

23. Smith, "China Queen Dianne Feinstein Used Her Senate Power to Push Most-Favored-Nation Status for the CCP's Corrupt Dictatorship. Why?"

24. Williams, "Husband Invested in China as Feinstein Pushed Trade."

25. Bunting, "Feinstein, Husband Hold Strong China Connections"; Kai Strittmatter, *We Have Been Harmonized: Life in China's Surveillance State* (New York: Custom House, 2020), 294.

26. Bunting, "Feinstein, Husband Hold Strong China Connections."

27. Daniel Klaidman, "Cracking a Chinese Code: Inside Beijing's Plan to Influence U.S. Politics," *Newsweek*, June 9, 1997, https://www.newsweek .com/cracking-chinese-code-173492; Mark Hosenball, "A Hobbled Presi-

dent?," *Newsweek*, March 23, 1997, https://www.newsweek.com/hobbled -president-170610.

28.   Douglas Stanglin and Shaheena Ahmad et al., "Secret Mission," *U.S. News & World Report* 123, no. 14 (1997): 19, http://search.ebscohost.com/login.aspx?d irect=true&db=asn&AN=9710091332&site=ehost-live.

29.   Roger Faligot, *Chinese Spies: From Chairman Mao to Xi Jinping* (London: Hurst, 2019), 157–58.

30.   Nina J. Easton, "Forget the Thelma and Louise Thing: Barbara Boxer and Dianne Feinstein Are Way Beyond the Election-Year Road Show," *Los Angeles Times*, November 19, 1995, https://www.latimes.com/archives/la-xpm -1995-11-19-tm-4900-story.html.

31.   Areddy, "A Conversation with Dianne Feinstein"; home page, Beijing Municipal, on Internet Archive, accessed June 16, 2021, https://web.archive.org /web/20141129112611/http://eng.bjgaj.gov.cn/ (the screenshot of the site was captured on November 29, 2014).

32.   Hosenball, "A Hobbled President?"

33.   Samuel Wagreich, "Lobbying by Proxy: A Study of China's Lobbying Practices in the United States 1979–2010 and the Implications for FARA," *Journal of Politics and Society* (2013): 145, 151.

34.   Quoted in Rush Doshi, *The Long Game: China's Grand Strategy to Displace American Order* (Oxford: Oxford University Press, 2021), 134, 147.

35.   Hosenball, "A Hobbled President?"; Edward Walsh and Roberto Suro, "Clinton Fund-Raiser Huang to Offer Guilty Plea," *Washington Post* (archives), May 26, 1999, https://www.washingtonpost.com/wp -srv/politics/special/campfin/stories/huang052699.htm; "House of Representatives—Tuesday, July 22, 1997," Congressional Record—House, July 22, 1997, https://www.gpo.gov/fdsys/pkg/GPO-CRECB -1997-pt11/pdf/GPO-CRECB-1997-pt11-2-2.pdf.

36.   Robert Pear, "FBI Warned of Donations from China, Senator Says," *New York Times* (archives), March 10, 1997, https://archive.nytimes.com/www .nytimes.com/library/politics/0310campaign-finance.html.

37.   Debbie Howlett, "President's Uncle Shares Bush Family Ties to China," *USA Today*, February 18, 2002, https://usatoday30.usatoday.com/news /washington/2002/02/19/usat-prescott-bush.htm.

38.   John Sutherland, "Best If the Americans Apologise Now—Soon the Chinese Could Rule the U.S.," *Guardian*, April 8, 2001, https://www.theguardian .com/world/2001/apr/09/china.usa.

39.   "The Dianne Feinstein Appease-China Award," *Weekly Standard*, September 29, 1997, https://www.washingtonexaminer.com/weekly-standard/the -dianne-feinstein-appease-china-award.

40.   Dianne Feinstein, "Opinion: U.S. Must Act in Face of Saudi Human Rights Violations," *Mercury News*, October 17, 2018, https://www.mercurynews .com/2018/10/17/opinion-feinstein/; "Subcommittee on Human Rights and the Law," Senate Committee on the Judiciary, accessed June 15, 2021, https:// www.judiciary.senate.gov/about/subcommittees/subcommittee-on-human -rights-and-the-law.

41. John Pomfret, "China's Influence on U.S. Congress Growing Steadily," *Austin American-Statesman*, last updated September 27, 2018, https://www.statesman .com/news/20120901/chinas-influence-on-us-congress-growing-steadily.

42. Faligot, *Chinese Spies*, 164; Easton, "Forget the Thelma and Louise Thing: Barbara Boxer and Dianne Feinstein Are Way Beyond the Election-Year Road Show."

43. Bunting, "Feinstein, Husband Hold Strong China Connections"; Ken Silverstein, "Their Masters' Voice: The Women's Shill Caucus," *Multinational Monitor* 18, no. 4, April 1997, https://www.multinationalmonitor.org/mm1997/ 041997/voice.html.

44. Silverstein, "Their Masters' Voice: The Women's Shill Caucus."

45. Weingarten, "Feinstein's Real Insider Trading Scandal Is Selling America Out to China."

46. Williams, "Husband Invested in China as Feinstein Pushed Trade."

47. Richard Simon, "Husband's Business Ties to China Dog Feinstein," *Los Angeles Times* (archives), October 20, 2000, https://www.latimes.com/archives /la-xpm-2000-oct-20-mn-39450-story.html.

48. Smith, "China Queen Dianne Feinstein Used Her Senate Power to Push Most-Favored-Nation Status for the CCP's Corrupt Dictatorship. Why?"

49. Williams, "Husband Invested in China as Feinstein Pushed Trade."

50. Simon, "Husband's Business Ties to China Dog Feinstein."

51. Robin Marriott, "CB Richard Ellis Invests in China," PERE, May 2, 2008, https://www.perenews.com/cb-richard-ellis-invests-in-china/; Jenny Auw-Yong, "CB Richard Ellis Expands in Northern China with New Office Presence in Dalian," PR Newswire, June 22, 2007, https://www.prweb.com /releases/2007/06/prweb534684.htm; "Richard Blum," Global Development Council, Obama White House Archives, accessed June 15, 2021, https:// obamawhitehouse.archives.gov/administration/advisory-boards/global -development-council/members/blum.

52. "20071035: Francisco Partners II, L.P.; Aeroflex Incorporated," Federal Trade Commission, April 11, 2007, https://www.ftc.gov/enforcement/premerger -notification-program/early-termination-notices/20071035.

53. Warren Ferster, "U.S. Satellite Component Maker Fined $8 Million for ITAR Violations," *Space News*, September 5, 2013, https://spacenews.com/37071us -satellite-component-maker-fined-8-million-for-itar-violations/.

54. Tish Drake, "Aeroflex Inks Deal in China," *Aviation Today*, August 29, 2007, https://www.aviationtoday.com/2007/08/29/aeroflex-inks-deal-in-china/.

55. John Shiffman and Duff Wilson, "RPT—SPECIAL REPORT—How China's Weapon Snatchers Are Penetrating U.S. Defenses," Reuters, December 17, 2013, https://www.reuters.com/article/breakout-sting/rpt -special-report-how-chinas-weapon-snatchers-are-penetrating-u-s-defenses -idUSL3N0JW3EG20131217.

56. Ferster, "U.S. Satellite Component Maker Fined $8 Million for ITAR Violations."

57. Dianne Feinstein, Public Financial Disclosure, July 15, 2005, https://pfds .opensecrets.org/N00007364_2004.pdf; "ZTE Selects Agere Network

Processors for Next-Gen DSL," ChinaTechNews, October 24, 2005, https://www.chinatechnews.com/2005/10/24/2903-zte-selects-agere-network-processors-for-next-gen-dsl; "ZTE to Show Its Cdma 2000 1x EV-DO System for the First Time at 3G World Congress," ZTE, December 12, 2003, https://www.zte.com.cn/global/about/magazine/zte-technologies/2002/6/en_335/161175.html.

58. USCC Research Staff, "The National Security Implications of Investments and Products from the People's Republic of China in the Telecommunications Sector," U.S.-China Economic and Security Review Commission Staff Report, January 2011, 22, https://www.uscc.gov/sites/default/files/Research/FINALREPORT_TheNationalSecurityImplicationsofInvestmentsandProductsfromThePRCintheTelecommunicationsSector.pdf.

59. "Lenovo's Links to China Government Under Scrutiny for Spying," *Aryavarth Express*, February 18, 2021, https://www.thearyavarthexpress.com/business/lenovos-links-to-china-government-under-scrutiny-for-spying/.

60. Tim Bajarin, "How a Chinese Company Became a Global PC Powerhouse," *Time*, May 4, 2015, https://time.com/3845674/lenovo-ibm/.

61. Adi Robertson, "Lenovo Reportedly Banned by M16, CIA, and Other Spy Agencies over Fear of Chinese Hacking (Update)," Verge, July 30, 2013, https://www.theverge.com/2013/7/30/4570780/lenovo-reportedly-banned-by-mi6-cia-over-chinese-hacking-fears.

62. Michael Singer, "Lenovo Gets Infusion of U.S. Cash," InternetNews.com, March 31, 2005, http://www.internetnews.com/ent-news/article.php/3494106/Lenovo+Gets+Infusion+of+U.S.+Cash.htm.

63. Richard C. Blum, "Conversations with Richard C. Blum: Businessman, Philanthropist, President Emeritus Board of Regents University of California," interviews conducted by Victor Geraci, Ann Lage, and Lisa Rubens, 2010–14, https://digitalassets.lib.berkeley.edu/roho/ucb/text/blum_richard_2015.pdf.

64. *USA v. Ehab Ashoor*, United States District Court, Southern District of Texas, Houston Division, No. H-09-CR-307, filed on January 9, 2010, https://assets.bwbx.io/documents/users/iqjWHBFdfxIU/r9dKMMM0Gi5I/v0.

65. Carla Marinucci, "A Busy Newsom Connects with China's Elite/Feinstein Helped Him Meet Ex-President, Shanghai Mayor," *San Francisco Chronicle*, last updated January 17, 2012, https://www.sfgate.com/politics/article/A-busy-Newsom-connects-with-China-s-elite-2590264.php; Rachel Gordon, "SAN FRANCISCO/Newsom Joins Feinstein on Sister-City Trip to Shanghai/Hong Kong and Beijing Also on Mayor's Itinerary," *San Francisco Chronicle*, last updated January 17, 2012, https://www.sfgate.com/politics/article/SAN-FRANCISCO-Newsom-joins-Feinstein-on-2592929.php.

66. Zach Dorfman, "How Silicon Valley Became a Den of Spies," *Politico*, July 27, 2018, https://www.politico.com/magazine/story/2018/07/27/silicon-valley-spies-china-russia-219071/; "Details Surface About Sen. Feinstein and the Chinese Spy Who Worked for Her," CBS San Francisco, August 1, 2018, https://sanfrancisco.cbslocal.com/2018/08/01/details-chinese-spy-dianne-feinstein-san-francisco/; Bill Gertz, "Inside the Ring: China Targeted

Dianne Feinstein Staff Member," *Washington Times*, August 8, 2018, https://www.washingtontimes.com/news/2018/aug/8/china-targeted-dianne-feinstein-staff-member/.

67. Dorfman, "How Silicon Valley Became a Den of Spies."

68. Marc A. Thiessen, "Opinion: The Poetic Justice in Eric Swalwell's Relationship with a Chinese Spy," *Washington Post*, December 10, 2020, https://www.washingtonpost.com/opinions/2020/12/10/poetic-justice-eric-swalwells-relationship-with-chinese-spy/.

69. Bethany Allen-Ebrahimian, "Exclusive: Suspected Chinese Spy Targeted California Politicians," Axios, last updated December 8, 2020, https://www.axios.com/china-spy-california-politicians-9d2dfb99-f839–4e00–8bd8–59dec0daf589.html; Amber Phillips, "What We Know About Rep. Eric Swalwell's Ties to an Alleged Chinese Spy," *Washington Post*, December 11, 2020, https://www.washingtonpost.com/politics/2020/12/11/what-we-know-about-rep-eric-swalwells-ties-an-alleged-chinese-spy/.

70. Bill Gertz, "Eric Swalwell's China Views Raise Security Questions," *Washington Times*, December 9, 2020, https://www.washingtontimes.com/news/2020/dec/9/eric-swalwells-china-views-raise-security-question/.

71. Robert Salladay, "Pelosi on China: A Voice in the Global Wilderness?," *San Francisco Chronicle*, last updated February 6, 2012, https://www.sfgate.com/news/article/Pelosi-on-China-A-voice-in-the-global-wilderness-3082494.php.

72. Congresswoman Nancy Pelosi, Testimony Before the Ways and Means Committee on the U.S.-China Bilateral Trade Agreement and the Accession of China to the WTO, February 16, 2000, https://pelosi.house.gov/sites/pelosi.house.gov/files/pressarchives/releases/prwymnchin.htm.

73. "Pelosi Statement on Amendment to Block Chinese Bid to Acquire Unocal," Congresswoman Nancy Pelosi, California's 12th District, press release, June 30, 2005, https://pelosi.house.gov/news/press-releases/pelosi-statement-on-amendment-to-block-chinese-bid-to-acquire-unocal.

74. Glenn Thrush, "Pelosi Still Hammers China," *Politico*, March 18, 2009, https://www.politico.com/story/2009/03/pelosi-still-hammers-china-020151.

75. Shai Oster, "Pelosi, in China, Seeks Consensus on Warming," *Wall Street Journal*, May 27, 2009, https://www.wsj.com/articles/SB124333266470153987.

76. Paul Singer, "Pelosi's Expert Was Also Business Partner," *Roll Call*, December 16, 2011, https://www.rollcall.com/2011/12/16/pelosis-expert-was-also-business-partner/.

77. Evan A. Feigenbaum, "Who's Behind China's High Technology 'Revolution'? How Bomb Makers Remade Beijing's Priorities, Policies, and Institutions," *International Security* 24, no. 1 (Summer 1999): 124.

78. Janet Yee, "Asian Leaders Plan for High-tech Success," ZDNet, November 19, 1999, https://www.zdnet.com/article/asian-leaders-plan-for-high-tech-success-5000104210/.

79. "Matthews China Fund," Matthews Asia, last updated March 31, 2021, https://www.matthewsasia.com/funds/asia-growth/china-fund/.

80. Singer, "Pelosi's Expert Was Also Business Partner."

81. "Former Carey CEO Founds China Concierge Service," *Travel Weekly*, April 28, 2008, https://www.travelweekly.com/Travel-News/Corporate-Travel /Former-Carey-CEO-founds-China-concierge-service; "Vince Wolfington," biography, Georgetown Basketball History Project, accessed June 16, 2021, http://www.hoyabasketball.com/players/v_wolfington.htm.

82. Congresswoman Nancy Pelosi, "Pelosi Calls Upon Congress to Oppose China's 2008 Olympic Bid," U.S. House of Representatives, press conference transcript, March 21, 2001, https://pelosi.house.gov/sites/pelosi.house.gov /files/pressarchives/releases/prchinaolympic3-21-01.htm.

83. Nancy Pelosi, Public Financial Disclosure, May 15, 2009, https://disclosures -clerk.house.gov/public_disc/financial-pdfs/2009/8140536.pdf; "Speaker Pelosi on the 2008 Olympic Games in Beijing," Nancy Pelosi Speaker of the House (blog), March 28, 2008, https://www.speaker.gov/newsroom/speaker -pelosi-on-the-2008-olympic-games-in-beijing.

84. Nancy Pelosi, Public Financial Disclosure, May 15, 2009, https://disclosures -clerk.house.gov/public_disc/financial-pdfs/2008/8135973.pdf; United States Securities and Exchange Commission, Form D, OMB No. 3235– 0076, received by CityCar Services LLC on January 11, 2006, https:// www.sec.gov/Archives/edgar/vprr/0602/06020318.pdf; Jake Sherman and John Bresnahan, "Who's Wealthiest in the House?," *Politico*, June 17, 2013, https://www.politico.com/story/2013/06/nancy-pelosi-eric-cantor -lead-list-of-wealthiest-house-leaders-092918; United States Securities and Exchange Commission, Form N-1A, filed by Matthews International Funds on October 29, 2010, https://www.sec.gov/Archives/edgar/data/923184 /000114420410056387/v200210_485bpos.htm.

85. "Paul Pelosi Jr. Joins Tree Top Industries Advisory Board," GlobeNewswire, June 22, 2010, https://www.globenewswire.com/fr/news-release/2010 /06/22/423607/12278/en/Paul-Pelosi-Jr-Joins-Tree-Top-Industries- Advisory-Board.html; "Tree Top Industries and Greenparts International, Inc. Evaluating Synergies," July 15, 2010, GlobeNewswire, https://www .globenewswire.com/news-release/2010/07/15/425183/12278/en/Tree-Top -Industries-and-Greenparts-International-Inc-Evaluating-Synergies.html.

86. "GTII Receives Final Audit Results from GoFun Group Holdings, Ltd.," Yahoo Finance, December 12, 2016, https://finance.yahoo.com/news/gtii -receives-final-audit-results-154500612.html; United States Securities and Exchange Commission, Forms S-1/A, Global Tech Industries Group, Inc., filed on August 18, 2021, https://www.marketwatch.com/investing/stock /gtii/SecArticle?guid=15176351.

87. "Global Tech Team Makes Trip to Hong Kong and China to Further Solidify Agreement with GoFun Group Holdings, Ltd.," Global Tech Industries Group, Inc., accessed September 4, 2021, http://gtii-us.com/2016/09/12 /global-tech-team-goes-to-hong-kong-and-china/.

88. Jerry Kronenberg, "SPAC Backed by House Speaker Nancy Pelosi's Son Inches Up after $200M IPO," *Seeking Alpha*, July 29, 2021, https://seekingalpha .com/news/3721798-spac-backed-by-house-speaker-nancy-pelosi-son-ipo.

89. Josh Rogin, *Chaos Under Heaven: Trump, Xi, and the Battle for the 21st Century*

(New York: HMH, 2021), 286; Associated Press, "WATCH: House GOP Say Democrats Are 'Stonewalling' COVID-19 Origins Probe," PBS, July 22, 2021, https://www.pbs.org/newshour/politics/watch-live-house-gop -members-hold-news-briefing-on-covid-delta-variant.

90. Peter Schweizer, *Secret Empires: How the American Political Class Hides Corruption and Enriches Family and Friends* (New York: Harper, 2019), 77–78.
91. "Jiang Zemin Meets U.S. Guests," Xinhua News Agency, December 30, 1993 (Lexis).
92. Schweizer, "McConnell and Chao: From China with Profits," in *Secret Empires*, 75–89.
93. "Foreign Influence? How McConnell Got Rich Off China," WorldNetDaily, March 18, 2018, https://www.wnd.com/2018/03/foreign-influence-how -mcconnell-got-rich-off-china/.
94. As quoted in Schweizer, *Secret Empires*, 84.
95. Michael Forsythe, Eric Lipton, Keith Bradsher, and Sui-Lee Wee, "A 'Bridge' to China, and Her Family's Business, in the Trump Cabinet," *New York Times*, June 2, 2019, https://www.nytimes.com/2019/06/02/us/politics/elaine -chao-china.html.
96. Schweizer, *Secret Empires*, 85.
97. "Foremost Group Adds to Orderbook with Kamsarmax Pair at Oshima," *IHS Fairplay Daily News*, July 25, 2018 (Lexis).
98. "H-Line Orders Largest LNG-Powered Bulk Carriers," Riviera, October 15, 2018, https://www.rivieramm.com/news-content-hub/news-content-hub/h -line-orders-largest-lng-powered-bulk-carriers-23048.
99. Schweizer, *Secret Empires,* 85.
100. Daniel Alderman and Rush Doshi, "Civil-Military Integration Potential in Chinese Shipbuilding," in *Chinese Naval Shipbuilding: An Ambitious and Uncertain Course*, ed. Andrew Erickson (Annapolis, MD: Naval Institute Press, 2016), 145–46.
101. Ibid.
102. Schweizer, *Secret Empires*, 84.
103. Ibid., 86.
104. Department of Transportation, Office of Inspector General, Letter to Chairman Peter DeFazio, Committee on Transportation and Infrastructure, U.S. House of Representatives, March 2, 2021, https://www.oig.dot.gov/sites/ default/files/DOT%20OIG%20Letter%20to%20Chairman%20Peter%20 DeFazio_2021-03-02.pdf.
105. Ibid.
106. "Directors and Board of Directors," Bank of China, accessed September 4, 2021, https://www.boc.cn/en/investor/ir6/201504/t20150402_4830133. html.
107. James Manyika, William H. McRaven, and Adam Segal, "Innovation and National Security: Keeping Our Edge," Council on Foreign Relations, Independent Task Force Report No. 77, 2019, accessed September 4, 2021, https://www.cfr.org/report/keeping-our-edge/pdf/TFR_Innovation_ Strategy.pdf.

108. Nathan Picarsic, "U.S. Investment in China's Capital Markets and Military-Industrial Complex," U.S.-China Economic and Security Review Commission, March 19, 2020, https://www.uscc.gov/sites/default/files/2021-03/Nate_Picarsic__Testimony.pdf.

109. Ryan Mac, Rosalind Adams, and Megha Rajagopalan, "US Universities and Retirees Are Funding the Technology Behind China's Surveillance State," BuzzFeed News, last updated June 5, 2019, https://www.buzzfeednews.com/article/ryanmac/us-money-funding-facial-recognition-sensetime-megvii.

110. Schweizer, *Secret Empires*, 79–80.

111. Olivier Knox, "Senate Passes China Currency Bill," IndustryWeek, October 11, 2011, https://www.industryweek.com/the-economy/article/21939588/senate-passes-china-currency-bill.

112. "Beijing," Squire Patton Boggs, accessed June 16, 2021, https://www.squirepattonboggs.com/en/locations/beijing; Tim Reid and Susan Cornwell, "Exclusive: China Launches Lobbying Push on Currency Bill," Reuters, October 12, 2011, https://www.reuters.com/article/us-usa-china-lobbying-newspro/exclusive-china-launches-lobbying-push-on-currency-bill-idUSTRE79B5PX20111012.

113. Knox, "Senate Passes China Currency Bill."

114. Scott N. Paul, "Paul: The High Cost of Our Addiction to China," CNBC, May 3, 2012, https://www.cnbc.com/id/47284584.

115. Justin Sink, "Republican Lawmakers Break with Boehner on China Currency Bill," *Hill*, October 5, 2011, https://thehill.com/blogs/blog-briefing-room/news/185755-republican-lawmakers-question-boehner-on-china-currency-bill.

116. Zhu Qiwen and Xin Zhiming, "Exchange Rate Could Float in a Wider Band," *China Daily*, last updated May 26, 2007, http://www.chinadaily.com.cn/china/2007-05/26/content_880766.htm; Lee Taylor Buckley, "China's Response to U.S. Pressure to Revalue the RMB," China Research Center, June 14, 2012, https://www.chinacenter.net/2012/china_currents/11-1/chinas-response-to-u-s-pressure-to-revalue-the-rmb/; Reid and Cornwell, "Exclusive: China Launches Lobbying Push on Currency Bill."

117. "John A. Boehner," Squire Patton Boggs, accessed June 16, 2021, https://www.squirepattonboggs.com/en/professionals/b/boehner-john.

118. U.S. Department of Justice, Supplemental Statement Pursuant to the Foreign Agents Registration Act of 1938, as amended, Squire Patton Boggs (U.S.) LLP, received January 29, 2021, https://efile.fara.gov/docs/2165-Supplemental-Statement-20210129-35.pdf.

119. Opensecrets.org, "Lobbying Firm Profile: Squire Patton Boggs," 2018, https://www.opensecrets.org/federal-lobbying/firms/summary?cycle=2018&id=D000067299; Opensecrets.org, "Lobbying Firm Profile: Squire Patton Boggs," 2019, https://www.opensecrets.org/federal-lobbying/firms/summary?cycle=2019&id=D000067299; Opensecrets.org, "Lobbying Firm Profile: Squire Patton Boggs," 2020, https://www.opensecrets.org/federal-lobbying/firms/summary?cycle=2020&id=D000067299; Opensecrets.org,

"Lobbying Firm Profile: Squire Patton Boggs," 2021, https://www.open secrets.org/federal-lobbying/firms/summary?cycle=2021&id=D000067299.

120. "Nick Chan Confirmed as Elected Member of the National People's Congress of the People's Republic of China," Squire Patton Boggs, May 17, 2019, https://www.squirepattonboggs.com/en/news/2019/05/nick-chan -confirmed-as-elected-member-of-the-national-peoples-congress-of-the -peoples-republic-of-china.

121. Company Profile of Squire Patton Boggs, Belt and Road, accessed June 16, 2021, https://beltandroad.hktdc.com/en/service-providers/squire-patton -boggs.

122. Steve Herman, "U.S. Seen Falling Short Countering China's Geopolitical Rise," States News Service, March 23, 2021, https://www.voanews.com/usa /us-politics/us-seen-falling-short-countering-chinas-rising-geopolitical-clout; "Trump Targets Belt And Road Initiative With US$60 Billion International Finance Development Corporation," Silk Road Briefing, October 22, 2019, https://www.silkroadbriefing.com/news/2019/10/22/trump-targets-belt-road -initiative-us60-billion-international-finance-development-corporation/.

123. Lily Kuo and Alicia Chen, "Chinese Workers Allege Forced Labor, Abuses in Xi's 'Belt and Road' Program," *Washington Post*, April 30, 2021, https://www .washingtonpost.com/world/asia_pacific/china-labor-belt-road-covid/2021 /04/30/f110e8de-9cd4-11eb-b2f5-7d2f0182750d_story.html.

124. "TikTok Case to Undermine U.S. Competitiveness Among Foreign Compa- nies, Says U.S. Lawyer," Shine, September 27, 2020, https://www.shine.cn /biz/company/2009276938/; "Trade Tensions Slowing Foreign Invest- ment in S. California: Business Leaders," Xinhuanet, May 22, 2019, http:// www.xinhuanet.com/english/2019-05/22/c_138080663.htm.

125. Opensecrets.org, "Client Profile: Alibaba Group," 2020, https://www.open secrets.org/federal-lobbying/clients/lobbyists?cycle=2020&id=D000064488.

126. "Tencent Security Forges Cyber Partnership with Qi An Xin," Intelligence Online, January 13, 2021, https://www.intelligenceonline.com/corporate -intelligence/2021/01/13/tencent-security-forges-cyber-partnership-with-qi -an-xin,109633901-art.

127. "Edward Royce," BallotPedia, accessed June 16, 2021, https://ballotpedia .org/Edward_Royce; Opensecrets.org, "Client Profile: Tencent Holdings," 2020, https://www.opensecrets.org/federal-lobbying/clients/lobbyists?cycle =2020&id=D000073651.

128. Alex Sherman, "TikTok Reveals Detailed User Numbers for the First Time," CNBC, August 24, 2020, https://www.cnbc.com/2020/08/24/tiktok-reveals -us-global-user-growth-numbers-for-first-time.html.

129. Matt Schrader, "Friends and Enemies: A Framework for Understanding Chi- nese Political Interference in Democratic Countries," Alliance for Securing Democracy, April 22, 2020, 10, https://securingdemocracy.gmfus.org/wp -content/uploads/2020/05/Friends-and-Enemies-A-Framework-for -Understanding-Chinese-Political-Interference-in-Democratic-Countries.pdf.

130. Kevin McCauley, "Breaux, Lott Lobby for TikTok," O'Dwyer's, January 19, 2021, https://www.odwyerpr.com/story/public/15516/2021-01-19/breaux

-lott-lobby-for-tiktok.html; Robin Toner, "PUBLIC LIVES; Deal-Making Adds the Spice to a Cajun Senator's Career," *New York Times*, June 28, 1999, https://www.nytimes.com/1999/06/28/us/public-lives-deal-making-adds-the-spice-to-a-cajun-senator-s-career.html.

131. Opensecrets.org, "Client Profile: ByteDance Inc.," 2020, https://www.open secrets.org/federal-lobbying/clients/lobbyists?cycle=2020&id=D000073174.

132. Christopher Balding, "ZTE's Ties to China's Military-Industrial Complex Run Deep," *Foreign Policy*, July 19, 2018, https://foreignpolicy.com/2018 /07/19/ztes-ties-to-chinas-military-industrial-complex-run-deep/; Open secrets.org, "Client Profile: ZTE Corp," 2019, http://www.opensecrets.org /federal-lobbying/clients/lobbyists?cycle=2019&id=D000071131.

133. Opensecrets.org, "Client Profile: Huawei Technologies," 2015, http://www .opensecrets.org/federal-lobbying/clients/lobbyists?cycle=2015&id =D000051951.

134. Faligot, *Chinese Spies*, 287.

135. Opensecrets.org, "Client Profile: China Ocean Shipping Group," 2019, http://www.opensecrets.org/federal-lobbying/clients/lobbyists?cycle =2019&id=D000073066.

136. Karl Evers-Hillstrom, "Huawei Hires Three New Lobbying Firms," *Hill*, July 7, 2021, https://thehill.com/business-a-lobbying/561979-huawei-hires -three-new-lobbying-firms.

137. John Collingridge, "Huawei's Founder Declares 'War' on West," *Times*, June 7, 2020, https://www.thetimes.co.uk/article/huaweis-founder-declares -war-on-west-95xfwh0dw; Sherisse Pham, "Who Is Huawei Founder Ren Zhengfei?," CNN Business, last updated March 14, 2019, https://www.cnn .com/2019/03/13/tech/huawei-ren-zhengfei/index.html.

138. Opensecrets.org, "Lobbyist Profile: Jack Kingston," 2017, https://www .opensecrets.org/federal-lobbying/lobbyists/summary?cycle=2017&id =Y0000051697L.

139. Anna Lehman-Ludwig, "Hikvision, Corporate Governance, and the Risks of Chinese Technology," Center for Strategic & International Studies, August 6, 2020, https://www.csis.org/blogs/technology-policy-blog/hikvision-corporate -governance-and-risks-chinese-technology.

140. Chris Buckley and Paul Mozur, "How China Uses High-Tech Surveillance to Subdue Minorities," *New York Times*, May 22, 2019, https://www.nytimes .com/2019/05/22/world/asia/china-surveillance-xinjiang.html.

141. Stephanie Grace, "Grace Notes: Vitter's Lobbying Firm Lands Big Contract; Former Colleague Raises Big Questions," *Advocate*, August 30, 2018, https://www.theadvocate.com/baton_rouge/opinion/stephanie_grace/ article_30abe60e-ac66-11e8-8cd2-0f1d7236b71e.html; Opensecrets.org, "Client Profile: Hikvision," 2019, https://www.opensecrets.org/federal -lobbying/clients/lobbyists?cycle=2019&id=F227731.

142. Lachlan Markay, "Scoop: Biden Inaugural Returns Cash from Ex-Senator-Turned-Foreign Agent," Axios, January 12, 2021, https://www.axios.com /barbara-boxer-biden-inaugural-foreign-agent-6022f95b-e6bd-44cc-b43c -2b7d50ffaca1.html; Caitlin McFall, "Barbara Boxer 'Deregisters' as Foreign

Agent for Chinese Surveillance Company That Targeted Uyghurs," Fox News, January 12, 2021, https://www.foxnews.com/politics/barbara-boxer -deregisters-as-foreign-agent-on-behalf-of-chinese-surveillance-company.

143. "Hong Kong Leader Resigns," CNN, March 10, 2005, http://edition.cnn .com/2005/WORLD/asiapcf/03/10/hongkong.tung/; Bethany Allen-Ebrahimian, "This Beijing-Linked Billionaire Is Funding Policy Research at Washington's Most Influential Institutions," *Foreign Policy*, November 28, 2017, https://foreignpolicy.com/2017/11/28/this-beijing-linked-billionaire -is-funding-policy-research-at-washingtons-most-influential-institutions -china-dc/.

144. Kris Cheng, "Central Gov't Exercises Overall Jurisdiction over Hong Kong, Says Xi Jinping in Communist Congress Speech," *Hong Kong Free Press*, October 18, 2017, https://hongkongfp.com/2017/10/18/central-govt-exercises -overall-jurisdiction-hong-kong-says-xi-jinping-communist-congress-speech/.

145. Clive Hamilton and Mareike Ohlberg, *Hidden Hand: Exposing How the Chinese Communist Party Is Reshaping the World* (London: Oneworld Publications, 2020), 83.

146. China–United States Exchange Foundation, 2019 Annual Report, 5.

147. Alexander Bowe, "China's Overseas United Front Work: Background and Implications for the United States," U.S.-China Economic and Security Review Commission, Staff Research Report, August 24, 2018, https://www .uscc.gov/node/551.

148. Larry Diamond and Orville Schell, eds., "Chinese Influence and American Interests: Promoting Constructive Vigilance," Hoover Institution, Stanford University, November 29, 2018, 60.

149. Bowe, "China's Overseas United Front Work: Background and Implications for the United States"; Opensecrets.org, "China-U.S. Exchange Foundation," Annual Lobbying Totals: 1998–2020, https://www.opensecrets.org/orgs/china -us-exchange-foundation/lobbying?id=D000048641.

150. Hamilton and Ohlberg, *Hidden Hand*, 210.

151. China–United States Exchange Foundation, Annual Report, 2019.

152. Center for American Progress, "The Next Phase: CAP Trip Report and Findings on the Future of U.S.-China Relations," November 2009, 1, https:// www.americanprogress.org/issues/security/reports/2009/11/12/6909/the -next-phase/; Allen-Ebrahimian, "This Beijing-Linked Billionaire Is Funding Policy Research at Washington's Most Influential Institutions."

153. Center for American Progress, "The Next Phase: CAP Trip Report and Findings on the Future of U.S.-China Relations."

154. "John Podesta," Georgetown Law, accessed June 16, 2021, https://www.law .georgetown.edu/faculty/john-podesta; "Todd Stern," Brookings, accessed June 16, 2021, https://www.brookings.edu/experts/todd-stern.

155. "Podesta Defends China Solar Biz," Jack O'Dwyer's Newsletter, February 13, 2012 (Lexis).

156. Liz Peek, "China's Rising Emissions Prove Trump Right on Paris Agreement," *Hill*, June 5, 2018, https://thehill.com/opinion/energy-environment/390741 -chinas-rising-emissions-prove-trump-right-on-paris-agreement.

157. Latika Bourke, "Podesta: Quad Will Demand Australia Does More on Climate Change," *Sydney Morning Herald*, April 28, 2021, https://www.smh.com.au/world/europe/podesta-quad-will-demand-australia-does-more-on-climate-change-20210427-p57mwa.html.

158. Myriam Robin and Joe Aston, "Rear Window," *Australian Financial Review*, July 16, 2021.

159. Caroline Downey, "Pelosi: U.S. Must Work with China on 'Overriding' Climate Issue Despite Uyghur Genocide," *National Review*, September 16, 2021, https://www.yahoo.com/now/pelosi-u-must-china-overriding-202019541.html.

160. Callie Patteson, "John Kerry Prioritizes Climate Change, Not Uyghur Abuses, with China," *New York Post*, September 23, 2021, https://nypost.com/2021/09/23/john-kerry-says-climate-change-is-priority-with-china/.

161. "China," Climate Action Tracker, September 21, 2020, https://climateactiontracker.org/countries/china/pledges-and-targets/.

162. "China Has Militarised the South China Sea and Got Away With It," *Economist*, June 21, 2018, https://www.economist.com/asia/2018/06/21/china-has-militarised-the-south-china-sea-and-got-away-with-it.

163. Kenneth Rapoza, "How China's Solar Industry Is Set Up to Be the New Green OPEC," *Forbes*, March 14, 2021, https://www.forbes.com/sites/kenrapoza/2021/03/14/how-chinas-solar-industry-is-set-up-to-be-the-new-green-opec/?sh=322823011446.

164. Opensecrets.org, "Client Profile: China-U.S. Exchange Foundation," 2015, https://www.opensecrets.org/federal-lobbying/clients/lobbyists?cycle=2015&id=D000048641 (see also: Reports for 2016, 2017).

165. Steven Musil, "China's ZTE Pleads Guilty to Selling U.S. Tech to Iran," CNET, March 22, 2017, https://www.cnet.com/news/chinas-zte-pleads-guilty-to-selling-us-tech-to-iran/.

166. Opensecrets.org, "Client Profile: ZTE Corp," 2016, https://www.opensecrets.org/federal-lobbying/clients/lobbyists?cycle=2016&id=D000071131 (see also: Report for 2017).

167. Charles Arthur, "China's Huawei and ZTE Pose National Security Threat," *Guardian*, October 8, 2012, https://www.theguardian.com/technology/2012/oct/08/china-huawei-zte-security-threat.

168. Richard Pollock, "EXCLUSIVE: Tony Podesta Made $500K Lobbying for Chinese Firm Convicted of Illegal Sales to Iran," *Daily Caller*, March 27, 2017, https://dailycaller.com/2017/03/27/exclusive-tony-podesta-made-500k-lobbying-for-chinese-firm-convicted-of-illegal-sales-to-iran/.

169. Karl Evers-Hillstrom, "Lobbyist Tony Podesta Returns to Work for Huawei," *Hill*, July 23, 2021, https://thehill.com/business-a-lobbying/business-a-lobbying/564573-lobbyist-tony-podesta-returns-to-work-for-huawei.

170. "China's Huawei Hires Democratic Lobbyist Tony Podesta," Huawei, July 23, 2021, https://consumer.huawei.com/ph/community/details/China-s-Huawei-Hires-Democratic-Lobbyist-Tony-Podesta/topicId_139786/.

171. Adam Behsudi, "Boustany Making Bid for Top Trade Spot," *Politico*, December 1, 2016, https://www.politico.com/blogs/donald-trump-administration/2016/12/charles-boustany-trump-trade-232085.

172. U.S. Department of Justice, Exhibit B to Registration Statement Pursuant to Foreign Agents Registration Act of 1938, as amended, Capitol Counsel LLC, received January 15, 2019, https://efile.fara.gov/docs/6328-Exhibit -AB-20190115-8.pdf.

173. "Former Congressional Leaders Tour China 2019–2019," China–United States Exchange Foundation, accessed June 16, 2021, https://www.cusef.org. hk/en/what-we-do/in-country-programs/engaging-with-american-leaders /former-congressional-leaders-tour-china.

174. "Former Rep. Charles Boustany Calls for Immediate End to Chinese Trade War," Louisiana Radio Network, December 14, 2018, https://louisianaradio network.com/2018/12/14/former-rep-charles-boustany-calls-for-immediate -end-to-chinese-trade-war/.

175. U.S. Department of Justice, Exhibit B to Registration Statement Pursuant to Foreign Agents Registration Act of 1938, as amended, Capitol Counsel LLC, received March 30, 2019, https://efile.fara.gov/docs/6328-Exhibit-AB -20190320-10.pdf; Keturah Hetrick, "Caught Our Eye," Legistorm, March 1, 2018, https://www.legistorm.com/pro_news/2121/ex-rep-boustany -registers-as-chinese-and-turkish-agent.html.

176. "Governor Haley Barbour," BGR Group, accessed June 16 2021, https:// bgrdc.com/team-member-post/governor-haley-barbour/; "Lester Munson," BGR Group, accessed June 16, 2021, https://bgrdc.com/team-member-post /lester-munson/; Opensecrets.org, "Lobbying Firm Profile: BGR Group," 2019, https://www.opensecrets.org/federal-lobbying/firms/summary? cycle=2019&id=D000021679.

177. "Fontheim International, LLC," LinkedIn profile, accessed June 17, 2021, https://www.linkedin.com/company/fontheim-international-llc/about/.

178. Lee Fang, "Clinton, Rubio, Cruz Receive Foreign Policy Advice from the Same Consulting Firm," Intercept, December 18, 2015, https://theintercept. com/2015/12/18/beacon-global-strategies/; John Dotson, "The China-U.S. Exchange Foundation and United Front 'Lobbying Laundering' in American Politics," Jamestown Foundation, September 16, 2020, https://jamestown.org /program/the-china-u-s-exchange-foundation-and-united-front-lobbying -laundering-in-american-politics/; Opensecrets.org, "Lobbying Profile: Fon- theim International," 2009, https://www.opensecrets.org/federal-lobbying /firms/summary?cycle=2009&id=D000033739.

179. "The 2016 Power 100," Washington Life Magazine, May 4, 2016, 52, https:// issuu.com/washingtonlife/docs/wl0516-digital; Fang, "Clinton, Rubio, Cruz Receive Foreign Policy Advice from the Same Consulting Firm."

180. "Leon Panetta," Beacon Global Strategies, accessed June 16, 2021, https:// bgsdc.com/team_member/leon-panetta/; "Michael Morell," Beacon Global Strategies, accessed June 16, 2021, https://bgsdc.com/team_member/michael -morell/.

181. Home page, Beacon Global Strategies, accessed June 16, 2021, https:// bgsdc.com/.

182. Fang, "Clinton, Rubio, Cruz Receive Foreign Policy Advice from the Same Consulting Firm."

183. "Michael Allen," Meridian, accessed June 16, 2021, https://www.meridian
     .org/profile/michael-allen/.

184. Don Clark, "AMD to License Chip Technology to China Chip Venture,"
     Wall Street Journal, April 21, 2016, https://www.wsj.com/articles/amd-to
     -license-chip-technology-to-china-chip-venture-1461269701?mod=article
     _inline.

185. Ibid.; Kate O'Keeffe and Brian Spegele, "How a Big U.S. Chip Maker Gave
     China the 'Keys to the Kingdom,'" *Wall Street Journal*, June 27, 2019, https://
     www.wsj.com/articles/u-s-tried-to-stop-china-acquiring-world-class-chips
     -china-got-them-anyway-11561646798.

186. Ibid.

187. Ibid.

188. Ibid.

189. O'Keeffe and Spegele, "How a Big U.S. Chip Maker Gave China the 'Keys
     to the Kingdom'"; Paul Alcorn, "U.S. Will Add AMD's China Joint Venture
     to Entity List, Cut Access to U.S. Technology (Updated)," Tom's Hardware,
     June 21, 2019, https://www.tomshardware.com/news/amd-joint-venture
     -partner-banned-us-trade-war,39703.html.

190. Ian King, Ben Brody, and Saleha Mohsin, "Qualcomm Outspent Broadcom
     About 100 to 1 in Washington Lobbying," Bloomberg, last updated March 15,
     2018, https://www.bloombergquint.com/technology/qualcomm-outspent
     -broadcom-about-100-to-1-in-washington-lobbying.

191. Chris Sanders, "U.S. Sees National Security Risk from Broadcom Qual-
     comm Deal," Reuters, March 6, 2018, https://www.reuters.com/article
     /us-qualcomm-m-a-broadcom/u-s-sees-national-security-risk-from
     -broadcoms-qualcomm-deal-idUSKCN1GI1S8; Steve McCaskill, "Broadcom
     Forecasts Lower Revenues After Huawei Ban," Techradar.pro, June 14,
     2019, https://www.techradar.com/news/broadcom-forecasts-lower
     -revnues-after-huawei-ban.

192. Ibid.

193. King, Brody, and Mohsin, "Qualcomm Outspent Broadcom About 100 to 1
     in Washington Lobbying."

194. Chloe Aiello, "Trump Blocks Broadcom-Qualcomm Deal, Citing National
     Security Concerns," CNBC, last updated March 13, 2018, https://www
     .cnbc.com/2018/03/12/trump-issues-order-prohibiting-broadcoms-bid-to
     -take-over-qualcomm.html.

4: Silicon Valley

1. Matt Sheehan, *The Transpacific Experiment: How China and California Collaborate
    and Compete for Our Future* (Berkeley, CA: Counterpoint, 2019), 118.

2. Associated Press, "Obama Hosts Lavish Dinner for China's President Xi Jinping,"
    NBC News, September 26, 2015, https://www.nbcnews.com/politics/white
    -house/obama-hosts-lavish-state-dinner-chinas-president-xi-jinping-n434126;
    Terry Mulcahy, "Delicacies and Decadence: The Chinese State Dinner," *Polit-
    ico*, September 26, 2015, https://www.politico.com/gallery/2015/09
    /chinese-state-dinner-gallery-002117?slide=1; Veronica Toney, "Complete

Guest List for the State Dinner in Honor of Chinese President Xi Jinping," *Washington Post*, September 25, 2015, https://www.washingtonpost .com/news/reliable-source/wp/2015/09/25/complete-guest-list-for-the-state -dinner-in-honor-of-chinese-president-xi-jinping/; Sheehan, *The Transpacific Experiment*, 119.

3. Ibid., 117.
4. Lu Wei, biography, China Vitae, https://www.chinavitae.com/biography /Lu_Wei; Joshua Phillipp, "Google Calls Out Chinese Internet Authority for Cyberattack," last updated April 17, 2015, https://www.theepochtimes.com /google-calls-out-chinese-internet-authority-for-cyberattack_1298038.html.
5. Sheehan, *The Transpacific Experiment*, 91.
6. Matthew Bell, "China's Internet Censor-in-Chief Gets a Warm Welcome at Facebook Headquarters," The World, December 9, 2014, https://www.pri .org/stories/2014-12-09/chinas-internet-censor-chief-gets-warm-welcome -facebook-headquarters.
7. Xi Jinping, *The Governance of China* (Mainland China: Foreign Languages Press, 2014), https://www.google.com/books/edition/_/wpn5oQEACAAJ?hl=en.
8. Rory Stott, "Facebook Moves into New Headquarters with the 'Largest Open Floor Plan in the World,'" *ArchDaily*, March 30, 2015, https:// www.archdaily.com/614515/facebook-moves-into-new-headquarters -with-the-largest-open-floor-plan-in-the-world; Sheehan, *The Transpacific Experiment*, 117.
9. Sheehan, *The Transpacific Experiment*, 117.
10. David P. Goldman, *You Will Be Assimilated: China's Plan to Sino-form the World* (New York: Bombadier, 2020), 140; Tarun Chhabra, Rush Doshi, Ryan Hass, and Emilie Kimball, "Global China: Technology," Brookings, April 2020, https://www.brookings.edu/research/global-china-technology/.
11. Anna B. Puglisi, "The Myth of the Stateless Global Society," in William C. Hannas and Didi Kirsten Tatlow, eds., *China's Quest for Foreign Technology: Beyond Espionage* (New York: Routledge, 2021) (emphasis in original), 75–76.
12. "Military-Civil Fusion and the People's Republic of China," U.S. Department of State, accessed June 19, 2021, https://www.state.gov/wp-content /uploads/2020/05/What-is-MCF-One-Pager.pdf.
13. Hao Xiaoming, Kewen Zhang, and Huang Yu, "The Internet and Information Control: The Case of China," *Electronic Journal of Communication* 6, no. 2 (1996), http://www.cios.org/EJCPUBLIC/006/2/00625.HTML.
14. Sheehan, *The Transpacific Experiment*, 70.
15. Ibid.; Robert McMillan, "Bill Gates: Internet Censorship Won't Work," *New York Times* (archives), February 20, 2008, https://archive.nytimes.com /www.nytimes.com/idg/IDG_002570DE00740E18882573F50010C487 .html?ref=technolog.
16. "Undermining Freedom of Expression in China: The Role of Yahoo!, Microsoft and Google," Amnesty International UK, July 2006, 20–21, https://www.amnesty.org/en/documents/POL30/026/2006/en/.
17. Joseph Cox, "Bing Censors Image Search for 'Tank Man' Even in U.S.," Vice, June 4, 2021, https://www.vice.com/en/article/qj8v9m/bing-censors

-tank-man; Julia Carrie Wong, "Microsoft Blocks Bing from Showing Image Results for Tiananmen 'Tank Man,'" *Guardian*, June 4, 2021, https://www
.theguardian.com/technology/2021/jun/04/microsoft-bing-tiananmen-tank
-man-results.

18. "Bill Gates Bats for China," Embassy of the People's Republic of China in the United States of America, accessed June 19, 2021, http://www.china-embassy
.org/eng/xw/t654165.htm.

19. Bobbie Johnson, "Web Censorship in China? Not a Problem, Says Bill Gates," *Guardian*, January 25, 2010, https://www.theguardian.com/technology/2010
/jan/25/bill-gates-web-censorship-china.

20. "Undermining Freedom of Expression in China: The Role of Yahoo!, Micro-soft and Google."

21. Brier Dudley, "Microsoft Plans to Outsource More, Says Ex-Worker," *Seattle Times*, September 3, 2005, https://www.seattletimes.com/business/microsoft
-plans-to-outsource-more-says-ex-worker/.

22. Steven Schwankert, "Bill Gates Named to Influential Foreigner List in China," NetworkWorld, August 3, 2006, https://www.networkworld.com
/article/2305536/bill-gates-named-to-influential-foreigner-list-in-china.html.

23. Mike Gudgell, "Chinese President Meets Bill Gates First," ABC News, April 20, 2006, https://abcnews.go.com/International/story?id=1857539&page=1.

24. Madhumita Murgia and Yuan Yang, "Microsoft Worked with Chinese Military University on Artificial Intelligence," *Financial Times*, April 10, 2019, https://www.ft.com/content/9378e7ee-5ae6-11e9-9dde-7aedca0a081a; Alex Joske, "The Chinese Military's Exploitation of Western Tech Firms," Strate-gist, April 12, 2019, https://www.aspistrategist.org.au/the-chinese-militarys
-exploitation-of-western-tech-firms/.

25. Adam Clark Estes, "Why Microsoft Is Letting Chinese Censors Spy on Skype Users," Vice, March 8, 2013, https://www.vice.com/en/article/bmmkyz
/skype-cant-be-stopped; Vernon Silver, "Cracking China's Skype Surveillance Software," Bloomberg, March 8, 2013, https://www.bloomberg.com/news
/articles/2013-03-08/cracking-chinas-skype-surveillance-software#p1.

26. "U.S. Tech Companies and Their Chinese Partners with Military Ties," *New York Times*, October 30, 2015, https://www.nytimes.com/interactive/2015
/10/30/technology/US-Tech-Firms-and-Their-Chinese-Partnerships.html; Gregg Keizer, "Microsoft Partners with Chinese State-Owned Defense Con-glomerate to Promote, Sell Windows 10 to Government," Computerworld, December 18, 2015, https://www.computerworld.com/article/3016921
/microsoft-partners-with-chinese-state-owned-defense-conglomerate-to
-promote-sell-windows-10-to-gove.html; Gregg Keizer, "Microsoft Wraps Up Special Windows 10 Edition for China's Government," Computerworld, March 28, 2016, https://www.computerworld.com/article/3048752
/microsoft-wraps-up-special-windows-10-edition-for-chinas-government
.html.

27. Jay Yarow, "Bill Gates Steps Down as Microsoft Chairman to Become a 'Technology Advisor,'" Business Insider, February 4, 2014, https://www
.businessinsider.com/bill-gates-2014-2; Raymond Li, "Gates Teams Up with

China to Build Nuclear Reactor," *South China Morning Post*, December 5, 2011, https://www.scmp.com/article/986859/gates-teams-china-build -nuclear-reactor; "About Us," TerraPower, accessed June 19, 2021, https:// www.terrapower.com/about/.

28. William Freebairn, "TerraPower Advances Design, Moves to Share Information with China," Platts Nucleonics Week, May 15, 2014 (Lexis); J. Michael Waller, "U.S. Gives China the Advantage in Next-Generation Nuclear Technology," Center for Security Policy, July 13, 2020, https://www.centerfor securitypolicy.org/2020/07/13/us-gives-china-the-advantage-in-next -generation-nuclear-technology/.

29. Dr. Christopher Ashely Ford, Assistant Secretary, Bureau of International Security and Nonproliferation, "Competitive Strategy Vis-à-vis China: The Case Study of Civil-Nuclear Cooperation," U.S. Department of State, Remarks to the Project 2049 Institute, June 24, 2019, https://2017-2021.state. gov/competitive-strategy-vis-a-vis-china-the-case-study-of-civil-nuclear -cooperation/index.html; Liz George, "Bill Gates' Nuclear Firm Collaborated with Chinese Military-linked Company," *American Military News*, July 30, 2020, https://americanmilitarynews.com/2020/07/bill-gates-nuclear-firm -collaborated-with-chinese-military-linked-company/.

30. Stephen Chen, "China Hopes Cold War Nuclear Energy Tech Will Power Warships, Drones," *South China Morning Post*, December 5, 2017, https:// www.scmp.com/news/china/society/article/2122977/china-hopes-cold-war -nuclear-energy-tech-will-power-warships; Waller, "U.S. Gives China the Advantage in Next-Generation Nuclear Technology."

31. Bethany Allen-Ebrahimian and Zach Dorfman, "Defense Department Produces List of Chinese Military-Linked Companies," Axios, June 24, 2020, https://www.axios.com/defense-department-chinese-military-linked -companies-856b9315-48d2-4aec-b932-97b8f29a4d40.html; Wang Xiaoyu, "Despite 'Setback,' Gates Pledges to Work with China on Nuclear Energy," *China Daily*, November 23, 2019, https://www.chinadaily.com.cn/a/201911 /23/WS5dd88706a310cf3e35579711.html.

32. Ibid.

33. Rebecca Fannin, *Tech Titans of China: How China's Tech Sector Is Challenging the World by Innovating Faster, Working Harder, and Going Global* (Boston: Nicholas Brealey, 2019), 208; Mark L. Clifford, "China's BYD and Korea's Samsung: Can Two Battery Kings Forge a Profitable Partnership?" *Forbes*, July 20, 2016, https:// www.forbes.com/sites/mclifford/2016/07/20/chinas-byd-and-koreas-samsung -can-two-battery-kings-forge-a-profitable-partnership/?sh=324afbc03c8d; Cong Mu, "Star Power Graces BYD Event," *Global Times*, September 30, 2010, https:// www.globaltimes.cn/content/578736.shtml.

34. "Building the China Dream: BYD & China's Grand Strategic Offensive," Radarlock, October 2019, https://www.americanmanufacturing.org/wp -content/uploads/2020/03/BYD.pdf; Curtis J. Milhaupt and Wentong Zheng, "Beyond Ownership: State Capitalism and the Chinese Firm," *Georgetown Law Journal* 103, no. 665 (March 1, 2015): 719, https://www-cdn.law .stanford.edu/wp-content/uploads/2017/04/103GeoLJ665.pdf.

35. Zhang Niansheng, "Bill Gates: 'I Am Impressed of How Hard President Xi Works,'" people.cn, April 6, 2017, http://en.people.cn/n3/2017/0406 /c90000-9199651.html.

36. "Bill Gates Elected as a Member of China's Top Academic Institution," people.cn, November 27, 2017, http://en.people.cn/n3/2017/1127/c90000 -9297429.html; Lorand Laskai, "Civil-Military Fusion and the PLA's Pursuit of Dominance in Emerging Technologies," *China Brief* 18, no. 6 (April 2018), https://jamestown.org/program/civil-military-fusion-and-the-plas-pursuit -of-dominance-in-emerging-technologies/; Ryan Fedasiuk, Emily Weinstein, Ben Murphy, and Alan Omar Loera Martinez, "Chinese State Council Budget Tracker," https://statecouncil.cset.tech/.

37. "Bill Gates Elected . . ."

38. "Xi's Thought Enshrined in CPC Constitution," Chinese Academy of Engineering, October 25, 2017, http://en.cae.cn/en/Important%20Events /Year%202017/2017-10-25/12159.html.

39. "China's Nuclear Weapon R&D Founder Remembered," Chinese Academy of Engineering, March 1, 2012, http://en.cae.cn/en/Important%20Events /Year%202012/2012-04-11/11542.html.

40. Cui Jia, "Gates Added to Top-Tier Chinese Academy," *China Daily Europe*, last updated December 1, 2017, https://europe.chinadaily.com.cn/epaper /2017–12/01/content_35149688.htm.

41. Chen Huanhuan, "The Third Meeting of 'Great Wall Engineering Science and Technology Conference' Focuses on Artificial Intelligence," ScienceNet. cn, June 26, 2017, http://news.sciencenet.cn/htmlnews/2017/6/380507.shtm; Elsa B. Kania, Testimony Before the U.S.-China Economic and Security Review Commission Hearing on Trade, Technology, and Military-Civil Fusion, "Chinese Military Innovation in Artificial Intelligence," Center for a New American Security, June 7, 2019, https://www.uscc.gov/sites/default/files /June%207%20Hearing_Panel%201_Elsa%20Kania_Chinese%20Military %20Innovation%20in%20Artificial%20Intelligence_0.pdf.

42. China Military Online, "PLA Navy Signs Partnership Agreement with Chinese Academy of Engineering," english.people.cn, October 25, 2012, http:// en.people.cn/90786/7990307.html.

43. Murgia and Yang, "Microsoft Worked with Chinese Military University on Artificial Intelligence."

44. Gordon Corera, "China Accused of Cyber-Attack on Microsoft Exchange Servers," BBC News, July 19, 2021, https://www.bbc.com/news/world-asia -china-57889981.

45. Aylin Woodward, "At Least 5 People in China Have Disappeared, Gotten Arrested, or Been Silenced After Speaking Out About the Coronavirus–Here's What We Know About Them," Business Insider, February 20, 2020, https:// www.businessinsider.com/china-coronavirus-whistleblowers-speak-out -vanish-2020–2#when-i-saw-them-circulating-online-i-realized-that-it -was-out-of-my-control-and-i-would-probably-be-punished-li-told-cnn-6; Nectar Gan and Natalie Thomas, "Chen Qiushi Spoke Out About the Wuhan Virus. Now His Family and Friends Fear He's Been Silenced," CNN,

February 9, 2020, https://www.cnn.com/2020/02/09/asia/wuhan-citizen
-journalist-intl-hnk/index.html; Mairead MCardle, "Chinese Doctor Dis-
appears After Blowing the Whistle on Coronavirus Threat," *National Review*,
April 1, 2020, https://www.nationalreview.com/news/coronavirus
-china-doctor-disappears-warned-about-covid-19-threat/; Ryan Pickrell,
"Chinese Official Says U.S. Army May Have 'Brought the Epidemic to Wuhan,'" Military.com, March 12, 2020, https://www.military.com/daily
-news/2020/03/12/chinese-official-says-us-army-may-have-brought
-epidemic-wuhan.html; Jackie Salo, "Bill Gates Says China 'Did a Lot of
Things Right' with Coronavirus Response," *New York Post*, April 27, 2020,
https://nypost.com/2020/04/27/bill-gates-defends-chinas-response-to
-coronavirus/.

46. Tyler O'Neil, "Gates Foundation Helped 'Raise China's Voice of Governance' in Africa, Emails Show," Foxbusiness.com, August 29, 2021, https://
www.foxbusiness.com/technology/gates-foundation-helped-raise-chinas
-voice-of-governance-in-africa-newly-released-emails-show.

47. William Yuen Yee, "Google Parent Company Alphabet Is Back in China
(Because It Never Left)," SupChina, June 18, 2020, https://supchina
.com/2020/06/18/google-parent-company-alphabet-is-back-in-china
-because-it-never-left/.

48. Quoted in Steven Levy, *In the Plex: How Google Thinks, Works, and Shapes Our
Lives* (New York: Simon & Schuster, 2011), 2, 288.

49. Levy, *In the Plex*, 305, 310.

50. Yee, "Google Parent Company Alphabet Is Back in China (Because It Never
Left)."

51. Sam Shead, "Google Is Opening a New AI Research Centre in China
(GOOG)," Yahoo News, December 13, 2017, https://www.yahoo.com/news
/google-opening-ai-research-centre-101919947.html.

52. James Vincent, "Google Opens Chinese AI Lab, Says 'Science Has
No Borders,'" Verge, December 13, 2017, https://www.theverge.
com/2017/12/13/16771134/google-ai-lab-china-research-center.

53. Graham Webster, Rogier Creemers, Paul Triolo, and Elsa Kania, China State
Council, "Full Translation: China's 'New Generation Artificial Intelligence
Development Plan' (2017)," translation provided by New America, August 1,
2017, https://www.newamerica.org/cybersecurity-initiative/digichina/blog
/full-translation-chinas-new-generation-artificial-intelligence-development
-plan-2017/.

54. Belinda Robinson, "Too Early to Pick Artificial Intelligence Winner," *China
Daily*, August 27, 2019, https://www.chinadaily.com.cn/a/201908/27
/WS5d654a0ca310cf3e355682fc.html.

55. Peter Thiel, "Good for Google, Bad for America," *New York Times*, August 1,
2019, https://www.nytimes.com/2019/08/01/opinion/peter-thiel-google
.html.

56. Idrees Ali and Patricia Zengerle, "Google's Work in China Benefiting China's
Military: U.S. General," Reuters, March 14, 2019, https://www.reuters.com
/article/us-usa-china-google/googles-work-in-china-benefiting-chinas

-military-u-s-general-idUSKCN1QV296; Amanda Macias, "America's Top Defense Officials Say Google's Work in China Benefits Beijing's Military," CNBC, March 14, 2019, https://www.cnbc.com/2019/03/14/americas-top -defense-officials-say-googles-work-in-china-benefits-chinese-military.html.

57. Aaron Gregg, "Google Bows Out of Pentagon's $10 billion Cloud-Computing Race," *Washington Post*, October 9, 2018, https://www.washingtonpost.com/business /2018/10/09/google-bows-out-out-pentagons-billion-cloud-computing-race/.

58. "Final Report," National Security Commission on Artificial Intelligence, 27, https://www.nscai.gov/wp-content/uploads/2021/03/Full-Report-Digital-1. pdf.

59. Ibid., 741; Richard Nieva, "Eric Schmidt, Who Led Google's Transformation into a Tech Giant, Has Left the Company," CNET, May 9, 2020, https:// www.cnet.com/news/eric-schmidt-who-led-googles-transformation-into-a -tech-giant-has-left-the-company/.

60. Joske, "The Chinese Military's Exploitation of Western Tech Firms"; Celia Chen and Sarah Dai, "How 'China's MIT' Tsinghua University Drives the Country's Tech Ambitions," *South China Morning Post*, May 6, 2018, https:// www.scmp.com/tech/china-tech/article/2144741/how-chinas-mit -drives-countrys-tech-ambitions; Elsa B. Kania (@EBKania), "I wanted to share . . . ," Twitter, March 17, 2019, 6:41 p.m., https://twitter.com/EBKania /status/1107411735818969088.

61. Roslyn Layton, "Commerce Allows Sales to Memory Chip Maker YMTC Despite Ties to Chinese Military," *Forbes*, May 13, 2021, https://www.forbes .com/sites/roslynlayton/2021/05/13/commerce-allows-sales-to-memory -chip-maker-ymtc-despite-ties-to-chinese-military/?sh=10c271c69c96.

62. "U.S. Tech Companies and Their Chinese Partners with Military Ties."

63. Speech by You Zheng (尤政), vice president of Tsinghua University, "The Road of Military-Civil Fusion for Artificial Intelligence Development," June 8, 2018, translated at https://www.battlefieldsingularity.com/post/tsinghua-s -approach-to-military-civil-fusion-in-artificial-intelligence.

64. Xu Wei, "Google to Set Up AI Lab with Chinese University as Second China App Comes out," Yicai Global, June 1, 2018, https://www.yicaiglobal.com /news/google-to-set-up-ai-lab-with-chinese-university-as-second-china-app -comes-out.

65. Samuel Wade, "U.S. Companies Fuel Surveillance in China," China Digital Times, March 22, 2019, https://chinadigitaltimes.net/2019/03/u-s -companies-fuel-surveillance-in-china-as-chinese-companies-export-it/.

66. Elsa B. Kania (@EBKania), "Tsinghua vice president You Zheng . . . ," Twitter, March 17, 2019, 7:06 p.m., https://twitter.com/ebkania/status /1107417838971768837.

67. Kai Strittmatter, *We Have Been Harmonized: Life in China's Surveillance State* (New York: Custom House, 2020), 298.

68. "'Wisdom' Wins the Era, See How This Young Teacher Researches for War and 'Calculates' for Victory," kknews.cc, December 29, 2016, https://kknews .cc/zh-sg/military/g2jbqre.html; Alex Joske, "The Chinese Military and Exploitation of Western Technology Firms," SLDinfo.com, April 17, 2019,

https://sldinfo.com/2019/04/the-chinese-military-and-exploitation-of
-western-technology-firms/.

69. "China Eyeing Google's Touchscreen Tech for Stealth Fighters?," *Week*
     (India), July 6, 2019, https://www.theweek.in/news/sci-tech/2019/07/06
     /china-eyeing-google-touchscreen-tech-for-stealth-fighter.html; Liu Zhen,
     "J-20 vs F-22: How China's Chengdu J-20 'Powerful Dragon' Compares
     with U.S.' Lockheed Martin F-22 Raptor," *South China Morning Post*, July 28,
     2018, https://www.scmp.com/news/china/diplomacy-defence/article
     /2157275/powerful-dragon-v-raptor-how-chinas-j-20-stealth; Stephen Chen,
     "Google Denies Link to China's Military over Touch-Screen Tools That May
     Help PLA Pilots," *South China Morning Post*, July 4, 2019, https://www.scmp
     .com/news/china/science/article/3017141/google-denies-link-chinas-military
     -over-touch-screen-tools-may.

70. Chen, "Google Denies Link to China's Military over Touchscreen Tools That
     May Help PLA Pilots."

71. Ibid.; "China Eyeing Google's Touchscreen Tech for Stealth Fighters?"

72. Ramish Zafar, "Did Google Help China Develop Targeting Tech For 5th
     Gen Fighters?," WCCF Tech Inc., July 10, 2019, https:/wccftech.com/google
     -china-j-20-touchscreen/.

73. "Horizon Robotics Carves Place Among China's Leading AI Firms," Intelli-
     gence Online, December 16, 2020, https://www.intelligenceonline.com
     /international-dealmaking/2020/12/16/horizon-robotics-carves-place
     -among-china-s-leading-ai-firms,109628150-gra.

74. "What's the Future of AI?—A Talk with Dr. Kai-Fu Lee and Dr. Olaf Groth,"
     Robin.ly, February 1, 2019, https://www.robinly.info/post/whats-the-future
     -of-ai-kaifu-lee-olaf-groth.

75. Tyler Schnoebelen and Leena Kamath, "More Data Beats Better Algorithms—
     By Tyler Schnoebelen," TechTarget, September 23, 2016, https://www.data
     sciencecentral.com/profiles/blogs/more-data-beats-better-algorithms-by-tyler
     -schnoebelen.

76. Yee, "Google Parent Company Alphabet Is Back in China (Because It Never
     Left)"; "SF Holding Signs Deal to Help Modernise China's Military Logis-
     tics," Reuters, October 25, 2017, https://www.reuters.com/article/china
     -sfholding-military/sf-holding-signs-deal-to-help-modernise-chinas
     -military-logistics-idUSL4N1N048A.

77. "Technology Can Help Realize Communism: JD.com CEO," *Global Times*,
     August 20, 2017, https://www.globaltimes.cn/content/1062242.shtml.

78. Matt Day, "Behind the Photo of China's Xi Jinping, Tech CEOs," *Seattle Times*,
     September 24, 2015, https://www.seattletimes.com/business/microsoft/behind
     -the-photo-of-chinas-xi-jinping-and-the-tech-ceos/.

79. "U.S. Tech Companies and Their Chinese Partners with Military Ties."

80. Sun Peilin, "Possibility of Retaliation Forces Cisco to Change Tune," *Global
     Times*, December 27, 2012, https://www.globaltimes.cn/content/746839.
     shtml.

81. Geoffrey Jones and Emily Grandjean, "John Chambers, Cisco and China:
     Upgrading a Golden Shield," Harvard Business School, 9–318–158 (last revised

April 14, 2020), 10; "The Great Firewall of China: Background," Torfox, June 1, 2011, https://cs.stanford.edu/people/eroberts/cs181/projects/2010–11 /FreedomOfInformationChina/the-great-firewall-of-china-background /index.html; "The Internet in China: A Tool for Freedom or Suppression?," Joint Hearing Before the Subcommittee on Africa, Global Human Rights, and International Operations and the Subcommittee on Asia and the Pacific of the Committee on International Relations, House of Representatives, 109th Cong. (2006), 6, 127, 188.

82. "Breaking Through the 'Golden Shield,'" Open Society Institute, 2009, https://www.opensocietyfoundations.org/uploads/e7d8b223-df0a-4975 -b40b-c9914a58b626/china-internet-censorship-20041101.pdf.

83. "Huawei: The Company That Spooked the World," *Economist*, August 4, 2012, https://www.economist.com/briefing/2012/08/04/the-company-that -spooked-the-world.

84. Jones and Grandjean, "John Chambers, Cisco, and China: Upgrading a Golden Shield."

85. Ibid., 12.

86. Brad Reese, "Cyber Attacks: Cisco Appears to Embrace China While Google Fights China," Network World, January 13, 2010, https://www.network world.com/article/2233108/cyber-attacks--cisco-appears-to-embrace-china -while-google-fights-china.html.

87. Jones and Grandjean, "John Chambers, Cisco, and China: Upgrading a Golden Shield," 7.

88. "About Cisco," Expo 2010 Shanghai China, accessed June 21, 2021, https:// www.cisco.com/c/dam/global/zh_cn/assets/expo/en/pdf/cisco_china_back grounder.pdf.

89. Wei Bing, "Cisco CEO Addresses on His China Strategy," *China Daily*, December 13, 2007, http://www.chinadaily.com.cn/bizchina///////2007–12/13 /content_6326325.htm.

90. Phil Hochmuth, "Chambers Lectures on China, Buyouts," Network World, September 12, 2005, https://www.networkworld.com/article /2314591/chambers-lectures-on-china--buyouts.html.

91. Pete Barlas, "Cisco, HP Paying Cyberspying Price in China," *Investor's Business Daily*, June 22, 2015, https://www.investors.com/news/technology /china-policies-hit-cisco-hp-sales/.

92. Adi Robertson, "Cisco and Other US Tech Companies Lobbied for Huawei Investigation, Says Washington Post," Verge, October 11, 2012, https://www.theverge.com/2012/10/11/3488632/cisco-huawei-national -security-lobbying.

93. Shai Oster and Danielle Muoio, "Cisco Pledges $10 Billion China Investment to Regain Ground," Bloomberg, June 17, 2015, https://www.bloomberg.com /news/articles/2015–06–17/cisco-to-invest-10-billion-in-china-to-create -jobs-promote-r-d.

94. Christiane Amanpour, "The Power of Art and the Internet for Chinese Dissident," CNN, transcript, March 16, 2010, http://transcripts.cnn.com/TRANSCRIPTS /1003/16/ampr.01.html.

95. Associated Press, "Twitter's New Censorship Plans Rouses Global Furor," *Deseret News*, January 27, 2012, https://www.deseret.com/2012/1/27/20247832 /twitter-s-new-censorship-plan-rouses-global-furor.

96. "With Google and Twitter Still Blocked in China, Executives Woo Beijing," *Los Angeles Times*, November 3, 2015, https://www.latimes.com/world/asia /la-fg-china-google-twitter-20151102-story.html.

97. "Twitter's Chief in China Raises Eyebrows over Military Past and Résumé," *New York Times*, April 18, 2016, https://www.nytimes.com/2016/04/19 /world/asia/china-twitter-kathy-chen.html; Josh Horwitz, "Twitter's New China Head Was a People's Liberation Army Engineer Who Worked on Military Security," Quartz, April 18, 2016, https://qz.com/664004/twitters -new-china-head-is-a-communist-party-ex-engineer-who-worked-on -military-security/; Jon Russell, "Twitter's Controversial Head of China Is the Latest Exec to Leave the Company," Tech Crunch, January 2, 2017, https://techcrunch.com/2017/01/01/twitters-controversial-head-of-china -is-the-latest-exec-to-leave-the-company/.

98. "Twitter's New China Head Wants to 'Work Together' with State Media," *Sino Daily*, April 18, 2016, https://www.sinodaily.com/reports/Twitters _new_China_head_wants_to_work_together_with_state_media_999.html.

99. "Twitter's Chief in China Raises Eyebrows over Military Past and Résumé."

100. Russell, "Twitter's Controversial Head of China Is the Latest Exec to Leave the Company."

101. Olafimihan Oshin, "Academic Who Mocked China's Xi Says Twitter Account Was Restricted," *Hill*, July 6, 2021, https://thehill.com/policy/international /asia-pacific/561655-academic-who-mocked-chinas-xi-says-twitter-account-was.

102. Stephen L. Miller, "Twitter Is in China's Pocket," Spectator, December 2, 2020, https://spectator.us/life/twitter-china-pocket-jack-dorsey-marco-rubio/.

103. "Hundreds of Fake Twitter Accounts Linked to China Sowed Disinformation Prior to the U.S. Election–Report," Cardiff University, January 28, 2021, https://www.cardiff.ac.uk/news/view/2491763-hundreds-of-fake-twitter -accounts-linked-to-china-sowed-disinformation-prior-to-the-us-election, -with-some-continuing-to-amplify-reactions-to-the-capitol-building-riot -report.

104. Tom Ozimek, "Hundreds of Twitter Accounts Linked to China Sowed Discord Around U.S. Election," *Epoch Times*, last updated February 2, 2021, https://www.theepochtimes.com/hundreds-of-twitter-accounts-linked-to -china-sowed-discord-around-us-election_3679956.html.

105. Miller, "Twitter Is in China's Pocket."

106. Ryan Lovelace, "Jack Dorsey, Twitter CEO, Defends Crackdown on Trump's Mail-in Voting Tweets," *Washington Times*, October 28, 2020, https://www .washingtontimes.com/news/2020/oct/28/jack-dorsey-twitter-ceo-defends -crackdown-trumps-m/.

107. Adam Shaw, "Twitter Says Chinese Government's Tweets Denying 'Forced Labor' in Xinjiang Don't Break Its Rules," Fox News, January 14, 2021, https://www.foxnews.com/politics/twitter-chinese-governments-tweets -forced-labor-rules.

108. Ryan Gallagher, "Twitter Helped Chinese Government Promote Disinformation On Repression Of Uyghurs," Intercept, August 19, 2019, https://theintercept.com/2019/08/19/twitter-ads-china-uighurs/.

109. "Twitter's Hiring of China-Linked AI Expert Sparks Concern," Radio Free Asia, May 20, 2020, https://www.rfa.org/english/news/china/concern-05202020134312.html.

110. Keoni Everington, "Petition Calls for Investigation into Twitter Censorship After Hiring of Li Fei-Fei," Taiwan News, May 25, 2020, https://www.taiwannews.com.tw/en/news/3940206.

111. Sam Shead, "Twitter Adds Former Google VP and A.I. Guru Fei-Fei Li to Board As It Seeks to Play Catch Up with Google and Facebook," CNBC, May 12, 2020, https://www.cnbc.com/2020/05/12/twitter-adds-former-google-vp-and-ai-guru-fei-fei-li-to-board.html; Jessi Hempel, "Fei-Fei Li's Quest to Make AI Better for Humanity," Wired, December 13, 2018, https://www.wired.com/story/fei-fei-li-artificial-intelligence-humanity/.

112. Shead, "Twitter Adds Former Google VP and A.I. Guru Fei-Fei Li to Board as It Seeks to Play Catch Up with Google and Facebook"; Everington, "Petition Calls for Investigation into Twitter Censorship After Hiring of Li Fei-Fei."

113. Sean Ross, "Elon Musk's Best Investments," Investopedia, last updated May 15, 2021, https://www.investopedia.com/articles/investing/031316/elon-musks-5-best-investments-tsla-pypl.asp.

114. Morgan McFall-Johnsen and Dave Mosher, "Elon Musk Says He Plans to Send 1 Million People to Mars by 2050 by Launching 3 Starship Rockets Every Day and Creating 'a Lot of Jobs' on the Red Planet," Business Insider, January 17, 2020, https://www.businessinsider.com/elon-musk-plans-1-million-people-to-mars-by-2050-2020-1.

115. Dave Mosher, "Elon Musk's Plan to Blanket Earth in High-Speed Internet May Face a Big Threat: China," Business Insider, November 21, 2016, https://www.businessinsider.com/spacex-internet-satellite-constellation-china-threat-2016-11.

116. Wayne Duggan, "Elon Musk's Thoughts About China, Tariffs, and Import Duties: 'Like Competing in Olympic Race Wearing Lead Shoes,'" Benzinga, March 8, 2018, https://www.benzinga.com/government/18/03/11329957/elon-musks-thoughts-about-china-tariffs-and-import-duties-like-competing-i.

117. Jerry Rogers, "Will China Steal Its Way to a Space Race Victory?," National Interest, May 6, 2021, https://nationalinterest.org/blog/buzz/will-china-steal-its-way-space-race-victory-184574.

118. Jayson Derrick, "Elon Musk Clarifies China Comments, Says Gigafactory in India Would Make Long-Term Sense," Benzinga, October 26, 2015, https://www.benzinga.com/news/15/10/5942799/elon-musk-clarifies-china-comments-says-gigafactory-in-india-would-make-long-term.

119. Matthew Campbell, Zhang Chunying, Haze Fan, David Stringer, Emma O'Brien, and Dana Hull, "Elon Musk Loves China, and China Loves Him Back—for Now," Bloomberg Businessweek, January 13, 2021, https://www.bloomberg.com/news/features/2021-01-13/china-loves-elon-musk-and-tesla-tsla-how-long-will-that-last.

120. Dana Hull, Chunying Zhang, and Tian Ying, "Elon Goes to China," *Bloomberg Businessweek*, October 28, 2019 (EBSCO); "Tesla Confirms $1.6 Billion in China Bank Financing for Factory," Bloomberg, December 26, 2019, https://www.bloomberg.com/news/articles/2019–12–26/tesla -confirms-1–6-billion-in-china-bank-financing-for-factory.

121. Angus Whitley, "In China, Elon Musk Sure Felt the Love That Was Missing at Home," Bloomberg.com, January 11, 2019 (EBSCO); David Welch and Crystal Chui, "China Wants Elon Musk to Help Promote Stable Ties with the U.S.," Bloomberg, January 9, 2019, https://www.bloomberg.com/news/articles /2019-01-09/beijing-urges-musk-to-promote-u-s-china-ties-boost-ev -market; David Marino-Nachison, "Elon Musk Goes to China at a Vital Time for Tesla and the U.S.," *Barron's*, January 10, 2019, https://www.barrons.com /articles/tesla-elon-musk-goes-to-china-at-vital-time-us-trade-tensions -51547146159.

122. Teddy Ng and Wendy Wu, "Elon Musk Praises Chinese 'Energy and Vigour' in Beijing," *Korea Times*, August 12, 2021 (Lexis).

123. Neer Varshney, "From 'Made in China' to 'Designed in China:' Tesla Is Hiring Staff to Design Models in a New Local Research Center," Benzinga, January 16, 2020, https://www.benzinga.com/news/20/01/15132527/from -made-in-china-to-designed-in-china-tesla-is-hiring-staff-to-design-models -in-a-new-local-resear.

124. Matthew Campbell, Zhang Chunying, Haze Fan, David Stringer, Emma O'Brien, and Dana Hull, "A Match Made in China," *Bloomberg Businessweek*, January 18, 2021.

125. Ibid.

126. Dylan Donnely, "Elon Musk Hails China 'More Responsible' Than US in Bizarre Pro-Beijing Confession," *Express*, January 4, 2021, https://www.express .co.uk/news/world/1379203/Elon-Musk-news-china-us-Tesla-technology -ethics-regulation-xi-jinping-ont.

127. "Elon Musk's Praise of China's Government for Being 'Very Responsible' to Its People's Needs and Happiness Is Objective: Chinese FM," *Global Times*, January 8, 2021, https://www.globaltimes.cn/page/202101/1212242.shtml.

128. Lora Kolodny, "Elon Musk Says 'China Rocks' While the U.S. Is Full of 'Complacency and Entitlement,'" CNBC, July 31, 2020, https://www.cnbc .com/2020/07/31/tesla-ceo-elon-musk-china-rocks-us-full-of-entitlement .html.

129. Liza Lin, "Tesla Boss Elon Musk's China Charm Offensive Rolls on With Praise for Climate Plans," *Wall Street Journal*, March 23, 2021, https://www .wsj.com/articles/elon-musks-china-charm-offensive-rolls-on-with-praise -for-its-climate-plans-11616497720.

130. Sun Chi, "Musk: China to Be Tesla's Largest Market," *China Daily*, March 23, 2021, http://global.chinadaily.com.cn/a/202103/23/WS60599aaea31024ad 0bab10d5.html.

131. Elon Musk (@elonmusk), "The economic prosperity that China has achieved is truly amazing . . . ," Twitter post, 6:44 p.m., June 30, 2021, https://twitter

.com/elonmusk/status/1410413958805270533; "Elon Musk Praises China Once Again, Here's Why," *Indian Technology News*, July 3, 2021, https://times ofindia.indiatimes.com/gadgets-news/elon-musk-praises-china-once-again -heres-why/articleshow/84085952.cms.

132. Kate Duffy, "Elon Musk's SpaceX Keeps Winning U.S. Military Contracts— Here's Why, According to an Aerospace Expert," Business Insider, October 18, 2020, https://markets.businessinsider.com/news/stocks/elon-musk-spacex -military-contracts-dod-space-force-2020–10; Amy Thompson, "SpaceX Launches Classified US Spy Satellite, Sticks Rocket Landing to Cap Record Year," Space.com, December 19, 2020, https://www.space.com/spacex -launches-nrol-108-spy-satellite-lands-rocket.

133. Issac Stone Fish, "Can Elon Musk Keep Beijing and Washington Happy," *Barron's*, November 13, 2020, https://www.barrons.com/articles/can-elon -musk-keep-beijing-and-washington-happy-51605293737.

134. Ibid.

135. Ji Xi, "Tesla Faces Backlash in China from Viral Video," VOAnews.com, May 8, 2021, https://www.voanews.com/east-asia-pacific/voa-news-china/tesla -faces-backlash-china-viral-video; "Professor Maochun Miles Yu," United States Naval Academy, accessed September 4, 2021, https://www.usna.edu /Users/history/yu/index.php.

136. Nectar Gan and James Griffiths "Latest Area of Competition between the U.S. and China—Saving the World," CNN Wire, April 23, 2021, https:// www.cnn.com/2021/04/23/china/china-us-climate-mic-intl-hnk/index .html.

137. PR Newswire, "LinkedIn Co-founder Reid Hoffman Outlines China Strat- egy," CEIBS-LinkedIn Forum, May 26, 2014, https://www.prnewswire.com /news-releases/linkedin-co-founder-reid-hoffman-outlines-china-strategy -260635291.html.

138. Emily Rauhala and Elizabeth Dwoskin, "U.S. Companies Want to Play China's Game," *Washington Post*, December 22, 2016, https://www.washingtonpost .com/world/asia_pacific/us-companies-want-to-play-chinas-game-they-just -cant-win-it/2016/12/22/0fffa35a-b7f3-11e6-939c-91749443c5e5_story.html.

139. "U.S. Companies Want to Play China's Game," *Washington Post*, December 22, 2016; Julie Makinen, Yingzhi Yang, Alexandra Li, "'Freedom Requires Strict Order': China Preps for Second World Internet Conference," *Los Ange- les Times*, December 15, 2015, https://www.latimes.com/world/asia/la-fg -china-internet-20151215-story.html; C. Custer, "China's World Internet Conference Is Still a Sham, and Facebook Is Still Playing Ball," TechinAsia, November 15, 2016, https://www.techinasia.com/chinas-world-internet -conference-sham-western-companies-playing-ball; "RSF Calls for Boycott of China's World Internet Conference," Reporters Without Borders, December 11, 2015, https://rsf.org/en/news/rsf-calls-boycott-chinas-world -internet-conference.

140. Mansoor Iqbal, "LinkedIn Usage and Revenue Statistics (2021)," Business- ofApps, last updated May 21, 2021, https://www.businessofapps.com/data

/linkedin-statistics/; Baijia Liu, "LinkedIn China Users More Than Triple to 13 Million in Two Years," LinkedIn, December 15, 2015, https://www .linkedin.com/pulse/linkedin-china-users-more-than-triple-13-million-two -years-baijia-liu.

141. John McDuling, "LinkedIn Is Doing What Facebook, Google, and Twitter Can't: Expanding in China," Bamboo Innovator, March 1, 2014, https:// bambooinnovator.com/2014/03/01/linkedin-is-doing-what-facebook-google -and-twitter-cant-expanding-in-china/.

142. Megha Rajagopalan, "LinkedIn Censored a Pro-Democracy Activist's Profile in China," BuzzFeed News, January 4, 2019, https://www.buzzfeednews .com/article/meghara/china-linkedin-zhou-fengsuo.

143. Jessi Hempel, "Now We Know Why Microsoft Bought LinkedIn," *Wired*, March 14, 2017, https://www.wired.com/2017/03/now-we-know-why -microsoft-bought-linkedin/.

144. Ryan Gallagher, "Microsoft's LinkedIn Accused by Noted China Critic of Censorship," Bloomberg, May 11, 2021, https://www.bloomberg.com/news /articles/2021-05-12/microsoft-s-linkedin-accused-by-noted-china-critic-of -censorship.

145. Nathan Gardels, "Chinese President Xi Jinping Meets the 21st Century Council in Beijing," Berggruen Institute, November 3, 2015, https://www .berggruen.org/activity/chinese-president-xi-jinping-meets-the-21st-century -council-in-beijing/.

146. "Full Transcript: Greylock Partner Reid Hoffman on Recode Decode," Re-code, July 18, 2017, https://www.vox.com/2017/7/18/15992344/transcript -greylock-partner-reid-hoffman-linkedin-win-future-recode-decode.

147. Scott Maucione, "Ash Carter Brings on More Innovators to Upgrade DoD," Federal News Network, June 10, 2016, https://federalnewsnetwork.com /defense/2016/06/ash-carter-brings-innovators-upgrade-dod/.

148. Reid Hoffman and Chris Yeh, *Blitzscaling: The Lightning-Fast Path to Building Massively Valuable Companies* (New York: HarperCollins, 2018), 274.

149. Scott Cendrowski, "China's Xi Spreads Censorship Ideals at Internet Confer-ence," *Fortune*, December 16, 2015, https://fortune.com/2015/12/16/chinas-xi -spreads-censorship-ideals-at-internet-conference/; "General Secretary Xi Jinping Cares About Wuzhen," Community of Shared Future in Cyber-space, November 2015, http://www.cac.gov.cn/files/pdf/zazhiwlcb /zazhiwlcb201511.pdf; Kirsty Styles, "China Hosts the World's Most Confusing Tech Conference . . . Again," Next Web, December 16, 2015, https://thenextweb.com/insider/2015/12/16/chinas-hosting-the-worlds -most-confusing-tech-conference-again/.

150. Xinhua Economic News Service, "China Focus: What to Expect When China Hosts 3rd World Internet Conference," Beijing Economic-Technological Development Area, November 25, 2016, http://www.chinadaily.com.cn /regional/bda/2016-11/25/content_27552142.htm; "China Holds First World Internet Conference, Urges Better Governance," *Global Times*, November 20,

2014, https://www.globaltimes.cn/content/892739.shtml; http://www.cac
.gov.cn/2015-12/18/c_1117631445.htm.

151. Rauhala and Dwoskin, "U.S. Companies Want to Play China's Game."
152. Strittmatter, *We Have Been Harmonized: Life in China's Surveillance State*, 322.
153. Custer, "China's World Internet Conference Is Still a Sham, and Facebook Is Still Playing Ball."
154. Press Trust of India, "World Internet Conference: Sundar Pichai Makes Strong Case for Google's Return to China," *Hindustan Times*, December 4, 2017, https://tech.hindustantimes.com/tech/news/world-internet-conference-sundar-pichai-makes-strong-case-for-google-s-return-to-china-story-Tz6pvlv3cFz0L6630yTc2N.html.
155. "#WorldInternetConference," Facebook, accessed September 6, 2021, https://www.facebook.com/hashtag/worldinternetconference?source=feed_text.
156. "Xi's Speech: Reactions from the Ground," *China Daily*, last updated December 18, 2015, https://www.chinadaily.com.cn/china/2015–12/18/content_22744020.htm.
157. Daniel Sneider, "Everyone Wants to Crack Down on China–Except Silicon Valley," *Wired*, September 13, 2020, https://www.wired.com/story/crack-down-china-except-silicon-valley/.
158. Jack Beyrer, "Peter Thiel Blasts Silicon Valley's 'Useful Idiots' for Selling Out to China," *Washington Free Beacon*, April 7, 2021, https://freebeacon.com/national-security/peter-thiel-blasts-silicon-valleys-useful-idiots-for-selling-out-to-china/.
159. Nicole Hao and Cathy He, "Chinese Leader Xi Jinping Lays Out Plan to Control the Global Internet: Leaked Documents," *Epoch Times*, May 2, 2021, https://www.theepochtimes.com/chinese-leader-xi-jinping-lays-out-plan-to-control-the-global-internet-leaked-documents_3791944.html.
160. Lin Yang, "How Facebook's Zuckerberg Went from Courting to Criticizing Beijing," VOA News, September 5, 2020, https://www.voanews.com/silicon-valley-technology/how-facebooks-zuckerberg-went-courting-criticizing-beijing.
161. Paresh Dave and Katie Paul, "Facebook Makes a New Ad Sales Push in China After Zuckerberg Criticizes the Country," CNBC, January 7, 2020, https://www.cnbc.com/2020/01/07/facebook-makes-a-new-ad-sales-push-in-china.html.
162. Justin Sherman, "The U.S.-China Battle over the Internet Goes Under the Sea," *Wired*, June 24, 2020, https://www.wired.com/story/opinion-the-us-china-battle-over-the-internet-goes-under-the-sea/.
163. Ibid.; "Dr. Peng Bristles After Being Dropped from Hong Kong Undersea Cable Project," Intelligence Online, September 9, 2020, https://www.intelligenceonline.com/corporate-intelligence/2020/09/09/dr-peng-bristles-after-being-dropped-from-hong-kong-undersea-cable-project, 109605067-bre.

164. "The Nixon Seminar," Nixon Seminar on Conservative Realism and National Security, transcript, April 6, 2021, https://nixonseminar.com/2021/04/the-nixon-seminar-april-6-2021-transcript/.

165. Noam Cohen, *The Know-It-Alls: The Rise of Silicon Valley as a Political Powerhouse and Social Wrecking Ball* (New York: New Press, 2017), 177.

166. Ibid.

5: Wall Street

1. Sam Dangremond, "Steve Schwarzman Hosted an Epic 70th Birthday Party in Palm Beach," *Town & Country*, February 13, 2017, https://www.townandcountrymag.com/the-scene/parties/news/a9556/steve-schwarzman-birthday-party/; Clive Hamilton and Mareike Ohlberg, *Hidden Hand: Exposing How the Chinese Communist Party Is Reshaping the World* (London: Oneworld Publications, 2020), 45.

2. Steve Schwarzman, "25 Most Powerful People in Business," *Fortune* (archives), accessed June 24, 2021, https://archive.fortune.com/galleries/2007/fortune/0711/gallery.power_25.fortune/19.html; Dan Primack, "Investors: You Can't Count on Private Equity to Bail You Out," *Fortune*, February 23, 2011, https://fortune.com/2011/02/23/investors-you-cant-count-on-private-equity-to-bail-you-out/.

3. Hamilton and Ohlberg, *Hidden Hand*, 45.

4. Ibid., 312.

5. Megan Davies and Jessica Hall, "Beijing Fund to Hike Stake in Blackstone: Source," Reuters, October 16, 2008, https://www.reuters.com/article/us-blackstone-bwil/beijing-fund-to-hike-stake-in-blackstone-source-idUSTRE49F8TI20081016; Francesco Guerrera, "Blackstone Boosts IPO as China Buys In," *Financial Times*, May 21, 2007, https://www.ft.com/content/8a131f0a-07cc-11dc-9541-000b5df10621.

6. Hamilton and Ohlberg, *Hidden Hand*, 44.

7. Guerrera, "Blackstone Boosts IPO as China Buys in."

8. Katsuji Nakazawa, "Xi Jinping's Back Channel to Donald Trump," *Nikkei Asia*, February 3, 2017, https://asia.nikkei.com/Economy/Xi-Jinping-s-back-channel-to-Donald-Trump.

9. Hamilton and Ohlberg, *Hidden Hand*, 44.

10. "Annual Conference of Financial Street Forum 2020 Held in Beijing CIC Co-Hosted the Parallel Forum of Financial Opening and Market," China Investment Corporation, October 22, 2020, http://www.china-inv.cn/chinainven/Media/2020-10/1001852.shtml.

11. Hamilton and Ohlberg, *Hidden Hand*, 45.

12. Greg Earl, "Blackstone Chief Plays Down China Market Turmoil," *Australian Financial Review*, January 13, 2016, https://www.afr.com/markets/blackstone-chief-plays-down-china-market-turmoil-20160112-gm4c5m.

13. Hamilton and Ohlberg, *Hidden Hand*, 45.

14. "Blackstone CEO Predicts China Will Invest More in the U.S.," *China Daily*, last updated April 22, 2015, https://usa.chinadaily.com.cn/business/2015-04/22/content_20504398.htm.

15. "CNBC Transcript: Blackstone Group Founder, CEO & Chairman Stephen Schwarzman Speaks with CNBC's 'Squawk Box' from Davos Today," CNBC, January 21, 2020, https://www.cnbc.com/2020/01/21/cnbc -transcript-blackstone-group-founder-ceo-chairman-stephen-schwarzman -speaks-with-cnbcs-squawk-box-from-davos-today.html.

16. "Hu's Colloquialism Delivers Unambiguous Message," 18th National Congress of the Communist Party of China, November 9, 2012, http://www .china.org.cn/china/18th_cpc_congress/2012-11/09/content_27063700.htm.

17. BizTalk Programs, CCTV.com, accessed July 2, 2021, http://cctv.cntv.cn/lm /biztalk/program/.

18. Andrew Browne and Lingling Wei, "Schwarzman Backs China Scholarship," *Wall Street Journal*, April 21, 2013, https://www.wsj.com/articles/SB10001424 127887323551004578436494052747764.

19. George Chen, "Once Rejected by Rhodes, Now He Launches His Own," LinkedIn, November 26, 2014, https://www.linkedin.com/pulse /20141126045429–5299727-once-rejected-by-rhodes-now-he-launches -his-own/.

20. Browne and Wei, "Schwarzman Backs China Scholarship."

21. "Tsinghua Establishes Institute for Xi JinPing Thought on Socialism with Chinese Characteristics for a New Era," Tsinghua University News, accessed June 25, 2021, https://news.tsinghua.edu.cn/en/info/1002/7989.htm.

22. Greg Earl, "Two Australians Win Valuable New Schwarzman China Scholarships," *Australian Financial Review,* January 12, 2016, https://www.afr.com /policy/health-and-education/two-australians-win-valuable-new-schwarzman -china-scholarships-20160112-gm3x5u.

23. "Tsinghua University's Schwarzman Scholar Delivers Speech at the Plenary Session of the 7th Annual U.S.-China High-level Consultation on People-to-Pe," Schwarzman Scholars, June 8, 2016, http://en.sc.tsinghua.edu.cn /newsletter/429.jhtml.

24. Christopher Bodeen, "U.S. Tycoon's China Scholarship Program Opens Doors in Beijing," Associated Press, September 10, 2016, https://apnews.com /article/ac63a1bf721143689fba69e2b6a6ea87.

25. Schwarzman, *What It Takes*, 297–98; "Current Administrators," Tsinghua University, accessed June 25, 2021, https://www.tsinghua.edu.cn/en/About /Current_Administrators.htm.

26. Bethany Allen-Ebrahimian, "The Moral Hazard of Dealing with China," *Atlantic*, January 11, 2020, https://www.theatlantic.com/international/archive/2020/01 /stephen-schwarzman-china-surveillance-scholars-colleges/604675/.

27. Ibid.

28. Hamilton and Ohlberg, *Hidden Hand*, 210.

29. "For Whom Mr. Bell Tolls," China Media Project, November 28, 2012, https://chinamediaproject.org/2012/11/28/for-whom-mr-bell-tolls/.

30. Echo Xie, "Chinese President Xi Jinping Says Corurption Remains Biggest Threat to Communist Party," *South China Morning Post*, January 23, 2021, https://www.scmp.com/news/china/politics/article/3118964/chinese -president-xi-jinping-says-corruption-remains-biggest.

31. "For Whom Mr. Bell Tolls."
32. "Daniel Bell," Berggruen Institute, accessed June 25, 2021, https://www
.berggruen.org/people/daniel-bell/.
33. "Chinese President Xi Jinping and U.S. President Barack Obama Sent Congratulations to Convocation Ceremony of Schwarzman College, Tsinghua
University," Schwarzman Scholars, September 14, 2016, http://en.sc
.tsinghua.edu.cn/newsletter/436.jhtml.
34. "Theory and Practice of Socialism with Chinese Characteristics,"
Schwarzman Scholars, accessed July 2, 2021, https://www.schwarzman
scholars.org/curriculum/theory-and-practice-of-socialism-with-chinese
-characteristics/.
35. "Chinese President Xi Jinping and U.S. President Barack Obama Sent Congratulations to Convocation Ceremony of Schwarzman College, Tsinghua
University."
36. "Tsinghua University's Schwarzman Scholar Delivers Speech at the Plenary
Session of the 7th Annual U.S.-China High-level Consultation on People-
to-Pe."
37. Zhou Xin, ed., "Opening Up of China Means Win-win Cooperation for
World: President Xi," Xinhua Net, October 31, 2017, http://www.xinhuanet
.com//english/2017-10/31/c_136715797.htm.
38. Li Yuan, "Facebook, Take Note: In China's 'New Era,' the Communist
Party Comes First," *Wall Street Journal*, November 2, 2017, https://www.wsj
.com/articles/facebook-take-note-in-chinas-new-era-the-communist-party
-comes-first-1509615006.
39. Allen-Ebrahimian, "The Moral Hazard of Dealing with China."
40. "Steve Schwarzman and Jon Gray's Statement on Racial Injustices," Blackstone, June 1, 2020, https://www.blackstone.com/insights/article/steve
-schwarzman-and-jon-grays-statement-on-racial-injustices/.
41. Hayley C. Cuccinello, "Blackstone Billionaire Stephen Schwarzman Optimistic on U.S.-China Trade Talks but Not the Wealth Tax," *Forbes*, November 6, 2019, https://www.forbes.com/sites/hayleycuccinello/2019/11/06
/blackstone-stephen-schwarzman-us-china-trade-talks-wealth-tax/
?sh=ee16f7b330ef.
42. Michael Kranish, "Trump's China Whisperer: How Billionaire Stephen
Schwarzman Has Sought to Keep the President Close to Beijing," *Washington
Post*, March 12, 2018, https://www.washingtonpost.com/politics/trumps
-china-whisperer-how-billionaire-stephen-schwarzman-has-sought-to-keep
-the-president-close-to-beijing/2018/03/11/67e369a8-0c2f-11e8-95a5
-c396801049ef_story.html.
43. "Board & Committees," Blackstone, accessed September 6, 2021, https://
ir.blackstone.com/corporate-governance/default.aspx.
44. Stephen A. Schwarzman, *What It Takes: Lessons in the Pursuit of Excellence*
(New York: Avid Reader Press, 2019), 319; see 311–24.
45. Julia Fioretti, "JD Logistics $3.5 Billion IPO Draws SoftBank, Temasek,"
Bloomberg, May 14, 2021, https://www.bloomberg.com/news/articles
/2021-05-14/jd-logistics-3-5-billion-ipo-is-said-to-draw-softbank-temasek;

Alexandra Stevenson, "JD Logistics, the Delivery Arm of the Chinese E-Commerce Giant, Gains in Its I.P.O.," *New York Times*, May 28, 2021, https://www.nytimes.com/2021/05/28/business/jd-logistics-the-delivery -arm-of-the-chinese-e-commerce-giant-gains-in-its-ipo.html.

46. "SF Holding Signs Deal to Help Modernise China's Military Logistics," Reuters, October 25, 2017, https://www.reuters.com/article/china-sfholding -military-idUSL4N1N048A; Chad Peltier, "China's Logistics Capabilities for Expeditionary Operations," U.S.-China Economic and Security Review Commission, accessed September 6, 2021, https://www.uscc.gov/sites /default/files/2020-04/China%20Expeditionary%20Logistics%20Capabilities %20Report.pdf.

47. Kranish, "Trump's China Whisperer."

48. Barbara Demick, "Xi Jinping on Track to Become China's Next President," *Los Angeles Times*, October 19, 2010, https://www.latimes.com/archives/la -xpm-2010-oct-19-la-fg-china-xi-20101019-story.html.

49. Eric Levitz, "In Appeal to Hard Left, Bloomberg Praises Chinese Communism," *New York Intelligencer*, December 2, 2019, https://nymag.com /intelligencer/2019/12/michael-bloomberg-china-pbs-climate-xi-dictator .html.

50. Ding Ying, "Building All-Dimensional China-U.S. Relations," *Beijing Review*, http://www.bjreview.com.cn/World/201801/t20180119_800114876 .html.

51. Carl E. Walter and Fraser J. T. Howie, *Red Capitalism: The Fragile Financial Foundation of China's Extraordinary Rise* (Hoboken, NJ: Wiley, 2012), 179.

52. Dealbook, "The People from 'Government Sachs,'" *New York Times*, March 16, 2017, https://www.nytimes.com/2017/03/16/business/dealbook/goldman -sachs-goverment-jobs.html.

53. "Expanding Its Commitment to China, Goldman Sachs Opens Offices in Beijing and Shanghai," Goldman Sachs, accessed June 25, 2021, https://www .goldmansachs.com/our-firm/history/moments/1994-beijing-shanghai.html.

54. Eric Ellis, "No Fools, These Children of the Revolution," *Australian Financial Review*, May 13, 1994, https://www.afr.com/politics/no-fools-these-children -of-the-revolution-19940513-jfkjh.

55. Jamil Anderlini and Sundeep Tucker, "The Rise of China's Ultimate Dealmaker," *Financial Times*, May 13, 2009, https://www.ft.com/content/=8efd 3718-3fe6-11de-9ced-00144feabdc0.

56. "Goldman Sachs Blazes New Trail with Debt Restructuring of over U.S.$5 Billion for Provincial Investment Trust in China," Goldman Sachs, accessed June 25, 2021, https://www.goldmansachs.com/our-firm/history/moments /2000-guangdong-enterprises-restructuring.html.

57. Cathy Chan and Adrian Cox, "China Gambit Paying Off for Goldman Sachs," *International Herald Tribune*, October 24, 2006, http://www.iht.com /articles/2006/10/23/bloomberg/sxgoldman.php.

58. Dominic Barton and Richard He Huang, "Governing China's Boards: An Interview with John Thornton," McKinsey Quarterly, on Scribd, Issue 1, 2007, https://www.scribd.com/document/12882500/Governing-China-s-Boards.

59. "Top 5 Water Users in Palm Beach," *Wall Street Journal*, July 10, 2011, https://www.wsj.com/articles/SB10001424052702304803104576428183030837332.

60. Landon Thomas Jr., "The Last Old Boy: John O'Hara Would Have Loved This Guy, John Thornton," *New York Observer*, January 15, 2001, https://observer.com/2001/01/the-last-old-boy-john-ohara-would-have-loved-this-guy-john-thornton/; Bethany McLean, "Inside the Money Machine Wall Street's Most Celebrated—and Secretive—Firm Is Nothing Like You'd Imagine It to Be," *Fortune* (archives), September 6, 2004, https://archive.fortune.com/magazines/fortune/fortune_archive/2004/09/06/380330/index.htm.

61. Mark Landler, "Wall Street Goes Hunting for Treasure in China," *New York Times*, December 17, 2000, https://www.nytimes.com/2000/12/17/business/business-wall-st-goes-hunting-for-treasure-in-china.html.

62. Chan and Cox, "China Gambit Paying Off for Goldman Sachs."

63. "Beijing Mayor Meets U.S. Guest," Xinhua General News Service, December 5, 2002 (Lexis).

64. Landon Thomas and Joseph Kahn, "Co-President at Goldman Announces His Retirement," *New York Times*, March 25, 2003, https://www.nytimes.com/2003/03/25/business/co-president-at-goldman-announces-his-retirement.html.

65. Chan and Cox, "China Gambit Paying Off for Goldman Sachs."

66. Graham Turner, "People Around the Globe Long for What the Americans Have," *Daily Telegraph*, June 17, 2003, https://www.telegraph.co.uk/news/worldnews/northamerica/usa/1433333/People-around-the-globe-long-for-what-the-Americans-have.html.

67. Thomas and Kahn, "Co-President at Goldman Announces His Retirement" (Note: The *Times* refers to the university as "Qinghua."); "John Thornton to Succeed James A. Johnson as Chairman of the Brookings Board," Brookings, news release, June 11, 2003, https://www.brookings.edu/news-releases/john-thornton-to-succeed-james-a-johnson-as-chairman-of-the-brookings-board/.

68. Kathy Chen, "Wall Street Exec Seeks Great Wall," *Globe and Mail* (Canada), March 26, 2003, https://plus.lexis.com/document?crid=f5834681-073b-4781-80ef-c3a95a867ab3&pddocfullpath=%2Fshared%2Fdocument%2Fnews%2Furn%3AcontentItem%3A4KWT-X6G0-TXJ2-N1VB-00000-00&pdsourcegroupingtype=&pdcontentcomponentid=303830&pdmfid=1530671&pdisurlapi=true.

69. "Business & Media: Trading Places: Goldman Graduates," *Observer* (London), June 11, 2006, https://advance.lexis.com/api/document?collection=news&id=urn:contentItem:4K75-7Y00-TX6W-837T-00000-00&context=1519360.

70. "Exec's Move Could Be Gold for Goldman Sachs in China," *Nikkei Weekly* (Japan), April 28, 2003.

71. "About the John L. Thornton China Center," Brookings Institution, accessed June 25, 2021, https://www.brookings.edu/about-the-china-center/; "John L. Thornton," Brookings Institution, accessed June 25, 2021, https://www.brookings.edu/author/john-l-thornton/.

72. "Professor John L. Thornton Honored Friendship Award," School of Economics and Management, Tsinghua University, October 13, 2008, http://www.sem.tsinghua.edu.cn/en/News1/TZ_36101.html.

73. David Goldman, *You Will Be Assimilated: China's Plan to Sino-form the World* (New York: Bombardier Books, 2020), 2–3.

74. "Our Team," Silk Road Finance Corporation, accessed June 25, 2021, https://www.silkroad-finance.com/our-team; "Belt and Road," accessed June 2, 2021, https://www.silkroad-finance.com/belt-road.

75. "Unique and Differentiated Strengths," Silk Road Finance Corporation, acccesed June 25, 2021, https://www.silkroad-finance.com/our-strengths.

76. "Strategic Shareholders," Silk Road Finance Corporation, accessed June 25, 2021, https://www.silkroad-finance.com/strategic-shareholders.

77. "Our Team," Silk Road Finance Corporation.

78. Kerry R. Bolton, "'One Belt, One Road,' China, Globalization and the International Oligarchy," *Foreign Policy Journal*, October 19, 2017, https://www.foreignpolicyjournal.com/2017/10/19/one-belt-one-road-china-globalization-and-the-international-oligarchy/.

79. Steve Herman, "U.S. Seen Falling Short Countering China's Geopolitical Rise," States News Service, March 23, 2021, https://www.voanews.com/usa/us-politics/us-seen-falling-short-countering-chinas-rising-geopolitical-clout.

80. Lily Kuo and Alicia Chen, "Chinese Workers Allege Forced Labor, Abuses in Xi 's 'Belt and Road' Program," *Washington Post*, April 30, 2021, https://www.washingtonpost.com/world/asia_pacific/china-labor-belt-road-covid/2021/04/30/f110e8de-9cd4-11eb-b2f5-7d2f0182750d_story.html.

81. Hamilton and Ohlberg, *Hidden Hand*, 206–7.

82. Ibid., 105.

83. Alex Frew McMillan, "U.S. Banks Delist Hong Kong Derivatives Linked to Chinese Military," Real Money, January 11, 2021, https://realmoney.thestreet.com/investing/global-equity/u-s-banks-delist-hong-kong-derivatives-linked-to-chinese-military-15534813.

84. Frances Yoon, "Chinese Companies in Pentagon Spotlight Hire Global Banks to Sell Dollar Bonds," *Wall Street Journal*, September 15, 2020, https://www.wsj.com/articles/chinese-companies-in-pentagon-spotlight-hire-global-banks-to-sell-dollar-bonds-11600165226.

85. "Trump's China Inc. Onslaught Leaves Key Decisions for Biden," *Financial Post*, January 15, 2021, https://financialpost.com/pmn/business-pmn/trumps-onslaught-on-china-inc-leaves-key-decisions-for-biden.

86. Tom Huddleston Jr., "Billionaire Ray Dalio Bought His First Stock at Age 12—Here's His Lesson for Young Investors," CNBC, last updated May 1, 2019, https://www.cnbc.com/2019/05/01/billionaire-ray-dalio-bought-his-first-stock-at-age-12.html; Stephen Taub, "Here's What Ray Dalio Made in Bridgewater's Impressive 2018," *Institutional Investor*, January 15, 2019, https://www.institutionalinvestor.com/article/b1cpywndrkcyzk/Here-s-What-Ray-Dalio-Made-in-Bridgewater-s-Impressive-2018.

87. Ray Dalio, "Why and How Capitalism Needs to Be Reformed," Harvard

Law School Forum on Corporate Governance, October 13, 2020, https://
corpgov.law.harvard.edu/2020/10/13/why-and-how-capitalism-needs-to-be
-reformed/.

88. Christopher Beddor, "BREAKINGVIEWS—What's with Ray Dalio's Wang
Qishan Obsession?," Thomson Reuters Foundation News, September 12,
2017, https://news.trust.org/item/20170912210850-oxqhc.

89. Ray Dalio, *Principles* (New York: Simon & Schuster, 2017), 107–8.

90. "Hedge Funds Bridgewater, Winton Plan to Launch Products in China,"
CGTN, last updated July 7, 2018, https://news.cgtn.com/news/3d3d514f775
9544e78457a6333566d54/index.html; Wu Yan, "2018's Most Popular Translated Books in China," CGTN, last updated December 28, 2018, https://
news.cgtn.com/news/3d3d674d32456a4e31457a6333566d54/share_p.html.

91. "The Devil, or Mr Wang," *Economist*, March 26, 2015, https://www.economist
.com/china/2015/03/26/the-devil-or-mr-wang.

92. News Wires, "China Proposes Lifting Term Limit for Communist Party
Leaders," France24, February 25, 2018, https://www.france24.com/en
/20180225-china-proposes-lifting-term-limit-communist-party-leaders
-president-xi-jinping.

93. Michael Forsythe, David Enrich, and Alexandra Stevenson, "Inside a Brazen
Scheme to Woo China: Gifts, Golf and a $4,254 Wine," *New York Times*,
October 14, 2019, https://www.nytimes.com/2019/10/14/business/deutsche
-bank-china.html?smid=tw-nytimes&smtyp=cur; Clive Hamilton and
Mareike Ohlberg, "The Red Square Mile: Jobs in City Firms for Children
of Party Leaders and the County's Critics Banned from the Lord Mayor's
Show . . . How China's 'Red Aristocracy' Has Sneaked Its Way into the Heart
of Britain's Financial Powerhouses," *Daily Mail* (UK), July 12, 2020, https://
www.dailymail.co.uk/news/article-8515719/How-Chinas-red-aristocracy
-sneaked-way-heart-Britains-financial-powerhouses.html.

94. "Special Measures," Human Rights Watch, accessed June 27, 2021, https://
www.hrw.org/report/2016/12/06/special-measures/detention-and-torture
-chinese-communist-partys-shuanggui-system.

95. Shi Jiangtao, "'No Separation of Powers': China's Top Graft-Buster Seeks
Tighter Party Grip on Government," *South China Morning Post*, March 6,
2017, https://www.scmp.com/news/china/policies-politics/article/2076501
/no-separation-powers-chinas-top-graft-buster-seeks.

96. "United States: SAFE's Billions Slipping into US, Foreign Markets," Ten-
dersInfo, March 15, 2010 (Lexis).

97. "Foreign Minister Yang Jiechi Meets with President Ray Dalio of Bridgewater
Associates Inc.," Embassy of the People's Republic of China in the United
States of America," May 13, 2011, http://www.china-embassy.org/eng
/zmgx/t822807.htm.

98. John Cassidy, "Mastering the Machine," *New Yorker*, July 18, 2011, https://
www.newyorker.com/magazine/2011/07/25/mastering-the-machine.

99. Bloomberg, "Bridgewater Booming in China," *Pensions & Investments*, November 10, 2020, https://www.pionline.com/money-management/bridgewater

-booming-china; Allen T. Cheng, "How Ray Dalio Broke into China," *Institutional Investor*, December 18, 2017, https://www.institutionalinvestor.com /article/b15yw0fcgtz1l8/how-ray-dalio-broke-into-china.

100. Linette Lopez, "It's Time to Stop Listening to Ray Dalio on China," Business Insider, January 3, 2019, https://www.businessinsider.com/ray-dalio-time-to -stop-listening-to-him-china-2019-1.

101. "Ray Dalio Sides with Chinese Regulators over Jack Ma," Chief Investment Officer, November 12, 2020, https://www.ai-cio.com/news/ray-dalio -sides-chinese-regulators-jack-ma/; Rob Davies and Helen Davidson, "The Strange Case of Alibaba's Jack Ma and His Three-Month Vanishing Act," *Guardian*, January 23, 2011, https://www.theguardian.com/business /2021/jan/23/the-strange-case-of-alibabas-jack-ma-and-his-three-month -vanishing-act.

102. Ray Dalio, "Don't Be Blind to China's Rise in a Changing World," LinkedIn, October 26, 2020, https://www.linkedin.com/pulse/dont-blind-chinas -rise-changing-world-ray-dalio/.

103. Huaxia, ed., "Anti-China Bias 'Has Blinded Too Many for Too Long to Opportunities': UK Newspaper," Xinhua Net, October 25, 2020, http://www .xinhuanet.com/english/2020-10/25/c_139466569.htm.

104. Shalini Nagarajan, "Billionaire Ray Dalio Reviewed Bitcoin, Praised China, and Explained His Thoughts on the Outlook for Financial Markets in a Reddit Session. Here Are His 10 Best Quotes," Business Insider, December 9, 2020, https://markets.businessinsider.com/news/currencies/ray-dalio-bitcoin-china -stocks-markets-reddit-best-quotes-2020-12.

105. "Bridgewater's Dalio Supports Ant IPO Suspension, Bullish on China," Reuters, November 11, 2020, https://www.reuters.com/article/us-china -bridgewater-invest/bridgewaters-dalio-supports-ant-ipo-suspension -bullish-on-china-idUSKBN27R0IR.

106. "Acting DHS Sec. Chad Wolf Describes His Visit to Portland amid Violence," Fox News, transcript, July 26, 2020, https://www.foxnews.com/transcript /acting-dhs-sec-chad-wolf-describes-his-visit-to-portland-amid-violence.

107. Shuli Ren, "To Ray Dalio, $US10m for China Is Pocket Change," *Financial Review*, February 18, 2020, https://www.afr.com/markets/debt-markets/to -ray-dalio-us10m-for-china-is-pocket-change-20200218-p541y7.

108. Nancy Qu, "Bridgewater Launches Second PFM Product in China," Fund Selector Asia, October 6, 2020, https://fundselectorasia.com/bridgewater -launches-second-pfm-product-in-china/.

109. "The Rise of BlackRock," *Economist*, December 5, 2013, https://www .economist.com/leaders/2013/12/05/the-rise-of-blackrock.

110. Ibid.; Andrew Ross Sorkin, "BlackRock's Message: Contribute to Society, or Risk Losing Our Support," *New York Times*, January 15, 2018, https:// www.nytimes.com/2018/01/15/business/dealbook/blackrock-laurence -fink-letter.html.

111. Suzanna Andrews, "Larry Fink's $12 Trillion Shadow," *Vanity Fair*, April 2010, https://www.vanityfair.com/news/2010/04/fink-201004.

112. Ibid; Christine Williamson, "BlackRock's BGI Acquisition 10 Years Ago Fuels Rapid Growth," *Pensions & Investments*, June 11, 2019, https://www.pionline.com/article/20190611/ONLINE/190619948/blackrock-s-acquisition-of-bgi-10-years-ago-fuels-breakneck-growth-of-investment-giant.

113. Annie Massa and Caleb Melby, "In Fink We Trust: BlackRock Is Now 'Fourth Branch of Government,'" Bloomberg, last updated May 22, 2020, https://www.bloombergquint.com/businessweek/how-larry-fink-s-blackrock-is-helping-the-fed-with-bond-buying.

114. Larry Fink, "A Sense of Purpose," Harvard Law School Forum on Corporate Governance, January 17, 2018, https://corpgov.law.harvard.edu/2018/01/17/a-sense-of-purpose/.

115. Barbara Novick, "A Fundamental Reshaping of Finance," Harvard Law School Forum on Corporate Governance, January 16, 2020, https://corpgov.law.harvard.edu/2020/01/16/a-fundamental-reshaping-of-finance/.

116. "CNBC Exclusive: CNBC Transcript: BlackRock Chairman and CEO Larry Fink Speaks with CNBC's 'Squawk Box' Today," CNBC, transcript, October 16, 2018, https://www.cnbc.com/2018/10/16/cnbc-exclusive-cnbc-transcript-blackrock-chairman-and-ceo-larry-fink-speaks-with-cnbcs-squawk-box-today.html; "Jamal Khashoggi: All You Need to Know About Saudi Journalist's Death," BBC News, February 24, 2021, https://www.bbc.com/news/world-europe-45812399.

117. Tony Boyd, "BlackRock CEO Larry Fink on Housing, Banks and Investing," *Australian Financial Review*, October 31, 2017, https://www.afr.com/chanticleer/blackrock-ceo-larry-fink-on-housing-banks-and-investing-20171031-gzc5u3.

118. Ibid.

119. Lingling Wei, Bob Davis, and Dawn Lim, "China Has One Powerful Friend Left in the U.S.: Wall Street," *Wall Street Journal*, December 2, 2020, https://www.wsj.com/articles/china-has-one-powerful-friend-left-in-the-u-s-wall-street-11606924454.

120. Enda Curran and Christopher Anstey, "A Year After Security Law, Hong Kong Finance Hub Status Endures," BNN Bloomberg, July 26, 2021, https://www.bnnbloomberg.ca/a-year-after-security-law-hong-kong-finance-hub-status-endures-1.1633148; Scott Murdoch and Samuel Shen, "Exclusive: Goldman, Other Financial Firms Add China Staff, Eyeing Growth," Reuters, February 10, 2021, https://www.reuters.com/world/china/exclusive-goldman-other-financial-firms-add-china-staff-eyeing-growth-2021-02-11/.

121. Report to Congress of the U.S.-China Economic and Security Commission, 113th Cong. (2013), 55, https://www.govinfo.gov/content/pkg/GPO-USCC-2013/html/GPO-USCC-2013-1.htm.

122. "2020 Investment Climate Statements: China," U.S. Department of State, accessed June 27, 2021, https://www.state.gov/reports/2020-investment-climate-statements/china/.

123. Office of the United States Trade Representative Executive Office of the President, "Findings of the Investigation into China's Acts, Policies, and Prac-

tices Related to Technology Transfer, Intellectual Property, and Innovation Under Section 301 of the Trade Act of 1974," March 22, 2018, https://ustr .gov/sites/default/files/Section%20301%20FINAL.PDF.

124. "Zacks Investment Research: BlackRock (BLK) to Expand in China with Majority Owned JV," 2019, accessed via ProQuest on June 23, 2021, https:// www.proquest.com/blogs-podcasts-websites/zacks-investment-research -blackrock-blk-expand/docview/2329722698/se-2?accountid=187973.

125. Terence Corcoran, "The People vs. ESG on China," *National Post*, March 12, 2021, accessed via ProQuest on June 23, 2021, https://www.proquest.com /newspapers/people-vs-esg-on-china/docview/2500698674/se-2?accountid =187973.

126. "Zacks Investment Research: BlackRock (BLK) to Expand in China with Majority Owned JV."

127. Filipe B. Areno et al., "Holding Foreign Companies Accountable Act Poised to Be Signed into Law," Skadden, Deember 3, 2020, https://www.skadden .com/insights/publications/2020/12/holding-foreign-companies-accountable. A site search of BlackRock.com on July 1, 2021, yields no mention of the act.

128. "BlackRock Puts Gunmakers on Notice After Florida School Shooting," CGTN, February 23, 2018, https://news.cgtn.com/news/7a596a4e34677 a6333566d54/index.html.

129. "Summary of the Risk Profile and U.S. Capital Markets Footprint of China Communications Construction Company and Its Subsidiaries," RWR Advisory Group, August 28, 2020, https://cccc.rwradvisory.com/pdf/CCCC -Risk-Profile-and-Capital-Markets.pdf.

130. Steve Goldstein, "George Soros Says Blackrock Is on Wrong Side of 'Life and Death' Conflict with China," Marketwatch.com, September 7, 2021, https:// www.marketwatch.com/story/george-soros-criticizes-blackrock-for-a-second -time-on-china-11631006083?mod=emerging-markets.

131. Novick, "A Fundamental Reshaping of Finance."

132. Josh Siegel and Abby Smith, "Daily on Energy: China's Coal Use Is Soaring," *Washington Examiner*, March 29, 2021, https://www.washingtonexaminer.com /policy/energy/daily-on-energy-chinas-coal-use-is-soaring.

133. Lingling Wei, Bob Davis, and Dawn Lim, "China Has One Powerful Friend Left in U.S.: Wall Street," *Wall Street Journal*, December 2, 2020, https://www .wsj.com/articles/china-has-one-powerful-friend-left-in-the-u-s-wall-street -11606924454?mod=hp_lead_pos6.

134. Yu Nakamura, "More Companies Are Writing China's Communist Party into Their Charters," *Nikkei Asia*, August 24, 2017, https://asia.nikkei.com /Politics/More-companies-are-writing-China-s-Communist-Party-into -their-charters.

135. Jennifer Hughes, "BlackRock and Fidelity Put China's Communists into Company Law," *Financial Times*, September 7, 2017, https://www.ft.com /content/e91270a8-9364-11e7-bdfa-eda243196c2c.

136. Alex McMillan, "China Communist Party Has Just Become Besties with Hong Kong," TheStreet, September 12, 2017, https://www.thestreet.com

/markets/emerging-markets/china-communist-party-controls-companies -14301678.

137. Tamar Groswald Ozery, "Illiberal Governance and the Rise of China's Public Firms: An Oxymoron or China's Greatest Triumph?" *University of Pennsylvania Journal of International Law* 42, no. 4, 60, https://papers.ssrn.com/sol3 /papers.cfm?abstract_id=3616513.

138. Rebecca Ungarino, "Here Are 9 Fascinating Facts to Know About Black-Rock, the World's Largest Asset Manager," Business Insider, June 10, 2021, https://www.businessinsider.com/what-to-know-about-blackrock-larry-fink -biden-cabinet-facts-2020–12; Mark Segal, "Biden Taps Brian Deese, Global Head of Sustainable Investing at BlackRock, to Lead National Economic Council," ESG Today, December 4, 2020, https://www.esgtoday.com/biden -taps-brian-deese-global-head-of-sustainable-investing-at-blackrock-to-lead -national-economic-council/.

139. "China, U.S. Vow Full Implementation of Paris Agreement," State Council, People's Republic of China, last updated August 25, 2016, http://english.www.gov .cn/state_council/vice_premiers/2016/08/25/content_281475425407669.htm.

140. "Chinese Experts Cautiously Optimistic on China-U.S. Trade Relation Following Biden's Economic Picks," *Global Times*, December 1, 2020, https:// www.globaltimes.cn/content/1208586.shtml.

141. "China Gives BlackRock Green Light to Start Mainland Operations," *China Economic Review*, May 13, 2021, https://chinaeconomicreview.com/china-gives -blackrock-green-light-to-start-mainland-operations/.

142. Gabe Collins and Eric Anderson, "Resources for China's State Shipbuilders," in Andrew S. Erickson, ed., *Chinese Naval Shipbuilding: An Ambitious and Uncertain Course* (Annapolis, MD: Naval Institute Press, 2016), 69.

143. Joel Gehrke, "White House: California Pension Fund Subsidizing Chinese Plans to 'Overmatch' U.S. Military," *Washington Examiner*, March 11, 2020, https://www.washingtonexaminer.com/policy/defense-national-security /white-house-california-pension-fund-subsidizing-chinese-plans-to-overmatch -us-military.

144. Ibid.

145. Ibid.

146. "CCP Expert Di Dongsheng: We Can't Fix Trump Via Wall Street, but with Biden . . . ," Jennifer's World (blog), accessed June 27, 2021, https://www .jenniferzengblog.com/home/opening-up-financial-sector-as-goodwill-to -biden-as-we-cant-fix-trump-via-wall-street; "Six Rounds of Laughter and Applause During Di Dongsheng's Speech," Jennifer's World (blog), accessed June 27, 2021, https://www.jenniferzengblog.com/home/2020/12/15/six -rounds-of-laughter-and-applause-during-di-dongshengs-speech.

147. Hamilton and Ohlberg, *Hidden Hand*, 99–100.

148. Ibid., 100.

6: Diplomats

1. John Schrecker, "'For the Equality of Men—For the Equality of Nations': Anson Burlingame and China's First Embassy to the United States, 1868," *Jour-*

nal of American-East Asian Relations 17 (2010): 9–34, https://www.burlingame
.org/library/Anson%20Burlingame/Burlingame%20JAEAR.pdf.

2. Ibid.
3. Secretary Colin L. Powell, "Swearing-in New Class of Foreign Service Officers," U.S. Department of State, February 15, 2001, https://2001-2009.state.gov /secretary/former/powell/remarks/2001/588.htm.
4. Quoted in Richard McGregor, *Xi Jinping: The Backlash* (London: Penguin, 2019), 80.
5. "Blood Meridian," *Economist*, September 25, 2013, https://www.economist .com/books-and-arts/2013/09/25/blood-meridian.
6. Quoted from Henry Kissinger memo to Richard Nixon, "My Asian Trip," February 27, 1973, 6, quoted in James Mann, *The China Fantasy: Why Capitalism Will Not Bring Democracy to China* (London: Penguin Books, 2008), 71.
7. A. G. Noorani, "Kissinger's China," *Hindu* (India), July 1, 2011, https://front line.thehindu.com/other/article30176004.ece.
8. Andrei Gromyko, *Memoirs* (New York: Doubleday, 1990), 394; Bernard Gwertzman, "Books of The Times; Gromyko's Memoirs, with a Fillip for Americans," *New York Times*, March 27, 1990, https://www.nytimes.com /1990/03/27/books/books-of-the-times-gromyko-s-memoirs-with-a-fillip -for-americans.html.
9. Ibid.
10. Ibid.
11. "Tiananmen Square Protest Death Toll 'Was 10,000,'" BBC News, December 23, 2017, https://www.bbc.com/news/world-asia-china-42465516.
12. Noorani, "Kissinger's China."
13. Eric Alterman, *Sound and Fury: The Making of the Punditocracy* (Ithaca, NY: Cornell University Press, 1999), 161.
14. Noorani, "Kissinger's China."
15. Ibid.
16. Alterman, *Sound and Fury*, 162.
17. George Archibald, "U.S.: Old Hands Hold Hands with Beijing on Trade Policy," *Washington Times*, March 3, 1997, https://corpwatch.org/article/us -old-hands-hold-hands-beijing-trade-policy.
18. Ibid.
19. Ibid.
20. Henry A. Kissinger, "China: Containment Won't Work," *Washington Post*, June 13, 2005, https://www.henryakissinger.com/articles/china-containment -wont-work/.
21. Heather Timmons and Ilaria Maria Sala, "At 93, Henry Kissinger Is Still Doing Deals and Courting Controversy in China," Quartz, April 5, 2017, https://qz.com/950103/at-age-93-henry-kissinger-appears-to-have-played-a -cruical-role-in-the-xi-jinping-donald-trump-summit/.
22. Ibid.
23. Ibid.
24. Clive Hamilton and Mareike Ohlberg, *Hidden Hand: Exposing How the Chinese Communist Party Is Reshaping the World* (London: OneWorld Publications, 2020),

29; Jane Perlez, "China Creates a World Bank of Its Own, and the U.S. Balks," *New York Times*, December 4, 2015, https://www.nytimes.com/2015/12/05 /business/international/china-creates-an-asian-bank-as-the-us-stands-aloof .html.

25. Hamilton and Ohlberg, *Hidden Hand*, 221.
26. Ibid., 40.
27. Ibid., 223.
28. Ibid.
29. "John Brennan," Swiss Re, profile, accessed July 4, 2021, https://www.swissre .com/profile/John_Brennan/ep_cb2b7a.
30. Jeff Wallenfeldt, "John Brennan," *Encyclopaedia Britannica*, accessed July 4, 2021, https://www.britannica.com/biography/John-Brennan; "Towercrest Plaza," Thumbs Up Real Estate, accessed July 4, 2021, https://www.thumbsup -realestate.com/building/34.html; Eamon Javers, "In John Brennan's Private Sector Stint, a China Connection," CNBC, February 6, 2013, https://www .cnbc.com/id/100440555.
31. "Biographies of the Secretaries of State: Alexander Meigs Haig Jr. (1924–2010)," Office of the Historian, accessed July 4, 2021, https://history.state.gov /departmenthistory/people/haig-alexander-meigs.
32. Archibald, "U.S.: Old Hands Hold Hands with Beijing on Trade Policy."
33. Mann, *The China Fantasy*, 98.
34. Madeleine Albright, *Madam Secretary: A Memoir* (Westport, CT: Hyperion, 2003), 435.
35. Mann, *The China Fantasy*, 84.
36. Sarah Chayes, *On Corruption in America: And What Is at Stake* (New York: Knopf, 2020), 100.
37. Ibid.
38. Quoted in Mann, *The China Fantasy*, 60.
39. "China," Albright Stonebridge Group, accessed July 5, 2021, Albrightstonebridge .com/regions/china.
40. "Jin Ligang," Albright Stonebridge Group, accessed July 5, 2021, Albrightstonebridge.com/team/jin-ligang.
41. "Amy P. Celico," Albright Stonebridge Group, accessed July 7, 2021, Albrightstonebridge.com/team/amy-p-celico.
42. "Best Frenemies: China, the U.S., and the Future of the 21st Century," Rev.com, transcript, August 1, 2019, https://aspen-ideas-festival-production .s3.us-east-2.amazonaws.com/nullc933be4b-617a-421d-af5c-02a8bbbdcd85 /BestFrenemiesChina%2CtheUS%2CandtheFutureofthe21stCentury.pdf.
43. Roger Faligot, *Chinese Spies: From Chairman Mao to Xi Jinping* (London: Hurst, 2019), 287–88.
44. Jerry Dunleavy, "Biden Nominee for UN Ambassador Calls Speech at Confucius Institute a 'Huge Mistake,'" *Washington Examiner*, January 27, 2021, https://www.washingtonexaminer.com/news/biden-ambassador -nominee-speech-confucius-institute-huge-mistake; Josh Rogin, "Opinion: Biden's U.N. Ambassador Nominee to Face Criticism for Past Praise of China," *Washington Post*, January 27, 2021, https://www.washingtonpost

.com/opinions/2021/01/27/linda-thomas-greenfield-china-biden-united
-nations-ambassador/.

45. Luke Patey, *How China Loses: The Pushback Against Chinese Global Ambitions* (Oxford: Oxford University Press, 2021), 119.

46. Bartholomew Sparrow, *The Strategist: Brent Scowcroft and the Call of National Security* (New York: PublicAffairs, 2015), 500; "Regional Expertise," Cohen Group, accessed July 5, 2021, https://www.cohengroup.net/regional/china.

47. "Regional Expertise."

48. "Cohen in China," *Wired*, January 19, 1998, https://www.wired.com/1998/01/cohen-in-china/.

49. "President Jiang Zemin Greets Secretary and Mrs. William S. Cohen at Zhongnanhai in Beijing, China," U.S. Department of Defense, photograph, accessed July 5, 2021, https://www.defense.gov/observe/photo-gallery/igphoto/2001239591/.

50. "The Cohen Group Opens Offices in China," PR Newswire U.S., June 18, 2007 (Lexis); "James Mattis," Cohen Group, profile, accessed July 5, 2021, https://www.cohengroup.net/our-people/james-mattis.

51. Yang Shilong and Zhang Zhihuan, "(Along Belt & Road) Interview: Belt and Road Initiative to Boost Sustainable Economic Development–Former U.S. Diplomat," Xinhuanet, April 28, 2017, http://www.xinhuanet.com//english/2017-04/28/c_136241610.htm.

52. Ibid.

53. "Belt and Road Receives Global Backing," *China Daily*, last updated May 11, 2017, http://www.chinadaily.com.cn/china//////2017-05/11/content_29301049_22.htm.

54. Shilong and Zhihuan, "(Along Belt & Road) Interview."

55. "Zeng Peiyan Meets with William Cohen of the Cohen Group," China Center for International Economic Exchanges, July 26, 2011, http://english.cciee.org.cn/Detail.aspx?newsId=3019&TId=46.

56. "Cohen Group to Expand Business in Shandong," *China Daily*, last updated September 29, 2020, http://shandong.chinadaily.com.cn/2020-09/29/c_542121.htm.

57. "Xiao Yaqing, Yan Xiaofeng Meet with William Cohen, Former U.S. Defense Secretary and Chairman and CEO of William Cohen Group," State-owned Assets Supervision and Administration Commission of the State Council, last updated October 2, 2018, http://en.sasac.gov.cn/2018/10/02/c_486.htm.

58. "William Cohen," U.S. Chamber of Commerce, profile, accessed July 5, 2021, https://www.uschamber.com/william-cohen.

59. Book review, "William S. Cohen, *Dragon Fire*," Kirkus Reviews, release date August 22, 2006, https://www.kirkusreviews.com/book-reviews/william-s-cohen/dragon-fire/.

60. "William Cohen," U.S. Chamber of Commerce.

61. Zen Soo and Sarah Dai, "How Did Huawei Fall Foul of the U.S. Government and Find Itself at the Epicentre of a New Tech War?," *South China Morning Post*, April 6, 2020, https://www.scmp.com/tech/enterprises

/article/3078451/how-did-huawei-fall-foul-us-government-and-find
-itself-epicentre.

62. Mann, *The China Fantasy*, 60–61.

63. U.S. Department of Commerce, Bureau of Industry and Security, Annual
Report to the Congress for Fiscal Year 2007, accessed July 7, 2021, https://
www.bis.doc.gov/index.php/documents/policy-guidance/919-bis-annual
-report-fy-2007/file; "Rice: U.S. Doesn't Have a Posture Against China,"
Embassy of the People's Republic of China in the United States of America,
March 16, 2005, http://www.china-embassy.org/eng/zmgx/zmgx/Political
%20Relationship/t187646.htm.

64. "Remarks by Secretary Gates to the Business Executives for National Security
on the U.S. Export Control System," U.S. Department of Defense, April 20,
2010, https://fas.org/sgp/news/2010/04/gates-export.html.

65. "Anja Manuel," Rice, Hadley, Gates & Manuel LLC, profile, accessed July 5,
2021, https://www.rhgm.com/anja-manuel/.

66. "Work," Rice, Hadley, Gates & Manuel LLC, accessed July 5, 2021, https://
www.rhgm.com/work/.

67. "Remarks by Secretary Gates to the Business Executives for National Security
on the U.S. Export Control System."

68. "Work 2," Rice, Hadley, Gates & Manuel LLC, accessed July 5, 2021, https://
www.rhgm.com/work-2/.

69. "Condoleezza Rice Brings Asia and Silicon Valley Closer Together," Intelligence Online, March 28, 2019, https://www.intelligenceonline.com
/corporate-intelligence/2019/03/28/condoleezza-rice-brings-asia-and
-silicon-valley-closer-together,108350979-art.

70. Graham Hand, "John Malloy: Why Time Is Now for Emerging Markets,"
Firstlinks, December 9, 2020, https://www.firstlinks.com.au/john-malloy
-why-time-is-now-for-emerging-markets.

71. "Global Emerging Markets and Artificial Intelligence," RWC Partners, investor letter, Q2 2017, May 2017, 10, http://www.rwcdr.co.uk/Docs/17.05
_RWC_Emerging_&_Frontier_Markets_-_Q2_Investor_Letter.pdf.

72. Industry and Security Bureau, "Addition of Certain Entities to the Entity
List," Federal Register, October 9, 2019, https://www.federalregister.gov
/documents/2019/10/09/2019-22210/addition-of-certain-entities-to-the
-entity-list; James Kynge and Demetri Sevastopulo, "U.S. Pressure Building
on Investors in China Surveillance Group," *Financial Times*, March 29, 2019,
https://www.ft.com/content/36b4cb42-50f3-11e9-b401-8d9ef1626294;
Calum MacLeod, "China Surveillance Targets Crime—and Dissent," *USA
Today*, January 3, 2013, https://www.usatoday.com/story/news
/world/2013/01/03/china-security/1802177/.

73. MacLeod, "China Surveillance Targets Crime—and Dissent." Pertinent
quote: "Human rights groups say the cameras are increasingly relied on to
monitor and intimidate political dissidents, and China's two most restive
ethnic groups: the Tibetans in the southwest and *Uighurs* in the northwest.
China's video surveillance technology has grown more sophisticated,
focusing on biometrics research. . . . Skynet has expanded in Tibetan

areas and Xinjiang, says Qian Hao, public security department manager at Hikvision Digital Technology, one of China's largest CCTV specialists. Police use *Hikvision's* 'raindrop-style grid' management system to follow suspects and trace back their movements for the previous two hours, he says . . . [emphasis mine]."

74. See "The Next Generation of Emerging Markets," RWC Partners, investor letter, Q1 2019, May 2019, 3, https://rwcpartnershub.com/wp-content /uploads/2019/06/19.05-RWC-Emerging-Frontier-Markets-Strategy-Update -Next-Generation-of-EM.pdf; "Global Emerging Markets and Artificial Intelligence," RWC Partners, investor letter, Q2 2017.

75. "Opportunities in China," RWC Partners, February 2019, https://www .rwcpartners.com/uk/wp-content/uploads/2019/02/19.02-rwc-emerging -frontier-markets-strategy-update-opportunities-in-china-9.pdf.

76. "Industrial," Han's Laser, accessed July 5, 2021, https://us.hanslaser.net /application/industrial.html.

77. "Huawei Technology May Face Tougher U.S. Chip Ban," MT Newswires Live Briefs PRO, May 21, 2020, https://advance.lexis.com/document/?pd mfid=1519360&crid=29baa3c2–85fe-48e9–929a-de99f158dbb1&pddocfu llpath=%2Fshared%2Fdocument%2Fnews%2Furn%3AcontentItem%3A5 YYB-H3S1-JBH1-X2WG-00000–00&pdcontentcomponentid=410393& pdteaserkey=sr0&pditab=allpods&ecomp=yzynk&earg=sr0&prid=4c1acdae –1878–4a41-abcb-860236a255f6; Jack Hawke, "Britain Bans Huawei from Its 5G Network and Will Remove Existing Equipment by 2027," ABC, July 14, 2020, https://www.abc.net.au/news/2020–07–14/uk-set-to-exclude -huawei-from-telecommunications-networks/12455930.

78. Anja Manuel, "Chinese Tech Isn't the Enemy," *Atlantic*, August 1, 2018, https://www.theatlantic.com/international/archive/2018/08/america-needs -china-in-tech/566516/.

79. United States Securities and Exchange Commission, Schedule 13D, Money- gram International Inc., November 25, 2020, https://ir.moneygram.com /node/21466/html; Greg Roumeliotis, "U.S. Blocks MoneyGram Sale to China's Ant Financial on National Security Concerns," Reuters, January 2, 2018, https://www.reuters.com/article/us-moneygram-intl-m-a-ant -financial/u-s-blocks-moneygram-sale-to-chinas-ant-financial-on-national -security-concerns-idUSKBN1ER1R7.

80. "About the Governor," Governor Gary Locke's website, accessed July 5, 2021, https://www.digitalarchives.wa.gov/governorlocke/bios/bio.htm.

81. Andrew Zajac, "Locke's Ties to China May Be Selling Point," *Los Angeles Times* (archives), March 1, 2009, https://www.latimes.com/archives/la-xpm-2009 -mar-01-na-locke1-story.html; Michelle Malkin, "He's No 'Mr. Clean,'" *New York Post*, February 28, 2009, https://nypost.com/2009/02/28/hes-no-mr-clean/.

82. Lee Fang and Jon Schwarz, "A 'Desperate' Seller," Intercept, August 3, 2016, https://theintercept.com/2016/08/03/gary-locke-ambassador-to-china -house-sale-chinese-tycoon/; Kristi Heim, "Forging Ties with China," *Seattle Times*, September 8, 2006, https://www.seattletimes.com/seattle-news /forging-ties-with-china-suits-locke/.

83. Gary Locke, Public Financial Disclosure Report, March 12, 2009, https://www.documentcloud.org/documents/3761684-lockepfd1.html#document/p34/a355954; Lee Fang, "Shadowy Chinese Conglomerate Cultivated Ties to the Most Powerful U.S. Politicians," Intercept, June 2, 2017, https://theintercept.com/2017/06/02/hna-group-corruption-scaramucci-trump-jeb-bush-clinton-guo-wengui/.

84. Heim, "Forging Ties with China."

85. Zajac, "Locke's Ties to China May Be Selling Point."

86. "Secretary Locke Meets with Chinese Foreign Minister Yang Jiechi," United States Department of Commerce, January 5, 2011, https://2010–2014.commerce.gov/blog/category/1157.html.

87. Fang and Schwarz, "A 'Desperate' Seller"; Lee Fang, Jon Schwarz, and Elaine Yu, "Power Couple," Intercept, August 3, 2016, https://theintercept.com/2016/08/03/chinese-couple-million-dollar-donation-jeb-bush-super-pac/.

88. Ibid.

89. Fang and Schwarz, "A 'Desperate' Seller."

90. Ibid.

91. Melinda Liu, "Blind Injustice," Newsweek, May 14, 2012, https://www.newsweek.com/chen-guangchengs-blind-injustice-64983.

92. Chen Guangcheng, The Barefoot Lawyer (New York: Henry Holt, 2015), 277, 281–86.

93. Ibid., 289, 294, 303.

94. Kate Woodsome, "Alternative Account of Chen Guangcheng Drama Unfolds on Twitter," VOA News, May 1, 2012, https://www.voanews.com/a/alternate-account-of-chen-drama-unfolds-on-twitter-149883735/370328.html.

95. Guangcheng, The Barefoot Lawyer, 319.

96. Drew Atkins, "Former Gov. Gary Locke's 'Highly Inappropriate' Home Sale," Crosscut, August 9, 2016, https://crosscut.com/2016/08/former-governor-gary-locke-faces-major-ethical-questions.

97. Ibid.

98. Steve Wilhelm, "Gary Locke Joins Seattle Law Firm," Puget Sound Business Journal, September 21, 2015, https://www.dwt.com/files/Uploads/Documents/Publications/PSBJ_Locke_FINAL.pdf; Ahmed Elbenni, "An Interview with Gary Locke, Former U.S. Ambassador to China," Politic, June 5, 2017, https://thepolitic.org/an-interview-with-gary-locke-former-u-s-ambassador-to-china/.

99. Cecily Liu, "President Xi Jinping Has Done an Excellent Job as President. He Has Great Presence and Visibility Around the World," China Daily, last updated September 18, 2017, https://www.chinadaily.com.cn/opinion/5year scorecard/2017-09/18/content_32147461.htm.

100. "Gary Locke and John Zeng Join AMC Entertainment Holdings, Inc. Board of Directors," Business Wire, February 17, 2016, https://www.businesswire.com/news/home/20160217006600/en/Gary-Locke-and-John-Zeng-Join-AMC-Entertainment-Holdings-Inc.-Board-of-Directors.

101. "Wanda Group Completes Acquisition of AMC Entertainment Holdings,

Inc.," Business Wire, September 4, 2012, https://www.businesswire.com
/news/home/20120904006119/en/Wanda-Group-Completes-Acquisition-of
-AMC-Entertainment-Holdings-Inc.

102. "Wang Jianlin," Wanda Group, profile, accessed July 5, 2021, https://www
.wanda-group.com/aboutwanda/Wan_Jianlin/.

103. Beatrice Verhoeven, "Washington Post Warns That China's Hollywood Inva-
sion Is a 'Propaganda' Play," *Wrap*, October 6, 2016, https://www.thewrap
.com/washington-post-warns-that-chinas-hollywood-invasion-is-a-propaganda
-play/; Brent Lang and Gene Maddaus, "Lawmakers Raise Questions About
Chinese Investment in Hollywood," *Variety*, September 22, 2016, https://
variety.com/2016/film/news/wanda-lawmakers-raise-questions-about-chinese
-investment-in-hollywood-1201868250/.

104. Ed Lin, "AMC Insiders Sold $13 Million in Stock in June as Share Price Dou-
bled," *Barron's*, June 15, 2021, https://www.barrons.com/articles/amc-stock
-insider-sales-51623687972.

105. "Gov. Gary Locke to Chair NW Innovation Works' Global Advisory Board,"
December 20, 2016, https://nwinnovationworks.com/news/gov-gary-locke
-chair-nw-innovation-works-global-advisory-board.html.

106. Hal Bernton, "How a Chinese Businessman Is Going Toe-to-Toe with Pacific
Northwest Environmentalists on Methanol," *Seattle Times*, July 6, 2017, https://
www.seattletimes.com/seattle-news/environment/the-chinese-businessman
-behind-the-18b-plan-to-make-methanol-in-washington-state/.

107. "Company Profile," Cas Holdings, accessed July 5, 2021, http://english.
holdings.cas.cn/cp/.

108. "CASH Holds Interaction Between National Strategy and Corporate Strategy
Workshop," Cas Holdings, October 15, 2015, http://english.holdings.cas.cn
/English/NF/201601/t20160105_158438.html.

109. "Corporate Governance," Cas Holdings, accessed July 5, 2021, http://english
.holdings.cas.cn/English/AC/CG/; "Company Profile," Cas Holdings,
accessed July 7, 2021, http://english.holdings.cas.cn/English/AC/CP/.

110. Elsa B. Kania, "Chinese Military Innovation in Artificial Intelligence," Tes-
timony Before the U.S.-China Economic and Security Review Commission
Hearing on Trade, Technology, and Military-Civil Fusion, Center for a New
American Security, June 7, 2019, https://www.uscc.gov/sites/default/files
/June%207%20Hearing_Panel%201_Elsa%20Kania_Chinese%20Military
%20Innovation%20in%20Artificial%20Intelligence_0.pdf.

111. United States Senate, "Threats to the U.S. Research Enterprise: China's
Talent Recruitment Plans," Staff Report, Permanent Subcommittee on Investigations, November 18, 2019, https://www.hsgac.senate.gov/imo/media
/doc/2019-11-18%20PSI%20Staff%20Report%20-%20China's%20Talent
%20Recruitment%20Plans.pdf.

112. Kevin Liptak and Kylie Atwood, "Biden Administration Off to a Combative
Start with Tough Rhetoric on Russia, China," CNN, March 20, 2021,
https://www.cnn.com/2021/03/20/politics/biden-russia-china-tough
-rhetoric-foreign-policy/index.html.

113. Tom Lutey, "Two Weeks Out of Office, Baucus Still Working on China,"

Billings Gazette, January 29, 2017, https://billingsgazette.com/news/state-and
-regional/govt-and-politics/two-weeks-out-of-office-baucus-still-working
-on-china/article_a2ea910a-31c1-5c93-9338-0bd0969bb2d5.html.

114. "How Chinese Companies Facilitate Technology Transfer from the United
States," U.S.-China Economic and Security Review Commission, May 6,
2019, https://www.uscc.gov/research/how-chinese-companies-facilitate
-technology-transfer-united-states.

115. "Aides: Max Baucus Has Long Been Fascinated with China," *Wall Street
Journal*, last updated December 19, 2013, https://www.wsj.com/articles/BL
-CJB-20056.

116. Thomas L. Friedman, "Senator Asks End to Threats Against China," *New
York Times*, January 27, 1994, https://www.nytimes.com/1994/01/27/world
/senator-asks-end-to-threats-against-china.html; Zachary Evans, "The Retired U.S. Senator and Diplomat Shilling for China's Propaganda Machine,"
National Review, May 25, 2020, https://www.nationalreview.com/2020/05
/coronavirus-china-max-baucus-shilling-for-beijing-propaganda-machine/.

117. Evans, "The Retired U.S. Senator and Diplomat Shilling for China's
Propaganda Machine"; "WTO: Will China Keep Its Promises? Can It?,"
Congressional-Executive Commission on China, transcript, June 6, 2002,
https://www.cecc.gov/events/hearings/wto-will-china-keep-its-promises
-can-it.

118. Evans, "The Retired U.S. Senator and Diplomat Shilling for China's Propaganda Machine."

119. "About," Baucus Group, accessed July 5, 2021, https://www.baucusgroupbeta
.com/about/.

120. Evans, "The Retired U.S. Senator and Diplomat Shilling for China's Propaganda Machine"; Sidney Leng, "HNA Holds Its Own Communist Party
Congress to Rally Support Amid Debt Woes," *South China Morning Post*,
February 9, 2018, https://www.scmp.com/news/china/economy/article
/2132724/hna-holds-its-own-communist-party-congress-rally-support-amid.

121. Evans, "The Retired U.S. Senator and Diplomat Shilling for China's Propaganda Machine."

122. "About the Institute," Max S. Baucus Institute, University of Montana,
accessed July 6, 2021, https://www.umt.edu/law/baucus-institute/about
-institute/default.php.

123. Dillon Kato, "UM Ushers in the Chinese Year of the Horse," *Missoulian*,
February 2, 2014, https://missoulian.com/news/local/um-ushers-in-the
-chinese-year-of-the-horse/article_e21b33f6-8c70-11e3-a7c7-0019bb2963f4
.html.

124. Jon King, "Professor Criticizes Beijing Censorship at University of Montana's
Confucius Institute," Newstalk KGVO, July 26, 2017, https://newstalkkgvo
.com/professor-criticizes-beijing-censorship-at-university-of-montanas
-confucius-institute/.

125. Anand Naidoo, "COVID-19: Fallout from U.S. Attacks on China," CGTN
America, May 15, 2020, https://america.cgtn.com/2020/05/15/covid-19
-fallout-from-u-s-attacks-on-china-amb-max-baucus.

126. Timothy P. Carney, "When Max Baucus Calls Trump Hitler, We Should Remember Who's Paying Max Baucus," *Washington Examiner*, May 21, 2020, https://www.washingtonexaminer.com/opinion/when-max-baucus-calls -trump-hitler-we-should-remember-whos-paying-max-baucus.

127. Zachary Evans, "Former Obama Ambassador to China Compares Trump to Hitler on Chinese State TV," *National Review*, May 21, 2020, https://www .nationalreview.com/news/former-obama-ambassador-to-china-compares -trump-to-hitler-on-chinese-state-tv/.

128. Evans, "The Retired U.S. Senator and Diplomat Shilling for China's Propaganda Machine."

129. "Anti-China Rhetoric Similar to That in McCarthy Era, Says Former U.S. Ambassador," Xinhua Net, May 8, 2020, http://www.xinhuanet.com/english /2020-05/08/c_139039096.htm; "Anti-China Rhetoric Similar to That in McCarthy Era, Says Former U.S. Ambassador," *Global Times*, May 8, 2020, https://www.globaltimes.cn/content/1187745.shtml; "Anti-China Rhetoric Similar to That in McCarthy Era, Says Former U.S. Ambassador," *People's Daily*, May 8, 2020, http://en.people.cn/n3/2020/0508/c90000-9687826 .html.

130. Yuichiro Kakutani, "Obama's Man in China Now Beijing's Man in Washington," *Washington Free Beacon*, May 21, 2020, https://freebeacon.com/national -security/obamas-man-in-china-now-beijings-man-in-washington/.

131. Ibid.

132. Lia Zhu, "Chinese Firms Advised to Stay in U.S. as Regulation Tightens," *China Daily*, September 18, 2020, http://epaper.chinadaily.com.cn/a/202009/ 18/WS5f63ef99a31099a2343506bb.html.

133. "Sanctions on China Tend to Cause More Problems, Says Former U.S. Ambassador," CNBC, March 24, 2021, https://www.cnbc.com/video/2021/03 /24/sanctions-on-china-tend-to-cause-more-problems-ex-us-ambassador.html.

134. Yuan Yuan, "China-U.S. Relations: What Now, What Next?," *Beijing Review*, July 18, 2019, http://www.bjreview.com/World/201907/t20190715 _800173469.html.

135. "Melodee Hanes," LinkedIn profile, accessed July 6, 2021, https://www .linkedin.com/in/melodee-hanes-1646b623/.

136. "Binance Hires Former U.S. Senator Max Baucus as Policy and Government Relations Advisor," Binance (blog), March 11, 2021, https://www.binance .com/en/blog/421499824684901776/binance-hires-former-us-senator-max -baucus-as-policy-and-government-relations-advisor.

137. Tom Schoenberg, "Binance Faces Probe by U.S. Money-Laundering and Tax Sleuths," Bloomberg, May 13, 2021, https://www.bloomberg.com/news /articles/2021-05-13/binance-probed-by-u-s-as-money-laundering-tax -sleuths-bore-in.

138. Binyamin Appelbaum, "Terry Branstad, Iowa Governor, Is Trump's Pick as China Ambassador," *New York Times*, December 7, 2016, https://www.nytimes .com/2016/12/07/us/politics/terry-branstad-china-ambassador-trump.html; Anthony Kuhn, "How the U.S. Ambassador to China May Have Xi Jinping's Ear," NPR, February 18, 2018, https://www.npr.org/sections/parallels/2018

/02/18/586371119/how-the-u-s-ambassador-to-china-may-have-xi-jinpings
-ear.

139. "Why Is the South China Sea Contentious?," BBC News, July 12, 2016,
https://www.bbc.com/news/world-asia-pacific-13748349; "2016 Report
to Congress," U.S.-China Economic and Security Review Commission,
accessed July 6, 2021, https://www.uscc.gov/annual-report/2016-annual
-report-congress.

140. Alex Isenstadt, Matthew Nussbaum, and Brent Griffiths, "Trump Picks Branstad as Ambassador to China," *Politico,* December 7, 2016, https://www
.politico.com/blogs/donald-trump-administration/2016/12/terry-branstad
-trump-china-ambassador-232298.

141. "An 'Old Friend' of Xi Jinping Will Be America's Next Ambassador to China,"
Economist, December 8, 2016, https://www.economist.com/democracy-in
-america/2016/12/08/an-old-friend-of-xi-jinping-will-be-americas-next
-ambassador-to-china.

142. Christina Sterbenz, "Why China's President Loves Iowa," Business Insider,
May 5, 2015, https://www.businessinsider.com/a-rural-town-in-iowa
-helped-chinas-president-xi-jinping-rise-to-power-2015-4.

143. Associated Press, "Terry Branstad Cities Trade Deal as Biggest Achievement
of His Time as Ambassador to China," *Gazette,* September 17, 2020, https://
www.thegazette.com/subject/news/nation-and-world/terry-branstad
-cites-trade-deal-as-biggest-achievement-of-his-time-as-ambassador-to
-china-20200917; Eva Dou, "U.S. Envoy to China Feels the Heat from Trade
Fight," *Wall Street Journal,* last updated July 19, 2018, https://www.wsj.com
/articles/u-s-envoy-to-china-feels-the-heat-from-trade-fight-1532019960.

144. "Lobbying Principal, American Chemistry Council," Eye on Lobbying, accessed July 6, 2021, https://lobbying.wi.gov/Mobile/PrincipalInformation
/2019REG/Information/8093.

145. "U.S. Chemicals Industry Responds to Escalating Trade Tensions Between
the United States and China," American Chemistry Council, August 23,
2019, https://www.americanchemistry.com/Media/PressReleasesTranscripts
/ACC-news-releases/U.S.-Chemicals-Industry-Responds-to-Escalating
-Trade-Tensions-Between-the-U.S.-and-China.html.

146. Lee Fang, "Chinese State-Owned Chemical Firm Joins Dark Money Group
Pouring Cash into U.S. Elections," Intercept, February 15, 2018, https://
theintercept.com/2018/02/15/chinese-state-owned-chemical-firm-joins-dark
-money-group-pouring-cash-into-u-s-elections/; Alexander H. Tullo,
"C&EN's Global Top 50 Chemical Companies of 2018," *Chemical & Engineering News,* July 29, 2019, https://cen.acs.org/business/finance/CENs-Global
-Top-50-chemical/97/i30.

147. Kuhn, "How the U.S. Ambassador to China May Have Xi Jinping's Ear."

148. "Eric Branstad," Mercury, accessed July 6, 2021, https://www.mercuryllc.com
/experts/eric-branstad/.

149. "China Commerce Chamber in Chicago Holds Annual Gala, Awards Con-

tributors," *Global Times*, June 30, 2017, http://globaltimes.cn/content
/1054317.shtml.

150. Mara Hvistendahl and Lee Fang, "China's Man in Washington," Intercept,
October 15, 2020, https://theintercept.com/2020/10/15/eric-branstad
-trump-china-ambassador/.

151. Ibid.

152. Ibid.

153. Ibid.; James T. Areddy, "Eric Branstad, Son of U.S. Envoy to China, Used
Trump Ties to Lure Business," *Wall Street Journal*, June 29, 2018, https://
www.wsj.com/articles/son-of-u-s-envoy-to-china-used-trump-ties-to-lure
-business-1530306803.

154. Hvistendahl and Fang, "China's Man in Washington."

155. Opensecrets.org, "Mercury Public Affairs: Registrants," 2019, http://www
.opensecrets.org/fara/registrants/D000071638/clients?cycle=2019.

7: The Bush and Trudeau Dynasties

1. Joel Gehrke, "China Experts Criticize Neil Bush for Support of Communist
Regime Against Trump," *Washington Examiner*, July 19, 2019, https://www
.washingtonexaminer.com/policy/defense-national-security/china-experts
-criticize-neil-bush-for-support-of-communist-regime-against-trump.

2. "U.S. Congress Ill-Informed on HK Freedoms: Neil Bush," *China Daily*, last
updated December 2, 2019, https://www.chinadaily.com.cn/a/201912/02
/WS5de5164ba310cf3e3557b6e0.html.

3. Jen Gerson, "At Toronto Fundraiser, Justin Trudeau Seemingly Admires
China's 'Basic Dictatorship,'" *National Post*, November 8, 2013, https://national
post.com/news/politics/justin-trudeau-seemingly-admires-chinas-basic
-dictatorship-at-toronto-fundraiser; Terry Milewski, "Justin Trudeau Ap-
plauds China—But Then, So Does Stephen Harper," CBC, November 11,
2013, https://www.cbc.ca/news/politics/justin-trudeau-applauds-china-but
-then-so-does-stephen-harper-1.2422068.

4. Aaron Kaiser-Chen, "Using the Old to Serve the Present, and the Foreign to
Serve China: Chinese Nationalism and Chinese Identity in Cultural Revolution Media," Columbia University, 2016, https://worldhistory.columbia
.edu/content/using-old-serve-present-and-foreign-serve-china-chinese
-nationalism-and-chinese-identity.

5. "George H. W. Bush: Biography," George H. W. Bush Presidential
Library and Museum, accessed July 9, 2021, https://www.bush41.org/bush
/biography.

6. George H. W. Bush, *The China Diary of George H. W. Bush: The Making of a
Global President* (Princeton, NJ: Princeton University Press, 2008), xvii, 6;
"George H. W. Bush: Biography."

7. Curtis Stone, "Americans Gather to Mourn Bush, an Old Friend of China,"
People's Daily Online, December 6, 2018, http://en.people.cn/n3/2018/1206
/c90000-9525922.html; Wang Li, "Chinese Diplomat Accompanies Bush on

His 1977 China Tour," China.org.cn, November 26, 2003, http://www.china
.org.cn/english/2003/Nov/80776.htm.

8. "The Bush Family in China," *China Daily*, May 31, 2009, https://www
.chinadaily.com.cn/china/09usofficials/2009–05/31/content_7956346_2
.htm (Note: article mistakenly calls Prescott Bush Jr. the younger brother of
George H. W. Bush).

9. Anahad O'Connor, "Prescott Bush Jr., Scion of a Political Family, Dies at 87,"
New York Times, June 24, 2010, https://www.nytimes.com/2010/06/25/us
/politics/25bush.html.

10. Michael Isikoff, "As Race Heats Up, So Does Scrutiny of Bush's Family,"
Washington Post, July 4, 1992, https://www.washingtonpost.com/archive
/politics/1992/07/04/as-race-heats-up-so-does-scrutiny-of-bushs-family
/be6db80b-e311-4e39-8acd-7f07c1d90e10/; "The Bush Family in China";
"Shanghai Course Demolished as Crackdown Continues," Golf Course Industry, March 22, 2016, https://www.golfcourseindustry.com/article
/shanghai-china-golf-crackdown/; Warren Vieth and Lianne Hart, "U.S.:
Bush's Brother Has Contract to Help Chinese Chip Maker," *Los Angeles
Times*, November 27, 2003, https://corpwatch.org/article/us-bushs-brother
-has-contract-help-chinese-chip-maker.

11. Isikoff, "As Race Heats Up, So Does Scrutiny of Bush's Family."

12. "Bush's Uncle in China on Business," CNN, April 4, 2001, http://edition
.cnn.com/2001/US/04/04/bush.uncle/index.html.

13. Rita Beamish, "White House Denies China Ties with President's
Brother," Associated Press, December 13, 1989, https://apnews.com
/article/62331a288953aebbd0ff16a29e05fd3a; Joe Conason, "The Chinese
Connection Has Bipartisan Roots," *Observer*, June 7, 1999, https://observer
.com/1999/06/the-chinese-connection-has-bipartisan-roots/.

14. Isikoff, "As Race Heats Up, So Does Scrutiny of Bush's Family."

15. Paul De La Garza, "Arms Deal Will Test Bush Ties," *Tampa Bay Times*
(archives), September 9, 2005, https://www.tampabay.com/archive/2001/04
/23/arms-deal-will-test-bush-ties/?outputType=amp.

16. "Membership Benefits," United States of America–China Chamber of Commerce, accessed July 9, 2021, https://www.usccc.org/membership-benefits.

17. Global Crossing Ltd. and GC Acquisition Limited, Before the Federal
Communications Commission, August 27, 2003, https://ecfsapi.fcc.gov/file
/6514782450.pdf.

18. James Mann, *The China Fantasy: Why Capitalism Will Not Bring Democracy to
China* (London: Penguin Books, 2008), 85.

19. "Directors and Senior Management," excerpt from Plus Holding Limited
2005 Annual Report, 13, https://www1.hkexnews.hk/listedco/listconews
/sehk/2005/1124/01013/EWF106.pdf.

20. "Profile of Mr. Prescott S. Bush, Jr.," Telecom Plus Holdings Limited, on
Internet Archive, accessed July 10, 2021, https://web.archive.org
/web/20040210073451/http://www.telecomplus.com.cn/englishversion
/Profile.htm (the screenshot of the site was captured on February 10, 2004).

21. Debbie Howlett, "President's Uncle Shares Bush Family Ties to China," *USA*

Today, February 19, 2002, https://usatoday30.usatoday.com/news/washington
/2002/02/19/usat-prescott-bush.htm; David Lague, "Obituary: Rong Yiren,
89, China's Famed 'Red Capitalist,'" *New York Times*, October 27, 2005,
https://www.nytimes.com/2005/10/27/world/asia/obituaryrong-yiren-89
-chinas-famed-red-capitalist.html.

22. Howlett, "President's Uncle Shares Bush Family Ties to China."
23. De La Garza, "Arms Deal Will Test Bush Ties."
24. John Pomfret, "Jiang Has Caution for U.S.," *Washington Post* (archives), March
24, 2001, https://www.washingtonpost.com/archive/politics/2001/03/24
/jiang-has-caution-for-us/4c7429b5-c02d-4d44-849f-ddc86fd438a6/.
25. Warren Vieth and Lianne Hart, "Bush's Brother Has Contract to Help Chinese Chip Maker," *Los Angeles Times* (archives), November 27, 2003, https://
www.latimes.com/archives/la-xpm-2003-nov-27-na-neilbush27-story.html.
26. David Corn and Dan Moldea, "Influence Peddling, Bush Style," *Nation*
(archives), October 5, 2000, https://www.thenation.com/article/archive
/influence-peddling-bush-style/.
27. Will Connors, "Sinopec Makes Offer for Ghana Offshore Oil Stake," *Wall
Street Journal*, October 26, 2009, https://www.wsj.com/articles/SB100014240
52748704335904574497421597586980.
28. "Neil Bush," George H. W. Bush Foundation for U.S.-China Relations,
accessed July 11, 2021, https://bushchinafoundation.org/people/neil-bush/.
29. Gehrke, "China Experts Criticize Neil Bush for Support of Communist
Regime Against Trump."
30. "About Us," SingHaiyi Group, accessed July 11, 2021, https://www.singhaiyi
.com/directors.html.
31. Bethany Allen-Ebrahimian, "Chinese Oligarch's Company with Ties to
George W. Bush's Brother Plunges in Value," Axios, October 13, 2020,
https://www.axios.com/neil-bush-china-hong-kong-finance-investment
-cbe8fec2-ae8a-4c59-a2ee-6be5b51adc1a.html; "Neil Bush," George H. W.
Bush Foundation for U.S.-China Relations.
32. Lee Jeong-ho, "U.S. Must Stop Treating China as an Enemy, Says Son of
Former President George HW Bush," *South China Morning Post,* July 10, 2019,
https://www.scmp.com/news/china/diplomacy/article/3018077/us-must
-stop-treating-china-enemy-says-son-former-president; "About," U.S.-China
Trade and Economic Relations Forum: What Now, What Next, China–
United States Exchange Foundation, accessed July 11, 2021, https://www
.chinausfocus.com/2019forum/about/.
33. Lachlan Markay and Bethany Allen-Ebrahimian, "Scoop: Bush Family Nonprofit's $5 Million Deal with China Influence Group," Axios, June 5, 2021,
https://www.axios.com/scoop-bush-family-nonprofits-5-million-deal-with
-china-influence-group-886e7d7a-36c3-471b-a582-31b0c2e50eeb.htmlf.
34. Howlett, "President's Uncle Shares Bush Family Ties to China."
35. Ibid.; "Jeb Bush's Private Equity Ventures Resemble Mitt Romney's," *Kansas
City Star*, December 11, 2014, https://www.kansascity.com/news/politics
-government/article4423275.html.
36. "Xi Meets Jeb Bush, Calls for Closer Cooperation Between China, U.S.,"

Embassy of the People's Republic of China in the United States of America, January 17, 2012, https://www.fmprc.gov.cn/ce/ceus/eng/zmgxss/t897342 .htm.

37. Lulu Ramadan, "From Jeb Bush to Trump: How Cindy Yang's China-linked Circle Gained Access," *Palm Beach Post*, March 23, 2019, https://www.palm beachpost.com/news/20190322/from-jeb-bush-to-trump-how-cindy-yangs -china-linked-circle-gained-access.

38. Lee Fang, "Shadowy Chinese Conglomerate Cultivated Ties to the Most Powerful U.S. Politicians," Intercept, June 2, 2017, https://theintercept .com/2017/06/02/hna-group-corruption-scaramucci-trump-jeb-bush -clinton-guo-wengui/; Joshua Green and Miles Weiss, "Jeb Bush Has a Mitt Romney Problem," Bloomberg, December 11, 2014, https://www .bloomberg.com/news/features/2014-12-11/jeb-bush-has-a-mitt-romney -problem; Kai Strittmatter, *We Have Been Harmonized: Life in China's Surveillance State* (New York: Custom House, 2020), 311.

39. Fang, "Shadowy Chinese Conglomerate Cultivated Ties to the Most Powerful U.S. Politicians"; Green and Weiss, "Jeb Bush Has a Mitt Romney Problem."

40. "Jeb Bush's Private Equity Ventures Resemble Mitt Romney's."

41. Ibid.

42. Brett LoGiurato, "Jeb Bush: Here's How I'd Deal with China," Business Insider, December 14, 2015, https://www.businessinsider.com/jeb-bush-china -foreign-policy-2015-12.

43. "About Us," SingHaiyi Group (Note: Huaidan Chen, aka Celine Tang).

44. Lee Fang, Jon Schwarz, and Elaine Yu, "Power Couple," Intercept, August 3, 2016, https://theintercept.com/2016/08/03/chinese-couple-million-dollar -donation-jeb-bush-super-pac/.

45. Ginger Gibson, "Election Commission Fines Jeb Bush Super PAC, Chinese Company," Reuters, March 11, 2019, https://www.reuters.com/article/us -usa-election-china/election-commission-fines-jeb-bush-super-pac-chinese -company-idUSKBN1QS2LM.

46. Ramadan, "From Jeb Bush to Trump: How Cindy Yang's China-Linked Circle Gained Access."

47. Ibid.

48. Ibid.

49. Ibid.

50. Jim Bronskill, "CSIS Destroyed Secret File on Pierre Trudeau, Stunning Historians," *National Post*, June 15, 2019, https://nationalpost.com/news/canada /csis-destroyed-secret-file-on-pierre-trudeau-stunning-historians?r.

51. David Curtis Wright, *Pacific Affairs* 88, no. 3 (2015): 692–94, accessed February 4, 2021, http://www.jstor.org/stable/43591192.

52. Bob Plamondon, *The Truth About Trudeau* (Ottowa: Great River Media, 2013), 230.

53. "Chiang Kai-shek," History, last updated August 21, 2018, https://www .history.com/topics/china/chiang-kai-shek.

54. William Borders, "Trudeau to Go to China to Better Special Ties," *New York*

Times, October 7, 1973, https://www.nytimes.com/1973/10/07/archives /trudeau-to-go-to-china-to-better-special-ties-expected-to-see-mao .html.

55. Pierre Elliott Trudeau and Jacques Hébert, *Two Innocents in Red China* (Van-couver: Douglas & McIntyre, 2007), 3, 10; Paul Adams, "Canada's China Syndrome," iPolitics, November 13, 2013, https://ipolitics.ca/2013/11/13 /canadas-china-syndrome/.

56. Quoted in Dirk de Vos, *Cobblestones: A Personal and Political Journey* (Victoria: Friesen Press, 2015), 219.

57. Trudeau and Hébert, *Two Innocents in Red China*, see photo captions, 107–11; Erik Eckholm, "After 50 Years, China Youth Remain Mao's Pioneers," *New York Times*, September 26, 1999, https://www.nytimes.com/1999/09/26 /world/after-50-years-china-youth-remain-mao-s-pioneers.html.

58. Cleo Paskal, "In U.S. Backyard: How China Embedded Itself in Canada," *Sunday Guardian* (India), January 2, 2021, https://www.sundayguardianlive .com/news/u-s-backyard-china-embedded-canada (Note: Chou En-lai alter-natively Zhou Enlai).

59. Ivan Head and Pierre Trudeau, *The Canadian Way: Shaping Canada's Foreign Policy, 1968–1984* (Toronto: McClelland & Stewart, 1995), 233–34; Austin Ramzy, "China's Cultural Revolution, Explained," *New York Times*, May 14, 2016, https://www.nytimes.com/2016/05/15/world/asia/china-cultural -revolution-explainer.html.

60. Joseph Hnatiuk, "China Chronicles," *Winnipeg Free Press*, September 17, 2016, https://www.winnipegfreepress.com/arts-and-life/entertainment/books/china -chronicles-393747141.html.

61. Head and Trudeau, *The Canadian Way*, 223.

62. "The Red China of Two Naïve Guys," *Toronto Star*, October 16, 2005, https:// www.pressreader.com/canada/toronto-star/20051016/282364035071812.

63. "Pierre Trudeau," Biography.com, last updated June 23, 2020, https://www .biography.com/political-figure/pierre-trudeau.

64. Jussi M. Hanhimaki, *The Flawed Architect: Henry Kissinger and American Foreign Policy* (Oxford: Oxford University Press, 2004), 108, https://www.google .com/books/edition/The_Flawed_Architect/pPjrpGUe7CEC?hl=en.

65. Paskal, "In U.S. Backyard: How China Embedded Itself in Canada."

66. Martin Patriquin, "China Memories," *Maclean's* 126, no. 41 (October 21, 2013): 66–71, EBSCO, http://search.ebscohost.com/login.aspx?direct=true& db=plh&AN=90642603&site=ehost-live.

67. Charles Burton, "Chapter 3, The Canadian Policy Context of Canada's China Policy Since 1970," in Huhua Cao and Vivienne Poy, eds., *The China Challenge: Sino-Canadian Relations in the 21st Century* (Ottawa: University of Ottawa Press, 2011), https://books.openedition.org/uop/880?lang=en.

68. Head and Trudeau, *The Canadian Way*, 236.

69. Peter C. Newman, "Paul Desmarais' Latest Power Play," *Maclean's*, October 23, 2006, https://archive.macleans.ca/article/2006/10/23/paul-desmarais -latest-power-play.

70. Jonathan Manthorpe, *Claws of the Panda: Beijing's Campaign of Influence and Intimidation in Canada* (Toronto: Cormorant Books, 2019), 128.

71. Ibid., 125; Paskal, "In U.S. Backyard: How China Embedded Itself in Canada."

72. Manthorpe, *Claws of the Panda*, 126.

73. Jonathan Manthorpe, "Crisis Liberates Canada's Asia Policy from Its China Fixation," *Vancouver Sun*, December 7, 2020, https://vancouversun.com /opinion/op-ed/jonathan-manthorpe-crisis-liberates-canadas-asia-policy -from-its-china-fixation.

74. Manthorpe, *Claws of the Panda*, 126–27.

75. "Power Player: In Making Power Corp. a Business Pioneer in China, Paul Desmarais Sr. Positioned the Company to Become a Leader Among a Network of Canadian Companies There," *Gazette* (Montreal), September 24, 2005 (Lexis).

76. "Trudeau Plans Business Tour of the Far East," *Toronto Star*, July 25, 1985, EBSCO.

77. "Confucius Say . . . Welcome," *Toronto Star*, April 17, 1986, EBSCO.

78. Trudeau and Hébert, *Two Innocents in Red China*, 10–11.

79. Ibid., 11–12.

80. Trudeau and Hébert, *Two Innocents in Red China*, 15.

81. Gerson, "At Toronto Fundraiser, Justin Trudeau Seemingly Admires China's 'Basic Dictatorship.'"

82. Charles Burton, "Relations with China Should Hinge on More than Short-Term Economic Value," *Globe and Mail*, October 26, 2015, https://www .theglobeandmail.com/report-on-business/rob-commentary/relations -with-china-should-hinge-on-more-than-short-term-economic-value/ article26967437/; Deborah Jaremko, "Nexen Name to Disappear as Subsidiary Absorbed into CNOOC International," J-W Power Company, January 16, 2019, https://www.jwnenergy.com/article/2019/1/16/nexen-name -disappear-subsidiary-absorbed-cnooc-int/.

83. Zhaohui Luo, "Opening a New Chapter," *China Daily*, last updated January 9, 2016, http://usa.chinadaily.com.cn/world/2016-01/09/content_23008728 .htm.

84. "Foreign Relations: Father's Legacy Casts Shadow of Great Expectations over Trudeau Visit to China," *Globe and Mail*, August 30, 2016 (Lexis).

85. Steven Chase, "Justin Trudeau's Book Was Republished by a Chinese State-Owned Company after He Became Prime Minister," *Globe and Mail*, September 14, 2021, https://www.theglobeandmail.com/politics/article-the -legend-continues-how-a-state-owned-company-republished-justin/.

86. "Foreign Relations: Father's Legacy Casts Shadow of Great Expectations over Trudeau Visit to China."

87. Robert Fife and Steven Chase, "Trudeau Attended Cash-for-Access Fundraiser with Chinese Billionaires," *Globe and Mail*, November 22, 2016, https://www.theglobeandmail.com/news/politics/trudeau-attended-cash -for-access-fundraiser-with-chinese-billionaires/article32971362/.

88. Tom Blackwell, "Alleged Mastermind of Lavish Mansion Casino Raided by Police Met Twice with Prime Minister Justin Trudeau," *National Post*, October 8, 2020, https://nationalpost.com/news/canada/alleged-mastermind-of-lavish-mansion-casino-raided-by-police-met-twice-with-prime-minister-justin-trudeau.

89. Ibid.; David Cochrane, "8 Things to Know About the Pierre Elliott Trudeau Foundation," CBC News, last updated November 26, 2016, https://www.cbc.ca/news/politics/pierre-elliott-trudeau-foundation-questions-1.3868049; Claire Brownell and Zane Schwartz, "Money Began to Rain on Trudeau Foundation Once Justin Took over Liberals, Analysis Shows," *National Post*, last updated December 14, 2016, https://nationalpost.com/news/politics/money-began-to-rain-on-trudeau-foundation-once-justin-took-over-liberals-analysis-shows; "Across Canada," *China Daily*, last updated June 10, 2016, http://usa.chinadaily.com.cn/world/2016-06/10/content_25668569_3.htm.

90. "Across Canada."

91. Marie-Danielle Smith, "Canadian Businesses Look to Capitalize on Popularity of 'Handsome' Trudeau—or 'Little Potato'—in China," *National Post*, September 3, 2016, https://nationalpost.com/news/politics/canadian-businesses-look-to-capitalize-on-popularity-of-handsome-trudeau-or-little-potato-in-china; "Prime Minister Concludes Successful First Official Visit to China," Prime Minister of Canada Justin Trudeau, September 6, 2016, https://pm.gc.ca/en/news/news-releases/2016/09/06/prime-minister-concludes-successful-first-official-visit-china.

92. Yu Lintao, "Back on the Right Track," *Beijing Review*, October 6, 2016, http://www.bjreview.com/Current_Issue/Editor_Choice/201610/t20161004_800068700.html.

93. Andy Blatchford, "Canada Not Perfect on Human Rights Either, Trudeau Tells Chinese Leaders," CTV News, September 6, 2016, https://www.ctvnews.ca/politics/canada-not-perfect-on-human-rights-either-trudeau-tells-chinese-leaders-1.3059625.

94. Catherine Tsalikis, "A Barbarian Abroad: Alexandre Trudeau and the Call of China," Open Canada, September 23, 2016, https://opencanada.org/barbarian-abroad-alexandre-trudeau-and-call-china/.

95. Rex Murphy, "Cubans Deserve Our Support, but the Left Would Rather Embrace Murderous Dictators," *National Post*, July 20, 2021, https://nationalpost.com/opinion/rex-murphy-cubans-deserve-our-support-but-the-left-would-rather-embrace-murderous-dictators.

96. "Offer China a Carrot, Trudeau's Son Says," *Record* (Kitchener/Cambridge/Waterloo), May 31, 2007 (Lexis).

97. "Alexandre Trudeau," CPAC, accessed July 11, 2021, https://www.cpac.ca/episode?id=e4c4ff16-c79a-457b-8a84-4c7bf8608f86.

98. Hattie Klotz, "Alexandre Trudeau's Memoir—a Barbarian Lost in the 'Biggest Human Story,'" *Ottawa*, September 8, 2016, https://ottawamagazine.com/arts-and-culture/alexandre-trudeaus-memoir-is-as-a-barbarian-lost-in-the-biggest-human-story.

99. Linda Renaud, "Alexandre Trudeau: The Once-Reclusive Member of Canada's Trudeau Dynasty Emerges to Promote His Personal Brand," *Montrealer*, November 3, 2016, https://themontrealeronline.com/2016/11/alexandre-trudeau/.

100. June Chua, "Q&A with Alexandre Trudeau on His China Book, His Famous Brother & Politics," Yahoo News, September 14, 2016, https://ca.news.yahoo.com/qa-with-alexandre-trudeau-on-his-china-book-his-154706884.html.

101. Szu-chien Hsu and J. Michael Cole, *Insidious Power: How China Undermines Global Democracy* (Manchester: Eastridge Books, 2020), 120.

102. Steven Chase, "Liberals Reverse Course on Chinese Takeover of Montreal High-Tech Firm," *Globe and Mail*, March 27, 2017, https://www.theglobeandmail.com/news/politics/liberals-reverse-course-on-chinese-deal/article34441975/.

103. Hsu and Cole, *Insidious Power*, 123.

104. Jolson Lim, "Global Affairs Warned Trudeau Gov't About Chinese Development Bank Canada Has Joined," iPolitics, February 26, 2020, https://ipolitics.ca/2020/02/26/global-affairs-warned-trudeau-govt-about-chinese-development-bank-canada-has-joined/.

105. Clive Hamilton and Mareike Ohlberg, *Hidden Hand: Exposing How the Chinese Communist Party Is Reshaping the World* (London: OneWorld Publications, 2020), 50.

106. Diane Francis, "Trudeau Fiddles Around as China Burns Canada," *Montreal Gazette*, November 20, 2020, https://www.pressreader.com/canada/montreal-gazette/20201120/28212.

107. Mark Katkov, "China Charges 2 Canadians with Espionage in Case Tied to U.S. Prosecution of Huawei," NPR, June 19, 2020, https://www.npr.org/2020/06/19/880741322/china-charges-2-canadians-with-espionage-in-case-tied-to-u-s-prosecution-of-huaw.

108. Tom Blackwell, "Chinese Diplomat Blasts Justin Trudeau, Says He Ruined Relations with China and Is a U.S. 'Running Dog,'" *National Post*, March 29, 2021, https://nationalpost.com/news/politics/chinese-diplomat-blasts-justin-trudeau-says-he-ruined-relations-with-china-and-is-a-u-s-running-dog.

109. Tristin Hopper, "A Self-centered Giant Baby: How China Is Bashing Canada," *National Post*, April 6, 2021, https://nationalpost.com/news/canada/a-self-centred-giant-baby-how-china-is-bashing-canada; Jeremy Nuttall and Joanna Chiu, "Claims of Uyghur Genocide in China Are 'Lies,' Adviser to B.C. Premier Says," *Toronto Star*, April 6, 2021, https://www.thestar.com/politics/federal/2021/04/06/claims-of-uyghur-genocide-in-china-are-lies-adviser-to-bc-premier-says.html.

110. Brian Lilly, "Trudeau Bet on China over Canada at Height of Pandemic," *Toronto Sun*, March 23, 2021, https://torontosun.com/opinion/columnists/lilley-trudeau-bet-on-china-over-canada-at-height-of-pandemic.

111. Josh Rogin, "How an Attempted Canadian Concession to China Backfired,"

Washington Post, April 15, 2021, https://www.washingtonpost.com/opinions/global-opinions/how-an-attempted-canadian-kowtow-to-china-backfired/2021/04/15/fa887e3e-9e2a-11eb-8005-bffc3a39f6d3_story.html; Keoni Everington, "Trudeau Pushing HFX to Drop Taiwan Award to Avoid Angering China," *Taiwan News*, April 12, 2021, https://www.taiwannews.com.tw/en/news/4174600.

8: Higher Education

1. Chris Patten, "Nathan Law," *Time*, September 22, 2020, https://time.com/collection/100-most-influential-people-2020/5888201/nathan-law/.

2. Isaiah Schrader, "Schrader: Beijing Comes to Yale," *Yale Daily News*, August 28, 2019, https://yaledailynews.com/blog/2019/08/28/schrader-beijing-comes-to-yale/; Jasmine Siu, "Joshua Wong and Other Jailed Hong Kong Student Leaders See Political Careers Halted," *South China Morning Post*, August 17, 2017, https://www.scmp.com/news/hong-kong/politics/article/2107216/occupy-activists-joshua-wong-and-nathan-law-jailed-hong-kong; Nathan Law, "Why I've Fled My Home in Hong Kong Aged 26 to Keep Fighting the Tyrants of Beijing: A Rousing Message to the World from a Young Leader of the Pro-Democracy Protesters Bravely Defying China," *Daily Mail* (UK), July 4, 2020, https://www.dailymail.co.uk/debate/article-8490243/A-rousing-message-world-young-leader-pro-democracy-protesters-defying-China.html.

3. "Yale and China: A Centuries-Old Partnership," Yale University, July 31, 2018, https://world.yale.edu/news/yale-and-china-centuries-old-partnership-0.

4. Hana Davis, "No Lux or Veritas," *Yale Daily News*, January 24, 2020, https://yaledailynews.com/blog/2020/01/24/no-lux-or-veritas/.

5. Ibid.

6. "Our Center," Paul Tsai China Center, Yale Law School, accessed July 19, 2021, https://law.yale.edu/china-center/about-us/our-center.

7. "Yale Law School Receives $30 Million for China Center," Philanthropy News Digest, March 23, 2016, https://philanthropynewsdigest.org/news/yale-law-school-receives-30-million-for-china-center.

8. Michael Morand, "President Salovey and Alumnus Tsai Talk Tech in Silicon Valley," *Yale News*, July 8, 2015, https://news.yale.edu/2015/07/08/president-salovey-and-alumnus-tsai-talk-tech-silicon-valley.

9. Sopan Deb and Li Yuan, "Nets Owner Joe Tsai Didn't Seem Political. Until Now," *New York Times*, October 7, 2019, https://www.nytimes.com/2019/10/07/sports/joe-tsai-nba-china.html.

10. Duncan Clark, *Alibaba: The House That Jack Built* (New York: HarperCollins, 2016), 119.

11. Ibid., 97; "Yale Law School Receives $30 Million for China Center"; "Leadership," Alibaba Group, accessed July 19, 2021, https://www.alibabagroup.com/en/about/leadership.

12. "How Lacrosse-Playing Tsai Became Alibaba's Mega-Dealmaker," *China Daily*, September 1, 2014, https://www.chinadaily.com.cn/business/2014-09/01/content_18519991.htm.

13. Michael Forsythe, "Alibaba's I.P.O. Could Be a Bonanza for the Scions of Chinese Leaders," *New York Times*, July 21, 2014, https://dealbook.nytimes.com/2014/07/20/alibabas-i-p-o-could-be-a-bonanza-for-the-scions-of-chinese-leaders/.

14. Jay Somaney, "Chinese Governement Has a Huge 'Stake' in Alibaba," *Forbes*, October 18, 2015, https://www.forbes.com/sites/jaysomaney/2015/10/18/chinese-government-has-a-huge-stake-in-alibaba/?sh=e40c7e725b86.

15. Joe McDonald, "Alibaba Post-IPO Structure Gives Insiders Control," *Washington Examiner*, September 18, 2014, https://www.washingtonexaminer.com/alibaba-post-ipo-structure-gives-insiders-control.

16. Ibid.

17. Alibaba Group Holding Ltd., GovernanceMetrics Reports—Analysis, September 12, 2014, https://www.msci.com/documents/10199/c4ffe535-12da-480f-acd7-871d1cc6ea93.

18. Clive Hamilton and Mareike Ohlberg, *Hidden Hand: Exposing How the Chinese Communist Party Is Reshaping the World* (London: OneWorld Publications, 2020), 98; "Tiananmen Square Protest Death Toll 'Was 10,000,'" BBC News, December 23, 2017, https://www.bbc.com/news/world-asia-china-42465516.

19. Blake Schmidt and Venus Feng, "Ex-Alibaba Chair Helps Repair China's Image by Donating Medical Supplies," Bloomberg via *Detroit News*, April 8, 2020, https://www.detroitnews.com/story/news/world/2020/04/08/alibaba-ceo-jack-ma-repair-china-image/111527270/; Sam Peach, "Why Did Alibaba's Jack Ma Disappear for Three Months?," BBC News, March 20, 2021, https://www.bbc.com/news/technology-56448688.

20. Clark, *Alibaba: The House That Jack Built*, 31.

21. Ibid., 42–43.

22. Ibid., 143.

23. Reuters, "Alibaba Is Behind Hit Chinese Communist Party's Propaganda App," VentureBeat, February 18, 2019, https://venturebeat.com/2019/02/18/alibaba-is-behind-hit-chinese-communist-partys-propaganda-app/.

24. "Alibaba and Ant Group: Involvement in China's Military-Civil Fusion Initiative," RWR Advisory Group LLC, October 2, 2020, 2, https://www.rwradvisory.com/wp-content/uploads/2020/10/RWR-Report-Ant-MilCiv-Fusion-10-2020.pdf.

25. Agence France-Presse, "Alibaba Joins China Arms Maker to Offer Location Services," *Industry Week*, August 20, 2015, https://www.industryweek.com/technology-and-iiot/article/21965757/alibaba-joins-china-arms-maker-to-offer-location-services.

26. Zak Doffman, "Huawei Employees Linked to China's Military and Intelligence, Reports Claim," *Forbes*, July 6, 2019, https://www.forbes.com/sites/zakdoffman/2019/07/06/huawei-employees-linked-to-chinas-state-intelligence-agencies-report-claims/?sh=4d649b4b4b24; Nicolas Vega, "Joe Tsai Says U.S. Being 'Extremely Unfair' to Huawei," *New York Post*, January 25, 2019, https://nypost.com/2019/01/25/joe-tsai-says-us-being-extremely-unfair-to-huawei/.

27. Jasmine Moheb, "U.S.-China Symbiosis: A Conversation with Joe Tsai," prospectjournal.org, February 27, 2019.

28. Saheli Roy Choudhury, "Alibaba Co-Founder Claims Many Americans 'Want to Stop China' from Upgrading Its Tech," CNBC, May 31, 2018, https://www.cnbc.com/2018/05/31/alibaba-joe-tsai-claims-many-americans -want-to-stop-china-from-upgrading-its-tech.html.

29. Josh Chin and Gillian Wong, "China's New Tool for Social Control: A Credit Rating for Everything," *Wall Street Journal*, November 28, 2016, https://www .wsj.com/articles/chinas-new-tool-for-social-control-a-credit-rating-for -everything-1480351590.

30. Gary Robbins and Paul Sisson, "Billionaire Joseph Tsai Gives San Deigo $1.6 Million in Critical Medical Supplies to Fight Covid-19," *San Diego Union-Tribune*, April 20, 2020, https://www.sandiegouniontribune.com /news/education/story/2020-04-20/san-diego-billionaire-joseph-tsai -donates-1-6-million-in-medical-supplies.

31. "Alibaba Completes South China Morning Post Acquisition," Alizila, April 5, 2016, https://www.alizila.com/alibaba-completes-south-china-morning -post-acquisition/.

32. Timothy McLaughlin, "A Newsroom at the Edge of Autocracy," *Atlantic*, August 1, 2020, https://www.theatlantic.com/international/archive/2020/08 /scmp-hong-kong-china-media/614719/.

33. Ibid.

34. Laine Higgins, "Alibaba's Joseph Tsai to Buy Rest of Brooklyn Nets," *Wall Street Journal*, August 14, 2019, https://www.wsj.com/articles/alibabas-joseph -tsai-to-buy-rest-of-brooklyn-nets-11565811497.

35. Daniel Roberts, "Why the NBA Really Needs China," Yahoo, November 1, 2019, https://www.yahoo.com/lifestyle/nba-needs-china-revenue-growth -leverage-170102327.html.

36. Scott Neuman, "Houston Rockets GM Apologizes for Tweet Supporting Hong Kong Protesters," NPR, October 7, 2019, https://www.npr.org/2019 /10/07/767805936/houston-rockets-gm-apologizes-for-tweet-supporting -hong-kong-protesters.

37. Roberts, "Why the NBA Really Needs China."

38. "How Not to Do Business in China," *Economist*, October 12, 2019, https:// www.economist.com/united-states/2019/10/12/how-not-to-do-business-in -china.

39. Sheila Dang, "Nets-Lakers Game in China Sidesteps Hong Kong in NBA Preseason Marked by Tension," Reuters, October 10, 2019, https://www .reuters.com/article/china-basketball-nba-media-idUKL2N26U1O7.

40. "How Not to Do Business in China."

41. Deb and Yuan, "Nets Owner Joe Tsai Didn't Seem Political. Until Now."

42. Ibid.

43. Mark Witzke, "The Houston Rockets Are China's Favorite NBA Team," Asia Matters for America, July 15, 2019, https://asiamattersforamerica.org/articles /the-houston-rockets-are-chinas-favorite-nba-team.

44. "LeBron James on Daryl Morey's Tweet Supporting Hong Kong Protesters: 'He Wasn't Educated on the Situation,'" CBS Los Angeles, October 15, 2019, https://losangeles.cbslocal.com/2019/10/15/lebron-james-rockets-gm-daryl-morey-tweet-hong-kong-controversy/.

45. Merrit Kennedy, "Back from China, LeBron James Speaks Out on NBA Controversy," NPR, October 15, 2019, https://www.npr.org/2019/10/15/770305688/back-from-china-lebron-james-speaks-out-on-nba-controversy; "LeBron James Plans to Keep Speaking Out on Social Issues," NBA, August 29, 2018, https://www.nba.com/news/lebron-james-los-angeles-lakers-vows-speak-out-social-issues.

46. Richard Thomaselli, "All the King's Men," *Advertising Age*, July 17, 2006 (Proquest).

47. Brian Windhorst, "The New King of Marketing: Sees Potential in Asia: James Has the Goal of Being the First Athlete Billionaire," *National Post*, August 26, 2006.

48. Jonathan Zimmerman, "On Darfur, LeBron James Drops the Ball," *Christian Science Monitor*, May 24, 2007, https://www.csmonitor.com/2007/0524/p09s01-coop.html; Bruce Arthur, "James Won't Use His Power for Good; Star Refuses to Sign Teammate's Latter on Darfur Killings," *National Post*, June 9, 2007, https://www.pressreader.com/canada/national-post-latest-edition/20070609/282853661528275.

49. Shelley Smith, "LeBron James Breaks Silence on Darfur," ABC News, June 18, 2008, https://abcnews.go.com/Sports/story?id=4886373&page=1.

50. Angela Doland, "The China Syndrome: The People's Republic Is Complicated but Most U.S. Brands Can't Afford to Walk Away," *Advertising Age*, October 28, 2019 (Proquest).

51. "China Gets James' Shoe 1st," *South Florida Sun-Sentinel*, November 12, 2005 (Lexis); John Kim, "Chamber of Fear to Terracotta Warrior: The History of Nike LeBron 'China' Editions," *Sneaker News*, August 28, 2013, https://sneakernews.com/2013/08/28/chamber-of-fear-to-terracotta-warrior-the-history-of-nike-lebron-china-editions/.

52. United States Securities and Exchange Commission, Form 20-F, Xinhua Sports & Entertainment Limited, accessed July 20, 2021, https://www.sec.gov/Archives/edgar/data/1389476/000095012310065648/c03211e20vf.htm; Xinhua Sports & Entertainment Limited, "XSEL Secures Exclusive China Rights to More Than a Game from Lionsgate Movie to Be Distributed by China Film Group in Late 2009," PRNewswire, September 28, 2009, https://en.prnasia.com/releases/global/XSEL_Secures_Exclusive_China_Rights_to_More_Than_A_Game_from_Lionsgate_Movie_to_be_Distributed_by_China_Film_Group_in_Late_2009-23709.shtml.

53. David Minsky, "LeBron James Promotes Pork Donuts and Ice Cream in China," *Miami New Times*, March 8, 2012, https://www.miaminewtimes.com/restaurants/lebron-james-promotes-pork-donuts-and-ice-cream-in-china-6604628.

54. "China Gets James' Shoe 1st"; Mario Briguglio, "LeBron James Debuts the

Nike LeBron Soldier 10 'Camo' in China," Sneaker Bar Detroit, September 13, 2016, http://sneakerbardetroit.com/lebron-james-nike-lebron-soldier-10 -camo-china/; "LeBron James Debuts Nike Ambassador V During Asia Tour in Beijing," NikeLeBron.net, August 22, 2012, https://nikelebron.net /lebron_james_debuts_nike_ambassador_v_during_asia_tour_in_beijing/.

55. Brian Lewis, "David Levy Shockingly Out As Nets CEO After 55 Days," *New York Post*, November 12, 2019, https://nypost.com/2019/11/12/david -levy-shockingly-out-as-nets-ceo-after-55-days/.

56. Schrader, "Schrader: Beijing Comes to Yale."

57. Yi-Ling Liu, "Unwrapping Major Gifts," *New Journal*, September 8, 2017, http://www.thenewjournalatyale.com/2017/09/unwrapping-major-gifts/.

58. Davis, "No Lux or Veritas."

59. "China 2015 Report: Discussion," Coutts, accessed July 19, 2021, https:// philanthropy.coutts.com/en/reports/2015/china/discussion.html; "Channel Islands 'Among Worst Tax Havens' Worldwide," BBC News, May 29, 2019, https://www.bbc.com/news/world-europe-jersey-48354081.

60. Form F-1, Alibaba Group Holding Limited, as filed with the Securities and Exchange Commission, May 6, 2014, https://www.sec.gov/Archives/edgar /data/1577552/000119312514184994/d709111df1.htm.

61. "The Joe and Clara Tsai Foundation," Opencorporates, accessed July 19, 2021, https://opencorporates.com/companies/us_ca/C3639665; "Joe and Clara Tsai Charitable Foundation Limited," Opencorporates, accessed July 19, 2021, https://opencorporates.com/companies/hk/2093497; "Joe and Clara Tsai Foundation Limited," Opencorporates, accessed July 19, 2021, https:// opencorporates.com/companies/gg/1-58899.

62. Qi Xu, "Law School Receives $30 Million Donation to Rename China Center," *Yale Daily News*, March 28, 2016, https://yaledailynews.com/blog/2016 /03/28/law-school-receives-30-million-donation-to-rename-china-center/.

63. "The Joe and Clara Tsai Foundation," ProPublica, Nonprofit Explorer, accessed July 19, 2021, https://projects.propublica.org/nonprofits/organizations /464577561.

64. Institutional Compliance with Section 117 of the Higher Education Act of 1965, U.S. Department of Education Office of the General Counsel, October 2020, 1, https://www2.ed.gov/policy/highered/leg/institutional-compliance -section-117.pdf.

65. Liz Teitz and Linda Lambeck, "Yale Preps Response to Federal Probe of Foreign Funding Sources, Says Failure to Report Was 'Oversight,'" *New Haven Register*, February 13, 2020 (Lexis).

66. Form 20-F, Alibaba Group Holding Ltd., Annual and transition report of foreign private issuers [Sections 13 or 15(d)], Securities and Exchange Commission, May 24, 2016, https://sec.report/Document/0001047469-16-013400.

67. Note: immediately following an inquiry by our researchers as to this confusingly named set of corporations, Joe and Clara Tsai Foundation Limited (Guernsey) trademarked "Joe and Clara Tsai Foundation," https://uspto .report/company/Joe-Clara-Tsai-Foundation-L-T-D.

68. Alan P. L. Liu, "Rebirth and Secularization of the Central Party School in China," *China Journal* 62 (July 2009), accessed July 19, 2021, https://www .journals.uchicago.edu/doi/10.1086/tcj.62.20648116; Zhao Tingting, "Wang Yong Takes Helm at SASAC," *China Daily*, last updated August 25, 2010, https://www.chinadaily.com.cn/business/2010-08/25/content_11200917 .htm; "Li Qiang," Yale Law, on Internet Archive, accessed July 21, 2021, https://law.yale.edu/li-qiang (the screenshot of the site was captured on March 9, 2021).

69. M. Taylor Favel et al., "Opinion: China Is Not an Enemy," *Washington Post*, July 3, 2019, https://www.washingtonpost.com/opinions/making-china -a-us-enemy-is-counterproductive/2019/07/02/647d49d0-9bfa-11e9-b27f -ed2942f73d70_story.html.

70. Paul Gewirtz, "What China Means by 'Rule of Law,'" *New York Times*, October 19, 2014, https://law.yale.edu/sites/default/files/documents/pdf /Intellectual_Life/What_China_Means_by_Rule_of_Law_NYTimes.pdf.

71. Jamie Horsley, "China's Orwellian Social Credit Score Isn't Real," *Foreign Policy*, November 16, 2018, https://foreignpolicy.com/2018/11/16/chinas -orwellian-social-credit-score-isnt-real/.

72. Jamie P. Horsley, "China Promotes Open Government As It Seeks to Re-invent Its Governance Mode," Wilson Center, February 23, 2016, https:// www.wilsoncenter.org/article/china-promotes-open-government-it-seeks -to-reinvent-its-governance-mode.

73. Jamie P. Horsley, "Challenging China to Make Good Project Governance a Centerpiece of the Belt and Road Initiative," Yale Law School, working paper, December 2018, https://law.yale.edu/sites/default/files/area/center /china/document/horsley_china_bri_good_governance_infrastructure.pdf.

74. "Paul Tsai China Center Virtual Open House," Yale Law School, February 5, 2021, https://law.yale.edu/yls-today/yale-law-school-events/paul-tsai-china -center-virtual-open-house?date=2021–02–05T12%3A10%3A00–05%3A00.

75. Blake Schmidt and Venus Feng, "Trump's 'Friend' Jack Ma Helps Repair China's Image After Virus," Bloomberg, April 8, 2020.

76. M. J. Prest, "Joe and Clara Tsai Foundation Commits $50 Million for Social Justice (Grants Roundup)," *Chronicle of Philanthropy*, September 2, 2020, https://www.philanthropy.com/article/joe-and-clara-tsai-foundation-commits -50-million-for-social-justice-grants-roundup.

77. "Clara Wu and Joe Tsai Commit $50 Million to Social Justice, Equality," *Philanthropy News Digest*, August 26, 2020, https://philanthropynewsdigest .org/news/clara-wu-and-joe-tsai-commit-50-million-to-social-justice -equality.

78. "Tsai Foundation Social Justice Fund Announces Inaugural Recipients," *Philanthropy News Digest*, December 23, 2020, https://philanthropynews digest.org/news/tsai-foundation-social-justice-fund-announces-inaugural -recipients.

79. "Social Justice Commitment Statement," BSE Global, August 25, 2020, https://www.bseglobal.net/social-justice-commitment-statement/.

80. Leonard Greene, "Brooklyn Nets Owners Score Points with Social Justice

Fund," *New York Daily News*, December 16, 2020, https://www
.nydailynews.com/new-york/ny-nets-social-justice-fund-20201216
-urk6phhimzh7nmorru7lecac64-story.html; "Social Justice Commitment
Statement."

81. "Clara Wu Tsai," Reform Alliance, accessed July 20, 2021, https://reform
alliance.com/meet-reform/clara-wu-tsai/#; "Our Work," Reform Alliance,
accessed July 20, 2021, https://reformalliance.com/our-work/#; "Who Are
the Uyghurs and Why Is China Being Accused of Genocide?" BBC News,
June 21, 2021, https://www.bbc.com/news/world-asia-china-22278037.

82. "CNBC Exclusive: CNBC Transcript: Alibaba Co-Founder, Executive Vice
Chairman & Brooklyn Nets Owner Joe Tsai Speaks with CNBC's 'Squawk
Box' Today," CNBC, June 15, 2021, https://www.cnbc.com/amp/2021
/06/15/cnbc-exclusive-cnbc-transcript-alibaba-co-founder-executive-vice
-chairman-brooklyn-nets-owner-joe-tsai-speaks-with-cnbcs-squawk-box
-today.html.

83. Avi Asher-Schapiro, "Chinese Tech Patents Tools That Can Detect, Track
Uighurs," Thomson Reuters Foundation News, January 14, 2021, https://
news.trust.org/item/20210113195157-jq6lj/.

84. Sarah Coble, "Alibaba Facial Recognition Tech Picks Out Uyghur Minorities," Info Security, December 18, 2020, https://www.infosecurity-magazine
.com/news/alibaba-tech-uyghur-alert/.

85. Paul Mozur, "One Month, 50,000 Face Scans: How China Is Using A.I. to
Profile a Minority," *New York Times*, April 14, 2019, https://www.nytimes
.com/2019/04/14/technology/china-surveillance-artificial-intelligence
-racial-profiling.html.

86. Davis, "No Lux or Veritas."

87. Ibid.

88. Matt Apuzzo, "Chinese President Hu to Cap U.S. Tour with Yale Speech,"
Associated Press International, April 21, 2006, http://archive.boston.com
/news/education/higher/articles/2006/04/21/chinese_president_hu_to_cap
_us_tour_with_yale_speech/?rss_id=Boston.com+%2F+News.

89. Davis, "No Lux or Veritas."

90. Hamilton and Ohlberg, *Hidden Hand*, 245.

91. "Globalization Was Key Focus at Inaugural China-Yale Youth Leaders
Dialogue," *Yale News*, April 16, 2013, https://news.yale.edu/2013/04/16/
globalization-was-key-focus-inaugural-china-yale-youth-leaders-dialogue;
Zhuang Pinghui, "How China's Communist Party, Founded by Young People, Continues to Engage Youth," *South China Morning Post*, May 26, 2021,
https://www.scmp.com/news/china/politics/article/3134774/role-young
-people-chinas-communist-party.

92. "Summary of Yale University's Collaborations and History with China," Yale
University, accessed July 21, 2021, 40, 53; "University of Science and Technology of China," Australian Strategy Policy Institute, last updated May 13,
2021, https://unitracker.aspi.org.au/universities/university-of-science-and
-technology-of-china/.

93. Davis, "No Lux or Veritas."

94. Ibid.

95. Ibid.

96. Ibid.

97. Ibid.

98. David Ho, "How China's Zhang Li, the Billionaire Tencent and JD.com Tech Investor, Went from Selling Instant Noodles to Buying Stake in Amazon," *South China Morning Post*, December 10, 2019, https://www.scmp.com /magazines/style/tech-design/article/3041233/how-chinas-zhang-lei-billionaire -tencent-and-jdcom-tech; Alexandra Stevenson, "The Chinese Billionaire Zhang Lei Spins Research into Investment Gold," *New York Times*, April 2, 2015, https://www.nytimes.com/2015/04/03/business/the-chinese-billionaire -zhang-lei-spins-research-into-investment-gold.html; "Hillhouse Capital Group," Crunchbase, accessed July 20, 2021, https://www.crunchbase.com /organization/hillhouse-capital.

99. Apuzzo, "Chinese President Hu to Cap U.S. Tour with Yale Speech."

100. Pan Yue, "Hillhouse Capital's Zhang Lei Establishes U.S.$43M Education Fund for Renmin University," China Money Network, June 26, 2017, https://www.chinamoneynetwork.com/2017/06/26/hillhouse-capitals -zhang-lei-establishes-us43m-education-fund-for-renmin-university; "Addition of Certain Entities to the Entity List," Federal Register, October 9, 2019, https://www.federalregister.gov/documents/2019/10/09/2019-22210 /addition-of-certain-entities-to-the-entity-list; Stevenson, "The Chinese Billionaire Zhang Lei Spins Research into Investment Gold."

101. "The Yale Endowment 2020," accessed July 20, 2021, https://static1.square space.com/static/55db7b87e4b0dca22fba2438/t/607e4da7bc999d01b4752ea2 /1618890160689/2020+Yale+Endowment.pdf; "The Yale Investments Office," Yale Investments Office, accessed July 20, 2021, https://investments .yale.edu/.

102. "Lei Zhang, B.A., '02 M.A. '02 M.B.A.," Yale, accessed July 21, 2021, https://web.archive.org/web/20160819184505/https://www.yale.edu/about -yale/president-leadership/yale-corporation/lei-zhang (the screenshot of the site was captured on August 19, 2016).

103. John Dotson, "The China-U.S. Exchange Foundation and United Front 'Lobbying Laundering' in American Politics," Jamestown Foundation, September 16, 2020, https://jamestown.org/program/the-china-u-s-exchange -foundation-and-united-front-lobbying-laundering-in-american-politics/; "Zhang Lei," Center for China & Globalization, accessed July 20, 2021, http://en.ccg.org.cn/archives/58926.

104. Natalie Winters, "EXC: Top TikTok Investor Funds Chinese Communist Party–Linked Artificial Intelligence Program," National Pulse, August 7, 2020, https://thenationalpulse.com/news/tiktok-ccp-investor/.

105. Annie Wu and Nathan Su, "How an Investor Managing America's Top College Endowments Funded an AI Research Institute Beneficial to China," *Epoch Times*, October 16, 2019, https://www.theepochtimes.com/how-an -investor-managing-americas-top-college-endowments-funded-an-ai-research -institute-beneficial-to-china_3092601.html; "Xu Yanhao," China Associa-

tion for Science and Technology, accessed July 20, 2021, http://english.cast
.org.cn/col/col570/index.html.

106. Ibid.

107. United States Senate, "China's Impact on the U.S. Education System," U.S.
Senate Permanent Subcommittee on Investigations, accessed July 21, 2021.

108. Institutional Compliance with Section 117 of the Higher Education Act of 1965,
U.S. Department of Education Office of the General Counsel, October 2020.

109. "Higher Education and National Security: The Targeting of Sensitive,
Proprietary, and Classified Information on Campuses of Higher Education," Federal Bureau of Investigation, U.S. Department of Justice, April
2011, 1, https://www.fbi.gov/file-repository/higher-education-national
-security.pdf/view.

110. Daniel Flatley, David McLaughlin, and Janet Lorin, "College Foreign Cash
at Risk as Senate Targets China's Clout," Bloomberg, last updated April 20,
2021, https://www.bloomberg.com/news/articles/2021-04-20/colleges
-foreign-cash-at-risk-as-congress-targets-china-s-clout.

111. Institutional Compliance with Section 117 of the Higher Education Act of
1965, U.S. Department of Education Office of the General Counsel, October
2020, 7–8.

112. United States Senate, "China's Impact on the U.S. Education System," 1.

113. Institutional Compliance with Section 117 of the Higher Education Act of
1965, U.S. Department of Education Office of the General Counsel, October
2020, 6, 9, 13.

9: Fighting Back

1. Quoted in Richard McGregor, *Xi Jinping: The Backlash* (New York: Penguin
eBooks, 2019), 80.

2. Alexander Hamilton, "The Same Subject Continued: Other Defects of the
Present Confederation," *New York Packet*, Federalist No. 22, December 14,
1787, https://guides.loc.gov/federalist-papers/text-21-30#s-lg-box-wrapper
-25493335.

3. Mark Boonshoft, "The Specter of Foreign Influence in Early American Politics," New York Public Library, November 8, 2016, https://www.nypl.org
/blog/2016/11/08/specter-foreign-influence-early-american-politics.

4. "Foreign Influence, [23 January] 1799," James Madison papers, Founders
Online, National Archives, January 23, 1799, https://founders.archives.gov
/documents/Madison/01-17-02-0140.

5. Ibid.

6. "Foreign Nationals," Federal Election Commission, June 23, 2017, https://
www.fec.gov/updates/foreign-nationals/; Opensecrets.org, "Foreign-
Connected PACs," accessed July 16, 2021, https://www.opensecrets.org
/political-action-committees-pacs/foreign-connected-pacs/2020.

7. "James Mann," James-mann.com, accessed July 16, 2021, https://james-mann
.com/bio/.

8. James Mann, *The China Fantasy: Why Capitalism Will Not Bring Democracy to
China* (New York: Penguin, 2007), 79.

9.   Clyde Prestowitz, *The World Turned Upside Down: America, China, and the Struggle for Global Leadership* (New Haven, CT: Yale University Press, 2021), 259.

10. Quoted in McGregor, *Xi Jinping: The Backlash*, 7.

11. "Blog," Keith Krach, accessed July 16, 2021, https://keithkrach.com/blog/.

12. Matt Schrader, "Friends and Enemies: A Framework for Understanding Chinese Political Interference in Democratic Countries," Alliance for Securing Democracy, April 22, 2020, https://securingdemocracy.gmfus.org/friends-and-enemies-a-framework-for-understanding-chinese-political-interference-in-democratic-countries/; "China Sentences Swedish Publisher to 10 Years in Prison," DW, February 25, 2020, https://www.dw.com/en/china-sentences-swedish-publisher-to-10-years-in-prison/a-52517293.

13. Derek Lidow, "Mark Zuckerberg and the Tech World Still Do Not Understand Ethics," *Forbes*, March 11, 2019, https://www.forbes.com/sites/dereklidow/2019/03/11/mark-zuckerberg-and-the-tech-world-still-do-not-understand-ethics/?sh=541f32085386.

INDEX

Advanced Micro Devices (AMD), 80–82
AEOW 2000 LP, 58
Aeroflex, 57–58
Agere Systems, 58
Airbnb, 83
Albright, Madeleine, 159–63
Albright Group, 160
Albright Stonebridge Group (ASG), 160, 161–62
Alderman, Daniel, 66
Aleman, Miguel, 15–16
Alibaba, 71, 178, 213–18, 223, 224–25, 230
Alibaba Cloud Computing, 215–16
All-China Youth Federation (ACYF), 231
Allen, Mike, 79, 80
Alphabet, 98
Alwaleed (prince), 106
Amazon, 83
AMC Entertainment, 174–75
Ameco Beijing, 57–58
American Chemistry Council (ACC), 182–83
American International Group (AIG), 154
American Pacific International Capital (APIC), 171–72, 196
Ant IPO, 140
APCO Worldwide, 72
Apple, 83, 85, 117
Archer, Devon, 13–14, 17–18, 22, 23, 25–26, 27, 29, 31
Arms Export Control Act, 58
Asia and America (A&A) Consultants, 192
Asian Infrastructure Investment Bank, 209
Asset Management International Financing and Settlement Ltd., 189–90
Assets Supervision and Administration Commission of China, 183
Atlantic Richfield, 154

Aviation Industry Corporation of China (AVIC), 24

Bachman, David, 171
Bacow, Lawrence, 232
Baker, James A., 190
Ballmer, Steve, 88
Bank of America, 53
Bank of China, 133, 209
Bao, JiaQi, 39–40
Barbour, Haley, 79
Barclays Global Investors, 142
Barshefsky, Charlene, 166
Baucus, Max, 29, 176–81
Baucus Group, 177–78
Beacon Global Strategies, 79–80, 81–82
Beau Biden Foundation, 31
Bell, Daniel, 126–27
Belt and Road Initiative (BRI)
    background, 31, 36, 70–71
    Cohen Group and, 164
    funding for, 135–36
    Horsley on, 227
    Locke on, 174
    Schwarzman on, 124
    Thomas-Greenfield on, 162–63
Berger, Sandy, 160–61
BH Global Aviation, 195
BH Logistics, 194–95
Biden, Hunter
    business model, 10–11, 13–17
    China Energy Fund Committee (CEFC) and, 33–40
    Chinese clients and investors, 17–25, 29–31, 33–40, 42–45
    Chinese political ties, 25–29
    family finances, 11–12, 36–37, 44–45, 250–51n9, 262n173
    information sources on business deals by, 12–13, 250–51n9, 251n14, 259n136
    real estate ventures, 31–33

Biden, James, 36, 38, 39, 43
Biden, Joseph Robinette (JRB)
  business model, 10–11, 14, 15–16
  China connection while vice-
    president, 10–11, 17–18, 22, 27, 30
  China policy while president, 42–43
  family finances, 11–12, 36–37,
    44–45, 250–51n9, 262n173
  presidential campaign, 40
  Promises to Keep, 18
Biden, Sara, 38
Biden Center, 40–42
Biden Foundation, 37
"big help with a little badmouth," 4, 43,
  65, 151
Bill and Melinda Gates Foundation, 95
Binance, 180–81
Bing search engine, 87–88
Black Lives Matter, 228
BlackRock, 141–48
Blackstone Group, 121–24, 129, 142
Blinken, Tony, 41, 42, 43
Blitzscaling (Hoffman), 116
Bloomberg, Michael, 130, 157
Blum, Richard, 48–51, 53–54, 56–59
BLUM Capital Partners, 57
Blum Family Partners LP, 58
Bobulinski, Tony, 13, 33–37, 251n14,
  259n136
Boehner, John, 69–71
Bohai Harvest RST (BHR), 20–24, 42
Bonderman, David, 49
Bonker, Don, 72
Borich, Joseph, 170
Boucher, Rick, 73
Boustany, Charles, 78
Bowes, Gregory, 160
Boxer, Barbara, 73
Brady, Anne-Marie, 3, 107
Branstad, Eric, 183–85
Branstad, Marcus, 182–83
Branstad, Terry, 181–85
Breaux, John, 72
Brennan, John, 157–58
Breyer, Jim, 67–68, 118, 129
Bridgewater, 137–41

Brin, Sergei, 96
Britton Hill Holdings, 194–95
Broadcom, 82
Brookings Institution, 134, 136
Brooklyn Nets, 218, 221, 228
Buffett, Warren, 92
Build Your Dreams (BYD), 92
Bulger, Billy, 16
Bulger, James "Jim" (nephew), 16, 17,
  21, 22, 27
Bulger, James "Whitey" (father), 16
Burlingame, Anson, 150
Burnham Asset Management, 27
Bush, George H. W., 188–90, 191, 197
Bush, George W., 190–92
Bush, Jeb, 171, 193–97
Bush, Neil, 186, 191–93
Bush, Prescott, Jr., 188–91
Bush China Foundation, 193
ByteDance, 71–72

California Public Employees'
  Retirement System (CalPERS), 148
Canada-China Business Council, 202,
  206–7
Canadian Halifax International
  Security Forum, 210
Capital, Albright, 160
Capitol Counsel, 78–79
Carter, Ash, 97, 116
Castro, Fidel, 207
Cathay Fortune, 42
CB Richard Ellis, 57
CEFC Infrastructure Investment LLC,
  38
Celico, Amy, 161–62
Center for American Progress (CAP),
  75
Central Military Commission, 94–95,
  100
Central Party School, 126
Chambers, John, 104–6
Champagne, François-Philippe, 209
Chan, Nick, 70
Chao, Angela, 67–68
Chao, Elaine, 64–67, 121

Chao, James, 64–67
Charoen Pokphand Group, 191
Chayes, Sarah, 160
Che Feng "The Super Chairman,"
   18–23
ChemChina, 70, 73
Chen, Huaidan, 171–72, 195–96
Chen, Kathy, 106–7
Chen, Wilson, 172
Chen Feng, 178
Chen Guangcheng, 172–74
Chen Xu, 125
Chen Yun, 51–52
Cheng, Maggie, 27
Chieffalo, Lee, 59
China Academy of Launch Vehicle
   Technology, 92
China Association for International
   Friendly Contact (CAIFC), 34, 75
China Association for Science and
   Technology, 196–97, 234
China Center at Yale Law School,
   212–13, 223
China Center for International
   Economic Exchange (CCIEE),
   156–57
China Construction Bank Corporation,
   145
China Cultural Industry Association,
   205
China Development Bank (CDB),
   156
China Development Research
   Foundation, 184
China Dream, The (Liu), 8
China Electronics Technology Group
   (CETC), 73, 90
China Energy Fund Committee
   (CEFC), 33–40
China Entrepreneur Club (CEC),
   25–27
China Film Group Corporation, 221
China Fund, 62
China General Nuclear Power
   Corporation (CGN), 23–24
China Institute of Culture, 34–35

China International Publishing Group,
   231, 234
China International Trust and
   Investment Corporation (CITIC),
   18, 29–30, 131, 202
China Investment Corporation (CIC),
   17, 29, 123, 144
China LPGA, 189
China Merchants Bank, 42
China Model, The (Bell), 126–27
China Molybdenum, 42
China National Petroleum
   Corporation, 158
China Ocean Shipping Corporation
   (COSCO), 30–31, 32, 72, 159
China Railway Rolling Stock
   Corporation, 70
China Securities Finance Corporation,
   119
China State Shipbuilding Corporation
   (CSSC), 66–67
China Telecom, 131
China Ventures, 154–55
Chinagate, 53–54, 169–70
China-U.S. Exchange Foundation
   (CUSEF), 74–75, 77–79, 130, 157,
   180, 192–93, 233
Chinese Academy of Engineering
   (CAE), 93–94
Chinese Academy of Sciences (CAS),
   58, 175
Chinese Academy of Sciences Holdings
   (CASH), 175
Chinese Communist Party (CCP).
   See Communist Party of China
Chinese Communist Party Youth
   League, 126
Chinese National Nuclear Corporation
   (CNNC), 91–92
Chinese National Offshore Oil
   Corporation, 204
Chinese National Overseas Oil
   Company (CNOOC), 61
Chinese People's Political Consultative
   Conference (CPPCC), 37–38,
   74–75, 192

Chinese State Council, 93
Chinese United Front, 11, 37–38, 74–75, 126, 157, 180, 197
Chou En-lai, 199
Christensen, Jon, 72
Christopher, Mike, 12
CIIC, 192
Cisco, 104–6
City Car Services (CCS), 63
Clinton, Bill, 52, 53, 159
Clinton, Hillary, 80, 156
Coalition for Affordable Solar Energy, 76
Cohen, Noam, 120
Cohen, William, 163–66
Cohen Group, 163–65
Coleman, Norman, 72
Comey, James, 139
Committee on Foreign Investment in the United States (CFIUS), 81
Communist Party of China (CPC)
  Alibaba and, 213–14
  China–United States Exchange Foundation (CUSEF) ties, 74–75
  Feinstein on, 55
  Gates and, 86–87
  Ma and, 214–15
  power concentration by, 225–26
  privatization of companies and, 131–32
  Schwarzman and, 122–29
  Tsai on, 216–17
  Wall Street and, 146–47, 148
  Yale University and, 231
  ZTE ties, 77–78
Confucius Institute, 162, 178
Cook, Tim, 83, 85, 117, 128
Cooney, Bevan, 12–13, 251n14
Coons, Chris, 244
COVID-19 virus
  Alibaba and, 227–28
  Baucus on, 178–80
  Canadian policies, 210
  origins, 63–64
Crime and Security Research Institute (CSRI), 107–8

Cruz, Ted, 80, 244
Cultural Revolution, 199–200

Dai, Xiaoming, 53, 54
Dalai Lama, 232
Dalio, Ray, 137–41
Davis Wright Tremaine, 170, 174
Deese, Brian, 147
DeLoche, John, 29
Demosisto, 211
Deng Xiaoping, 163, 188, 203
Denham, Jeff, 72
Desmarais, Paul, 201–2
Di Dongsheng, 9–10, 149
Dimitrijevic, Marko, 167
Docusign, 245
Dolma, Kelsang, 222
Dong, Gongwen, 37–38
Dorsey, Jack, 106–9
Doshi, Rush, 66
Dotson, John, 196, 197
Dr. Peng Telecom & Media Group, 119
Dragon Fire (Cohen), 165
Dreyer, Teufel, 197
Dunford, James, 97

Ellison, Larry, 53
Environmental, Social, and Governance (ESG) standards, 241
Erisman, Porter, 213
Eudora, 14
Evanina, William, 81
Everest Partners, 167
Export Control Reform Initiative, 166–67

Facebook, 83, 84–85, 119, 245
Faligot, Roger, 19
Falun Gong, 104
Fang, Christine (aka Fang Fang), 60
Fang Fenglei, 131
Fang Zheng, 133
FBI, 38–39, 44, 53–54, 59–60, 235
Federal Election Campaign Act (1974), 239

Feinstein, Dianne, 46–52, 53–55,
    56–60
Finergy Capital, 195
Fink, Larry, 141–49
First Boston, 142
Florida Association for the
    Reunification of China, 196
Fontheim, Claude, 79
Fontheim International, LLC, 79
Foreign Agents Registration Act
    (FARA) of 1938, 26, 155, 238–39
Foreign Language Bureau, of CCP, 231
Foremost Maritime, 64, 65–67
Founder, 19
Francisco Partners, 57
Free Enterprise Project, 242
Frelinghuysen, Rodney, 71
Friendship Award, 134
Fudan University, 99–100

Galanis, Jason, 13, 27, 29
Gallo, Ernest, 53
Gates, Bill, 86–95
Gates, Robert, 166, 167, 168
Gemini Investments, 32
George H. W. Bush Foundation for
    U.S.-China Relations, 192
Gewirtz, Paul, 226
Gilliar, James, 36
Gingrich, Newt, 155
Glenn, John, 51
Global Ambassador Concierge, 62
Global Strategies Group (GSG), 158
Global Tech Industries Group, 63
Global Times, 35
Goldman Sachs, 130–34, 136–37
Gong (prince), 150, 195
Google, 88, 95–101, 108, 117, 118, 119
Google AI China Center, 96, 108
Gordon, Bart, 72
Governance of China, The (Xi), 84–85
"Government Sachs," 130
Grace Semiconductor Manufacturing,
    191
Gracias, Antonio J., 113
Grassley, Charles, 36

Great Leap Forward, 198
Greece, 30–31
Greenberg Traurig, 71
Greene, Diane, 97
Gromyko, Andrei, 152
Grossman, Marc, 164
Guan Naiyang, 100
Guan Video (website), 9
Guang Yang, 195
Gui Congyou, 245

H. J. Heinz, 154
Hadley, Stephen J., 167
Haig, Alexander, 158–59
Hainan province, 193–94
Hambrecht, William, 62
Hamilton, Alexander, 237
Hamilton, Clive, 149, 157
Hanes, Melodee, 177–78, 180
Han's Laser, 168
Harvard University, 232, 235
Harvest Fund Management, 20
Harvest Global Investments, 20, 27
He Jianyu, 127
He Xin, 53
Heath, Edward, 152
Hébert, Jacques, 198–200
Heinz, Christopher, 13–14
Henniges Automotive, 24
Hidden Hand (Hamilton and Ohlberg),
    149
Higher Education Act (1965), 224
Hikvision, 73, 167–68, 185
Hillhouse Capital, 232–33
Hills, Carla, 166
Hills & Company, 166
HNA Group, 170, 178, 194–95
Ho, Allen, 24
Ho, Patrick, 39
Hoffman, Reid, 114–18
Holding Foreign Companies
    Accountable Act (2020), 145
Hong Kong, 186, 211, 218–19
Hong Kong Finance Investment
    Holding Group (HKFI) Ltd, 192
Horizon Robotics, 101

Horsley, Jamie, 226–27
Houston Rockets, 218–19
Howie, Fraser, 130
Hu Jintao, 67, 89
Huai Jinpeng, 234
Huang, John, 53, 169–70
Huawei, 70, 72–73, 78, 82, 105–6, 119, 162, 165, 209–10, 216
Hudson West, 40
Hudson West IV, 36
Hughes Aircraft, 189–90
Hui Chi Ming, 192
Humphrey, Peter, 115
Hutchison, Tim, 71
Hytera, 209

IBM, 58–59
IDG Capital, 67
Ingram Micro, 178
Innes, Martin, 108
Institute for China-America Studies, 157
Intel, 80, 101
Interlink Management Corporation, 191
International Finance Corporation, 50
International Media Acquisition Corp., 63
International Telephone and Telegraph (ITT), 154
International Traffic in Arms Regulation (ITAR), 58
Italian National Railway, 31
ITF Technologies, 209

James, LeBron, 219–21
JD Logistics, 129
Jennings, Peter, 153
Jeremic, Vuk, 32–33
Jia Chunwang, 20–21
Jia Liqing, 20–21
Jiang Zemin, 48, 49, 50–52, 59, 64, 133, 137, 189, 191
Jin Ligang, 161
Jiwei, Lou, 123
Joe and Clara Tsai Charitable Foundation (Hong Kong), 224–25

Joe and Clara Tsai Foundation (La Jolla), 223–25, 228, 325–326n67
Joe and Clara Tsai Foundation Limited (Guernsey), 224–25, 325–326n67
J.P. Morgan, 137

Kaldany, Rashad, 50
Kania, Elsa, 99
Kantor, Mickey, 166
Kaplan, Steven, 24
Karloutsos, Alex, 31
Karloutsos, Michael, 31
Kerry, John, 76
Khashoggi, Jamal, 143
Kingston, Jack, 73
Kissinger, Henry, 75, 152–58
Kissinger Associates, 152–53, 157–58
Kokorotsikos, Paris, 31
Koresh, David, 55
Krach, Keith, 245
Kuehmann, Charles, 113
Kushner, Jared, 121
Kuwata, Kam, 56

Lai Changxing, 34
Lam Ting Keung, 37–38
Lanza, Bryan, 183–84
Law, Nathan, 211–13, 221
Layton, Roslyn, 98
Le Corre, Philippe, 30–31
Lee, Kai-fu, 102
Legend (company), 58
Legend Continues, The (Trudeau and Hébert), 205
Lenovo, 58–59
Levin, Rick, 230
Levy, David, 221
Lew, Jack, 136
Li, David Daokui, 126
Li, Fei-Fei, 96, 108–9
Li, Jonathan, 22
Li, Zhonggang, 196–97
Li Deyi, 101
Li Keqiang, 111
Li Peng, 202
Li Qiang, 136

Li Shan, 136
Li Yang, 210
Lieberman, Joe, 72
Lin, Michael (aka Lin Junliang),
    16–17, 21
Lincoln, Abraham, 150
LinkedIn, 114–18
Lippo Group, 54
Liu Mingfu, 8
Liu Xiaobo, 56
Liu Yandong, 127
Liu Yunshan, 21, 117
Locke, Gary, 169–76
Locke Global Strategies, 174
Lott, Trent, 72
Lowe, Russell, 59–60
Lu Wei, 84–85, 116

Ma, Jack, 140, 213–15, 217, 223,
    227–28
Ma Jian, 19, 23
Ma Weihua, 25
Ma Yanli, 47
Mack, Connie, IV, 72
Madison, James, 238
Malloy, John M., 167
Manchin, Joe, 244
Mann, James, 159, 242–43
Manthorpe, Jonathan, 202
Manuel, Anja, 167, 168–69
Mao Tse-tung, 3, 51, 152, 198–200,
    201
Matthews International Capital
    Management, 62
Mattis, James, 163
Max S. Baucus Institute, 178
Mayer, Brown, Rowe, & Maw, 166
McCarthyism, 155, 179–80
McConnell, Mitch, 44, 64–65, 68,
    118
McFadden, Richard, 205
Mead, Walter Russell, 8
Menard, C. J., 221–22
Mercury, 183–84
Merrill Lynch, 137
Mexico, 15–16

Microsoft, 83, 86–91, 94–95, 115
Military Project Confidentiality Office,
    99
Ming, Yao, 219
Mnuchin, Steve, 121
Moffett, Toby, 73
More than a Game (film), 221
Morell, Mike, 79
Morey, Daryl, 218–21
most-favored-nation (MFN) trade
    status, 50, 53, 56, 61, 177
Mozur, Paul, 84
MSCI, 214
MSN Spaces, 87
Munson, Lester, 79
Musk, Elon, 109–14
Musk, Kimbal, 113

Nankai University, 165
National Council for Social Security
    Fund, 19
National People's Congress (NPC), 70
National University of Defense
    Technology (NUDT), 94–95
NBA, 218–21
NBA Foundation, 228
Netcom, 131–32
Newbridge Asia, 49–50
Newbridge Capital, 49–50, 59
Newman, Peter, 201
Newsom, Gavin, 59
Nexen, 204
Nike, 220
Niu Gensheng, 206
Norsat International, 209
North Dragon Iron & Steel Works, 50
Nuclear Threat Initiative, 91
Nunn, Sam, 51
NW Innovation Works (NWIW), 175
Nye, Joseph, 227–28

Obama, Barack, 75, 77, 127
O'Brien, Robert, 148
Ohlberg, Mareike, 149, 157
Oldaker, Biden, and Belair, LLP, 14
Olympics (2008), 62–63

One Belt One Road.
  See Belt and Road Initiative
O-Net, 208–9
Oracle, 53
Owasco, 14, 39
Ozery, Tamar Groswald, 147

Pacific Light Cable Network, 119
Page, Larry, 96
Palantir, 245
Panetta, Leon, 79
Paris Climate Accords, 75–77
Parker, Mark, 220
Patton Boggs, 69
Paul, Rand, 244
Paul, Scott, 69
Paul Tsai China Center, 212, 223, 225–27
Paulson, Hank, 130
Pelosi, Nancy, 60–64, 76
Pelosi, Paul, 62–63
Pelosi, Paul, Jr., 63
People's Daily Online, 89
People's Liberation Army Air Force, 129
People's Liberation Army Navy (PLAN), 94
People's Liberation Army (PLA), 34, 36, 52, 71, 90, 92, 145
PetroChina, 131, 133
Pichai, Sundar, 117
Piraeus (Greek port), 30–31
Plus Holdings, 190–91
Podesta, John, 75–76, 77
Podesta, Tony, 76, 77–78
Podesta Group, 77–78
Power Corporation, 201–3
Prescott, Jeff, 227
Prestowitz, Clyde, 243
Principles (Dalio), 137–38
Promises to Keep (Biden), 18

Qihoo 360, 68
Qualcomm, 82

Radiance Holdings, 37
Ralston, Joseph, 163

Rapp-Hooper, Mira, 227
Reagan, Ronald, 244
Red Capitalism (Walter & Howie), 130
Refinitiv, 124
REFORM Alliance, 229
Reines, Philippe, 79
Renmin University Gaoling School of Artificial Intelligence, 234
Reporters Without Borders, 106
Reynolds, Roger, 91
Rhodes Scholars, 125
Ricchetti, Steve, 41
Rice, Condoleezza, 166–69
Rice, Hadley, Gates, and Manuel (RHGM), 167–69
Richard C. Blum & Associates, 48–49
Right to Rise PAC, 196
Rong Yiren, 191
Roosevelt, Franklin D., 238
Rosemont Capital, 13
Rosemont Realty, 14, 31–32
Rosemont Seneca Advisors, 14
Rosemont Seneca Partners, 12, 13–18, 23, 37, 43–44
Rosemont Seneca Technology Partners, 14, 29
Ross, Wilbur, 121
Royce, Ed, 71
RSP Investments, 14
RSTP I, 14
RSTP II Alpha and Bravo, 14
Rubin, Robert, 75
Rubio, Marco, 80, 244
RWC Partners, 167–68

Salovey, Peter, 213, 232
San Francisco, 48–49, 50
Saudi Arabia, 143
Schmidt, Eric, 96, 98, 118
Schumer, Chuck, 244
Schwarzman, Stephen, 121–30
Schwarzman Scholars, 125–29
Schwerin, Eric, 11–12, 14–15, 18, 21, 27, 33
Science and Technology Research Institute, 99

Scissors, Derek, 195

Scowcroft, Brent, 166

Scowcroft Group, 166

Secret Empires (Schweizer), 13–14, 16–17, 21, 44, 65

Seneca Global Advisors, 14

SenseTime, 68, 129

Sensitive Compartmented Information Facility (SCIF), 46

Sequoia Capital China, 101

Shanahan, Patrick, 97

Shanghai, 48–49, 50

"Shanghai Classic" golf tournament, 189

Shanghai Investment and Trust Company, 49

Shanghai Pacific Partners, 49

Shanghai Stock Exchange, 131

shareholder activism, 241–42

Shenzhen Development Bank, 49–50

Silk Road Finance Corporation (SRFC), 135–36

Silk Road Planning Research Center, 135

Silverstein, Ken, 55

Sinclair, Upton, 245

SingHaiyi Group Ltd., 192

SinoHawk, 36

Sino-Ocean Land (now Sino-Ocean Group), 32

Sinopec, 192

Sioeng, Ted, 170

Skaneateles, 14

Skype, 90

Smithsonian Institution, 225

Soldiers Sortie (TV show), 215

Sorkin, Andrew Ross, 229

Soros, George, 145–46, 167

South China Morning Post (SCMP), 217–18

SpaceX, 110, 113–14

Spalding, Robert, 81

Squire Patton Boggs (SPB), 69, 70–71

Stanford University, 225, 235

State Administration of Foreign Exchange (SAFE), 138

Stearns, Cliff, 72

Stern, Tod, 75

Stonebridge, 161

Su, Ivan, 110

Sugon Information Industry Company, 80–82

Sullivan, Jake, 227

Sullivan, Russ, 177

Sun Ninghui, 81

Suntech Power Holding, 76

Swalwell, Eric, 60

Symasia Foundation Limited, 223

Taiwan, 48, 155, 200–201

Tan Xiangdong, 194

Tang, Gordon, 171–72, 195–96

Tang Xiao'ou, 128–29

Tang Xiaosong, 205

Tao, Grace, 111–12

Tao, Long, 35

Taobao website, 214, 219

Tariffs Hurt the Heartland, 78

Technorati, 83

Telecom, 133

Tencent, 71, 110, 233

TerraPower, 91

Terry, Lee, 72–73

Tesla, 109–12, 113–14

The Analysis Corporation (TAC), 158

Thiel, Peter, 97, 118, 119–20, 245

Thomas-Greenfield, Linda, 162–63

Thomson Reuters, 123–24

Thornton, John, 131–37

Thornton Group, 16–17

Tiananmen Square massacre (1989)
   Blum on, 49
   censorship of, 87–88, 107, 115, 124
   Feinstein on, 50, 55
   Jiang and, 51–52
   Kissinger on, 153–54
   Ma on, 214–15
   Pelosi on, 61
   Trudeau (Pierre) on, 203–4

Tianjin Municipal Government, 165

TikTok, 71

Tmall website, 214
TrainOSE, 30–31
Tree Top Industries, 63
Trina Solar, 76
Trudeau, Alexandre, 200, 203–4, 206, 207, 208
Trudeau, Justin, 187, 200, 202, 203, 204–10
Trudeau, Margaret, 201
Trudeau, Pierre, 197–205, 206, 207
Trudeau Foundation, 206
Trump, Donald J.
  coronavirus policies, 179–80
  Hoffman on, 117
  presidential campaign donations, 196, 197
  trade policy, 156, 161–62, 243
  on Wall Street's involvement in China, 137
Trump, Ivanka, 121
Tsai, Clara, 228, 229
Tsai, Joe, 212–19, 221–23, 227–28, 229–30
Tsai Center, 212, 225–27
Tsai Foundation, 224–25
Tsai Ing-wen, 156, 210
Tsang, Steve, 228
Tsinghua Tongfang, 98–99
Tsinghua University, 98–99, 125–29, 133–34
Tung Chee-hwa, 74, 130
Twitter, 106–9
Two Innocents in Red China (Trudeau and Hébert), 198–200

Umbrella Movement, 211
united front organizations, 11, 37–38, 74–75, 126, 157, 180, 197
United States Senate Oversight Committee Report, 12, 13
Universal Energy, 63
University of California, San Diego, 216
University of Pennsylvania, 40–42
University of Science and Technology of China (USTC), 231

Unocal, 61
U.S. Department of Education, 224, 234–36
U.S. Federal Communications Commission, 119
U.S. Federal Election Commission (FEC), 196
U.S. Senate Select Committee on Intelligence, 46
U.S.-China Bilateral Investment Treaty, 176
U.S.-China Business Council, 165
U.S.-China Chamber of Commerce (USCCC), 190
U.S.-China Transpacific Foundation (UCTPF), 78–79

Vitter, David, 73

Walter, Carl, 130
Wanda Group, 175
Wang, Jian, 175
Wang Jianlin, 175
Wang Lijun, 41
Wang Qishan, 137–38
Wang Weixing, 162
Wang Zhongyu, 25
Wanhua Chemical Group, 70, 183
Warner, Mark, 216, 244
Washington, George, 8, 237–38
Webb, David, 214
Wei Wei, 206
Weiwen, He, 147
Weizenbaum, Joseph, 120
Wen Jiabao, 134–35, 157
WestExec, 42
WilmerHale, 166
Wolfington, Vincent, 62–63
Wong, Benson, 205
World Bank, 50, 209
World Internet Conference, 116–18
World Trade Organization (WTO), 56, 155, 159–60, 166, 177
Wu, Harry, 65
Wu Lebin, 175
Wynn, Albert, 71

Xi Jinping
  on All-China Youth Federation, 231
  Belt and Road Initiative by, 30
  Biden (J.) and, 40, 43
  Branstad and, 181–82
  on Bush family, 194
  on China's re-ascension, 1, 7, 8
  concentration of power by, 6, 128,
    225–26
  Governance of China, The (Xi),
    84–85
  Locke on, 174
  military policy, 77
  Schwarzman on, 122, 130
  Schwarzman Scholars address by, 127
  Silicone Valley and, 83–86, 92–94,
    113, 116, 117, 118–19
Xianqin Qu, 196
Xinhua, 7–8
Xinhua Sports and Entertainment, 221
Xipei, Jiang, 25
Xu Erwen, 194
Xuexi Qiangguo (app), 215

Yale Endowment, 232–33
Yale Law School, 212–13, 223–24,
  225–27
Yale University, 211–13, 221–24,
  225–27, 230–34, 236
Yale-China Association, 232
Yang, Cindy, 196, 197
Yang Jiechi, 190
Ye Jianming, 33–39

Yiengpruksawan, Mimi Hall, 231
Yilin Press, 205
Yingli Green Energy Holding, 76
Yitu Technology, 233
You Zheng, 99
YouTube, 96
Youtz, David, 232
Yu, Miles, 114
Yu Kai, 101
Yu Yong, 42

Zaikin, David, 77
Zhai, Shumin, 100
Zhang, W. K., 49
Zhang Bin, 205
Zhang Lei, 233–34
Zhao, Changpeng, 180–81
Zhao, Henry, 27
Zhao, Li, 184
Zhao Jing, 87
Zhao Runlong, 38
Zhao Xuejun (aka Henry Zhao), 20,
  21, 23
Zhengfei, Ren, 73
Zhongnanhai, 51
Zhou Fengsuo, 115
Zhou Ji, 94
Zhu, Tom, 111
Zhu Guangya, 94
ZTE Corporation, 58, 72, 77–78,
  184–85
Zuckerberg, Mark, 83–85, 119, 128
Zuckerberg, Priscilla, 83

ABOUT THE AUTHOR

PETER SCHWEIZER is the president of the Government Accountability Institute and the former William J. Casey Research Fellow at the Hoover Institution, Stanford University. He is the author of the *New York Times* number one bestsellers *Secret Empires* and *Profiles in Corruption*, as well as the *Times* bestsellers *Clinton Cash, Throw Them All Out, Extortion,* and *Do As I Say (Not As I Do)*. He is the author of numerous other books on history and politics that have been translated into eleven languages. His investigative work has been featured on the front pages of the *New York Times* and the *Wall Street Journal* as well as CBS News' *60 Minutes*.

Peter received his BA from George Washington University and his MPhil from Oxford University. He lives with his wife in Florida.